WITHDRAWN

AVID

READER

PRESS

Madoff

The Final Word

Richard
Behar

AVID READER PRESS

New York   London   Toronto
Sydney   New Delhi

AVID READER PRESS
An Imprint of Simon & Schuster, LLC
1230 Avenue of the Americas
New York, NY 10020

First Avid Reader Press hardcover edition July 2024

AVID READER PRESS and colophon are
trademarks of Simon & Schuster, LLC

Simon & Schuster: Celebrating 100 Years of Publishing in 2024

For information about special discounts for bulk purchases,
please contact Simon & Schuster Special Sales at
1-866-506-1949 or business@simonandschuster.com.

The Simon & Schuster Speakers Bureau can bring authors to
your live event. For more information or to book an event, contact
the Simon & Schuster Speakers Bureau at 1-866-248-3049
or visit our website at www.simonspeakers.com.

Interior design by Lewelin Polanco

Manufactured in the United States of America

1   3   5   7   9   10   8   6   4   2

Library of Congress Control Number: 2024934288

ISBN 978-1-4767-2689-2
ISBN 978-1-4767-2691-5 (ebook)

For Rebecca
and for Isabel, always

Contents

Introduction

It's the largest theft by a private individual in financial history.

—STEPHEN HARBECK, PRESIDENT (2003–2019), SECURITIES INVESTMENT PROTECTION CORPORATION (SIPC), ESTABLISHED BY CONGRESS TO HELP BAIL OUT DEFRAUDED INVESTORS

You could investigate this case for fifty years and not be done, and not explore everything there is to explore, and not go down every avenue, and not get to all the truths. You could do this for fifty years and still leave a lot on the table.

—MATTHEW L. SCHWARTZ, LEAD "MADOFF FIVE" TRIAL PROSECUTOR

The first time that history's greatest financial fraudster contacted me was in January 2011, a month after his eldest son, Mark, hung himself from his dog's leash on the second anniversary of his father's arrest. The email's subject line read simply: "Inmate: MADOFF, BERNARD L." It came via the "Trust Fund Limited Inmate Computer System," operated by a private company, CorrLinks, that is contracted by the Bureau of Prisons to provide email service to all federal inmates. Prisoners pay a nickel a minute to use the system. They can afford it by earning wages for work starting at twelve cents per hour, or by receiving cash into their "email accounts" from outsiders—something that Bernie hit me up for on too many occasions in order for me to keep communicating with him. (It turns out that he had way more dough in that account than he needed from me.)

That first email, of what would become hundreds over the years, stated that Madoff was seeking to add me to his contacts list. I had the option of accepting or blocking him forever. In hindsight, I sometimes wish I'd chosen the latter—spending time with Bernie was a frequently tiresome exercise—but now, after more than fifteen years on the case, I am finally able to illuminate some of the most elusive questions in the whole saga: When did his Ponzi scheme begin? How, precisely, did it work? And, to paraphrase that oft-used line from the Watergate-scandal era, what did his family know, and when did they know it?

Besides, how could I say no? As a longtime financial investigative reporter, one with a special fondness for scammers, I could hardly pass up the chance to probe the unrivaled superstar of swindlers. Bernie was the architect of the world's biggest and longest-running Ponzi scheme. And now he was opening the door to me.

"Thank you for your kind card," the 2011 email began, referring to a note of condolence I'd sent him following his son's suicide. Bernie didn't know me in the slightest, but under the circumstances, and despite the number of his investors and their descendants whose financial lives were wrecked by the Ponzi, I felt at least some compassion for the man. Mark, forty-six, had not only chosen the second anniversary of his dad's 2008 arrest as the day to kill himself, but also he did it with his two-year-old son, Nick, sleeping in a nearby bedroom. Family members made it clear to Bernie—not even six months into a 150-year sentence in a North Carolina prison—that under no circumstances was he to show up at Mark's funeral, even if he could have gotten a pass from the warden to attend. (Four years later, he would also be barred from the funeral of his younger son, Andrew, who died at the age of forty-eight from a recurrence of lymphoma.) Losing your only children is a life sentence in itself, but to mourn them from a literal cage has to be unbearable, even for a financial cannibal.

My note had an ulterior motive, of course. I hoped that sending a card without explicitly requesting an interview might nudge open a line of communication. Madoff had been swamped with media requests since his arrest, and, after all he'd been through, I could hardly blame him for shunning reporters or even just wanting some peace. But it couldn't hurt to try.

My first letter to Bernie, in which I did request an interview, had been in early 2009, three months after his arrest. No answer. A year later, I sent another letter—a request to visit him in prison—which was also ignored. This time, finally, a response. (Throughout this book, I will quote Bernie's written communications verbatim, without corrections for grammar, spelling, punctuation, or formatting.):

I CAN ASSURE YOU THAT THE CIRCUMSTANCES THAT CREATED THIS DISASTER HAS YET TO BE TOLD. Richard, if you like to arrange a visit you must contact the Institution and ask for a special visit through the warden at Butner. Bregards, Bernie.

And so began a relationship with "Bregards, Bernie" that endured for a decade. It had its share of ups and downs, and periods of silence on both ends, but between that first message and my initial visit to the Federal Correctional Complex in Butner, North Carolina, in early 2011 and his death, at age eighty-two, on April 14, 2021, I received more than three hundred emails from Madoff and emailed him more than four hundred times. He also sent me dozens of handwritten letters (mostly to me, but sometimes copies of letters he had written to others or that others had sent him). We had roughly fifty phone conversations, which I recorded, and I was granted permission from subsequent wardens to visit him a second time in 2014, and a third time in 2019. Printed out, my Bernie communications file runs to more than a thousand single-spaced pages in 12-point type—much of it colorful, but too much of it useless. Such are the perils of spending a decade with a pathological liar.

Nevertheless, I have been able to triangulate between Bernie's slippery testimony and the memories and documentation of others to nail down for the first time what I feel confident are certain crucial truths about his case. In addition to reviewing more than 100,000 pages of documents—legal, personal, financial—in an effort to sort out the saga, I have drawn on more than three hundred interviews with everyone from current and former federal regulators, prosecutors, FBI and SEC agents, fund liquidators, and investigators working for a court-appointed trustee, to Wall Street experts, criminal defense lawyers, Madoff family members, former employees, and school classmates who knew both Bernie and Ruth, his future wife. All have helped me to put Bernie into perspective. The passage of time has proved helpful. And with that passage of time, more of them have been willing to speak.

It is hard to overstate the magnitude of what Bernie pulled off, or almost did. Louis Freeh, the former FBI director and federal judge who reviewed a small portion of the Madoff scheme, noted that in his decades of experience in federal investigations, he had "never seen such a sophisticated, elaborate infrastructure and operation for deceit and deception that served to protect an underlying fraud scheme of such mammoth proportions."

There are plenty of species of financial scams, but Bernie's—the Ponzi scheme—is a classic. In its simplest form, a Ponzi involves taking money from one investor (as an investment) and passing it to another investor (as a profit) in a zero-sum game of financial musical chairs. In other words, robbing Peter to pay Paul. It's a crime that's been around for thousands of years but finally got its enduring name from Charles Ponzi, a Boston con artist who ran a scheme for a mere eleven months, from 1919 to 1920. Charles did it with postal reply coupons (which can be exchanged for stamps), promising his investors a 50 percent profit within forty-five days or a 100 percent profit within ninety days. Madoff did it with fake trades of stocks and more modest but consistent returns, for decades. Most Ponzis fall apart after a year or two. The longest known Ponzi scheme prior to Madoff's arrest—launched in 1985 by a nobody named Dennis Helliwell, with an "exclusive fund" supposedly operated by a bank where he worked that turned out to be just his personal checking accounts—lasted for only eleven years and grew to just $5 million.

The mechanics are simple, but irresistible to the gullible. A Ponzi's architect uses the allure of fantastical returns to lure in the next wave of investors; each subsequent wave's money is then used to pay off the previous wave—although many investors choose not to redeem their purported profits but instead let them continue to "grow." So long as there is a sufficient supply of new money coming in at the bottom of the pyramid, the schemer can afford to pay other investors—especially those higher up—the promised returns. If, for whatever reason, the supply of new money dries up, and investors start requesting (or demanding) their money, that's when the plunderer either gets busted or flees. It's a story as old as the pyramids. Or at least pyramid schemes.

The broad outlines of Madoff's Ponzi and worldwide legacy are widely known. Early followers of the Bernie saga know much of the minutiae. And yet a new generation knows little to nothing about him. Prior to 2013, given a public clamor for details, a dozen books were published. At the time, FBI agent and spokesman James Margolin drew me a graph showing that the terrorist attacks of September 11, 2001, understandably, generated more media calls than any other event in the New York field office's history. Next up was the Madoff case. Everything below that barely registered on his graph.

But 2013 was far too soon for the saga to be understood. In the years since those books were published, the story has largely gone dark, with numerous questions still unanswered. And, in fairness, the early 2010s was far too early for outsiders to make sense of the story, including the fraud's origins. It was not until 2013 that the trial of the "Madoff Five" (the only criminal trial of any of his former employees) even began. All told, fifteen Madoff associates either pled or were found guilty between 2010 and 2015, only six of them ratting on others to reduce their sentences or avoid prison. And well over a hundred legal battles continue to unfold to this day, shedding occasional splotches of new light on the scandal as they crawl through the world's court systems.

Madoff began his company, Bernard L. Madoff Investment Securities (henceforth, BLMIS), in 1960 at the age of twenty-two. At the time of his arrest on December 11, 2008, his then-active 4,900 client accounts—held by individuals, family trusts, charities, colleges, pension funds, hedge funds (pools of money from the wealthy for high-risk investments), even banks—had an estimated $68 billion of assets on paper. Never mind that there was actually less than $300 million in Bernie's coffers; from his investors' point of view, Madoff made $68 billion disappear almost overnight. Freeh was essentially right: Bernie had engineered the greatest known fraud in human history.

In late 2023, fourteen years after Bernie's arrest, the US Department of Justice announced that its Madoff Victims Fund (MVP) would send the latest batch of recovered money to more than *twenty-four thousand* people worldwide who'd lost actual principal investing in funds that in turn had invested with Madoff. That lifted the total disbursements from the feds to $4.2 billion for more than forty thousand people worldwide. And that's separate from the thousands of other people who invested *directly* with Bernie, which a court-appointed trustee with a team of lawyers and investigators is responsible for locating, recovering, and distributing funds to customers who lost principal.

"9-11 was a terrorist attack," says Robert Fagenson, a former vice chairman of the New York Stock Exchange (NYSE), who recalls watching, in his thirty-ninth-floor office off Wall Street, one of the hijacked passenger jets crash into the World Trade Center—halting the markets for four days and changing the world forever. "Bernie's crime in many ways was also a terrorist attack. It was just a different type. I mean, if you think about the tens of thousands of victims and their families, they feel no less violated. In all my [fifty-seven] years in the business, he was probably the biggest surprise—and I've been through a lot of crises as the markets went up and down."

Those financially harmed—destroyed, in many cases—by Bernie reads like a Who's Screwed Who in the sports, business, entertainment, academic, and philanthropic worlds: publisher and real estate baron Mort Zuckerman; Baseball Hall of Fame hurler Sandy Koufax; actor John Malkovich; film director and producer Steven Spielberg; New York Mets co-owner Fred Wilpon; entertainment mogul David Geffen; Larry Silverstein, developer of the rebuilt World Trade Center; Home Depot cofounder Ken Langone; actors Kevin Bacon and his wife, Kyra Sedgwick; talk-show host Larry King; Bed Bath & Beyond cofounder Leonard Feinstein; New Jersey US senator Frank Lautenberg; actress Zsa Zsa Gabor; billionaire Norman Braman, a former owner of the Philadelphia Eagles; entertainment industry executive Jeffrey Katzenberg; L'Oréal heiress Liliane Bettencourt, the world's richest woman; prolific movie screenwriter Eric Roth; and organizations such as the International Olympic Committee, the American Jewish Committee, Yeshiva, Brandeis, and New York Universities, Boston's Museum of Fine Arts, the Hadassah Jewish women's charity, and on and on and on. "We thought he was God, we trusted everything in his hands," said Nobel Prize winner and Holocaust survivor Elie Wiesel, whose foundation was wiped out by "Bregards Bernie."

I was particularly eager to ask Madoff how he could possibly steal from Wiesel, the iconic witness and voice for the victims of the Nazi

death camps. Hadn't Elie, who made it through Auschwitz and Buch-
enwald—where his mother and younger sister were gassed to death,
and his father starved—suffered enough? Were there no boundaries
that Bernie, especially as a fellow Jew, wouldn't cross?

Wiesel declined to be interviewed, but I met him briefly at a
Jewish charity lunch several years before he died in 2016. I asked if
there is any healing after being fleeced by Bernie. "Never," he replied.
However, the camp survivor added, "We've been through worse."

In a phone conversation four years after we first met, Bernie
dodged the question of how he could possibly harm such a sym-
pathetic figure, and quickly came up with this instead: "Elie Wiesel
came in at the request of friends of mine, who I've known forever.
They put me under pressure to invest for him. Everyone put me
under pressure. I did have a dinner with him once. You can't even
have a conversation with Elie; you can't hear what he's saying. He's
full of shit, that guy. First of all, he didn't lose any money [principal],
like everyone else claims. He's counting the profits."

He went on to disavow any responsibility for the financial ca-
lamities he'd visited upon countless boldface names. "Celebrities I
never solicited or even met with. Steven Spielberg, David Geffen—
that group came in because they had a professional money manager
that handled them in California; some guy named Jerry something
from Beverly Hills. People like [John] Malkovich came in again
through a professional advisor who was a client of mine for years.
Kevin Bacon came in because his father-in-law, Kyra Sedgwick's
father, is a very major art dealer in New York who was a client
of mine for twenty-somewhat years. I never solicited anybody like
that because, quite frankly, I didn't want any high-profile people in
there. I turned down Michael Jordan. I turned down Derek Jeter.
Their financial advisor wanted me to take them; I just didn't want
them."

Mort Zuckerman? "I never even knew Zuckerman was a client. I never knew half these people. I never knew Larry King was a client of mine."

And so it goes, as Kurt Vonnegut would say. Or to paraphrase Chico Marx (in disguise as brother Groucho's character in *Duck Soup*): Who ya gonna believe, me or your own eyes?

Few Bernie clients did any due diligence; most weren't exactly trained to comprehend a trading statement, or bothered to read theirs carefully. "You show me a dress, being an old seamstress myself, I can tell you if it was put in by hand, by machine, if it's this kind of zipper or that," says octogenarian supermodel Carmen Dell'Orefice, who socialized regularly with Bernie and his wife, Ruth, for many years, She lost her life's savings. The stock market is "not my field, and I haven't thought about it or studied it in depth," Dell'Orefice tells me. "People who appear to be in the business and seem to be operative in—listen, if it was good enough for Elie Wiesel, it was good enough for me."

That kind of blind faith is a Ponzi scammer's lifeblood. Who among us with a brokerage or IRA account—be honest—has bothered to take thirty seconds to type their broker or investment manager's name into the search bar of Wall Street's database of "disciplinary actions" at the Financial Industry Regulatory Authority (FINRA), the self-regulatory organization for securities firms?

People spend more time researching a new TV purchase than they do a Ponzi's can't-lose proposition like Madoff's. (I actually did that FINRA search after I began the reporting for this book and found out that my eighty-three-year-old Merrill Lynch broker, Harold "Hal" Kahn, who has since died, committed a felony in 1968. According to the records, he helped his father-in-law omit income on his tax returns from the sales of securities. Hal pled guilty, paid a fine, and the case against his wife's dad was dropped. When I confronted Hal about it, he explained that he was trying to help his father-in-law out of a financial jam and regretted having broken the law. The answer satisfied me, and I kept my account with him because, well, I really liked and trusted Hal. But had he *made-off* with my IRA, I would have had nobody to blame but myself.)

Supermodel Carmen is in good company. Scores of institutions failed to do enough due diligence—or any at all. A legion of red flags was ignored. The biggest flag of all: month after month, year after year, decade after decade, in up markets and in down markets, Madoff returned between 15 percent and 20 percent "profits" to most of his customers. Those he especially liked "earned" as much as 50 percent on paper. Or more.

Those kinds of consistent profits are just not possible on Wall Street. Madoff lured in his investors—and kept them in—by keeping his club selective. Not everyone could join, causing many to beg for admittance, like gaggles of nightclub patrons standing outside the velvet rope and hoping to get picked by the doorman. The so-called smart money—professional investors; finance types in general—was, as a rule, excluded. A man of few words, Bernie had an almost cult-leader allure. Those he did accept were expected to keep quiet about their relationships with him. And if you asked too many questions about Madoff's delectable payouts, you could get shown the door—like *Seinfeld*'s Soup Nazi refusing to serve his spectacular concoctions to those who annoyed him.

In his 2009 book *Think Like a Champion: An Informal Education in Business and Life*, future president Donald Trump stated that Madoff solicited him to invest but that he declined. "He'd say, 'Why don't you invest in my fund?'" wrote Trump. "I didn't know much about him and I'm not a fund guy, so I said no. I had enough going on in my own businesses that I didn't need to be associated or involved with his." Countered Bernie, with a chuckle: "You know, he claimed that he never invested with me, which is true. And he said that I approached him, which is not true. I never approached him for anything. I played golf with him once at his golf club, [which] my brother was a member of. You know, that's typical Trump, to say he was smart enough not to invest." He chuckled again. Imagine that: a golf matchup between two of the world's greatest fabulists. In this case, I believed Bernie.

To understand the architecture of the fraud, it's essential to know that BLMIS was composed of four business units, three of them housed (starting in 1987) in 885 Third Avenue—the iconic Lipstick Building, so named because the thirty-four-story, red-granite sky-scraper resembles a giant tube of lipstick—and one based in London. Think of each unit as a separate company, for the most part, under Bernie's umbrella.

The nineteenth floor, the home of two of the units of BLMIS: the largely legitimate broker-dealer and proprietary trading wings. In "prop trading," as the latter is known in Wall Street parlance, traders buy and sell equities from the company's own inventory of stocks in order to produce profits. Bernie allowed those traders to keep 25 percent of their net trading gains, in line with most Wall Street firms' practices.

As for the broker-dealer unit, for decades it engaged in genuine trading with some of the biggest financial institutions in the world: Bear Stearns, Charles Schwab, Fidelity Investments, Merrill Lynch, Morgan Stanley, the Vanguard Group. Those firms acted on behalf of individual clients (people like you, perhaps); Bernie's broker-dealer unit simply executed trades in response to external orders. That's known on Wall Street as market making. For certain years in the 1990s, BLMIS was the sixth-largest market maker in the S&P 500 (the Standard & Poor's index tracking the stock performances of five hundred of the largest US companies) and accounted for 8 percent to 10 percent of the total volume of equities bought and sold on the New York Stock Exchange. This impressive feat is confirmed from interviews with credible Wall Street experts such as Alan "Ace" Greenberg, the late legendary chairman of Bear Stearns, as well as Harvey Pitt, the former chairman of the US Securities and Exchange Commission (SEC), who died in 2023.

Before Bernie's arrest, and even for years afterward, no one questioned the longtime legitimacy and legality of those two units, market making and prop trading, run by his younger brother, Peter, and Bernie's two sons, Mark and Andrew. Madoff used that legit side of the business as a kind of beard, leveraging his prominence to insinuate himself into major roles on Wall Street. He served on various committees of the SEC. For eight years, he chaired the National Association of Securities Dealers Automated Quotations (NASDAQ) exchange, a largely ceremonial post. In a letter to me, he proudly scribbled fifteen industry titles he'd held since the 1980s. Among them: chairman of the National Securities Clearing Corporation (NSCC), a company owned by banks and brokers that performs the actual post-trade exchanges of securities on behalf of buyers and sellers; member of an SEC trading committee; chairman, intermittently, of three NASD committees, on market surveillance, regulatory matters, and market automation. (The NASD, or National Association of Securities Dealers, was once a self-regulatory organization for the industry, replaced in 2007 by FINRA.)

A scale drawing of the nineteenth floor, dated July 2008 (five months before Madoff's arrest), shows the trading desk, with seats for (in order): Andrew, Peter, Bernie, and Mark. (Bernie, who barely knew how to look at a computer screen, rarely sat there—except to blab or have lunch with his sons.) On each side of the trading desk sat the firm's legit traders and others.

The nineteenth floor was also the location of large corner offices of both Bernie and his brother, Peter, BLMIS's senior managing director. Next to Peter were the offices of Mark and Andrew. And next to Bernie were the offices of a David Kugel, a longtime BLMIS trader, and Stanley Shapiro, a big investor and a nonstaffer. (Kugel was convicted and sent to prison. Nobody at BLMIS could figure out why Shapiro, another subject of Chapter Eight, even had an office there.) There were no other offices anywhere near Bernie's.

On the eighteenth floor was the office of Ruth Madoff, as well as the office of Sonny Cohn, who ran a boutique brokerage from his desk named Cohmad Securities Corp., which was one of the biggest conduits of investors into the Ponzi. That entity, whose name combines Cohn and Madoff, was also the home for a $60 million account for Ruth that she tried unsuccessfully to keep after the scheme collapsed. (Cohn is a subject of chapter 8.) And not far from Ruth, on the other side, was the office of Shana Madoff, who reported to her father, Peter, and who would narrowly escape an indictment.

The third unit of BLMIS was overseas: Bernie had a controlling stake in a brokerage firm in London called Madoff International Securities Limited (MSIL), in which other family members held minority stakes. Launched in 1988, it became one of the first US companies to belong to the London Stock Exchange, employing twenty-five people by 2008.

But all of those components of BLMIS rested on the foundation of the seventeenth floor, where the computer systems were known internally as "House 17." This was the home of the so-called investment advisory (IA) unit, or wealth management arm. This was where the Ponzi grew and thrived and spread throughout the world like a pandemic—and where most of the firm's money, it turns out, was earned and kept.

Like on a conveyor belt in a factory that manufactures rat poison, this unit was where fake documents were churned out robotically by a few longtime employees for thousands of customers, utilizing personal computers as well as an IBM computer system that was long obsolete. Computers that talked only to one another and were not even connected to the eighteenth or nineteenth floors or to MSIL in London—let alone to the stock exchanges.

While investors were often taken to the nineteenth floor for tours of the broker-dealer unit's state-of-the-art trading desk built by a proud Peter, a technophile, no one offered tours of seventeen. There wasn't even a BLMIS sign on the door; a special keycard, which few employees possessed, was needed to get inside. Not only that, but also in the last eight years of BLMIS's existence, if not earlier, Bernie was taking some $799 million in funds from his individual investors in the Ponzi scheme to help prop up the legitimate side of the business, which often lost money due to increased competition and technological advances on Wall Street. In that way, it all got intermingled in the end; a big, dirty financial hairball. Bernie denied intermingling, but the evidence is indisputable. Peter, a lawyer, not only co-headed the legit trading desk but also served as the company's chief of compliance—responsible for ensuring that the enterprise met outside regulatory and legal requirements, as well as internal policies and bylaws. In the end, Peter was sentenced to ten years in federal prison for clearly abdicating those fiduciary duties; daughter Shana, also an attorney, who worked as the firm's compliance counsel under her father, was never charged.

Ironically, says Fagenson, "[Bernie] Madoff became a poster child for competing with the 'Big Bad NYSE,' as the guy who championed electronic trading and the use of computers and the use of technology to compete." Thanks to propellerhead Peter, BLMIS was among the Wall Street firms on the cutting edge of automation—which makes those old House 17 machines look even more suspicious. Those relics used homegrown software programs coded specifically to backdate trades; they could be tweaked to deliver specific "profits" for specific clients. Printers spat out the statements, plus false trade-confirmation slips. It would all go into envelopes and be distributed by snail mail. Always snail mail. Quaint. Small-town. Old-fashioned. If it's on paper, well, it must be legit, right? Until the very end, in 2008, customers were unable to view their statements online. Nor could they email anyone on the seventeenth floor who was overseeing their accounts. That alone should have set off alarm bells. Instead, the bells jingled only every Christmas and Hanukkah, when Bernie Claus (so tagged in court by a prosecutor) would adjust the statements of favorite clients to gift them some extra gelt.

In retrospect, the money machine Bernie built was not that complicated—Ponzis rarely are. The central mechanism here was the backdated trade confirmation slip. In a legitimate stock trade, a buyer and a seller are connected through a broker (or market maker) to transfer ownership of a security at the stock's current price, minus a small margin that goes to the broker as a fee. The broker is transparent about the stock's buy-versus-sell price, and everyone knows what he or she is getting. Such a trade typically takes place in a matter of minutes or even fractions of a second.

Put simply, backdating literally meant having one of his seventeenth-floor puppets pick up the *Wall Street Journal* or (in later years) look at a Bloomberg computer terminal to see how the stocks of well-known companies performed on the prior day (their highs and lows)—and then picking prices within that range for the imaginary "buys" and "sells." It doesn't take a genius to predict the past.

"It was widely known within BLMIS that I had little technology skills," beamed Bernie in a 2013 email, during the Madoff Five trial. "The running joke within our firm was that I would never realize that my computer keyboard was disconnected. My only needs were to view the monitor to gauge the market movements. I even had to have the tech staff sign me in to start my computer if it turned off by mistake. My talents laid in trading and marketing and conception, and not tech, which was the province of my brother and sons and others."

He may not have known how to turn on his computer, but—over and over again—Bernie insisted to me that he single-handedly was a legitimate and successful options trader for his IA clients from not long after he launched his company in 1960 until 1992—when, he maintained, he made a "tragic mistake" that snowballed. (Briefly put, stock options are contracts between two parties that give the buyer the right to buy or sell a stock at a specific price and by a specific date.)

The tale of Bernie's alleged mistake, or "my problem," as he often downplayed it, is so convoluted that some investigators are still trying to unravel it. (At its crux, a Ponzi scheme is one of the simpler frauds there is. But little about Madoff's octopean universe was simple.) In parts of the book, I will be referring broadly to "investigators," in order to protect some identities, as many of them could face disciplinary actions or worse for having shared information. Where they can be named, they are.

Many questions still swirl around Madoff, but perhaps the most crucial is not only the ultimate scale of the fraud but also the scale of the complicity in it—among Bernie's investors, bankers, and family members alike. In other words, the enablers. In this book, I will try to provide clarity on the following unanswered questions:

> » When did the world's greatest fraud begin? Several years after the October 19, 1987, stock market crash known as Black Monday, as Madoff insisted? Or was it a fraud from the start of his career in the early 1960s?
> » How involved were his wife, brother, sons, and niece? What did they know?
> » Did his biggest investors lead to his downfall, as Bernie insisted?
> » Did Bernie shred the evidence, or do we have everything?
> » Why didn't anyone at JPMorgan Chase (JPMC), the long-time home of the Ponzi checking account, get indicted? And what are the largest foreign banks hiding?
> » Why were the only people tried for the Madoff fraud five mid-level employees with limited education and financial acumen?

» Why did some of Bernie's clients receive extra and strato-spheric returns?

» Why did those who directed clients to Madoff ignore the obvious?

» How did Wall Street heavyweights miss this so completely? (Or perhaps they didn't?) And did the SEC deserve the backlash?

» And Bernie's brain: How did he morph from a mild money manager into a historic sociopath? Or is it psychopath?

Over my decade with him, I gave Bernie the benefit of many doubts, as I went granular with him into the elaborate yarns he insisted were true. Some of his minor claims are indeed true, while the biggest and most important ones are as false as his customer statements.

I had to hang on to his tail for as long as the project needed to last. Most people tell white lies from time to time, so I cut him some slack on that. His explanations were astonishingly consistent for years, perhaps because he'd had plenty of time to rehearse them in his prison cell, or perhaps he'd concocted these alibis long before he was found out. Or maybe because he indeed believed things that never happened. I was not inside his head. And I'm unaware of any existing document or audio recording in which Bernie states that he will or has knowingly told a major lie—and I rarely caught him telling one. But with the passage of time, the inconsistencies give him away. Parsing them out has been a fifteen-year process. Several years before Madoff died, I told Arthur Levitt, the former chairman of the SEC, that Bernie and I are apparently both in prison for life. This book marks my escape. At least one of us made it out.

1

Bernie in Butner

| | | | | | | | | | | | |

What I did was terrible. I'll never forgive myself. But it's not like I planned it. If I did, I would have done it better [*chuckles*]. I'd have been somewhere like Montenegro with no extradition treaty. There were times I had four billion in cash sitting in the bank. When you have the money I had, and the banking connections I had, I could have disappeared. But I wanted to take responsibility, and at least try to get the money back for people.

—BERNIE FROM PRISON, IN BUTNER,
  NORTH CAROLINA, 2011

When the headlines started roaring in December 2008 that Bernard Lawrence Madoff was busted for running a $50 billion Ponzi scheme (upped later to $64.5 billion, and then to $68 billion), most Americans' first reaction was, undoubtedly, "Who?"

The global financial crisis, the worst since the Great Depression, was in full bloom at the time, leaving legendary giants such as Lehman Brothers bankrupt and the likes of Bear Stearns and Merrill Lynch so broke that they needed to be rescued. But Bernie, who became the human face of the crisis, was by no means a household name. He was little known outside certain circles of investors, brokerage houses, regulators, bankers, and top Wall Street executives (a number of whom believed he was a con man but kept their mouths shut). And that was the way Bernie wanted it. To the greater world, he was a nonentity, a nobody—a mediocre high school student from Queens with a nasal dialect and grades just high enough to get accepted to a mediocre Alabama college he dropped out of after one year.

The announcement of Bernie's arrest transformed him into a world-historical figure. Sixty-eight billion bucks, laid end to end in dollar bills, would encircle the Earth approximately 265 times. Now add another 104 circles to calculate the fraud's value in today's money: $100 billion, give or take a billion. That's nearly two million times what the average American worker earns in a year. It is fifty times the SEC's entire budget, which, as we'll see, is the real reason the much-maligned agency was unable to detect Madoff's fraud. With $100 billion, you could own Luxembourg (gross domestic product, $91 billion)—one of the countries that Madoff "feeder funds" used for funneling money to Bernie, thanks to their strict banking secrecy.

To put Bernie's arrest into further context, consider the Enron scandal of 2001, one of the largest accounting frauds in history, which dinged the energy behemoth's shareholders to the tune of $74 billion over the four years leading up to its demise. While that rip-off was slightly bigger than Bernie's, the Houston-based firm was widely known as one of America's largest publicly traded corporations, with two hundred thousand employees. So, too, WorldCom, once America's second-biggest phone company (with eighty thousand employees), which collapsed in 2002 in an $11 billion fraud. By comparison, BLMIS had less than two hundred employees. And Madoff accomplished his swindle with just a handful of untrained, largely untalented, and, in many cases, barely educated staffers; a few computers; and a floor of leased office space.

The $68 billion figure aggregates two distinct sums: an estimated $22 billion in loss of principal actually invested by customers, and $46 billion in phantom profits listed on their final monthly statements. Of the $22 billion, roughly 75 percent of it had been recovered by early 2024—some by the federal government but the vast majority of it by an eighty-two-year-old court-appointed trustee named Irving Picard ("the idiot Picard," as Bernie referred to him routinely). Picard, a veteran bankruptcy attorney with an iron will, is spending his golden years forcing so-called net winners to return their ill-gotten profits to the "net losers," who lost principal—a compensatory Ponzi in reverse, if you will, although few net winners feel it is fair.

Those recoveries, called clawbacks in industry jargon, continue to this day, a few tens of millions of dollars at a time. In February 2024, in what Picard called the fifteenth pro rata interim distribution to Madoff claims holders, he distributed $45.2 million to Bernie's losers, with more than eighty cases still to be litigated as of that date. Many of those cases are still being fought at every step by individuals and banks eager to hold on to their winnings. As of early 2024, banks all over the world—from Citibank, Credit Suisse, and HSBC to Natixis (France), Nomura (Japan), and the National Bank of Kuwait—that received the funds through what is known as "subsequent transfers" are also battling to fend off the tenacious trustee's claws.

At his investigation's peak, Picard had more than 200 lawyers, investigators, and industry experts working on the more than 1,000 lawsuits that he'd filed. Their work is overseen by the Securities Investors Protection Corp. (SIPC), which was formed in 1970 by an act of Congress in order to build confidence in the securities markets. By pooling fees from brokerage houses, SIPC protects investors from theft, in part by reimbursing them for missing securities up to $500,000 and financing any necessary liquidations and investigations.

How much will the world's losers ultimately get back per dollar invested with Bernie? Eighty cents on the dollar? Ninety? More? And how many total losers and winners are there in the world? "There is no possible answer to your question," says Kenneth Krys, the Cayman

Islands–based liquidator for Fairfield Sentry, the largest feeder fund into Madoff. That's because, in Picard's case, he's responsible for locating, recovering, and distributing money to *individual* losers who invested *directly* with Madoff—and by all accounts he has outperformed expectations, hauling in nearly $15 billion over the fifteen-plus years he's been on the job. But Picard isn't tasked with recovering money for people who lost their principal in funds invested in Madoff—that's the feds' job. And offshore feeder funds comprise yet another money pot, and they're overseen by a half dozen trustees (mini-Picards) in places such as Luxembourg and the British Virgin Islands. In short, says Krys, it may never be possible to come up with accurate totals.

But numbers tell only part of the Madoff story. To grasp the enormity of his "accomplishment," you need to envision the cosmos that Bernie had created. It was like an elaborate Hollywood set, propped up with poles, behind which stood . . . nothing. "The first term that came to me to describe this is that I was living in the Matrix," says a top trader who worked on BLMIS's prop-trading side. "But you can also view it a little bit like a Potemkin village. Everyone idolized Bernie until December 10 [the day before he was arrested]. As my wife said, it was a death. We all cried continuously for the first week. Obviously, he was brilliant at constructing legitimate businesses to provide cover. He manipulated everybody."

Bernie's Ponzi started with what's known in the law enforcement community as an affinity crime—which, in his case, meant robbing fellow American Jews before moving on to engulf other investors around the world like a financial tsunami. When Bernie was sentenced to what was essentially life plus on June 29, 2009, it was for eleven felony charges, including securities and investment advisor fraud, perjury, filing false statements with the SEC, and even theft from an employee benefit plan. From his cell, he denied none of it.

The days and weeks following Bernie's arrest triggered the bloodlust of the press. The *New York Post* called him "The Most Hated

Man in NY," in huge all-caps type on its front page. The *Wall Street Journal* published a list of thousands of investors who lost money—along with their mailing addresses—which angered and embarrassed many of them. News crews and apoplectic investors camped outside Bernie and Ruth's duplex penthouse, where they were holed up. ("Jump!" read one protester's sign on the street below.) Video surveillance and private guards followed him, as feds were worried he might either be killed by investors or by his own hand. He and Ruth would claim later, not entirely convincingly, that they tried to fatally overdose on the sleeping aid Ambien and maybe some Klonopin, a tranquilizer, which pharmacologists say is hard to do. Eleven blocks south, R. Thierry Magon de la Villehuchet, manager of a multibillion-dollar Madoff feeder fund, was more successful, cutting his wrists and biceps, and bleeding out into a wastebasket in his twenty-second-floor Madison Avenue office. Security officers discovered his body in a chair, with one leg propped up on his desk.

Before long, it became clear that Bernie had run nearly the entire Ponzi scheme out of a single checking account at JPMorgan Chase & Co., no. 140081703, nicknamed "the 703" by investigators after his arrest. Billions of dollars flowed through that lone account, with virtually none of the money used to buy or sell securities. It is estimated by Picard that JPMC made more than a half billion dollars in fees and profits from its relationship with Madoff, ignoring signs of fraud even as its due diligence unearthed evidence of it. (It's an aggressive estimate by the trustee, but it's the best we have.) Spokespeople for Chairman and CEO Jamie Dimon insisted that America's largest bank did nothing wrong, but clearly changed their tune in 2014 when the financial behemoth agreed to a set of damning facts in a "deferred prosecution agreement" with the feds that should be required reading for anyone hoping to become a banker. "The banks had to know," Bernie told me once, adding that he'd met multiple times with Chase's president, Robert Lipp. "Chase will have a hard time. The reality of it is, the complicity of the banks and the feeder funds is very clear."

Feeders are sub-funds that put all their investment capital into an umbrella fund for which a single investment advisor handles all the trading. Or is supposed to, anyway. Profits from this pooled money are then split proportionately to the feeder funds based on how much they had contributed to it.

Bernie, for his part, pleaded guilty—then refused to cooperate with criminal probes that could have fingered relatives, associates, and his biggest investors. Indeed, he went to his reward insisting that his wife, sons, brother, and niece knew nothing of his chicanery. At the same time, unable to resist playing the hero, Bernie would go so far as to claim later that it was he—not the authorities or "the idiot Picard"—who got most of the money returned to net losers, a feat he apparently pulled off by strong-arming two of his oldest, greediest investors from a pay phone by a highway while he was out on bail. He was like an arsonist who calls 911 after having set the fire and then sticks around to congratulate himself as the firefighters extinguish the flames.

Butner, North Carolina, home to Bernie's prison, is one of those proverbial towns that time forgot. On its main street, the abandoned Exxon station still advertised gas for $1.29 a gallon—in 2011, when the state's average price was nearly triple that.

There are several fast-food joints in Butner, but no supermarket. The most popular place to eat was Sam's, a dive that seated fifteen people, where beef tips with string beans, cabbage, grits, and a Diet Coke ran you $6. It wasn't exactly the *nodino sassi* being presented to diners at Primola, Bernie and Ruth's favorite Upper East Side restaurant. But none of this mattered to Bernie. He'd never see the town.

My first meeting at Butner was scheduled for February 2011.

At the prison, I went through an elaborate security process until a deputy warden approached and asked if I could step outside of the building with her. "I'm sorry, but Mr. Madoff changed his mind and won't see you," she said. "He says it's upon the advice of his lawyers and that he will explain in an email to you."

I flew home to New York and called Allan Dodds Frank, a retired CNN investigative reporter who was assisting me at the time. He alerted me that the *New York Times* had just published an exclusive online by a reporter who visited Bernie that very morning. In fact, she was already sitting with him when I showed up.

"Bernie screwed me," I said in dumb disbelief.

"Get in line," Allan said, laughing. "You're number 22,834."

It was illustrative, right out of the starting gate, of how Bernie operated.

"I am sorry for the mess up," began Bernie's next email to me. "I assumed that your visit would not happen for a while based on what has been the pattern with all visits for me, even my attorneys. While speaking to my attorneys last night, they advised me to not have any visits at this time due to the ongoing litigation. I will be able to see you as soon as these issues are resolved. I'm sorry for the inconvenience, but this is out of my hands."

Of course, that wasn't true.

"Bernie, I feel ill-used by you," I wrote back. "We both know it wasn't your lawyers who prevented you and I [*sic*] from further communications; it was your decision entirely. So what was it, and why? I really would like to know."

I learned later that Bernie routinely stovepiped reporters, just as he did employees and investors, limiting what they knew about what he was doing or saying. To take one trivial example: he periodically asked me to help fund his email account, and, given that I needed to communicate with him, I decided doing that was a necessary expense, however uncomfortable it made me as a reporter. ("I do feel like a schnorrer," Bernie wrote me after one of his requests, using the Yiddish word for beggar, or sponger. "I'm embarrassed but have little other options," he wrote on another occasion.) But during one of my visits, a prison spokesman named Chris McConnell told me that "Bernie has got all you reporters wrapped around his fingers. He has plenty of money. He tells reporters the same story." If information can be viewed as income, Bernie was running a mini–Ponzi scheme behind bars.

In July 2011 I went through Butner security again and this time got to see Bernie. It was the first of what would be three in-person visits over the course of the next eight years. Altogether I spent some six hours in Bernie's presence—the wardens at Butner seldom granted access to reporters—but that time doesn't include all the aforementioned phone calls, letters, and emails we exchanged over the course of the decade. What follows is a quasi-composite rendering of those one-on-one meetings, in the hope that I can convey a sense of the man while sparing the reader the redundancy of those interviews, in which I was compelled to revisit the same investigative ground again and again. And, really, who are we fooling here? The scenery doesn't change much in a medium-security prison from one year to the next. And except for Bernie's getting a little jowlier, a little wrinklier, and a little sicklier over those years, neither did he.

Because I was neither a family member, close friend, nor lawyer, my visits were deemed rare "special meetings," limited to two hours. I was told that I could provide nothing to an inmate of any value— not even a piece of paper or gum. But Bernie had written me in advance: "By the way, you are allowed to bring up to $20 in quarters for the vending machines." So I did.

There are few things more disturbing than visiting a prison, and while it was no supermax, Butner was plenty grim in its own way. A twelve-foot fence topped with razor wire gleamed like icicles in the blazing ninety-six-degree sun, with inmates penned inside like cattle with shivs. The heat only exacerbated the feeling that this place was hell. On the airplane down, my thoughts turned to Willie Bosket, a killer I'd visited in prison in 1989. Just as Bernie committed history's greatest fraud, Bosket was considered at the time to be the most violent criminal in New York State history. At age fifteen he shot to death two strangers riding a New York City subway. (He had also battered a reformatory teacher, knifed a half-blind man, beat up a psychiatrist, smashed a prison guard's skull, stabbed a second guard, and set his cell on fire seven times.) But he was more than a self-described "monster"; he was intelligent, well read, and sophisticated. And so dangerous that authorities had built him a special dungeon at the prison: a room lined with Plexiglas, with three video cameras tracking him. When I arrived, I found him chained backward to the inside of his cell door. When the door swung open, there was Bosket, pinned to the bars like a specimen in a bug collection. "I'm really a loving and caring person," he assured me later.

There were no chains for Bernie, although plenty of investors who called him a financial killer would have loved to see them. His routine seemed to soothe him: up at four in the morning, coffee in bed (he had an instant hot water machine in his cell), reading or listening to NPR on his radio until breakfast. No Internet access, however, so Bernie would sometimes ask for news stories about his crimes to be sent to him. Then it was time for his prison job: in the kitchen in the early years, then the laundry room, and later (and extremely improbably) overseeing the inmate computer and telephone room. Lunch was from ten thirty to eleven; dinner at five thirty.

What Bernie seemed to love best was sleeping or sitting outside in the prison courtyard. He pointed to his deep suntan, noting that he spent much of his time in the yard, soaking up the North Carolina rays and strolling with Carmine "the Snake" Persico and Nicodemo "Little

Nicky" Scarfo, "terrific guys" who'd been bosses of, respectively, the Colombo Mafia family in New York and the Scarfo family in Philly. "You adapt in prison," Bernie said with a shrug, explaining away his friendship with the two homicidal godfathers. (Astonishingly, both had received lighter sentences for their multiple murders than he had for his swindles.) "You're thrown together. No one asks about your crime. Never comes up in the slightest, and they never ask me about mine." Madoff would deliver the eulogy for Persico, who died while still behind bars in 2019.

As I approached on our first meeting, Bernie smiled, eyes twinkling behind gold-rimmed glasses. His short salt-and-pepper hair was neat and had been trimmed into a slight Transylvanian triangle on his forehead. He seemed gentle, warm, vulnerable—likable. In fact, he looked pretty good for a guy who had run a $68 billion fraud and was serving a 150-year sentence.

Bernie's hands were soft. His face betrayed no sign of the carnage he'd left behind. I felt the sudden urge to hug and comfort him, to give him whatever he wanted. Even in the clink, Madoff had that special power. I could see why so many investors (including a co-owner of a feeder fund that lost more than $7 billion in the Ponzi) referred to him as "Uncle Bernie."

He began our first meeting by apologizing again for my having flown down for nothing a few months earlier. This time he blamed not his lawyers but prison officials for not letting him know which day I was coming. "It's bureaucratic here, and difficult getting word about meetings," he said. "The assistant warden is a ballbuster; a blonde woman who likes to rattle her sword. She has a power struggle with me for some reason. The staff hates her, everyone hates her. Makes it difficult for my visits." Nonetheless, he said, he's a "celebrity of sorts" inside the prison, and "the staff joke with me about how the food compares to New York restaurants."

Our meeting had begun in a tiny visiting room, but we were

soon transferred to a large, empty conference room that featured happy-pink padded chairs as well as framed posters of nature scenes on the walls, with the words "Teamwork," "Performance," and "Challenge" on them. "You're getting the royal treatment," Bernie said.

Once seated, I placed the quarters on our conference table and motioned for Madoff to have at it. "No, you have to do it," he said. "I'll have a Diet Coke." Ouch. The greatest fraudster in history was not allowed to touch a coin. A billionaire who was once among the biggest market makers at the New York Stock Exchange not permitted now to get a soda for himself. But if he felt humiliated, he didn't show it.

It's tempting and perhaps common sense to dismiss everything Bernie says as bullshit. John Moscow, a former chief white-collar-crimes prosecutor for the Manhattan District Attorney's Office who worked on Madoff cases for Picard, certainly did: "If a word or two of truth passed his lips, he'll need medical care," Moscow once told me. Prosecutors felt the same: after just two sit-downs with Bernie, they concluded he was so unreliable that any potential cooperation from him was useless. Bernie's lawyer, a former SEC official named Ira (Ike) Sorkin, found this decision flabbergasting. Surely, he felt, his client could be of some help if he met regularly with the feds. But the feds disagreed. And yet: "The door was open, if Bernie was gonna be honest," says former federal prosecutor Lisa Baroni, who led the Madoff-related investigations at the time for the US Attorney's Office–Southern District of New York. "He certainly could have saved the government so many years of work, investigation, and expense, where we had to piece it together—literally document by document, witness by witness."

A team of Picard's investigators met with Bernie in prison in mid-2009. They came away feeling that he lied on some matters but told the truth on others—and so they used him simply to confirm or fill gaps in matters they knew already. That had been my experience, too, and often my strategy. At the same time, we all were convinced that in certain areas, Bernie believed what he was saying was true—even when it clearly wasn't.

Liar or not, Madoff was an infuriating interlocutor. Although willing to discuss just about anything, he tended to control conversations by ranting endlessly about certain subjects. It's a tactic that FBI psychologists told me is used by con men to throw off investigators. (So, too, the phrase "and so on and so forth," which Bernie would slap onto the end of many sentences.) I learned early on in phone interviews with him that I needed to limit questions to perhaps two, maybe three, for each fifteen-minute increment that the prison permits at one time. "I only get 300 minutes a month," Bernie complained early on, "and I pay five cents a minute, and I only receive a small salary here."

During our first meeting, Bernie spoke mainly about how and why (in his view) the Ponzi scheme began. He was especially fixated on how purported betrayals by key investors who'd been with him since the 1970s—the "Big Four," he called them—had driven him to it, exploiting him after the 1987 stock market crash, the sharpest market downtown since the Depression. "I knew the Big Four were generating false trades, backdated trades, tax losses, tax fraud," he told me, in a classic case of projection. Did they know it was a Ponzi? "Nobody wanted to acknowledge what they knew, or [they] didn't want to know. They had to know something was wrong, 'cos they knew backdating was wrong. And they knew I was desperate at times. These guys are so greedy, and so obsessed with not paying any taxes, you would not believe it." Take it from the decades-long tax cheat.

When he wasn't working in the prison's kitchen, Bernie said, he spent most of his time alone, mainly reading books. (Leon Uris's classic and mammoth 1953 novel *Battle Cry*, about US Marines fighting in the Pacific in World War II, was on his plate.) He told me that while he enjoyed hanging out in the prison yard with Persico ("a very sweet man") and Scarfo, he couldn't abide the infamous convicted spy Jonathan Pollard, an American who pleaded guilty in 1986 to spying for Israel and was sentenced to life. "I don't get along with him. I find him to be, you know, a total phony—he makes up these stories that he tells everybody about himself, and he walks around sort of kissing the ass of all the guards here. He's just a really despicable kind of a character, you know."

Our conversation ranged from the Ponzi's genesis story—a critical area, as we will see—to why he thought the SEC had been blamed unfairly for not catching him, a view I share. Bernie was adamant that he never took on customers who couldn't afford to lose all their money. How so? His earliest clients were extraordinarily wealthy and sophisticated, he claimed. But once he opened the doors to herds of clients, starting in the early 1990s, there was a minimum investment of $2 million, he insisted, and that number had to be no more than 50 percent of their liquid net worth. "They also signed documents attesting to that, and they also signed documents stating that this trading involved risks, and so on and so forth," he pointed out, shifting blame down the food chain. "Whether people read that . . ." He chuckled. "I mean, that's like any other disclaimer. Believe it or not, I also stated that there was always the possibility of fraud being committed by me or others."

Bernie let drop that certain schools had reached out to him to teach business ethics. "How can I teach ethics?!" he marveled, revealing some measure of self-awareness. He said he had also been asked by fellow inmates to lecture and tutor them about business—until "the word got out." A financial swindler teaching fellow incarcerated felons about finance did seem possibly ill-advised. "They don't want me to discuss that [business] with inmates here," he added, in case inmates "misinterpret" him as laying out a blueprint for a giant caper like his own. "So I was transferred from education to the commissary, which was actually a good move for me."

Many lies start small. Many snowball in a way that feels unstoppable to those who got them rolling in the first place. "I know it's hard to imagine, but I'm not a gambler," Bernie claimed. "It's not in my nature. I never played cards. Never bought lottery tickets." But events outstripped him, he told me, leaving him with no way out of the hole he had dug for himself by taking money from friends, relatives, and strangers—and attaching big promises to them.

"I started in the 1960s with trading," he said defensively. "Everyone thinks I woke up and decided to start to steal. I felt there's nothing you can't do with trading with my ability." According to Madoff, he began stealing only after markets and some major clients turned against him, maintaining "I just had no choice."

All that lying took a toll even on Bernie, at least to hear him tell it. "Oh, yeah. After awhile, you start bullshitting yourself to believe what you want to believe. 'I'm gonna get out of this mess.' And then you just block it out of your mind. I was going nuts. Sixteen years of doing this [Ponzi]. Not telling your wife and sons. I don't know how I stood the stress. There must be something wrong with me to be able [to handle] the pressure. I woke up every morning for sixteen years—certainly the last eight or nine of it—feeling I'm not coming out of it. I was hoping for some kind of miracle. The only time I relaxed was on weekends, when I was on my boat." (His biggest: an eighty-eight-foot megayacht aptly named *Bull,* which had a life-saving buoy named "Bullship.")

This struck me as odd. Mafia hitman Nicky "the Crow" Caramandi—the guy who ratted out Bernie's pal Scarfo—once told me that he hated to fly because "I think of all the rottenness I've done in my life when I'm on a fucking plane. All the evil." Wouldn't Bernie suffer the same pangs on a boat? His employees said Madoff was an absolute control freak at the office, and one could imagine he kept busy to avoid having to reflect on his fraud. But bobbing around on a boat in the open ocean? What else would even a con man have to do except stew in it all?

A former top FBI behavioral analysis expert named Joe Navarro understands why Bernie might have found some peace at sea. "The reason he felt safe on his boat is because he could see three hundred sixty degrees," says Navarro, a pioneer of the science of unraveling the verbal and nonverbal behaviors of criminals. "And there's no danger out on a boat alone. You can see all around you, and can see there's no threats, and 'Oh, I can relax—there's comfort all the way around.' It's the threat of being caught that he fears. And if there is a threat, 'I'm gonna see way out to the horizon so I'll have a lot of forewarning that a threat is coming.'"

I asked Bernie if he ever sought treatment for depression during all those years of running and concealing the Ponzi. "There was no way out, so I don't know if it would have helped," he told me. "Now I'm upset every day of this; I have periods of depression. I'm on medicine for it. Sometimes it's hard getting out of bed." Referring to his public image following his arrest, he added, "This 'evil monster' thing developed."

At times Bernie spoke of his Ponzi with almost a bemused detachment. "Ever since I've been here, this psychologist has really helped me a lot," he exclaimed happily during one phone call. "After awhile, you start believing what you're reading. Am I a sociopath? I had a lot of clients who were friends and family. How could I do this? It became a very personal crime." Did his psychologist tell him he's a sociopath? "No. She said people have the ability to compartmentalize. It's like, I never understood how Mafia people kill and go home and hold their kids. She said, 'You put it out of your mind.'" According to Bernie, his prison shrink never came up with a diagnostic label for him, at least not one that she shared with him. "Just compartmentalize," he repeated to me.

"So you're a compartmentalizer," I said.

"Exactly."

Bernie then moved from misery to victimhood: "All my friends are worried about clawback, which is why I think I didn't receive a single letter on my behalf to the court. Everyone ran for the hills. I have not received one letter from friends or family members since I've been here. Not one . . . All of these people were friends, and happy to take these returns before this happened. Now all of a sudden everybody is upset."

Unsurprisingly, Bernie felt he'd been railroaded, handed down a sentence seriously out of whack with the nature of his crimes. What *was* surprising was that I found myself agreeing with him. He hadn't killed anyone, after all, and Irving "Clawback" Picard and the feds had been extremely effective in getting money back for the Ponzi's net losers who'd been left holding the proverbial bag. But when I asked what justice for him would have looked like, Bernie responded dejectedly, "It's hard for me to tell. Even if [it had been] twenty years, I would have been ninety when I got out. Maybe the situation would have been different if I was sentenced after they saw what the net loss was."

Bernie said he gets twenty to thirty letters a day from people he doesn't know. "They want me to be a mentor, they want autographs. I don't answer them; I'm afraid they'll use it in the media." Or maybe sell it on eBay, where a cottage industry in Madoff paraphernalia and swag mushroomed for years and still exists to some degree.

A few months before my 2019 meeting with him, Bernie had requested clemency from then-president Donald Trump, the fellow yarn spinner he'd played golf with once in better days. He asked for a sentence commutation "simply as an act of mercy or grace." A former prosecutor on his case called it "the very definition of chutzpah." (In 2018 Bernie had made a previous request for clemency to Denny Chin, the judge who had sentenced him to the 150. Chin turned him down, saying that "it was fully my intent that he live out the rest of his life in prison.")

In his request to Trump, Bernie pointed out that he never denied his crimes, pled guilty immediately, that his losing (direct) investors had already gotten back 75 percent of their principal, and that due to kidney disease, his life expectancy was eight years, which he said he felt was "overly-optimistically generous." (He was right about that, as he'd be dead in two years.) Of course, it didn't help his case that Madoff refused to rat on underlings or help the feds in other ways. Although Trump was profuse with pardons for many crooks, he denied Bernie's request. A decade before, he had called Madoff "a Svengali for rich people" who "took their money like it was candy, chewed it up, and spit it out."

Bernie said often that he was counting on my book to set things straight and was upset that I still hadn't published it after a decade of work. He complained in an email that he'd probably be dead by the time it came out.

Madoff could become indignant when speaking of his crimes. He scoffed at those victims who were holding out for Picard to recoup their losses. Referring to a secondary market that had sprung up around the clawbacks—hedge funds offering to pay Bernie's victims now for the right to collect their settlement money later—he grew hot: "To show you how stupid or greedy my clients are," he told me, still speaking of them in the present tense, "they're offered eighty cents on the dollar by these hedge funds years ago and wouldn't take it. They feel they'll be rewarded for waiting. Claiming they're living in dumpsters and won't take the money . . . All clients lie. Every client would call me and ask if there were any tax things or scams I can do. Pay the fucking tax!"

During our first meeting in 2011, when I had Bernie in a calm, reflective mood, I asked whether he'd had any contact with Ruth, his wife of fifty-two years, who'd been hunkered down post-arrest alone in the Manhattan apartment they used to share. The feds eventually seized almost all of their assets, including the apartment, but were allowing Ruth to keep a small sum of money—which Picard nonetheless was trying to claw back. Ruth moved temporarily to Boca Raton, Florida, to live with her sister and brother-in-law (from whom Picard was also clawing profits).

"No," Bernie replied matter-of-factly. "Ruth visited two, three times at the beginning," in 2009. "I haven't seen her in a year."

At one point in our correspondence, in 2012, I noticed that Bernie was cc'ing Ruth on a number of emails he was sending me. Does she know? Does she care? A year later, he even addressed her directly in one of them: "Ruth, you may wonder why I risk annoying you, by copying you on these emails. It is only in the hope that they may help my grandchildren have some understanding of their grandfather. . . . I would like them to know the truth." Ruth replied: "I'll just save this. I don't know how to copy this."

Bernie told me several years later, in 2015, that he and Ruth were speaking a few times a week. The phone calls were monitored and—according to one investigator who reviewed confidential transcripts of them—the conversations were constant and always "loving." Nevertheless, she still hadn't visited him. "I don't want her to visit me," he said. "It's too hard for me to see her like this, and for her to see me this way."

It is difficult to parse the psychology of a marriage, as anyone who's married will attest. And it is difficult to predict what one spouse will let the other get away with, until they draw a line. So it is worth pointing out that Ruth, who always claimed she was a victim just like all the investors who lost money (and who said during a TV interview that "It took me awhile to realize that the same person I had lived with and loved for fifty years was the same person that destroyed all these lives"), remained married to him until the day Bernie checked out. Bernie's brother, Peter, apparently felt a similar loyalty, from his prison cell at the Federal Medical Center in Devens, Massachusetts, even though in a courtroom he'd blamed his own crimes on his allegiance to his older sibling and insisted that he was clueless about the Ponzi. Several years into their respective prison terms, Bernie forwarded me a letter he'd received in 2016 from his brother that ended, simply, "Love, Peter."

Ruth never agreed to speak with me, but in 2018 she used a life-long friend I had reached out to for an interview to convey a few shreds of information. The friend, who asked not to be named, spoke constantly with Ruth, and had forwarded her my questions, including: "Did Ruth suspect (or maybe should have suspected) that something wasn't quite right about Bernie through the years?"

The friend's reply, by phone, was simply: "All she cares about is that people know that she knew *nothing* about it [the fraud]."

I pressed, asking whether, in retrospect, Ruth saw at least *one* sign that something was off? "I don't think she could have seen," said the friend. "He fooled the most sophisticated of businessmen. He fooled the SEC. How could someone of my generation who trusted her husband *ever* know anything?"

I told her that I'd interviewed a dozen former classmates of theirs, and that many feel the opposite: that *they* surely would have seen some signs. "I married my high school sweetheart [too], and there are plenty of things that I don't know about him," she replied. "And there were plenty of things he didn't know about me. There would be no reason ever for Ruth to suspect because she was married to somebody who she knew to be a very hard worker, very industrious and clever at business . . . obsessive about business. And once your mind is set on one way of looking at someone, it stays that way until you hear the contrary. So, *A*, she loved him, and *B*, she had no reason not to trust him. . . . I know that Ruth is not a duplicitous person. She just isn't. It's out of the question that she would have any inkling."

"So Ruth says she can't look back now and see signs of anything suspicious?" I asked.

"No, she doesn't."

We will return to that question.

2

Solved: When the Fraud Began

| | | | | | | | | | | | | |

The Question: When did the world's greatest fraud begin? In the early 1990s, as Madoff insisted up to his last breath? Or was it a fraud from the start of his career in the early 1960s?

The Laurelton, Queens, of Bernie Madoff's childhood comes off as some sort of Hebraic version of the hometowns portrayed nostalgically in both George Lucas's 1973 film *American Graffiti* and TV's *Happy Days*, which debuted a few months later. The kids of Laurelton hung out at a soda fountain called Raab's right out of *Archie* comics. (Or it would have been, had Archie been Jewish.) They walked to see movies at the local theater, nicknamed "the Itch." The butcher delivered meat in a carriage. Dr. Diamond performed nose jobs for the neighborhood beauties. Teens sang doo-wop on the sidewalks. Vitalis men's hair tonic was a thing. And at Far Rockaway High School, Ruth and her girlfriends weren't allowed to wear pants.

Jews made up more than 30 percent of the town's population at the time; today very few remain. For them, the Laurelton Jewish Center was a major hub. Bernie's father, Ralph, served for a time as president of the temple, and his mother, Sylvia, was president of Hadassah, a major Jewish women's charity that later invested with Bernie. At home, they kept the kitchen kosher but weren't especially religious. Bernie's great-grandfather, Berel Miodownick, had immigrated to Scranton, Pennsylvania, in 1908 from Poland along with his wife and seven children. He changed his name to Barnett Madoff and found work as a tailor. Ralph moved from Scranton to Brooklyn, where he married Sylvia, and then settled in Laurelton.

"Quite frankly, it was an ideal household to grow up in," said Bernie. "Loving, very supportive parents, a very loving sister, a loving brother. The family was very idyllic." He added with a laugh: "At least, that's the way I thought about it."

But the Madoff house was clearly less than typical. Father Ralph ran a sporting goods business that went bust, resulting in an IRS tax lien on their modest three-bedroom brick home with detached garage on 228th Street. Ralph had put the house in Sylvia's name, under the mistaken belief that they couldn't lose it that way, something Bernie would try, fruitlessly, decades later for Ruth.

More significantly, Bernie's mother was listed by the SEC as the owner of a brokerage firm called Gibraltar Securities, with the Madoffs' house listed as its address. In 1963, three years after Bernie launched his own securities firm, Gibraltar was caught up in a sweep of forty-eight broker-dealers who had failed to file reports of their financial condition. It was a violation of a regulation (rule 17a-5 of the Securities Exchange Act of 1934) that brokers certainly didn't need a lawyer or accountant to know about. It would be akin to failing to file your personal tax returns—only worse, because in Sylvia's case, brokerage clients would have been vulnerable.

It was pretty much the same violation that Bernie himself would repeat over and over and over again in his career. Although in Bernie's case, it was hardly the only one.

SEC records from the 1960s are scant, but what is clear is that in

1964, one year after the agency's sweep, the firm's registration was revoked, as was that of another company listed at the Madoffs' home address, Second Gibraltar Corp. Yet the SEC dismissed administrative proceedings against Bernie's mother as long as she promised to stay out of the business.

It was a precursor of what was to come.

By all indications, Bernie was an unexceptionable student. After graduating from Far Rockaway High School in 1956, he headed off to the University of Alabama, which—then under pressure from the federal government to diversify its student body—was aggressively recruiting ethnic (but white) kids from the Northeast. Gay Talese, one of America's best writers, an Italian American, was a student there several years before Bernie arrived. He says his own high school grades were so awful that the principal visited his father at the family's home in New Jersey to tell him there was simply no way his son would be able to go to college. That is, until Alabama called. "You couldn't get into other colleges," says Talese. "That's why you went to Alabama."

But Bernie pined for his high school sweetheart, Ruth Alpern, and lasted only two semesters before hightailing it home.

Madoff enrolled at Long Island's Hofstra College, a mediocre school at the time. On November 28, 1959, during his senior year, he and Ruth were married at Laurelton Jewish Center by Rabbi Saul Teplitz.

In June 1960 Bernie graduated Hofstra with a degree in political science. We don't know exactly what gave him the idea, but later that same year, the twenty-two-year-old founded BLMIS. He operated it out of the Midtown Manhattan accounting office of Saul Alpern, Ruth's father, before hanging out his shingle on his own space at 39

Broadway, a four-minute walk from Wall Street. He soon had about a dozen clients, all of them friends, family, and clients of Saul's.

Soon enough, Bernie found himself in his first pickle. He told me that his father, Ralph, was the "finder" of some new-issue penny stocks—securities that are sold to investors for the first time. Bernie purchased some shares, only to watch the share prices crash within weeks. Bernie said he "felt so embarrassed and responsible" that he decided to buy back his clients' shares, booking a roughly $30,000 loss (the equivalent of about $300,000 today) that depleted his capital. "With my tail between my legs," he recounted in an email, "I tearfully asked my father-in-law, Saul, for a loan to recapitalize my firm." (Following his arrest in 2008, Bernie told the FBI that the experience was so humiliating that he vowed it would never happen again.)

Madoff blames the loss on the Cuban Missile Crisis of October 1962, of all things. He had developed enough retail business, he explained to me in 2012, to allow his capital to grow from $500 to $35,000. But just weeks later, US military reconnaissance discovered that the Soviet Union had been secretly constructing nuclear missile sites in Cuba, just ninety miles off the coast of Florida. President John F. Kennedy demanded that his Soviet counterpart, Premier Nikita Khrushchev, dismantle the weapons immediately. For thirteen excruciating days, the two superpowers remained locked in a tense showdown that could have plunged the entire world into nuclear Armageddon. On account of the Cold War confrontation, claimed Bernie, "the new issue [initial public offerings] market collapsed." And in a subsequent email: "The underwriters of the new issues as well as the market makers completely withdrew their support, and the stocks dropped."

Not plausible, says Jay Ritter, an economics professor known as "Mr. IPO" for his work and historical studies on initial public offerings. Ritter walked me through a statistical analysis of the IPO market of the 1960s. Bottom line: the missile crisis had nothing to do with any rise or decline in the IPO markets. As for Bernie's pinning his supposed loss on the crisis, Ritter says dismissively: "He's trying to come up with a source to blame rather than 'I had a bunch of cruddy companies that depend upon getting unsophisticated retail investors to buy them. And when people got cold feet, I could no longer find some other unsophisticated investor to foist 'em off on.'"

For the record, Bernie maintains that his bailout of clients was "perfectly legal." Well, not quite. It is against SEC rules for even a new broker to reimburse a client for trading losses. Whether that was Bernie's first violation of the law, we'll never know. It certainly wasn't his last. Who were those clients he'd made whole? It took years for Madoff to name them, but he finally did. Three were relatives: Saul himself, and his brothers Bill Alpern and Max Alpern, Ruth's uncles. The other two? Nonrelatives who Bernie said were his very first customers: Abraham "Abe" Hershson and Morris "Moe" Steinberg, both of them clients of Saul's and both of whom I'd eventually discover from FBI records were critical to the fraud's origin. (Bernie didn't mention him, but another initial investor was Marvin Weiner, an oral surgeon who was married to Bernie's sister, Sondra.)

In any case, by the early 1960s, there was Bernie, young, undereducated, and already in hock again to the tune of some $30,000. It isn't hard to see how a Ponzi would become almost irresistible. No one is left alive to tell us exactly what went down, but by Bernie's own admission, he had all the elements of his scheme in place within a couple years of opening up shop. At its center sat Bernie, Ralph, Saul, and a few other friends and relatives.

And, crucially, that web of investors began expanding almost immediately. In the early sixties Saul formed his own group of investors, consisting mainly of his accounting clients, to provide money to Madoff, which they did for decades to come. He told the people he recruited that investing with his son-in-law would yield them 20 percent returns. Saul took a cut along the way from those investors, essentially becoming one of Bernie's first feeders. It's easy to imagine how Saul and his cronies would see the opportunity to get their hooks into a young trader by underwriting his desk in exchange for Bernie's doing right by them down the road. Bernie's debt made him weak, vulnerable. And his lack of experience could well have rendered him exploitable to a financially savvy operator and veteran accountant like Saul.

"Saul was the incubator," says Steven Garfinkel, a former FBI agent who probed the Madoff family after Bernie's arrest. "Like a Silicon Valley venture capitalist putting tech people together, Saul brought con men together."

To hear Bernie tell it, he soon revealed himself to be a trading prodigy who "never had a year that lost money," as he put it to me in Butner. In fact, he said, referring to the bailout from Saul, "I was able to repay the loan within a year, which made both of us happy." If true, that alone seems to lend even more credence to the theory that the Ponzi was up and running early on. As Madoff told me, in what could be the epitaph for his entire financial career, "My clients were unaware of my actions due to their lack of market experience."

"I'm at the end of my rope," Bernie told his right-hand man in early December 2008. It was almost a half century into BLMIS's existence, and Madoff was in his office, catatonic in front of his computer screen. Frank DiPascali Jr., by then Bernie's longtime deputy-in-crime, had noticed that his boss had been under tremendous stress for the past few weeks; now he seemed to be cracking.

Frank later told a group of nine federal investigators that he wasn't sure what Bernie meant until he added: "I don't have any money. . . . The whole business has been a scam. It goes all the way back to Moe and goes back to Abe." Frank then provided the feds with their full names: Moe Steinberg and Abe Hershson—the same guys Bernie had told me were his first nonfamily clients.

A week later, Frank told investigators, he walked into Bernie's office to find him talking with Peter Madoff "about the history of BLMIS and how the fraud went all the way back to Abe and Moe" and that "Peter did not seem shocked by any of this." DiPascali also revealed that in the late 1970s, Bernie had about twenty to a hundred investment advisory (IA) clients, many of whom were friends of Saul Alpern. He rattled off only four names as examples, including Abe. Frank said he never knew who was performing these "trades" for them. Nobody, it turned out.

We'll come back to Moe and Abe, as they are ground zero to the origin of the fraud. But first, let's meet Frank DiPascali. After Bernie's arrest and guilty plea, DiPascali emerged as—or turned into—the key witness against him and numerous employees, including the Madoff Five, four of whom reported to Frank in the firm's hierarchy.

Frank had arrived on Bernie's doorstep in 1975 as an unemployed local punk; in the end, he was one of the longest-serving non-family-member employees of BLMIS. By the time the FBI rounded him up, DiPascali owned a $2 million boat (his fourth) and a seven-acre estate. Confronted with the choice of singing or going to jail, Frank asked the FBI to strike up a tune.

I obtained more than 100 pages of confidential FBI interview summaries (known in agency parlance as 302s) compiled during the many months that Frank sat with them, dishing dirt on Madoff and others. Each session was attended by as many as ten government investigators—FBI and SEC agents and federal prosecutors—and subsequently typed up by the FBI.

Reading those summaries, it's clear that in the nearly thirty-five years that DiPascali spent with Bernie, he'd become his main accomplice, essentially running the fraud with him. Obviously, that begs the question: How reliable a witness was DiPascali? The answer seems to be "surprisingly reliable!" Frank had more than seventy-five lengthy sessions (over a period of more than four years) with government investigators, who told me they never caught him in a lie, and considered him one of the best and most honest cooperators they ever worked with in their many collective years of prosecuting major financial crime cases. And after a jury in 2014 convicted all the defendants in the Madoff Five case—on every charge—more than half of the jurors agreed to be interviewed, and each told me they'd found DiPascali, who testified for sixteen days, to be entirely credible. I attended more than half of the six-month trial and felt the same way. Furthermore, in 2022 two federal judges presiding over a civil case in bankruptcy court deemed DiPascali's testimony not only reliable but also backed up by "voluminous evidence," including BLMIS books and records.

So, for lack of a better candidate, Frank, who died in 2015 of lung cancer at the age of fifty-eight, is our Virgil here—our guide to the early years (and the back rooms) of BLMIS.

Frank DiPascali grew up in Howard Beach, Queens, about a fifteen-minute drive from Bernie in Laurelton. He and Bernie had little in common, apart from both being crooks in training. Howard Beach was largely Italian and middle class, full of cops and firefighters; Laurelton was upper middle class, heavily Jewish. Frank spent his youth stealing coats from stores; Bernie was a lifeguard at prestigious country clubs. Like Bernie, Frank was an indifferent student. One of his classmates at a Catholic high school, Ray Kelly, grew up to become the longest-serving commissioner in the history of the New York City Police Department, while DiPascali would go on to withdraw from St. John's University in Queens after receiving five incompletes for his first semester. Frank was what we might call a delinquent, a wastrel—or, these days, a child with challenges. By his own admission, he drank and played cards excessively and spent too much time hanging out in the cafeteria and pledging a fraternity.

In 1975 Frank went to the US Army recruiting station in Jamaica, passed the physical, and enlisted to train at Fort Hamilton, in Brooklyn. He still had braces on his teeth, which an army dentist said would have to be removed prior to enlisting. But when the young man told his father he'd signed up, Frank Sr. nixed the whole idea. Frank Jr. withdrew his enlistment papers and had to hatch a new plan.

With Frank at loose ends, his dad approached their neighbor Annette Bongiorno (née Argese) to see if she could help Frank get a job at BLMIS, where she worked as a bookkeeper. Frank had known Annette since he was in second grade; she babysat him when he was younger, and Frank drove her dad's laundry delivery van when he was in his teens. Frank saw Bongiorno's nice car—her company even gave her a reserved parking space; a big deal for a kid from Howard Beach back then—and figured she must know something. He also figured it must have been easy work, since he didn't consider her to be very smart.

In August 1975 Bongiorno arranged an interview for him at BLMIS, something she would come to regret decades later when Frank's testimony would land her in prison. The company consisted of just a dozen employees. Bernie was in the Hamptons and asked his brother to handle the interview.

Peter seemed impressed by Frank's fluency with numbers and agreed to hire him and teach him the business. At nineteen, DiPascali became Peter's clerk. Ralph Madoff had died three years earlier; Frank inherited his office.

It seems fair to say that Frank did not thrive initially in his new environment. He was bored and got yelled at a lot. But he was a sharp-eyed observer. He occasionally spotted Ruth's father, Saul, at the office, or leaving for an apartment at Regency Towers, a luxury building, that Bernie gave to him for when he was in town. He also saw Ruth around the offices; she would come in part-time and perform bookkeeping duties that included preparing financial statements, "box counts" (a count of customer funds and securities), as well as "reconciliations"—an accounting term for matching account balances with transactions to find any discrepancies or omissions.

Frank started noticing signs early on that something was not quite right at BLMIS. He saw that his old friend Bongiorno kept old copies of the *Wall Street Journal* on a ledge in the tiny twenty-five-by-twenty-five-foot office that was home to the dozen workers. Sometimes the newspapers were spread out on the floor, with David Kugel, a senior trader in the company's legit side of the business (he would eventually plead guilty to securities and bank fraud), poring over the stock pages. Kugel was the firm's expert in convertible arbitrage, an investment strategy that entails simultaneously purchasing convertible securities and short selling the same issue's common stock. (In short selling, the trader sells the shares first and hopes to buy them back at a later time at a lower price than originally sold.) Frank saw Kugel, who started at BLMIS in 1970, take the old *Journals* home in a briefcase, returning the next day with formulas for Bongiorno based on the previous day's stock prices. "Where's my work?" she would ask him. "Give me my work." Annette would also write reminders to herself on scraps of paper, such as "Find Monies + % - Give David Figures. . . . Do setups."

Frank didn't know it yet, but he was watching the trench-level labor required to maintain an ever-growing Ponzi scheme.

Imagine trying to keep track of a hundred thousand lies a month. Let's say that you could use a computer, a printer, and you had the help of a handful of other people, but if you lost control of a single lie—one slip of the tongue, one misplaced shred of paper—you'd be hauled off to prison for the rest of your natural life. When Frank watched David

Kugel harvest those day-old stock prices and construct arbitrage formulas for them, and when he observed Bongiorno slap them into
three-ring binders of customer records, transpose them onto customer statements, attach trade confirmation slips to them, and then
mail the documents to each customer, he was watching them sweat
the details of each of BLMIS's lies.

By the time of his arrest, Frank had all the makings of a Martin
Scorsese capo à la the film *Goodfellas*: handsome in a hollowed-out
way, with an unruly crop of dark hair; slick, funny, fast-talking,
glad-handing, but with a surly streak. Frank preferred jeans to suits,
doted on his family, and was almost touchingly protective of the mis-
creants who worked for him on seventeen, to whom he delegated
almost all the scut work required to maintain Madoff's scheme.
Though ever eager to please Bernie, if given the choice, Frank would
have preferred to be out on his yacht off the Jersey Shore, fishing for
stripers. His catchphrase around the office was "Don't be a fucking
asshole," recalls JoAnn "Jodi" Crupi, one of the Madoff Five defendants he helped send to prison.

Frank proceeded to sketch for the FBI the elements of the perpetual money machine Bernie had built all but single-handedly in
that tiny room off Wall Street. It was a machine that would throw off
cash in unbelievable quantities—billions—for a half century, without a single client ever raising a complaint, let alone alerting the authorities that something might not be quite right.

But it's tough to keep a perpetual money machine running. A
Ponzi scheme that doesn't expand is a doomed Ponzi scheme. For
BLMIS to survive and grow, it needed massive, regular infusions of
cash to fuel it. Madoff could have raised money directly from US
institutional investors but knew that doing so might have subjected
BLMIS to the kind of strict regulatory scrutiny applied to banks
and pension funds. By contrast, the hedge fund arena was largely
unregulated. This friendlier environment led Madoff to turn to

"intermediaries"—hedge funds and funds of funds—which could, and did, deliver large amounts of cash. Parasitism on both sides. He also failed to register as an investment advisor (until 2006, as a result of an SEC investigation), which would have subjected him to a deeper level of SEC scrutiny than broker-dealers typically receive.

The proposition Madoff offered customers from the 1960s through the 1980s, whether directly or through those intermediaries, was that their funds would be employed in virtually risk-free convertible arbitrage transactions. What he didn't tell them was that it was hard to make much money in such a tiny market unless you were simply faking it. Starting in the early 1990s, Madoff informed his customers that their funds would now be invested in a basket of approximately thirty-five to fifty common stocks selected from the S&P 100 Index, which consists of publicly listed stocks of the hundred largest companies—common household names such as General Electric, Coca-Cola, and General Motors. He told them that the basket of stocks would closely mimic the price movements of the overall S&P 100 and be hedged (or risk-mitigated) by stock options that would limit potential losses. BLMIS would move in and out of the strategy as needed: buying and selling stocks, adjusting ratios and hedges. And when clients' money was not invested in securities, it would be parked safely in US Treasury notes.

Frank walked the FBI through the way Bernie took an initial handful of family and friends and used them to create an epic $68 billion fraud. He explained how Kugel and Bongiorno created a paper trail for paper profits by literally manufacturing fake trading records—using those old *Wall Street Journals* to find historical prices for stocks so that they could pretend to have bought low and, "later," sold high. Eventually other employees would join the company and find themselves swept into the charade in major or minor ways.

Bernie was a stickler, for a con man. He would not allow emails between customers and the seventeenth floor, telling DiPascali that

"emails have become the greatest tool a regulator has in his toolbox."
Meanwhile, those historical "buy" and fictional "sell" prices were fed
into a computer programmed in-house to produce replicas of legitimate trade confirmations, a paper "record" of each client's growing—
always growing—"investment." Sometimes Bernie would come down
to seventeen to hold documents up to the light to see if they looked
sufficiently real, and if not, have them reprinted or printed on different paper stock—especially if he was trying to match paperwork used
by real stock clearinghouses or the SEC. At one point, Madoff bought
a $20,000 IBM laser printer just to make sure the firm's work was up
to snuff. He "insisted on perfection," said Frank.

DiPascali related further how customers were required to pony
up at least $200,000 to join in the 1990s—sometimes even that wasn't
enough—the cash going into the Chase 703 checking account. (Bernie long insisted to me that $2 million was the minimum.) A Ponzi
is at its most vulnerable when people are pulling money *out* of it, so
Bernie made certain to maintain the 703 as an always-liquid pool,
ready to pay investors who wanted to cash out. But many, if not most,
preferred to receive quarterly "profit" checks, keeping their principal
with Bernie in order to keep the train running. If that hadn't been the
case, of course, the whole pyramid would have collapsed.

The payoffs varied with a client's proximity to the center of
the Ponzi. In essence, it was a caste system. The closest and oldest
pals—the insiders' club—were making 30 percent, 40 percent, even
50 percent returns. There was even a special name within the firm
for the juicy annual payoffs handed to this small slice of the clientele:
shtupping. To *shtup*, in Yiddish, means, well, to fuck. In this case, it
was a good thing.

Those percentages shrank as one moved out from the inner circle. On the outer perimeter of the Ponzi—if, say, you were the son
of a friend of a major feeder's Aunt Greta—you might net 14 percent
on your nut. But part of the way Bernie's scheme kept growing was

by promising special people the chance to boost their numbers by bringing in new money. Get Uncle Marty and his bridge club to sign over the bulk of their 401(k)s and you could find yourself goosed up into the high teens, maybe higher.

This, of course, led to a kind of fraudulent arms race. Bernie had to pay bigger returns in order to rake in more money to pay the even bigger earners—those who'd either gotten in early (like Abe and Moe), or those with big balances, or both. And that dynamic created ravenous animals that could be difficult to satisfy.

Given that Bernie confessed that the fraud went back to Abe and Moe, just who were these important players? Abraham Hershson was a highly successful rags-to-riches businessman, who immigrated to America from Poland when he was nineteen. He lived most of his life in Jamaica Estates, Queens, roughly twenty miles from the Madoff home in Laurelton. Hershson hit it rich as the founder in 1933 of a company named Hygiene Industries, which grew into the country's biggest manufacturer of shower curtains and bath accessories—with factories in five states and about a thousand employees by 1988. He died two years later at the age of eighty-nine in Palm Beach, Florida.

Abe's accountant was, not surprisingly, Bernie's father-in-law, Saul. And it was Bernie's father, Ralph, who had encouraged Hershson to give Bernie money to manage for him in the early 1960s, if not 1960 itself, the year Bernie set up shop in Saul's accounting office. (While still in high school, Bernie had started a business selling and installing underground lawn sprinkler systems, and he said that Abe was a customer of his.)

Hershson's number two at his manufacturing company was his son-in-law Noel Levine, who—at the time of Madoff's implosion in 2008—operated a real estate management and equity company on Lipstick's seventeenth floor, a few doors from the Ponzi's center.

According to Bernie, it was Levine, "who I've known forever," who brought Elie Wiesel aboard as an investor and, he added with a laugh, was "skimming off the top" of Wiesel's profits.

Frank told the feds that Levine spoke with him every December to make sure that his IA account was shtupped with extra profits by year-end, no matter the condition of the actual stock market that month. There is no evidence that Levine, who died in 2016, knew it was all a fraud, but he and his father-in-law, Abe, *should* have known—based on the extraordinary returns (more than 30 percent annually) that Madoff provided them.

Old SEC records show that in 1961 Hygiene Industries went public, raising about $1 million. The Hershson-Levine families invested some of the cash garnered in that deal into Bernie's IA business. Abe also invested in commercial real estate. Both men became major philanthropists while they lived, particularly to medical centers and Jewish charities. In 1985 Abe established a fund to help Polish émigrés in Israel. Noel, who also served as a director of the Bank of Greenwich, donated enough to the Metropolitan Museum of Art to have a gallery named for him.

Noel and his wife, Harriette, insisted they lost a fortune when Madoff collapsed, but that was based only on the final (and phony) account statement that Bernie had mailed them. Before they died, they were unable to recoup any of it. That's because they were deemed net winners.

Michael Jahrmarkt, a stepson of Hershson's, recalls that Abe "was a significant investor early on and who got into the belief that he couldn't lose." What's more, he had a lot of friends and got them to climb aboard the Madoff caravan with him. Thus, he was an early feeder. By all accounts, Hershson was a pretty mean guy, but if you paid him compliments, he could be very rewarding.

Jahrmarkt, who cofounded his own securities firm in 2002, says he knew Bernie well but never invested his own capital in the

Hershson family's accounts. When asked his view about whether Bernie's Ponzi began from the time his stepdad started investing in the early 1960s, he speculates, "I think it *had* to, because I don't think he ever really traded. I saw statements going back to the 1970s, and I think those statements were not dissimilar from the statements that everyone saw in 2008."

But Jahrmarkt says he didn't analyze them closely through the years, as the quarterly statements flowed to his mother and Abe. Jahrmarkt is in the private equity business, but he says he doesn't invest in stocks, nor is he an arbitrageur (which Bernie claimed to be doing for his individual customers). Nevertheless, he thinks he would have understood that the statements were fake "if I wanted to, but I guess it was almost as if I didn't want to. . . . I can only tell you I think my mother [Evelyn Hershson Jahrmarkt], who passed away eleven months before he was arrested, would have had a heart attack just because everybody believed Bernie walked on water. I'm sure others had their reservations, including me."

Abe was looked up to as a success story by fellow Jews who'd escaped Europe before or during the Holocaust. He told them that if they needed extra money, he'd show them how to do it. "These people were tailors or bakers, or whatever, and that extra money from Madoff was a lifesaver to them," says Jahrmarkt. "It was not deservedly their money, but the view was that 'Hershson did right by me.'" As for Abe's view of Bernie, says Jahrmarkt, he looked up to him, relied on him, "and thought he couldn't do wrong."

That was true—for Abe, at least.

What about Moe? As with Abe Hershson, there is no evidence that Steinberg committed fraud. Bernie once let on that Moe was his "first or second" client in the IA business, and that he was a Realtor who also owned a car dealership in Queens. And just as with Abe, Moe's accountant was Ruth's dad, the all-present Saul, who keeps popping up in all the right places throughout the Ponzi's early history.

Moe and his wife, Lillian, who died in 2003, were close friends with Bernie and Ruth, according to Phil Baum, a former head of the American Jewish Congress. Over decades, the Steinbergs provided the organization, founded in 1918 to fight anti-Semitism, massive funding in the form of Madoff IA accounts. Moe also helped Bernie take a spin as its treasurer—a glaring conflict of interest. Madoff even attended a meeting of the nonprofit's investment committee in November 2008, just weeks before he was arrested, when he knew the end was in sight. "There was no reason to suspect anything," said Baum in 2009. But *of course* there was, given the fanciful returns.

In 2003 the AJCongress sold its Manhattan headquarters building for $18 million and invested half the proceeds with—who else?—Bernie. Moreover, the Steinbergs, who were childless, left the charity two trusts valued at nearly $11 million; it, too, was invested with Madoff. The subsequent collapse of the Ponzi all but obliterated the organization financially, thanks largely to the Steinbergs, sweeping away $21 million, or 90 percent of its total assets.

In 2011 trustee Picard sued the AJCongress to recover more than $9.4 million in phony profits it had received; the sides eventually settled, with the nonprofit returning roughly $1 million.

There's little information in the public sphere about the Steinbergs. We do know that thanks to the Ponzi, they were major philanthropists. Files at the Gerald R. Ford Presidential Library in Ann Arbor, Michigan, show that both First Lady Betty Ford and Bernie spoke in 1976 at a dedication by the AJCongress of a Martin Steinberg Cultural Center for Jewish artists and musicians, on Manhattan's Upper East Side. Bernie is listed in the event's schedule as the donor of the Bernard L. Madoff Jewish Music Library.

By all accounts, the institutional memory of the AJCongress

(and the Steinbergs) is an eighty-one-year-old woman named Belle Faber, a former associate director of the charity who joined it in 1984. Faber was close to Moe's widow, Lillian; she also met Bernie on many occasions. As her story goes, Moe made an initial fortune in real estate and "staked" Bernie when the latter opened his brokerage business in 1960. "In other words, he gave him money to launch his business," says Faber. Lillian also revealed to her that Bernie, while in high school, began working for her husband part-time, perhaps helping out in his real estate business.

Faber recalls Lillian speaking often about Bernie. "She loved him." And why not, given the returns? The AJCongress was earning an annual average of at least 11 percent, in both up and down markets. "Everybody I knew there was invested" with Madoff, says Faber, who, fortunately, kept her own money out of it.

Abe and Moe aside, there is another crucial piece of evidence that the scheme was already in place by the early 1960s. This comes not from DiPascali's relaying to the feds what Madoff told *him*; it involves what Madoff himself told investigators following his arrest—and *before* deciding later to change his story.

On December 16, 2008, five days after his arrest, the fraudster sat in a conference room with about a half dozen investigators on the fifth floor of the US Attorney's Office in Lower Manhattan. One investigator who was present remembers that on at least two, maybe three, occasions during the meeting, Madoff confessed that he'd been running the Ponzi since at least the early 1960s. Bernie insisted to me he never said it, calling it "bullshit" and maintaining that either the feds lied or simply misheard or misunderstood him. But the investigator's memory is supported by an FBI 302 that was typed up two days after the interview.

According to that document, Madoff revealed that when he first began his business, he did initially engage in "some actual trades," but that he "soon" began to engage in fraud as to the entire business. Specifically, Bernie confessed, he stopped conducting *any* actual trading. What's more, "for virtually the entire life" of the business, he sent investors false account statements and false trade confirmations. "It was essentially a Ponzi scheme," he told them.

Madoff also recounted the $30,000 loss his handful of clients (friends and family) suffered in 1962, which his father-in-law bailed him out of. At roughly that time, he told the feds, he took in new clients—also friends and family—"and began to falsely report returns of thirty percent to forty percent to these customers." Bernie added that such rates of returns in the 1960s were "not unheard-of at legitimate firms." As the business grew in the 1970s, he continued, he was "paying ridiculously high returns in the range of 30%, 50 [*sic*], 40% per year" in order to attract more and more customers. He said he "began engaging in fraud in earnest in the 1970s."

On the one hand, Bernie admits that his fraud began in the early 1960s. Yet on the same hand, he claims that returns of 30 percent to 40 percent were "not unheard-of" in the sixties at legitimate firms. How true was that? Not true at all. Throughout the 1960s, the S&P 500 returned an annual average of only 5.2 percent—with the biggest years being 1961 (23.1 percent), 1967 (20.1 percent), and 1963 (18.9 percent). For three years in the 1960s, the returns ranged from *negative* 11 percent to negative 13 percent.

And the 1970s? Even worse: an average annual return of just 3.2 percent on the S&P 500. If Bernie *was* doing legitimate convertible arbitrage trading in those decades, as he long insisted, could he have returned 30 percent to 50 percent annually for his customers? Not likely. Traders in that segment of the industry could only employ limited amounts of capital for high returns. Otherwise everybody on Wall Street would have been doing it.

A subsequent interview by the feds was held inside Madoff's apartment on Manhattan's Upper East Side in February 2009, while Madoff was out on bail. At that session, Bernie explained that in the "early 1960s," he had taken money from friends and relatives to invest in the stock market, and lost it. "He admitted that it was all fake from *then*," says a federal investigator who was at the meeting. "He told us he decided that he didn't want to disappoint people anymore, and self-servingly created the illusion that he knew what he was doing [as a trader]." As for Madoff's stating subsequently that the fraud began in 1992, "that's totally bullshit," says the investigator. "The gist that we got from him was that he fucked up early on with his friends and relatives and was very embarrassed by it, and then he started making it all up [fake trades]. It was clear in my mind because I was kind of taken aback at his plea allocution [four months later in the court-room in 2009], when he said it only started in the early nineties. He changed his story when he realized the implication of it."

Bernie's response to this investigator's recollections: "He's bull-shitting. . . . What I have to do is disprove this cockamamie theory that I started from Day One to steal money and that I never wanted to do any trades. And my wife keeps saying to me, 'How can these people deny [the positive things] you've done for the industry?'"

What did the investigator mean by "the implication"? Why did Madoff care so much about this? Two reasons are likely. First, Bernie fought hard and endlessly to have his legacy include that he was a legitimate trader who made a "mistake" in 1992 that snowballed. Spend enough time with him, and it seems as if his ability to continue to breathe and function depends on this. It was pretty much the only subject he focused on during the last few years we were communicating. That's because if it was just a sham from Day One, then Madoff was never anything but a crook.

"Richard, you might wonder why I am so intent in establishing the starting date of my going off the tracks," he wrote me in 2018, laying out two reasons why this was important to him. First, he said, "It is crucial that people as well as my family understand that they came into and participated in a completely legitimate business and that their compensation was always awarded from that source." The second reason: "To confirm to my clients and friends who always relied on the trust and respect I earned from both them and my industry during the first 32 years of my career, as a successful trader and industry innovator. . . . I am relying on you to accomplish this. Thank you, Bernie."

That's all about pride and ego. But there's more. Investigators have concluded that once it became clear to Madoff (or, more likely, one of his attorneys told him) that *all* Ruth's assets could be stripped from her if the fraud could be shown to have begun from the get-go, Bernie decided that a 1990s fraud-origin date could prevent that from happening. That's because he and Ruth had bought homes in New York, Montauk, and Palm Beach in the 1980s. So, if the fraud began after those purchase dates, she would be able to keep the value of those assets. Moreover, Madoff had long asserted that a $60 million brokerage account in Ruth's name was initially seeded with $5 million in municipal bonds that Saul had gifted her (after Bernie had bought them for Saul in the 1970s). Investigators could find no records of the purchase of such bonds—that's because, as we'll see later, they never existed. Therefore, if the enterprise was a fraud from the 1960s, everything Ruth had in her name could be taken in a civil forfeiture. She could have been left penniless.

In the end, the US Attorney's Office agreed to allow 1992 as the fraud's start date. The prosecutors were also facing a time pressure to get Ruth's financial situation resolved in early 2009—specifically, a determination of how much money she could keep—or else Bernie would refuse to plead out. Moreover, despite having fessed up to the feds behind closed doors that the fraud started in the sixties, there was no hard evidence of it. "He would only plead back to a certain date [1992]," recalls an FBI agent on the case. "And we had to get it done so that we could move on to the other folks [Madoff's coconspirators]. You also have to remember that Bernie was not remanded [in jail] at this point, and the optics of having him living in his penthouse were not great."

The prosecutors agreed to let Ruth keep $2.5 million, although Picard subsequently filed a lawsuit to try to claw that back, as well as an additional $42 million that she would someday have to fork over if she ever came into riches again. That civil case settled only in 2019, ten years after her husband went to prison. It was among more than fifty proceedings that Irving Picard had deemed "bad-faith" cases, meaning that Ruth and the others knew or should have known it was a fraud.

Why did her case linger so long? "Frankly, she doesn't have a lot [of money], so that's kind of a low priority," explained Stephen Harbeck, president of SIPC—the overseer of Clawback Picard—in a phone interview in 2018, two years before he retired from the agency's helm. "It would be nice to tie a ring around that and say we're done with the family, but it's much more important from the standpoint of the victims to go after somebody who owes [more]."

For much of the past decade, Ruth, now eighty-two, lived in a lavish four-bedroom waterfront property in Connecticut, estimated today to be worth about $5 million. She shared it with the family of her former daughter-in-law Susan Madoff Elkin, Mark Madoff's first wife. Before Bernie died, he told me that Ruth's memory is deteriorating, which may account for why in 2020 she moved into an assisted-living facility.

After that second interview with Bernie—the meeting that took place in his Upper East Side apartment—the feds had little use for him. In part that's because he refused to rat out any underlings, which would have made the government's work a lot easier. Few white-collar-crime cases start with the man at the top confessing. They usually begin with a lower-level employee being nailed, and then getting him or her to roll on someone higher—with prosecutors and FBI agents working their way up the pyramid, getting underlings to "domino" their bosses. But this case was the reverse, and Bernie wasn't playing. He had refused even to roll on his deputy, DiPascali, in the days prior to Frank's coming clean. "They wanted me to give criminal evidence against these people; I said I'm not interested," explained Bernie. "I said I'm not interested in destroying more lives."

Bernie insisted that he couldn't have helped even if he'd wanted to. He maintained that, other than Frank, his employees were all unsophisticated and "didn't know anything." Instead, he told the feds and the trustee that he would help them get money back from investors. Bernie no longer had any power, but he was still going to try to control it his way.

He insisted he had "leverage" with his biggest individual investors and could threaten them to return billions in return for his silence about crimes he said they committed. To recover those funds, Bernie said early on that he gave the feds "blueprints of what they should do, what was done . . . and every one of them has settled, except the banks."

But there was never a blueprint that Bernie provided to authorities, either verbally or in writing. Nor is there any evidence that he threatened his biggest clients. Bernie took credit for "forcing" clients to return more than $8 billion, and whether he actually believed that may never be known.

As to when Madoff's fraud began, perhaps the last thing one needs is another "Moe" in the room. Nonetheless, in Las Vegas in 2010, I dined at the Red Rock Casino with Maurice "Moe" Rind, who went to prison for his role in one of the most legendary Ponzi schemes: ZZZZ Best, a 1980s Mafia-linked carpet-cleaning company. *This* Moe was an associate of Meyer Lansky, the most famous Jewish mobster in history.

Rind ran his own small brokerage on the same floor as Madoff from 1964 to 1970, when the latter was running his tiny operation at

39 Broadway, around the corner from the New York Stock Exchange. They sometimes did deals together, and Rind recalls Bernie surreptitiously "paying off" order clerks on Wall Street at the time, to get orders from big brokerage firms on certain stocks that his fledgling broker-dealer unit was trading. "He paid them off with green," says Rind. "That was the name of the game then because there were no computers."

According to Rind, he and Madoff never got along "because I thought he was a faker, and I used to say it to his face. He was a wannabe trader." Rind claims he once accused Madoff of cheating him on a stock deal. Is Rind telling the truth? Despite his own conviction decades ago, his lengthy knowledge of Madoff's staffers at the time does ring true. He also credits Madoff with once buying a great deal of stock in Forest Laboratories circa 1967 and making a huge profit from it—a fact Bernie confirmed to me after I asked him vaguely if he ever scored big in the early days with a pharmaceutical stock. He named Forest instantly.

"He lived and breathed that company and was the number one market maker in it," recalls Rind. "But when he was wrong on a stock, he committed fraud."

One of Madoff's strategies at the time was short selling, in which, as stated earlier, a position in a public company is taken by borrowing shares that the investor believes will fall in value. Only in Madoff's case, "If he sold short, and the stock price went up, then he would pull the shares from his clients," recalls Rind. Put another way, he'd use customer money to leverage *himself* when he was wrong regarding the market. "He would pull the stocks from their accounts."

In other words, he had a Ponzi scheme going.

Whether due to duplicity, greed, laziness, insecurity, or some combination of all of them, there is no evidence that Bernie actually bought or sold any stocks for his IA customers. He never bought or sold any Treasuries. And the firms feeding him their business were no better. Those feeder funds would tell their customers that they actively monitored Madoff's trading. But guess what? They didn't. Bernie even managed to hoodwink some of his seventeenth-floor employees for years, insisting that all the trading was happening upstairs on the nineteenth floor, or overseas. It wasn't.

Nevertheless, by 1987, the business was booming to the point where the company moved into seventeen thousand square feet in Manhattan's famed Lipstick Building. (Bernie's client Fred Wilpon, co-owner of the New York Mets, co-owned the building and gave him a sweet deal. Wilpon and his brother-in-law, Saul Katz, the other Mets co-owner, had some sweet deals of their own—with nearly 500 Madoff IA accounts during the life of the Ponzi.) As the years ticked by, new "strategies" were designed or updated to excite clients, with new computer programs written to keep on top of it all. The whole firm grew to more than one hundred and fifty employees, nearly twenty of whom worked on the seventeenth floor.

Toward the end of his run, for example, Bernie's biggest feeder-fund conduit, the Fairfield Greenwich Group, based in Connecticut, had over *$7 billion* invested (and ultimately lost). Desperate to keep the music playing, Madoff tried to entice FGG executives into investing more by telling them he had a new trading model available that would return a deliriously high 50 percent. The three coheads of FGG, who told him they'd name it the Emerald Fund, already kept prized racehorses, private jets, and fabulous mansions. One was a former SEC official; the other used his daughters and sons-in-laws to travel the globe, from Brazil to the Middle East, soliciting new investors. They flew on Gulfstream jets, threw extravagant parties, and went pheasant hunting with royalty. It was nice while it lasted.

To get a sense of the sprawling, incestuous nature of BLMIS, listen to one of Picard's investigators, who gave me a partial flyover of the operation during one of my many visits to the trustee's headquarters: "Everybody looks at it as a kind of amorphous web," he told me. "I see a spine. And the spine I see starts with Sonny Cohn [cofounder, with Bernie, of Cohmad, the boutique brokerage operation at BLMIS]. He brings in his friend Sonja Kohn [an Austrian Orthodox Jewish grandmother with numerous shell companies], who then starts her own bank [Bank Medici] that lures in the giant Bank Austria, which lures in Italy's UniCredit Bank. They bring in Grosso & Ceretti [Italy], who bring in the Benbassats [Switzerland, New York City, Ireland], who set up five European feeder funds based in the British Virgin Islands. If Cohmad got credit for part of Bank Medici, you wind up being able to bring in Herald and Primeo [Kohn-promoted funds]. Cohmad also separately brought in Fairfield."

Yes, that is unintelligible to the uninitiated. But if that was just the spine of BLMIS's illicit organization, imagine what the whole body looked like. Some eight thousand accounts came and went over the life of the Ponzi. One reason Fred Wilpon and his brother-in-law Saul Katz, co-owners of the Mets, had hundreds of accounts was to spread around the money so that each account's balance fell below the upper limit of $500,000 per account for SIPC's theft insurance.

Even the feeder funds had feeders. Some of them used leverage to grow, borrowing from banks to invest in Bernie—although some banks just cut to the chase and invested directly with him. Some feeders implemented huge, if quiet, marketing blitzes, flogging Bernie even as they told customers to not mention his name. There were feeders from Rye, New York, to Vienna, Austria; Rome to Geneva, Switzerland; Bermuda, to the Netherlands, to Ireland. Most feeder funds had their own sophisticated investment advisors and risk specialists, who simply closed their eyes. For fees paid to financial institutions—Citibank and Chase, as two examples—investors could make large "synthetic investments" in Madoff using the banks' balance sheets with a low upfront capital outlay by investors in relation

---

to the promised returns. "Those instruments typically included derivatives such as options contracts or an equity index and debt securities," according to the trustee's lawyers.

It definitely paid to have gotten in early. Bernie's four biggest individual clients—whom FBI agents would dub the Four Horsemen of the Apocalypse—got in during the 1970s and raked in astronomical returns for decades. One of them, Jeffry Picower, an unusual man beyond the unconventional spelling of his first name, ended up with $7.2 billion in his BLMIS account, all of which was later clawed back from his widow by both the feds and trustee Picard.

And so it went, a magical money machine that rolled on and on, making thousands of customers rich (in many cases grotesquely so). The Madoffs themselves were by no means the biggest winners but were by no means too proud to dip into the pool. And image was everything. There was a 10.5-carat diamond ring for Ruth. A Claes Oldenburg sculpture in the form of a "soft" screw that sat near Bernie's desk in his office. A vast collection of Rolexes for Bernie. The couple had a home on the beach in Montauk, another on a lake in Palm Beach, a villa on the French Riviera. They stayed in the finest suite at the Lanesborough, the most expensive hotel in London, and left suitcases of clothes behind, since they visited often. BLMIS's London office was in the posh Mayfair district, of course. They flew on the Concorde supersonic and, later, on two private jets he co-owned with one of his largest investors. "I lived well, but so what?" he said.

Bernie was a master at projection. People like SEC chairman Arthur Levitt and Senator Charles Schumer of New York, even borscht belt comedian and actor Alan King, were given tours of the state-of-the-art trading system on the nineteenth floor—a kind of movie set behind which stood little more than a pile of old *Journals* and a really expensive printer. But people loved the projection. They loved the smell of success. And the smell of money.

3

Solved: The Four Horsemen and the Hold-Harmless Hooey

| | | | | | | | | | | | |

The Question: Did Madoff's four biggest individual investors—Carl Shapiro, Stanley Chais, Norman Levy, and Jeffry Picower—cause his downfall, as Madoff insisted right up until his death? Or did Bernie spin a tale?

Buried deep inside the 2009 autopsy report of Jeffry M. Picower is a conclusion by the Palm Beach medical examiner that can't possibly be true. It reads: "Genitals: Unremarkable." The truth is that Picower had a remarkable set of balls. If Madoff's Ponzi scheme itself had been an actual registered company, Picower—one of the biggest multibillionaires whom few people had ever heard of—would have owned a controlling percentage of the shares. That's pretty remarkable. That is, until he drowned in his swimming pool from an apparent heart attack a year after Bernie's arrest.

For financial frauds, the biggest trail of money is what typically leads to the kingpin. In this case, the money trail didn't lead to Bernie. Picower's net worth at the time of his death—an estimated

$10 *billion*—came mostly from the Ponzi. Bernie and his family didn't pocket or spend even one-twentieth of that.

Bernie says his business relationship with Picower began in 1970, when they were introduced by Ruth's accountant father, Saul. By the 1980s, Picower had carved out a reputation in small business circles as a promotor of dubious tax shelters and as a "greenmailer"—a pun on *blackmailer,* used to describe someone who buys enough shares to threaten a hostile takeover unless the company repurchases its shares at a higher price. There is evidence that Picower also made a small fortune from buying bankrupt companies (including private banks) and liquidating them. He also partnered with the notorious Ivan Boesky, convicted of insider trading in 1986 and sentenced to three years in prison. Reached by phone at his home, Boesky hung up immediately before he could be asked about Picower.

Starting in the 1990s, he seems to have made at least $1 billion from savvy investments in medical device companies, but whether he had silent partners is not known. Picower began investing with Madoff in 1970, when, it's now clear, the Ponzi was under way. Thus, if the seeds of a tree count for anything, almost all of Picower's billions in net worth sprang from Madoff.

Picower, with plenty to hide, was reclusive. Only ten people attended his funeral, six of them family members, according to an attendee. He was estranged from his sister, his daughter, and other relatives. His final will, of nearly twenty that he had gone through, was written fifteen days before he died in the pool, his signature shaky from Parkinson's disease. He had only one real friend in the world (not Bernie, to whom he nonetheless left $1 million). His only child, Bree—a college professor and author committed to left-wing causes— has long wanted nothing to do with the family's money. Not long after her father's death, she pleaded with her widowed mother, Barbara, to keep the Picower surname off a new foundation that Barbara was launching. Barbara agreed, naming the charity the JPB Foundation. (Through a lawyer, neither of them agreed to be interviewed.)

Following a grueling multiyear negotiation with prosecutors and the court-appointed bankruptcy trustee, Barbara Picower in 2010 agreed to return $7.2 billion in ill-gotten gains. The largest civil forfeiture in federal history, it represented about 40 percent of the total estimated *net* losses suffered by *all* of Madoff's direct customers. Those billions held by Picower (90 percent of it parked at the investment firm Goldman Sachs) was for the most part in the form of a margin loan from Madoff, meaning that it was at least technically a "debt" that Jeffry Picower owed Bernie. While the reason for that remains shrouded in mystery, investigators have long wondered if Picower controlled the Ponzi scheme.

There is ample evidence that Picower knew certain frauds were being committed on his behalf, such as the backdating of trades. Over the years, the billionaire bailed out Bernie when the latter had liquidity problems. But he failed to rescue him in 2008, following the stock market collapse, for reasons unknown. "We believe Picower knew what was going on," said the SIPC's Harbeck in 2018, citing the trustee's ongoing investigations. "He knew that he could tell Bernie what returns he wanted and *get* them. I can't crawl inside his mind, but I do know that he knew something was seriously not turning square corners."

As for Barbara Picower's $7.2 billion settlement, added Harbeck, "I think Mrs. Picower did the right thing, the honorable thing, and the wise thing from her standpoint, of getting out from under that. And I think she knows where her next cheeseburger is coming from." If the estate had been held liable for collusion, if the facts of the complaint were provable—and Harbeck believes they were—the estate could have lost everything it had. In the end, the Madoff trustee and prosecutors generously left the estate $2 billion for the new JPB Foundation.

At first, Barbara Picower didn't want to return the funds, arguing that her husband did nothing wrong. She also felt that Jeffry, if alive, would have fought against a settlement. Once she was resigned to settling, according to insiders, she pushed hard to be allowed to donate the $7.2 billion to a charity of her choice (meaning, not the losing investors). But that didn't fly with the feds, who were astounded that she'd even suggest it.

Bernie claimed he reached out to Jeffry Picower after the Ponzi imploded. "I said, 'You have a choice. You have to return the money, or I will give evidence on you. I'm going down, I have nothing to lose. You have a serious tax evasion issue.' I said, 'Jeffry, it's not just you, there are other people involved; it's all this *shmay-dray* [Yiddish slang for a rotating swindle] you did between your various accounts and [prior] foundation. All I want is to make clients whole.'" He added smirkingly: "I probably gave him the heart attack."

Even if he didn't control the Ponzi, Picower's importance to it was towering. An anonymous well-placed source close to his business operations told me that the billionaire, given his obvious financial smarts and decades-long investment with Bernie, "must" have known that there was a fraud going on, whether he knew it was a Ponzi scheme or something else.

To show how much $7.2 billion is, consider that Goldman Sachs, where Picower kept the money, borrowed $10 billion from US taxpayers just to stay afloat during the fiscal crisis of 2008. Did Goldman ever ask Picower about the source of his treasure? The firm isn't saying. Commercial banks are supposed to comply with the KYC (Know Your Customer) requirements—established in the early 1990s by the US Treasury Department to fight money laundering—but investment banks such as Goldman have no such requirement. Six weeks after Picower's death, a Goldman partner named Eric Lane penned a "to whom it may concern" letter, presumably to portray both Goldman and Picower in a favorable light. But the letter was too brief (at twenty-six words) and too vague to be of value to whoever may have received it. It stated only that Picower was a valued client for nearly three decades and that over that period, "through primarily self-directed investments in public securities, he generated returns in excess of $2 billion."

In his calls, emails, and letters, and during my visits, Bernie raged about Picower. But this is one subject he had many reasons to lie about. There was too much at stake—perhaps stemming from anger and jealousy over the fact that Picower not only profited far more than he did from the Ponzi but also that Bernie suffered more because of it. Also, it may be more than a coincidence that Madoff tended to have the harshest things to say about those who are dead, as opposed to those who can still draw breath to defend themselves.

"Really a horrible character," Bernie said about Picower. "He didn't speak to anyone in his family. He was tough, conniving; how his wife managed with him, I don't know." Madoff claimed he never liked the man, and that—despite Picower's critical importance to the Ponzi—he tried to avoid socializing with him. He portrayed Picower as someone to whom he was reluctantly bound, especially as the scheme skyrocketed.

Given the symbiotic relationship between the two men, a natural question is whether Bernie himself served as a *front* for the Ponzi scheme, with Picower the true brains and even the owner of it. Or was Picower acting as Bernie's bagman in some way? Investigators, having spent many years grappling with those questions, have come away suspecting the latter role (bagman) more than the former.

FBI case agents are certain that, had he lived, Picower would have been indicted, due to evidence that he repeatedly made requests for backdated trades for extra profits, as well as requests for "losses" on his statements that could be deducted from his taxes. But the prosecutors, whose job was to act as the checks and balances on FBI agents, tell me they can't be certain. John Moscow, the former DA prosecutor who worked on some cases for Picard, is clearly in the FBI camp on this one. "Picower was in the position where dying is the best option and that will to live doesn't really even help a lot," says Moscow. "He was the major beneficiary of this fraud by large numbers. He was going to be going to prison and his world was going to collapse."

Whether there may have been enough evidence to convict a breathing Picower, he and Bernie clearly had enough damaging dope on each other to cost both men plenty of sleepless nights. "It was a Mexican standoff," Madoff acknowledged. "He knew he had me, and I knew I had him." Whenever Picower wanted to show tax losses, he'd have his deputy reach out to Bernie or some of his mid-level staffers on floor seventeen to backdate trades—which could have gotten both of them prosecuted for tax fraud. Bernie said that Picower and his three other biggest investors were constantly asking him to doctor his books on their behalf in order to fool the IRS. And, as we'll see, he cooked up a tale of mammoth proportions to accuse the four of causing his downfall.

From the 1970s until his arrest, Bernie's four largest IA customers—the Big Four, as he called the Four Horsemen—were Carl Shapiro, Boston-based founder of the Kay Windsor dressmaker; Los Angeles money manager Stanley Chais; Norman Levy, chairman of a large New York real estate brokerage, as well as his offspring; and Picower.

The net gains the Big Four were achieving on the fake trades were gargantuan, ranging from 30 percent to *700 percent* for decades. The men must have known something was wrong. In the real world, people don't win the lottery on a monthly basis. But did they know it was an actual *Ponzi*? In one of his sessions with the FBI, in June 2009, Frank DiPascali spoke specifically about Picower, Shapiro, and

Chais regarding Bernie's backdating of trades for them: "They knew the game he was playing," he said firmly.

In 2021, inside the police station in Palm Beach, the rich enclave where Jeffry Picower lived in a $35 million home, an officer held up a stack of more than one hundred small sheets of paper—each of them, as irony perhaps demands, roughly the same size as Bernie's four-by-eight-inch fake trade confirmation slips. And like those trade slips, there are checkboxes on them listing the value, quantity, units, and dates of items. But the police slips are not about phony stock sales, they are itemized lists of dozens of products found near Picower's palatial pool. "Pillow Case," "Used Tissue," "Skinsations Insect Repellant," "Mirado Black Warrior Pencil," "Liquid from Coffee Cup," "CamelBak Bottle Containing Clear Liquid."

Florida, like most states, has strict laws that include mandatory autopsies to confirm the cause of death in traumatic or violent deaths, including drownings (with any religious objections to autopsy handled on a case-by-case basis). And in this case, Palm Beach police were especially sensitized and were not going to miss creating an inventory of everything found at the scene, however innocuous the item.

In Picower's case, the slips also contained lists of drug bottles found, showing just how unhealthy the sixty-seven-year-old was. On the one hand, Picower had his $10 billion, but it wasn't easy for him to revel in it. Each day, he took twenty-eight different prescription meds for ailments ranging from depression, heart disease, high blood pressure, and Parkinson's, to irritable bowel syndrome, muscle disease, diabetes, and Addison's disease. He'd undergone two heart surgeries.

Jeffry was a walking pharmacy, and likely a floating time bomb. He didn't need any help drowning, despite conspiracy theories circulating through Palm Beach parties that he'd been murdered.

His wife, Barbara, told the police that the couple had finished breakfast and were lying by the pool. Jeffry decided to go for a swim, while she remained on a lounge chair on the north side of the pool. She was lying on her stomach, she said, and couldn't see him. After about fifteen minutes, she got up and found him lying face up at the bottom of the pool. Barbara yelled for her estate manager to come downstairs, where the manager hauled Jeffry out of the pool and tried to revive him with CPR.

Bernie insisted that Picower made *all* his billions through the Ponzi, and he also gives him a starring role in creating a situation that propelled Bernie to launch the Ponzi. One thing is clear: after the richest American billionaire that nobody had ever heard of came to an inglorious end, Bernie was free to say anything he wanted about him, no matter how improbable.

Bernie's promise in 2011 to reveal the fraud's "yet-to-be-told" truths turned out to be a serpentine story that he repeated for years—eventually contradicting himself on key facts. "There's no justification for allowing myself to get trapped into this thing [by the Horsemen]," he once said over the phone. "But it was not something where I said, 'Okay, I'm gonna do this so I can live well,' or 'I can make a lot of money, and screw everybody else.' And to me, that's a big difference."

Trapped into what thing, and how?

In addition to referring to them as the Big Four, Madoff also christened them "the Patriarchs" and "the Fathers." Prosecutors coined their own pejorative in-house nickname: "the Schleps"—the Yiddish word for clumsy or foolish people—which they devised by anagramming the first letters of the four men's last names: S, C, L, P.

Foolish, perhaps, but clever enough to keep their wealth under the radar. Each of the Big Four–Patriarchs–Fathers–Horsemen– cum–Schleps kept his Madoff-related wealth so hidden that when I joined the founding team of investigative reporters behind the Forbes 400 in the early 1980s, they weren't even among the thousands of names in overstuffed file cabinets under consideration for inclusion on our list of the richest people in America. As DiPascali's lead attorney Marc Mukasey, one of the country's top white-collar criminal lawyers, would ask me years later: "Who *are* these people? Had anybody ever *heard* of them?"

Bernie said that through the 1970s, he was making them super-rich. But come the 1980s, they wanted a new strategy. In an eight-page letter in 2011, he laid out the plan. "Richard, I am asking you to keep this info to yourself for now," it began. He then rambled on about how in 1980 the Big Four wanted an investment approach that would enable them to achieve trading profits that were not taxed as short-term gains, given that short-term gains are taxed at much higher rates than long-term gains. At the time, wrote Bernie, he was investing their monies in convertible bond arbitrage.

"My suggestion was a possible strategy of establishing a diversified portfolio of equities with the potential of long-term gains that would be taxed at the lower long-term capital gains rate. I explained that the equities required an 'up market' for that period which, although I was bullish at that time, there was certainly no guarantee of that happening." He says all four men gave their approval.

As luck had it, a private French financial institution called Union Bancaire Privée just happened to approach Bernie around the same time. So, too, a banker named Jacques Amsellem. They were joined by an industrialist and (of all things) Spinoza scholar named Alberto Igoin, who Bernie told DiPascali was a "good friend" and "mentor," as well as a rescuer of Jews in Nazi-occupied France.

Bernie flew to Paris, he recalled, to meet them all. He said they knew he was doing arbitrage trading, something they were also doing through Goldman Sachs traders. "I said I can hedge your portfolio of stocks, and can short another portfolio of stocks." The two men liked the idea, as did the French bank, said Bernie, and told him that they would make their money in francs, not dollars, "so we don't care if *you* make money—we just need to break even. This is the 1980s, and they weren't allowed to do something with the currency because of [French president François] Mitterrand or the socialists." And so on and so forth.

Bernie was thrilled, he said. On one side, he had the Schleps—Shapiro, Chais, Levy, and Picower—all of whom wanted to own a portfolio of stocks. He could use them as a "cross-hedge" with the French clients (Bank Privee, Amsellem, and Igoin) and make it a long-term agreement. "My negotiations were arms-length in nature and would not have been possible without the special family type relationship I had with the parties involved," he explained. "It required a great deal of good faith understanding and commitments." In other words, nothing was put in writing.

(The French clients, in short, were to be the counterparties—meaning those at the other side of a trade. Worth noting is that Bernie long admitted after his arrest that there were no actual trade counterparties in Europe or anywhere after 1992, but here he insisted that they existed up *until* then.)

Everything went along profitably, he said, until the stock market crash of 1987. Bernie maintains that three of the Big Four "started to panic." He advised them to honor their commitments and wait until the overseas French clients were ready to unwind—that is, to close out complex investment positions. But the Horsemen refused, he said, and "they forced me to sell their positions." (So much for that "special family type relationship.") "I complained that the premature unwinding was a violation of the agreement and would put me in a terrible position with my foreign clients, particularly in the current market environment," he recalled.

According to Madoff, their demand that he sell their stock put him in a jam because of his cross-hedge agreements with the French. But the Horsemen didn't much care, he said, which led him to do what he felt was right: to take on the hedges *himself.* This left Bernie, apparently the only honorable man in this cavalry, on the short side of the market, and as the stock market recovered, he was left holding the proverbial bag. In order to avoid lengthy litigation of the default "that would hurt the reputation of everyone," he explained, he decided to negotiate "an assumption of the necessary hedge position of the families who were forcing the sale."

To protect Bernie, he said, the Horsemen gave him "hold-harmless agreements," meaning that they would step in and bail *him* out if he suffered "any loss." Not only that, claimed Bernie, but two of them even changed their wills to ensure that their descendants would also be responsible for Madoff getting back what he was purportedly owed.

But as the jam continued to go bad for Bernie, the Horsemen *didn't* honor the hold-harmless agreements, leading Madoff to make what he called the worst "mistake" of his life: hatching a Ponzi scheme that he believed would be temporary until he could bail himself out of the crisis that the Schleps had caused. "Quite frankly my story and circumstances are not that complicated," he promised.

That's Bernie's story in a nutshell. To anyone with even a modicum of common business sense, that may sound like—well, horsefeathers—when boiled down to just a few paragraphs. But Bernie was consistent on the details for many years (and in volumes of letters and emails to me), even when challenged. Of course, he'd had a lot of time to rehearse it in the months following what he told the feds. And he knew that Ruth's fortunes following his arrest were tied to his maintaining the fiction that he'd built his fortune honestly for the first few decades of his career. What's more, once he got up in a courtroom and stated under oath that his fraud started in the early 1990s, to the best of his "recollection," there was no turning back. He was insisting that he was leading a life of *post-arrest* honesty. How could he ever concede that he had lied in court about when the fraud began?

"They betrayed you," I said during my first prison visit, repeating Bernie's words.

"These four were like good friends," he responded. "I made them all rich and never thought they would [betray me]." Note that by this time, three of the four had died and couldn't counter him: Levy, in 2005; Picower, in 2009; and Chais, in 2010. As for Carl Shapiro, he was ninety-eight and not of sound mind. The two Frenchmen purportedly on the other end of the hedges were also long dead.

Note also that Bernie fingered all four of his biggest clients initially, but, in later years, his story changed to only *two*, then *three*, and then back to four. "Who screwed you first?" I asked.

"Starting with Shapiro, and then Picower was the kibosh; he virtually was the one that took me down," he answered. "After the 1987 crash, they see the market is down twenty percent. They panic. Picower says, 'I want to take these gains and withdraw money.' I said, 'Wait, I have commitments on the other side.' He said, 'I want to ring the register on the gains.'"

As Madoff told it, Picower started withdrawing his money, and he was powerless to prevent it. "I *had* to do it—unwind their positions," he claimed. Prior to Black Monday, "They'd all honored their contracts, so I had no reason to believe these guys would not honor them. I said, 'Listen, I have huge losses that I'm responsible for.' Picower says, 'So what are they [the French] gonna do, *sue* you?' I said, 'You put me in a terrible position. I don't want to be put out of business.'"

So, it was only Shapiro and Picower who drove him into Ponziland? Not so fast.

"At first, I believed my four clients would honor their commitments, and then I hoped to earn enough money from the split strike," he said at a later time. Okay, we're back to four. And some years later, it's back to just two: "[I] was the victim of Carl and Picower's betrayal."

In phone conversations, emails, and handwritten letters over my decade with Bernie, he started consistently—but then flipped back and forth between two, three, and four, "everybody." And yet Levy "never betrayed me. He never forced me to close his trades prematurely like Picower, Shapiro, and Chais. Norman never withdrew his profits, either." Now it's a trifecta betrayal. It was like a jailhouse version of "Who's on First?," the classic 1930s Bud Abbott and Lou Costello comedy routine about the confusing last names of a fictional baseball team's players: "*Who's* on first, *What's* on second, *I Don't Know* is on third."

At first, it worked like a dream, Bernie once said. "Everybody was happy, including myself." But when the market crashed in October 1987, the Big Four—particularly Picower and Shapiro, but let's throw Chais into that pool, too—decided, "Listen, the market is crashing. The game is over." And so on and so forth.

FBI experts in behavioral analysis say that a con man's use of a word such as *everybody* in this context is known as a "text bridge," the purpose of which is to avoid going into essential details. Second, what are the odds of *each* of Bernie's four biggest clients wanting to bail on commitments they'd maintained with him following a stock market crash—when it was clear to any savvy investor that the market would recover? As it did, and quickly.

Did the four clients know that they were all joined together in this purported overseas hedge-counterparty arrangement with the French? Bernie contended they didn't. Why wouldn't he tell such close friends? He never explained why. Finally, were these overseas hedging "agreements" with any of the four clients put in writing? Nope, said Bernie, they were all verbal. While certainly possible, that would defy belief and basic business acumen, given the enormous amounts of money involved.

In the decade to follow, we would return to the subject repeatedly—whether I wanted to or not, as Bernie became increasingly obsessed with trying to get me to grasp it. The more he talked, the more I spotted the fissures. Even the greatest con man can't remember all his lies as time passes.

Moreover, Bernie made a critical mistake of sharing copies of a few letters with me that he'd sent to others, including a TV journalist, in which he altered the story just enough for me to conclude that he was providing false details to at least one of us.

One can and perhaps should excuse minor discrepancies in the nucleus of a crime story—even from a criminal. But how many are enough?

For example, in 2014 Bernie sent an email to a Harvard professor that he shared with me years later. In it, he told the professor that "when the four clients (primarily Picower and Shapiro)" started to balk at their original agreements, his choice was to litigate, which he said "would've been a nightmare [that] would ruin my relationship with everyone, particularly the foreign clients." So, he decided to assume the positions of the Big Four, "which put me in a naked short position as the market recovered and the hedges developed into huge losses. . . . The rest is my tragic history of never being able to recover."

But what of the so-called hold-harmless agreements that Bernie said the Four Horsemen agreed to? True, he conceded, they were only *verbal* promises. But in the wake of Black Monday, as they pressured him to lock in their profits, they agreed to put *in writing* that they would bail Bernie out of any future losses he might suffer. And this was enabled in part, he said, by each horseman having named him executor of their wills or laying this out in their family trust agreements.

In a letter to me, which Bernie requested that I keep confidential "for now," Bernie wrote that "due to the advanced age and poor health of the Patriarchs of the families, I asked to have their trust agreements and wills amended to protect my interests in the event of their demise." Nonetheless, he added, "the Fathers' greed began to get the upper hand."

Unfortunately, no such agreements were found by the FBI agents excavating his offices after the Ponzi imploded.

It sounds far-fetched on its face, but there's a big difference between calling something implausible and proving it so. As with all con men, there is usually a kernel of truth somewhere in their story that stirs doubt in those who have concluded that everything they say is false.

Bernie was indeed made the coexecutor of Norman Levy's estate, with JPMorgan Chase as the other coexecutor, sometime prior to Levy's death in 1995. (He also stole from the estate, according to prosecutors.) Stanley Chais's widow, Pamela, declines to comment on anything to do with Bernie. And the two remaining Horsemen? A credible source close to the Picower family points out that Jeffry changed his will *eighteen* times before he died, but the source says there is no evidence that Bernie was ever an executor or that anything was written into family trusts to cover any potential losses of his.

As for Carl Shapiro, family spokesman Elliot Sloan says that Madoff was never an executor of Shapiro's estate.

This denial by Sloan made Bernie explode over Shapiro. Post-arrest, he said, he phoned Carl and threatened to expose certain crimes that the apparel businessman allegedly committed—if Carl didn't return hundreds of millions of dollars to investors. Bernie also took credit for helping prosecutors recover *billions* for them.

The Shapiro family ultimately forked over $625 million. Their attorney, Stephen Fishbein, recalls government investigators pressuring the family for a settlement but says Bernie had nothing to do with that. Fishbein managed the settlement process start to finish and never heard of any such conversations. "I know Lisa Baroni [a key prosecutor] was going through hundreds of boxes in Bernie's offices, and as far as I know she was not taking instructions from Bernie," he says.

Baroni laughs over Bernie's claim, and says, "The idea that we were in conversation with Madoff about how to conduct our investigation in this case is absurd."

But Madoff dug in. "If you think that Barbara Picower was gonna give back seven billion on her own because she thought it was the right thing to do [*laughs*]—or that Carl Shapiro, as greedy as he is, was gonna turn over the six hundred fifty . . ." he said in a rant about the Big Four. Bernie maintained (and this is true) that the government had evidence of tax fraud on several of the Horsemen, as well as faxes the men sent to his office seeking backdated trades. "I gave them [the prosecutors] a blueprint," he said. "Quite frankly, the government felt, 'Listen, these people are ninety years old. Shapiro is like ninety-seven. Levy was already dead. Chais is dead.'" Thus, he said he told the feds, the government's only leverage was to blacken their names and reputations, since they were either dead or just about dead. "They will never serve a sentence, because they'll just keep appealing it till they die."

Bernie, on a roll now, insisted that all he wanted to do once he got busted was get money back for investors from the Horsemen. "And quite frankly, that's what I did. I got the seven billion back from Picower. I got the close-to-a-billion dollars back from Shapiro. Of the eleven billion that Picard collected, almost all of it came from me." Bernie said these settlements were negotiated by his placing a series of phone calls with the Patriarchs or their families while he was out on bail. "I made it clear to the parties involved that if their monies were not returned, I would turn over the condemning tax fraud information that they were well aware I possessed. As you can see, this was done, and all the parties have escaped prosecution."

As concerns Carl Shapiro, there does remain one question that his family or attorneys should address. An investigator reveals that, in a confidential 2009 deposition taken by the trustee, Shapiro spoke about how he first came to invest with Bernie in the 1960s. "Carl Shapiro was the one who I wanted to inject with truth serum," says the investigator. "He met for ten minutes with someone named Lieberbaum." That would be Mike Lieberbaum, a longtime Madoff friend. "He never speaks with him again but remembers his name years later. He says Lieberbaum encouraged him to invest with Madoff. Carl gives him ten thousand dollars without meeting him, and the money grows to thirty thousand in *three weeks*. How could that be when interest rates at the time were three percent? Then Carl gives him a hundred thousand dollars more. What was Carl thinking was going on?"

That answer is buried with Carl himself, who died in 2021 at age 108.

And what became of the hold-harmless agreements that Bernie insisted the Schleps gave him? In some emails, Bernie wrote that after he was arrested, he assumed that "all my customers would be MADE WHOLE" by those agreements. In other words, he believed that the Four Horsemen or their families would *finally* honor those purported contracts. He claimed he made phone calls to two of them, including Picower, to threaten them if they didn't. Investigators say there is no record of such calls.

In a letter to Peter Goldman, a trust and estate attorney for Ruth Madoff, that Bernie passed to me, he wrote that he'd been asked by the trustee if there was any way he could support his claims "of the COMPLICITY and HOLD HARMLESS agreements" with customers like Picower and Shapiro. Bernie told Goldman that the feds had the ability to subpoena the Horsemen's trust agreement and wills that contained those agreements, or subpoena their attorneys and accountants who drew up these documents. "There were also copies in my files."

No such copies were ever found in his files. And one can conclude that if they ever existed Bernie would consider them the most important papers he ever had to preserve.

Finally, who drew up these purported hold-harmless agreements? This is yet another point in his stories where Madoff pins an important aspect on someone who is no longer alive to counter him.

In 2015 Bernie wrote that the agreements were drawn up by Edward Kostin, Carl Shapiro's longtime friend and accountant, who was once a partner at PricewaterhouseCoopers, now known as PwC. "Kostin assured me that these agreements would be honored by all the parties involved because of how important I was to all of them," he said, before suggesting that I review an email years ago that had an "OFF THE RECORD" heading that apparently explained all this. "I'm curious why you seem to not give much attention to this which is certainly not the case with all the visiting attorneys as well as the business schools that have been studying my case. Bernie."

Kostin, of course, was not alive to confirm or deny Bernie's account, having died in 2005. I tracked down his widow, Susan, and told her the story about the hold-harmless agreements that Bernie said her husband had drawn up for him and the Horsemen after the '87 crash and how, according to Bernie, the Ponzi began after the Horsemen squeezed him.

"This is the first I'm hearing of it," she responded. "He claims that Ed *drafted* these agreements? He was also a lawyer, but he never practiced law. Carl Shapiro was Ed's biggest client and introduced him to Bernie." She went on to explain that in 1987, Ed was living in London, and Shapiro was no longer his client. "It just doesn't smell right to me," she said about Bernie's story. "Maybe he said it because he knew Ed died. I mean he came to Ed's funeral."

Madoff's story about Kostin was fresh in my mind in 2019 when Bernie reached out in the hopes that I might visit him again. He seemed lonely. There was a new warden, and it wasn't too hard to get approved for another special two-hour visit. He looked frail and was now residing in his own room in the prison's hospital building, as opposed to the normal cellblocks. His heart was weak; his kidneys failing. I told him that since he wasn't well and wouldn't live forever, maybe this was a good time to come clean on all the facts with his investors, many of whom are still desperately needing to know what happened and why.

His face tightened, and he said he'd always been straight with me. I brought up Ed Kostin and said that it's simply not true that he drew up any hold-harmless agreements for Bernie and the Big Four. The story was a fabrication, I said.

"Ed Kostin?" Bernie responded loudly. "He's dead!" Precisely, I said.

Bernie rose up from his chair for the first time during our meeting and grimaced. He said he gets shooting pains in his legs. He never sat down again. After a few minutes, he shuffled off with a walker and said he'd send me an email laying it all out, but I never heard from him again.

4

The Implosion

| | | | | | | | | | | | | |

Make sure you brush your teeth," Theodore Cacioppi told Bernie. It was December 11, 2008, and Cacioppi, then an eleven-year veteran agent with the FBI, knew all too well that there was nothing worse than having to spend hours interrogating a suspect with foul breath. Once Bernie had complied, Cacioppi placed handcuffs on the seventy-year-old and led him from his Upper East Side penthouse to a squad car.

The scene Ted encountered that morning was one he'll never forget. For one thing, it was seven o'clock in the morning, and Bernie was in his pajamas, while Ruth stood nearby dressed in blue jeans and a blouse, perfectly calm. That's odd, thought Cacioppi: Why wasn't Bernie dressed? And why was the house so serene? Usually in this sort of scenario, there would be tears, anger, chaos—*something*. After all, this was a man who'd supposedly confessed to his middle-aged sons Andrew and Mark the night before—even as he and Ruth were heading off to the company's annual holiday party—that the entire investment advisory business was a fraud. And according to the family's version of events, "the boys," as everyone in the Madoff empire called them, had responded by dutifully and secretly turning in their father by way of a phone call to a family lawyer, who, in turn, kicked the wheels into gear with a call to Marty Flumenbaum, a prominent criminal defense lawyer and former prosecutor. Flumenbaum, for his part, called the SEC.

Mark and Andrew were nowhere in sight the morning of their father's arrest. (Nor did they or any Madoff family member *ever* knock on the doors of the prosecutors to help in the investigations.) Yet there was Bernie, in his jammies, pretty much waiting for the feds to knock—and acting like it was the last thing he expected. It all seemed too cozy, wrapped up for the FBI like a holiday gift package. Prosecutors said later, as did Frank DiPascali, that they always believed it was a ruse by Bernie, a setup, to make the boys look like heroes.

Whatever the truth of the family's performance, after Flumenbaum reached the SEC the previous evening, phones were smoking across the city. Longtime SEC official Andrew Calamari, who took Flumenbaum's call on an Amtrak train, rang the chief of the securities fraud unit at the US Attorney's Office for the Southern District of New York (SDNY), Bill Johnson, who was still in his office at eight o'clock. Calamari proceeded to tell Johnson what Flumenbaum had revealed to him: Madoff's sons claimed their father had made a "confession of sorts" that he had been running a $50 billion Ponzi scheme. (In fact, when all the counting was done, it came to $68 billion.)

"Fifty million," said Johnson, sounding nonplussed.

"No, I said *billion*," responded Calamari. "That's billion. With a *B*!"

Calamari also sent an email to Alexander Vasilescu, chief of the SEC's trial unit in New York, asking if he was interested in working on an "emergency action." Vasilescu, who was at a Christmas party, said "Yeah," but he, too, was nonplussed, having initially misread the email as "just a" $50 million Ponzi scheme.

The magnitude of the true amount was not something anybody in the history of the office had dealt with before. But the account struck Johnson as credible. He then called Flumenbaum to confirm the tip firsthand. The conversation was brief, and Flumenbaum—now officially representing "the boys"—was guarded, not saying much. But he reiterated what he had told Calamari.

Johnson was sitting at his desk, trying to digest what he had just heard. It was a famous desk. Notorious insider trader Dennis Levine had stood, handcuffed, in front of it in 1986. But this time it didn't seem quite big enough. Now Johnson's boss, criminal division chief Lev Dassin, was walking through the door. "*What* are you doing about this thing?" he said upon entering Johnson's office.

"Look," Bill told him, "I'm going to call the FBI and send them over there to interview the guy [Madoff], and if he says the wrong thing, he's going to get arrested."

Given the limited information they had, Dassin was concerned that Johnson was "out over his skis on the case," as Johnson later told colleagues. It would likely be a "warrantless" arrest, based on nothing more than Flumenbaum's statement—but *only* if Madoff confirmed it with a confession.

Johnson told Dassin that under normal circumstances his office would develop more evidence before knocking on Madoff's door, but that if everything he'd been told was true, he was concerned that Madoff might flee or even kill himself. In his gut, Johnson believed the accusations. It's not every day that a father confesses to his sons, who are part of his company, to having committed a $50 billion fraud. If the facts were borne out, this would be the largest known fraud in world history.

The securities fraud chief considered having an FBI agent rap on Madoff's door that night. But he decided it could wait until the morning, as everything Flumenbaum had told him about his client suggested that Bernie wouldn't bolt or whack himself. And Johnson wanted to try to develop at least a little more evidence.

Johnson remained at his desk for a while, typing out a draft of the criminal complaint that might have to be filed, assuming that Bernie confessed or said anything that warranted arresting him on the spot. He googled Madoff but found only a few results, such as a BLMIS company website that required permission to access and some photos of the family's charitable events in the Hamptons. He then sent a text to the BlackBerry phone of a top FBI fraud chief, Patrick Carroll, who was at his home in suburban New Jersey after a long day overseeing the soon-to-be-famous case involving one of the world's largest hedge funds, Galleon Group. It would be shut down a year later in an insider trading scandal.

"Pat, we've got a huge one," the text read. "A $50 billion fraud." But, for the third time that night, Pat, too, misread it as $50 million and was unimpressed by the number. Nonetheless, he phoned Johnson and said to him, "Okay, fifty million, so let me call—"

Johnson cut him off and, echoing what he had told Andy Calamari earlier, raised his voice to say: "Pat, *listen* to me! Billion, not million. *Billion!* With a *B.*"

Across the Hudson River from Carroll, Agent Cacioppi was watching TV with his wife and dogs in their Upper West Side apartment when *his* BlackBerry flashed. Cacioppi had grown up on a farm on a dirt road in Vermont; he was now running the FBI's New York scuba team, where he'd become expert at fishing corpses and guns out of the East River. Little did he know that he'd soon be on the biggest case of his career. Cacioppi was exactly what Johnson needed here: an agent with a reputation for being firm and effective but also fair and gentle. While only thirty-five, he had also worked plenty of fraud cases.

"Call me right away," Carroll, his supervisor, had texted. He was told to visit Madoff in the morning and question him, and that it looked like a big case. But Carroll tried to play it down, to alleviate any unnecessary pressure. As for Johnson, he barely slept that night, keeping one eye on his cell phone in case Bernie panicked one way or the other.

At five in the morning, Cacioppi showed up at the bureau's Manhattan headquarters to sit and strategize with a team of eight FBI and SEC agents. The team's first stop was attorney Flumenbaum's office. Cacioppi arrived alone and was surprised to find a huge spread of coffee and bagels in a conference room. Was the lawyer confused about the purpose of the visit? It all seemed surreal.

Cacioppi got another surprise an hour or so later when he and a second agent turned up at Bernie's penthouse. Johnson had told Cacioppi to simply ask Bernie "if there was an innocent explanation." Standing there in his pj's, Bernie confessed there was not. Yes, he'd been running a "$50 billion" Ponzi scheme. *Fifty?* Why not tell the feds it was actually more than $65 billion? Even before the cuffs went on, Bernie was tweaking his story to make himself look a little better. As he explained to me two years later: "I said that there was $50 billion in client accounts. I was giving them a round number, because I was knocking off monies that I knew they were gonna get immediately."

Simultaneously, with Bernie's arrest, or very shortly after it, SIPC's Harbeck also found himself in the million-or-billion comicality. He was in a cab in Washington when he received a call from an official with the SEC's trading and markets division in New York. "He said somebody had stolen $50 million," Harbeck recalls. "I said, 'Jeez, how did you let *that* happen?' He said, 'No. $50 *billion.*' He said we needed action very quickly. The shock of the sheer size and scope and duration of that theft. It took a long time to sink in how it was conceivably possible for him to do that."

Back in New York, the two FBI agents put Bernie into the squad car, and the group drove downtown in silence to FBI headquarters at 25 Federal Plaza, a forty-two-story building surrounded by concrete bollards. Unlike Bernie, with his billions, multiple homes, and three yachts, FBI agents don't even get reserved parking spots. After many circles around the building's underground garage, Cacioppi finally tucked the car into an empty space, and the two agents walked Madoff upstairs.

They moved through one set of battered gray doors, water dripping onto corroded cement, then through another and into an elevator. Per FBI procedure, the handcuffed Madoff was facing the back of the elevator car as it climbed to the twenty-third floor. Staffers came and went, oblivious to the rather hollowed-out old man in their midst. The agents placed Bernie in a tiny five-by-ten-foot room called WCC Interview room number two and cuffed him to a stainless-steel railing. (WCC is the FBI's abbreviation for white-collar crime.)

After yet another confession, Madoff was taken to the twenty-sixth floor to place his thumbs and fingers on a LifeScan computer. Some ninety minutes after first arriving, Bernie was led out a back door and through a small public garden for the ten-minute walk to the US District Court for the Southern District of New York. Folks on benches looked up as he shuffled past along a section of Worth Street renamed "Avenue of the Strongest" to honor the city's sanitation workers. No longer was he the high-rolling head of one of the world's most successful investment funds. No longer could he claim to be one of JPMorgan Chase's most valued customers. He was simply case 08-325, and on his way to becoming federal inmate #61727-054.

Bernie had been having a rough 2008 even before his December arrest. By midyear, the world was in the throes of the greatest economic crisis since the Great Depression. Mortgage-backed securities tied to US real estate, as well as the vast web of derivatives linked to those securities, were collapsing in value. Stock prices were plummeting. Bear Stearns, the eighty-five-year-old investment bank, imploded in March. Financial institutions worldwide were hemorrhaging money, culminating in the bankruptcy of 158-year-old Lehman Brothers in September. By year's end, hedge funds were facing record losses.

Bernie's business, too, was bleeding out, as more and more customers began pulling their money out of their IA accounts to cover their losses in other investments. He kicked off the year with about $5 billion in the 703 account; by summer and fall, investors were withdrawing billions from their IA accounts. At the same time, his desperate efforts to attract new money were going nowhere. He became increasingly angry at the number and scale of the redemptions, which were leaving him on a progressively shaky footing. He told Frank DiPascali that he might go so far as to threaten to boot investors permanently if they continued, even once the fiscal crisis ended.

Around Thanksgiving, Madoff began creating a new investment fund for "special friends"—five investors—for a total of $500 million. Home Depot cofounder Ken Langone got pitched for it, but he declined. Frank and his crew on the seventeenth floor were increasingly worried, as the billions of dollars in the Chase account were dwindling rapidly throughout November, with too much money out and very little money in.

On November 25 Ruth suddenly withdrew $5.5 million from her Cohmad account, the tiny brokerage unit a few doors from Bernie's office, something she had never done before. (On the day prior to Bernie's arrest, before heading off to the firm's annual employee holiday party, she suspiciously yanked out another $10 million.)

Bernie's Ponzi was in so much trouble that he started taking cash from investors he had previously shunned. For example, three dozen New York labor unions had invested about $180 million in Bernie's IA account starting in 1989. But in 1997 Madoff refused to accept any more money from them. Why? Bernie said he had "reached capacity," which was a ploy he used often to make clients feel even more comfortable with him. After all, would any fraudster turn down money? But when Madoff was suddenly frantic for funds in late 2008, he threw open his door and let those unions invest more money. He needed more grist for the mill and no longer cared where it came from.

On December 1 Bernie asked Carl Shapiro to wire him $250

million, which father figure Carl did, of course, pushing up the total he and his family foundation had invested with Bernie that year to about $550 million. But Bernie knew that wasn't enough. December's slated redemptions were on pace to wipe out BLMIS, especially a $250 million payment scheduled to go out to a European hedge fund entity named Optimal Investment Services S.A. At that moment, there was only about $300 million in the 703 account.

Two days later, Bernie called Frank into his office and told him to close the door. It was late in the evening. This was when Bernie first revealed to him that the fraud went all the way back to Abe Hershson and Moe Steinberg, Madoff's first nonfamily investors in 1962. As DiPascali recalled years later, Bernie kept switching topics rapid-fire and was borderline incoherent. Frank described his own mental state that day as "crazed" and said his knees were buckling. Bernie asked Frank if he and his wife, Joanne, had enough money. As for his own wife, "Ruth will be okay," said Bernie, a phrase he kept repeating over and over again. "She's got sixty million dollars of her own money." He proceeded to tell DiPascali the sources of Ruth's assets—from the real estate he had put in her name, to millions of dollars that had been gifted to her by her father—and how he believed (incorrectly, as it turned out) she'd be able to keep them.

Frank told the FBI later that Bernie also spoke regretfully about his sons and brother. He said, "The boys will never work in the securities business again. My damn brother is probably going to get disbarred." Adding to the tragedy of what awaited Peter—forfeiture of his family's assets and a prison term—he had lost his thirty-two-year-old son, Roger, to leukemia just two years earlier.

DiPascali, terrified, kept yelling at Bernie, and Bernie kept telling him to calm down, that he was making a scene. Frank knew Bernie was right: he had to take a breath and start thinking. He felt they needed to "circle the wagons," but Bernie wanted to talk with his attorney before making any moves. Madoff also said that he just did not want to be "embarrassed." Frank got the feeling Bernie was planning to kill himself that weekend and confronted his boss about it.

"I'm not going to kill myself," Bernie assured him. "I know I'll spend the rest of my life in jail."

Bernie decided to tell Optimal, the European fund entity, that he would have to push back its $250 million redemption until the day after Christmas, hoping that the move would buy him enough time to explain to his family that he was broke and to sort through the legalities of how to surrender to authorities. Also, he told Frank, "I don't want to ruin anyone's Christmas."

Six days later, on December 9, Frank was back in Bernie's office. Peter was there, and the three men became obsessed with who should get the remaining $250 million in the 703. Turning it over to the feds didn't seem to enter their minds.

Over the next few days, Frank walked around the office compiling a list of people he felt should get most of the remaining money. He enlisted JoAnn Crupi, who oversaw the 703 checkbook—and who would later be convicted for it in the Madoff Five case—to gather information on these special IA investors. He and Crupi, who went by the name Jodi, also talked about what they would say to the authorities. Crupi said she was going to tell them that she thought the trades were being done overseas, which, in fact, was what she had been led to believe. Frank felt that story would not fly for his part, considering his level of knowledge; he admitted to Jodi that he did not know what he was going to say.

Jodi Crupi, with her thin lips and long blonde hair, could easily be mistaken for Jodie Foster (especially when Crupi was hounded like a Hollywood star by court photographers after her indictment). She had joined BLMIS in 1983 as a keypunch operator before being promoted to bookkeeper. Bernie did his best to keep her in the dark—he once refused her request to study to get a brokerage license ("I'll teach you what you need to know," he said)—and she slowly got sucked into assisting the fraud, getting paid excessively for what was basically clerical work.

Frank assured Crupi that he would convince Bernie, somehow, to forgo sending out disbursements to the large hedge funds and other wealthy investors and use the remaining funds at BLMIS to take care of family, employees, and other customers whose entire fortunes were invested with BLMIS. DiPascali knew these people, after all; as far as he was concerned, the other investors were anonymous, faceless.

On Monday, December 8, Frank's list of employees "to save" was taking shape. Crupi and Bongiorno were on the list, as was Frank's mother (who also had an IA account). However, Frank was surprised at how much financial exposure Bongiorno had when he saw her fake accounts: roughly $50 million. Frank reasoned that she always gave herself the maximum return.

Frank met with Peter in Bernie's office and produced the list of clients Bernie had asked him to prepare. They discussed how those accounts on the list with $500,000 or less would be covered in full by insurance from SIPC and were therefore not their problem, but that they would do their best to cover the others (minus the $500,000 already covered by SIPC). They called it the "Screw List," but it was the good kind of screwing, like shtupping!

Bernie had started going through the list, marking accounts with green ink to indicate the people he wanted to repay. Peter asked for his own list so that he could do the same for the clients he had brought in to BLMIS. The brothers seemed concerned only with who was going to get paid, Frank told the FBI. There was never any mention of freezing BLMIS assets or going to the SEC or other authorities. When Bernie mentioned again in front of Peter how Ruth was going to be okay because she had an account of her own worth $60 million, Peter suddenly started asking about his own wife, Marion's, finances.

He then started to scramble to take care of Marion with some of the remaining BLMIS assets.

Frank noticed that Bernie was still earmarking money for some of the richest investors and tried to wrest control of the list and the funds so that he could dole it out to "regular guys," as he called them. In fact, he practically threatened Bernie over the issue: "I'll be good goddamned before you send a wire to some foreign hedge fund where I don't even know who the manager is," Frank told his boss, "before you pay down these employees what you owe them."

On Wednesday, December 10, the day before Bernie's arrest, Ruth came into the office to hand out gifts to some of the women on the seventeenth floor, as she did every Christmas. "She looked horrible," Frank would tell the Madoff Five jury years later. "She looked like she had just been crying all day, and she—her eyes were red, and she was—and she was a very attractive woman who was always very well kept. So, there was a radical change to her look."

Frank concluded that Bernie had told her what was happening. Ruth proceeded to scurry around the office, dropping the gifts on various employees' desks, then walked out into the hallway and stepped into the elevator. "So, I chased her into the elevator, and she was catatonic," Frank recounted. "She couldn't look at me. She didn't say anything. She just stared straight ahead, and I touched her cheek, and I said, 'Ruthie, it's going to be okay.'"

In 2013, while testifying in the Madoff Five trial, one of the prosecuting attorneys asked him if he truly believed that everything was going to be "okay."

"No," he admitted.

"And what did you think was going to be happening very shortly?"

"There was going to be a black Escalade coming down the driveway to arrest me."

Before leaving the office, DiPascali began making out checks dated the following day for the group of lucky employees he had selected to pay. After sending the checks upstairs to be signed by Bernie the next day, he felt comfortable enough to go home early. Instead of attending the company Christmas party, he wanted to see his sons play together in a high school hockey game. Frank was still under the impression that he had until the following Tuesday, December 16, to get all this done, given that Bernie had told him he wouldn't confess for another week. Eleanor Squillari, Bernie's longtime secretary, told him that the boss had gone out with his own sons that night.

At approximately 7:40 a.m. the following morning, December 11, Frank received a call from Bernie on his cell phone. Frank, at home in New Jersey, was irritated because he had not slept. He was also surprised: Bernie did not usually call him that early. "Peter said the FBI is in the office," Bernie told him.

"Why are you calling me?!" DiPascali replied. Then he threw the phone across the room, enraged because he realized that Bernie had deviated from the plan and must have told his family everything the night before. Frank was also annoyed—inexplicably, given the circumstances—that his boss would call him and "drag him into this legal mess."

Assuming that the FBI would be showing up at his door any minute, Frank started deleting work files on his home computer. He also crushed a USB drive full of falsified Excel spreadsheets and scattered the tiny pieces in the woods on his property. At some point, however, he abandoned the effort because he realized that all the files would be on the BLMIS computers anyway. He knew full well "I was toast," he told the FBI. He then remembered an old pistol he had in the house that had been given to them by a relative. It was unregistered. Rather than risk a charge of illegal firearms possession on top of all his other problems, he threw the gun into the pond on his property.

It was time to face the music. DiPascali drove to Lipstick around ten thirty that Thursday morning. He walked into an eighteenth floor conference room to find Peter sitting with a group of people he didn't recognize. They were all FBI and SEC agents. Peter handed Frank a list of information requests on legal paper. Frank was to provide the investigators with the IA accounts, but as Frank compiled the data, things were clearly not adding up. DiPascali felt that BLMIS's compliance officer—none other than Peter's thirty-eight-year-old lawyer daughter, Shana Madoff Swanson—was misleading the SEC agents. She was in the process of explaining to them that the scope of the IA business included "some friends and family." What she didn't tell them was that it actually included more than four thousand accounts belonging to not only individuals but also to giant hedge funds, charities, pension funds, and banks on behalf of individuals.

Frank recalled getting angry. "Enough is enough!" he snapped. "You gotta stop about this 'friends and family' crap." He felt it was time for Shana and everyone else to stop bullshitting the government. "These are not all the accounts," he told the investigators.

As Frank came clean about the real number of customers, the investigators started to get an idea of the fraud's scope. Frank saw Shana going around the office collecting documents for the investigators. One of the items she was tasked with providing was the bank reconciliations for all BLMIS accounts. For this she had to go to operations chief Daniel Bonventre, who would later be convicted as part of the Madoff Five.

Frank was in the conference room when Bonventre, who eerily resembles Bernie, walked in carrying stacks of account records. Armed with an associate's degree in accounting he'd earned in night school at a community college, Bonventre had started at BLMIS in 1968 as a twenty-two-year-old clerk and risen through the ranks. He dropped the documents in the middle of the table and said softly to everyone present: "This is where all the secrets are."

Frank worked until nine in the evening retrieving records for the investigators. At one point, he was spotted vomiting in Bernie's bathroom on the nineteenth floor. Earlier in the day, he'd accompanied Peter through all the hallways, where the company chief compliance officer and senior managing director informed the employees that Bernie had been arrested. He said simply: "My brother has been arrested for securities fraud. I don't know what is going on. The firm is operating for now. I don't know what the future holds. Don't discuss this with anyone. Try to go on as best you can."

At some point during the day, DiPascali heard through the office grapevine that Bernie's sons had turned him in. Frank started to believe that Bernie had deceived him as to when he planned to surrender to authorities and had orchestrated the entire thing to provide maximum protection for his own family, setting up Mark and Andrew as the heroes who turned in their own father. Frank also felt Bernie was setting up Frank and the other BLMIS employees to take the fall. DiPascali realized that *he* could have been the hero by going to the authorities a week before. Now he regretted not having done just that.

At another point, he learned that one of the first things the feds found when they entered Bernie's office was a pile of about a hundred signed checks—totaling $173 million—ready to be sent out to lucky friends, family, and employees.

Surreally, as if in its own dream world, House 17 was still going about its fraudulent business for the first few hours that the feds were on the eighteenth and nineteenth floors. Nobody had told them yet that Bernie had been arrested or that investigators were upstairs.

"What do we say to the [IA] clients?" asked Crupi when she found out.

"Just tell them we don't know anything yet but that it's business as usual," Peter responded.

The news of Bernie's arrest didn't hit the Street until after the market closed, with the cable business news channel CNBC breaking the story. The phones and fax machines started raging, especially with investors wanting redemptions. By the next day, the lobby was filled with investors demanding money back.

The seventeenth floor crew worked until ten o'clock at night answering phones. All they would tell clients was: "Just send in your request" and "We don't know what's going on." Crupi thought the arrest was some huge misunderstanding; that's how swept up she was in being a seventeenth-floor automaton. When, a month after Bernie's arrest, the FBI told Crupi they wanted to talk to her and others on seventeen, she told them, "Peter Madoff told me I shouldn't talk to you." And that was what Peter apparently told *everyone* on seventeen. As Crupi, a quiet, naïve, and obedient soul, explained to her colleagues: "I'm gonna follow it, and I think you should too. I don't know what I'm supposed to do, but this is what he [Peter] said. I'm just doing what Peter said; he's an attorney." The feds were furious.

While investigators were prowling floors eighteen and nineteen on the day of Madoff's arrest, Frank saw an opportunity to scoot down to seventeen and shred some phony trade blotters that he had left behind on a table. The blotters, detailed records of trades for a given period of time, were from an audit by KPMG, a Big Four accounting firm that had been hired by HSBC Bank a year before to review Bernie's operation. But he had to stop destroying the documents when SEC agents returned to seventeen for another look.

Then Frank DiPascali went home, logged on to the Internet, and found himself an attorney. He came to work the next morning but soon left, telling the agents he'd be right back. Instead, he headed across town to meet with his lawyer, Marc Mukasey, and never returned to work again. Over the weekend of December 13–14, he decided to cooperate and turn on the others, including Annette Bongiorno, his childhood babysitter who'd introduced him to Bernie more than thirty years earlier.

5

Hoarding and Shredding

| | | | | | | | | | | | |

The Question: Did Madoff engineer a massive shredding operation, or did he keep just about everything?

Over the days, weeks, and months that followed, the BLMIS meltdown led to a flurry of events almost too dizzying for the press to track. Lawsuits started flying. A federal judge quickly froze Madoff's assets, and trustee Irving Picard was appointed to identify the so-called winners—those who were still in positive territory when the music stopped—and return some or all of that money to those deemed net losers.

Roughly 4,800 customers of Bernie's were exposed, although Bernie had almost twice as many during the life of the scam. By summer, investors had filed more than 15,400 claims to Picard, and, within a year, the trustee had filed more than 1,000 lawsuits to net winners to claw back their profits. The *Wall Street Journal* published its complete list of investors. For the cover of its March 2, 2009, issue, *New York* magazine put lipstick on a photoshopped image of

Madoff grinning grotesquely like *Batman*'s malevolent Joker. The cover line read:

BERNIE MADOFF, MONSTER

AND THE PEOPLE WHO ENABLED HIM.

He didn't necessarily deserve it, given the rampant, egregious behavior across Wall Street at the time—this was the subprime mortgage era, after all—but Bernie became the human face of the entire financial crisis. In Washington, DC, the US Senate Committee on Banking, Housing, and Urban Affairs held a January hearing on "How the Securities Regulatory System Failed to Detect the Madoff Investment Securities Fraud, the Extent to Which Securities Insurance Will Assist Defrauded Victims, and the Need for Reform." In Chicago, President-elect Barack Obama issued a statement blaming the fraud at least partly on ineffective regulators, adding that failures of oversight and accountability had put our entire economy at risk. (Obama didn't place an iota of blame on Bernie's see-no-evil investors.)

Global feeder funds started publicly bemoaning their losses. Spain's Banco Santander said its clients' exposure to Madoff funds topped $3 billion. Hong Kong–based HSBC put its number at around $1 billion. Royal Bank of Scotland claimed almost $600 million, while Japan's Nomura pegged its losses at half that. Meanwhile, Sonja Kohn—the grandmother we met briefly in chapter 2—resigned from Bank Medici, the small Austrian bank she'd founded that was one of the largest BLMIS feeders.

In London, the Serious Fraud Office announced it was opening an investigation into the operations of Madoff's unit there, even as the SEC in Washington launched a probe into how the agency was caught flat-footed. The state of Massachusetts filed an action alleging that Ruth had withdrawn funds just prior to the collapse. Which, of course, she had. Yeshiva University announced that the school had lost $110 million of its endowment—and later conceded that it shouldn't have had Madoff on its board, directing its investments. The $1 billion Picower Foundation—helmed by Jeffry Picower, one of the Four Horsemen—announced that it was shutting down, as its assets were managed by Madoff. Ezra Merkin, a major figure in New York's Jewish community and the chairman of GMAC (the financial arm of General Motors and known now as Ally Financial), said he ran a fund through Bernie that had lost $1.8 billion, nearly all its money.

Merkin, whose surname adorns Manhattan's prestigious Merkin Hall concert venue (thanks to a major gift from his parents), had held himself out as an investment guru in his own right; many investors (Mort Zuckerman among them) had no idea it was Madoff pulling the strings. It was the same charade, it turned out, that Stanley Chais—the Beverly Hills money manager who knew nothing about trading—had pulled off with his own customers. Not only that, DiPascali told the FBI, but "there had to be no risk to Stanley. No individual trade could *ever* result in a loss, even if the bottom line of the statement netted a gain." It's what Chais himself had insisted upon because he couldn't bear the thought that even just one of his clients might discover that he'd made a poor trade. Chais, Frank added, liked to see a 5.5 percent rate of return each quarter (or 22 percent per year), no matter the condition of the stock market. Picard, who sought $1.3 billion back from Chais's estate, settled for just one-quarter of that in 2016.

Meanwhile, Jewish country clubs from Long Island, to Minneapolis, to Palm Beach were decimated. In the latter community, a week after Bernie's arrest, a fistfight nearly broke out at Donald Trump's Mar-a-Lago Club between the founder of the Nine West shoe chain, Jack Fisher, who lost $150 million, and Bob Jaffe, a local bon vivant and Madoff feeder. "You dirty bastard!" the seventy-eight-year-old Fisher reportedly yelled at Jaffe, who was a son-in-law and partner of Carl Shapiro. Even a group of teenagers got in on the action: they called the *Palm Beach Post* to report that they had toilet papered Bernie's mansion there, claiming that they had lost their trust funds in the scheme and that "the prank was their retaliation."

Jaffe, it turned out, was also a former vice president and minority owner of Cohmad—the Lipstick's eighteenth-floor boutique brokerage (owned mainly by the Madoff and Sonny Cohn families)—through which, it was later discovered, some 20 percent of Bernie's active customer accounts had originated. In a lawsuit by the state of Massachusetts, Jaffe invoked his Fifth Amendment right not to testify. He claimed he was a victim but eventually coughed up $38 million to Picard in 2015.

At a New York panel discussion on the scandal, Elie Wiesel made his first and only public comments on the matter. "Remember, there was a myth he created around him," he said of Bernie, "that everything was so special, so unique, that it had to be secret." Asked what punishment Madoff should receive, Wiesel came up with something that only a Nazi death camp survivor could imagine: "I would like him to be in a solitary cell with only a screen, and on that screen for at least five years of his life, every day and every night, there should be pictures of his victims, one after the other after the other, all the time a voice saying, 'Look what you have done to this old lady, look what you have done to that child, look what you have done.' Nothing else."

With security guards and video cameras protecting him from murderous investors (and keeping him from going on the lam), Bernie holed up with Ruth in their $7 million Upper East Side apartment. Effectively imprisoned in the building where he once served as co-op board chairman, he apologized in a letter to the board for the "terrible inconvenience" of the hateful mobs out on the sidewalk. Prosecutors soon revealed that the Madoffs had distributed $1 million worth of jewelry and personal possessions to friends and relatives while they were for all intents under house arrest—a violation, they said, of the court order freezing their assets.

Bernie remained in his home for three months, until March, when he pled guilty and was locked up in a seven-by-seven-foot jail cell in downtown Manhattan. In addition to the 24/7 company of his cellmate, he was once visited by David Kotz, the inspector general of the SEC. As Kotz recalled to me in 2012, "He said he could feel vibrations while he was standing on the company's trading floor, and had a gut feel when stocks and bonds are going up and down." That same month, US authorities seized $69 million of assets held in Ruth Madoff's name, including the Manhattan penthouse and $17 million in a bank account.

Their personal accountant, David Friehling, was charged with fraud for having helped deceive investors by rubber-stamping BLMIS's books for seventeen years. The feds discovered stacks of blank letterhead that the accountant had given Bernie to use for deceiving investigators in the event that Friehling was unavailable. Not that the accountant had a ton of clients around the country to visit. He had operated out of an office in a strip mall next to a Chinese restaurant in Westchester County, and Bernie was his only client. DiPascali told the FBI that when Bernie broke the news to him that it was all a fraud, he asked, "Have you been paying Friehling loads of money all these years, or is he just the dumbest guy ever?" Bernie's odd response: "He is just the dumbest white fuck you'll ever meet." One FBI agent who worked on the Friehling case says, "I never met a dumber person in my life. It was the easiest case I ever worked. We didn't need Frank for it."

On the day of his arrest, Bernie had given his consent for the FBI to search his offices, where, he told agents, they'd find about fifty boxes of papers. Armed with that information, the bureau's white-collar-crime supervisor, Pete Grupe, arranged for a small truck carrying four agents to pick them up. When the group arrived, however, they were met by ten agents already at 885 Third Avenue.

"Hey, boss, we got a lot more than fifty boxes!" one agent called out to Grupe.

"How many?"

"About seven hundred just on the three floors, never mind the two thousand boxes in the basement!"

After consulting with *his* boss—Dave Cardona, who ran the entire New York FBI office—and after talks with the bureau's Evidence Recovery Unit, Grupe called a trucker in Brooklyn they often relied on for heavy work such as Mafia cases that entailed jackhammering to find entombed bodies. The trucker had tractor trailers at his disposal and always made it a point to be available 24/7 when the FBI needed him. One time, he'd supplied seventy-two Mack trucks for a single bureau operation. "No problem, Pete," he said. "We'll get the tractor trailer warmed up."

But there was a huge problem that the agents realized only later. The Fifty-Third Street entrance to the Lipstick Building's garage was too narrow for a semi. So, the crew did the only thing it could think of: the FBI wound up leasing all three floors housing Madoff's empire for the next several years. What began as a crime scene evolved into a field office/crime lab.

As it turned out, the biggest fraud in history also had one of the biggest hoards ever of documents for investigators to sift through: four terabytes, or some thirty million pages—nearly half the size of the printed material collection of the US Library of Congress. The sifting took a decade. In one giant warehouse in Queens, there were rows and racks of storage shelves crammed with banker boxes straight up to the ceiling. FBI agents wearing jeans and T-shirts would spend many days there climbing and sorting. One box, strangely enough, contained thousands of lottery tickets. (Bernie's? Couldn't be, given his claim that he'd never bought a lottery ticket in his life.) All told, there were two warehouses—one located ninety miles north of Manhattan—full of about ten thousand boxes of documents, as well as thousands of sheets of microfiche and reels of microfilm.

But hoarding paper wasn't Bregards Bernie's only obsession: he was also an enthusiastic shredder of said paper. Exactly when a given document transitioned from important to expendable isn't clear, but when it did, it was usually hauled down to Vinegar Hill, now a trendy neighborhood in Brooklyn, but for decades a quasi-wasteland overlooking the East River where strangers went unnoticed and rats knew no fear. Due to the chronic lack of physical space, storage is big business in New York, and Vinegar Hill was, for decades, one of the city's self-storage *kingdoms.* Manhattan's Upper East Side—where Bernie and Ruth enjoyed life in their palatial penthouse—was just six miles north, but it might as well have been in a different universe. Here in this unadorned corner of Brooklyn, with the stink of urine wafting through the empty streets, warehouses, paper companies, and storage yards lined the waterfront. Every building seemed stacked with secrets behind its sealed windows.

It was in this humble hood, inside a ten-story storage facility now called Tuck-It-Away, that much of Bernie's dirty work was completed—and those secrets destroyed forever. From the mid-1990s until 2004, according to an employee there, Madoff was the largest tenant, renting twenty-seven oversized rooms, each piled with paper. In one of those rooms—room 310—sat an oversized, five-foot-tall shredding machine.

Even before Bernie's arrest, the whole situation seemed fishy to Evans Harris, the office manager and field supervisor of a trucking company Madoff hired to cart boxes of documents from the Lipstick Building to Vinegar Hill. One morning about a year after Bernie got busted, Harris drove me to the Tuck-It Away, where a manager named Mohammad gave a tour. According to Harris, the operation worked this way: Every Tuesday, Harris and his team would appear at the Lipstick Building to pick up roughly three hundred boxes and burlap bags—often from the secretive seventeenth floor, where the Ponzi lived. They'd drive the paper across the Manhattan Bridge to the warehouse on John Street, where another team would come on Saturdays—led by Madoff's personal chauffeur, Lee Sibley, who showed up driving a Jaguar—to decide which boxes to save and which to feed through the monster shredder. Harris remembers seeing documents spread across the floor and could tell that they were customer and bank statements; many listed various stocks the customers (allegedly) held.

Interestingly, Mohammad says that in the aftermath of 9-11, the FBI showed up on John Street in search of "Muslims" in the storage industry to interview. "When we explained that Madoff had twenty-seven rooms—including an entire floor—they asked *a lot* of questions, such as who is Madoff, what is he storing, and why so many rooms," Mohammad told me. But they went away satisfied. Mohammad says that no other customer ever conducted shredding at the facility. Just Madoff.

The second part of the operation involved taking the shredded documents in burlap bags to a recycling plant in the Greenpoint section of Brooklyn. There were so many of those bags that several large trucks had to be used. Many of Bernie's secrets vanished this way, dissolving to mulch.

After 2004, in need of more space, Madoff moved the storage operation to a warehouse in Queens owned by a family by the name of Goldman. Harris says that after Madoff was arrested, the FBI showed up at this warehouse, too, but the staff there had been ordered not to say anything to law enforcement. That didn't stop the FBI from finding more than 250 boxes of documents there implicating feeder funds, as well as numerous other boxes of bank statements (including from Chase) that were carted off to the Department of Justice.

Harris says he routinely met Peter Madoff at the Lipstick Building—one time asking him for career advice. He was aware they were moving out massive amounts of documents. It turns out that the shredding operation, coordinated in part by the Jaguar-driving chauffer, was sped up dramatically in the weeks before Bernie confessed.

In Frank DiPascali's 2009 meetings with FBI agents, he revealed that a week before Bernie's arrest, his boss instructed him to "box up" compromising materials and label them for transport to the warehouse in Queens. "I got to get rid of it," said Bernie, referring to work that Frank and his team had created later that year. "There is stuff on that stuff that is damning." Bernie told him that chauffer Lee would then take the materials there to shred them. Twenty-eight boxes were destroyed, Frank estimated. He had initially explained to Bernie that the sheer magnitude of the material—reams and reams and reams of documents—was "not something you just throw in a wastepaper basket." At one point, Bernie remembered that DiPascali had a giant fire pit in his backyard, so he asked if Frank could stuff it all into his car and drive it to his house to burn it all. "That's not happening, boss," DiPascali replied, before Madoff reverted to his plan for Lee to take care of it.

What was in those boxes? For one thing, many records showing forged paperwork that served as a fictional record of Bernie's trades on behalf of clients—trades that never took place. A company called the Depository Trust & Clearing Corp. (DTCC), located in Lower Manhattan, provides clearing and settlement services for the financial markets—essentially, it is where proof of every trade is held for Wall Street. Bernie, Frank, and the latter's team on the seventeenth floor had created fake DTCC records to trick accounting giant KPMG, which had been retained earlier that year by the trillion-dollar-asset HSBC Bank to review Madoff's operations. The reason the men didn't shred *those* documents was because, well, according to Frank, they were pretty good forgeries, and the gang never knew when they could come in handy again!

As hard as that may be to believe, prosecutors never indicted anyone for the shredding. They decided it would have been DiPascali's word against theirs, with no other corroborating sources or materials. They worried a jury might not have felt the proof rose to the beyond-a-reasonable-doubt standard required for a criminal conviction. They probably also figured they had enough on this crew to put away the ones who really deserved it.

When the FBI decided to lease Bernie's three floors in the Lipstick Building, it more or less sealed off seventeen—the heart of the Ponzi—to prevent shredding or theft of incriminating materials. But the bureau's decision-makers allowed many employees to remain at the company, on the eighteenth and nineteenth floors, some of them for *months*. They did so for decent reasons: they figured that if they could keep the moneymaking (and supposedly legitimate) prop-trading businesses operating, they'd minimize the pain for the innocent members of BLMIS's staff, while maintaining access to employees who might be able to assist them in their investigation. Over time, they sent many home, some of whom they ended up indicting. Case in point: Peter Madoff, who was there for about a week until the feds sent him packing.

One investigator on the scene felt that every floor "should have been treated as a crime scene from Day One. But investigators didn't know the extent of the fraud, and they wanted to keep it operating because they thought a lot of people would get injured financially." If you get in early on an investigation, you can obtain voicemails, said this investigator. "That's where fraudsters leave stuff. If deleted, voicemails are backed up on most servers, but people don't know that."

In the Madoff case, however, the feds did not retrieve voicemails, because when the criminal seizure took place, "the FBI was using the phone system themselves. And it wasn't preserved because with voicemails, the systems overwrite the backups after sixty days, typically."

Would those voicemails have revealed critical material about the fraud? Would there have been any from Madoff family members that were incriminating? We'll never know, said that investigator. But voicemails aside, there were at least some vital records that were destroyed right before Bernie was arrested, "and they pretty much all had to do with the family," former Madoff Five prosecutor Matt Schwartz told me several years ago. "For example, there were binders that Peter maintained—compliance documents—where he, as the compliance officer, had to review trades."

How did prosecutors know they existed if they were destroyed? "We know that they used to exist," Schwartz clarified.

To their credit, investigators were able to utilize a cutting-edge software program—developed initially for the CIA and FBI to help track down terrorists—that analyzed phone calls, emails, faxes, and corporate events at BLMIS. In total, some *thirty million* documents were entered into the software system, according to an investigator who worked on the project.

Three years ago, these investigators provided me their findings in a series of talks in their Midtown Manhattan offices. They analyzed 3.2 million telephone call records, including from Bernie and Ruth's home phones, as well as the mobile phones of all his employees. They reverse engineered dozens of phone calls from the Swiss UBS bank's subsidiary in Luxembourg. They also found 13,310 text messages, 506,318 financial transactions, and evidence of 11,708 meetings.

The software helped investigators discover that on October 10, 2008—two months before Bernie's arrest—a $10 million credit was received into Madoff's Ponzi account from Fred Wilpon, then the co-owner of baseball's New York Mets. Oddly, November 7 saw a debit in the exact same amount. These transactions were juxtaposed in the data with lengthy conversations between the parties. What was going on? "This is the end of the line [for the company's fate], and it's juxtaposed with a long conversation," says one investigator. "Any forensic accountant will tell you that an account that zeros out is weird anyway."

We'll never know what it was about, as a $1 billion case brought by trustee Irving Picard against the Mets owners was settled, with Katz-Wilpon forking over more than $100 million for losing investors. Both men have long insisted they were victims and had no clue that it could all be a fraud. However, that is disputed by a Wall Street expert named Noreen Harrington, whom they once hired to perform due diligence on their funds. Harrington claims that in 1993 she told Katz that Madoff's returns had to be bogus. Under oath in a related case involving one of the feeder funds, she recalled telling Katz, "I don't believe the numbers are worth the paper they're printed on." She requested a meeting with Bernie but never received one. Katz responded angrily, Harrington testified, leading her to quit.

The $10 million circular Katz-Wilpon transaction did lead investigators to examine phone records during the first eleven days of October 2008, when 457 outbound phone calls were made from BLMIS. Five-second calls were not of interest to them, and most were three minutes long or less, but a few were lengthy. Why? Investigators probed it. They then matched it to events and found a Katz-Wilpon ribbon-cutting ceremony at a Long Island shopping center that Bernie and Ruth attended. No biggie.

From December 1 to December 12 (the day after Madoff's arrest), a flurry of phone calls came in from or went out to an assortment of interesting people, but investigators have not been able to figure out the significance of many of them. They are still trying. On December 8 Mark Madoff phoned Mike Minikes, a prominent executive at Chase, though Minikes declines to discuss anything about Madoff.

On December 9 there were thirty-six calls, one of them to the Picower Foundation lasting just twelve seconds. Another call originated from Fred Wilpon's car. At one point, secretary Eleanor Squillari spoke with Marion Madoff, Peter's wife, for about a minute. And on December 10, one day before Bernie's house of cards toppled, there were fifty-eight total phone calls involving either Bernie or Eleanor. Bernie spoke for three minutes with one of his accountants, Paul Konigsberg, who, in 2014, would plead guilty to falsifying the company's IA and broker-dealer records. Another call was from Noel Levine, of the Abe Hershson family. Madoff's lawyer, Ike Sorkin, spoke to Ruth via a pay phone. Shana Madoff rang her Uncle Bernie shortly before noon and spoke with him for about three minutes. The next morning, he was arrested.

For the month of December, prior to Bernie's arrest investigators found 840 financial transactions—and even a few on December 16, five days *after* his arrest. They attempted to match the transactions with the communications. One of the lengthiest calls placed, likely by Bernie himself, was from the BLMIS offices to Wilpon. (Investigators won't reveal the duration.)

Madoff had a private bathroom in his office with a private landline phone. The calls he made from it were usually brief. But shortly before the firm collapsed, someone made an atypically long, ten-minute call from there. As it turns out, $10 million was moved into an account when the call ended, followed quickly by $10 million moving from that account into a different one. Investigators probed what happened but won't reveal the results, if any. There were several examples of that.

"I always found it interesting that there seemed to be a spike in phone traffic to his Montauk phone right before; right when things were going to hell," says one investigator. Nonetheless, adds another prober, "You rarely found a specific smoking gun with the technology, but you do put together, like, a *silhouette* of a smoking gun. It can show you everything in the room *but* the smoking gun."

Some leading investigators look back on the Madoff affair and wonder if it should have been handled as a racketeering (RICO) case, in essence treating the *entire* enterprise as one would treat a Mafia operation. (RICO is an acronym for the Racketeer Influenced and Corrupt Organizations Act, passed by the US Congress in 1970.) That would have enabled law enforcement to sweep through the floors and arrest just about everybody (as many as one hundred employees), in the hopes that most of them would flip on one another. Case investigators wonder if the RICO approach could have led to yet more indictments and perhaps convictions—maybe even of family members. But it's easy to be a Monday-morning quarterback.

They didn't know in the early stages that Bernie had been pumping Ponzi money into the "legitimate" divisions, and the decision was made to let employees continue to work there until those divisions were sold. The price: a measly $1 million, which was roughly what the real trading platforms were worth. That said, to their credit, prosecutors scored convictions for thirteen Madoff employees, plus two outside accountants—far more than were taken down in the Enron and MCI cases.

Within two days of Bernie's confession, Frank DiPascali decided to flip on underlings. Within weeks, one employee after another was arrested: David Kugel, Madoff's longtime arbitrage trading expert; Kugel's son Craig; Enrica Cortellessa-Pitz, the controller; longtime employees Irwin Lipkin and his son Eric (who would flip on his own father); and, of course, the Madoff Five, whose trial is chronicled in chapters 12 and 13 (operations chief Bonventre, software programmers Jerry O'Hara and George Perez, and both Crupi and Bongiorno, DiPascali's top colleagues in the Ponzi).

Several of the FBI agents were old-school and aggressive. Early on in the cases, a group of law enforcers met at the US Attorney's Office with Eric Lipkin. An intimidating agent named Keith Kelly tossed two documents at him and said sharply, "It's time to stop the bullshit." One document was an IA investment account that Lipkin himself had at the company with millions in it. The second document was the account *opening* statement, which was dated *after* the account statement showing the funds. In other words, it had been backdated by Lipkin, just as tens of thousands of documents at BLMIS were backdated fakes over the decades. Lipkin's lawyer, a former prosecutor named Jim Filan, motioned for his client to step out of the room with him. Within minutes, Lipkin became a cooperator.

Another old-school G-Man was Steve Garfinkel ("Garf" to his colleagues). When he and other agents turned up at the Florida winter home of Madoff Five's Bongiorno, he told her, "We're taking everything! Every piece of furniture. You're not going to be left with anything!" Her response? She served them coffee. Annette's husband, Rudy, who would chortle for most of the trial, was in his boxer shorts at the time. He thought that he was being arrested and asked if he could get dressed. The agents laughed and reassured him they were there only for his wife.

At the height of its investigations in 2009, and for a couple of years thereafter, BLMIS's floors in the Lipstick building were humming with roughly fourteen FBI agents—an unprecedented number for a financial crime case. So much so that when Bernie was sentenced in June 2010, there weren't enough seats for all the agents in the front of the courtroom where the feds normally sit. "We were all pissed," recalls an agent. "They had to stand in line with the public and press to get in, and then had to stand in the back of the court."

But the bureau felt that the biggest scam in the history of

American finance deserved and needed each one of them. Inside Lipstick, they were joined by investigators from Picard's office, as well as agents from the SEC, the IRS, even the US Department of Labor. That translated into lots of empty pizza boxes and soda cans.

On the seventeenth floor, agents found a big bookcase filled with old *Wall Street Journals* going back years for cooking up the back-dated IA statements. And while agents Keith Kelly and Julia Hanish were rummaging through boxes, Hanish stumbled onto a handwritten "script" by O'Hara and Perez—who would ultimately be convicted of writing hundreds of computer software programs that were used to carry out the Ponzi. The script was their plan of action for how the men were going to confront Madoff to inform him that they would no longer write illegal programs. "*Holy shit*, Keith!" she exclaimed. "You're not gonna believe this."

The fake trading desk on the seventeenth floor is where FBI agents and prosecutors huddled regularly to debate (and sometimes argue) over who should or shouldn't be indicted. That scene would be akin to having the FBI move into the Ravenite Social Club on Mulberry Street in Little Italy—John Gotti's mob family hangout—to discuss which members of the Gambino family should be put in jail.

On another day at Lipstick, Andrew Madoff was going ballistic. He had shown up to collect some personal belongings and suddenly charged onto the nineteenth floor claiming that two of his metallic expensive fishing reels were missing. By then, there were so many people who had been walking around the floors, including Madoff employees, that anyone could have walked off with them. Astonishingly, Andrew started accusing FBI agent Garfinkel of having stolen them. People watching the scene were shocked and amused.

"*Well*, call the police," Garf suggested sarcastically. "*Oh*, I *am* the police! File a claim." Andrew's attorney, Flumenbaum, tried to calm his client. The biggest fraud in history, and this was what Andrew was worried about: his reels.

He had a similar skirmish with Agent Hanish—over yet another fishing reel. Andrew showed up one day to pick up personal belongings and was seen trying to lift a reel off a ledge in his office. Hanish stopped him. "But my *dad* gave it to me," he said, perhaps forgetting that the funds his father had used to buy the gift were tainted. "Put it back," Hanish said. "Anything your dad bought we are taking. You can take your personal papers, that's all." By all accounts, Andrew looked at her with hatred in his eyes. It was still early in their investigations and the agents and prosecutors were hoping that Andrew and Mark, as well as Peter, Ruth, and Shana, would cooperate and help the investigations. But none of them ever did.

At Ruth and Bernie's penthouse, agents Kelly and Garfinkel turned up one day with a forfeiture expert from the US Attorney's Office to create an inventory of their personal items. When Ruth asked if she could keep her new Nespresso machine, Garfinkel phoned prosecutor Baroni. "Lisa, you're not gonna believe this, but Ruth asked if she could keep the coffee maker. Can you believe this? What should I do?" Baroni asked what it was worth. "Ahhh, two hundred dollars," estimated Garf. They broke out laughing. "You can't have that, Ruth," said Garf. "The government's taking that. But you know what? I'll buy you a French press." Ruth also eyeballed some of her expensive cashmere sweaters, but those, too, would be put up for auction.

In her kitchen, a deflated Ruth lit a cigarette.

"Ruth, that's gonna kill you," warned Garf.

"If only," said Ruth.

Once the inventory was completed, Garf was preparing to give Ruth a ride to a cousin's house on Long Island. But with TV news trucks and photographers on the street waiting for their prey, he didn't feel she deserved to be put through that. "Well, I have a disguise," Ruth said. "I have a wig." Garf laughed. "That wig is the same style and color as your hair," he said.

He led her down the building's elevator to the basement, where one of several underground passageways led to a stationery store on Lexington Avenue. Once on the road (Kelly drove), Garf remarked, "You're like so skinny, Ruth. You need something to eat." He suggested a good Jewish deli in Woodmere, but she wasn't hungry. Instead, during the entire hour-long trip, Ruth didn't stop talking. It was a stream of consciousness ranging from Butner ("Bernie doesn't seem to mind prison. You know, he gets to read a lot") to how "the happiest times we ever had was when the family was out on the water, on the boat in Montauk." When the agents finally let her off, Garf turned toward Kelly and said, "No wonder Bernie doesn't mind prison. She won't shut the fuck up."

Months later, FBI agents were at the Madoffs' Montauk house, creating yet another inventory. Andrew, who allegedly was not on speaking terms with his mother at the time (as he claimed later), showed up to tell the agents that his mother was hoping she could keep an old bicycle. "You can have the bike," an agent sighed. But like Andrew's reels, the bike wasn't there. Andrew also wanted family photos. "You can have the photos," the same agent said. "But I'm taking the frames." Like the Nespresso, the sweaters, and everything else, those would be sold at auction, too.

Back in Manhattan, Andrew once entered his Chase bank branch in Lenox Hill on the Upper East Side. He needed cash and was irate when the bankers told him that his funds were frozen. He demanded to speak to the manager, refusing to accept that the government had frozen his money, and there was nothing the bank could do about it. He yelled and screamed, bankers there recall.

For most of his adult life, thanks to his dad, Andrew had millions in the bank, three luxury homes, and one of the best fishing boats money can buy (not to mention those fancy reels). Indeed, an email exchange between Andrew and his brother, Mark, from 2003 is illustrative of how privileged the boys were, and felt. The subject line: "Bonus." The text:

Andrew: How about $3mm (same as last year)? My apart-
ment is closing Wednesday. . . . I need the cash.

Mark: You've got my proxy. Begin the negotiations on behalf
of the two of us.

But six years later, their assets frozen, the brothers would need every dollar they could scrape up. In Andrew's case—a year before Bernie's arrest—he and his girlfriend, Catherine Hooper, had befriended a retired Secret Service agent who would be among the charitable souls to help him for free.

The agent, Scott Alswang, who had guarded several US presi-dents, says that Hooper once bragged to him over lunch that "I could make you a rich guy." How so? "She said her boyfriend had a lot of contacts." Indeed he did—his dad being first on any list. (Mark, for his part, used to say to Bernie, "Dad, can you? My friend wants to . . . [open an IA account]," according to a former employee.)

Following Bernie's arrest, Andrew and Catherine immediately summoned Alswang to their apartment. "Scott, can you help me out? I need my family protected," said Andrew. Responded Alswang: "The first thing you gotta do is put the fucking blinds down. I don't know how much of a threat case you are, but I don't think you're the most well-liked guy in America right now."

Alswang's firm proceeded to provide them security protection. Food, too. They often showed up at a diner he co-owns in Midtown Manhattan called Theatre Row. "They were like pariahs and had no friends. They would come to the diner, and I bought every meal be-cause they said they have no money and couldn't spend any money."

In 2014, when Andrew Madoff died of lymphoma, Catherine reached out to Alswang. Protection was needed again, she said, add-ing that Andrew's funeral service would be at a church, rather than a synagogue, to help circumvent reporters and others. He had thirty security guards dispatched to the church.

By the time the feds were done with Frank DiPascali, despite his being their star witness against many BLMIS employees, he'd be left in a lot worse financial shape than Ruth and the boys. On the morning of December 11, 2013, during the Madoff Five trial, he told the jury that he forfeited everything he owned to the feds, with the exception of his clothing. "We gave away real estate. We gave the government my boat. We gave the government the contents of my home, my kids' furniture."

When asked by a defense lawyer what he had left in terms of money, Frank replied, "the fourteen dollars that are in my pocket." That afternoon, he was asked if he spent anything for lunch. "I think I spent two dollars or so for coffee." And when the remaining twelve dollars is gone? "My sister will lend me another twenty dollars for coffee. . . . My mom and sister have been supporting me since June."

Frank's unraveling—his dispossession—was a long process that started three years earlier. That's when the first of his belongings were auctioned off in Morris County, New Jersey, about a thirty-minute drive from the lavish estate he used to call home.

The auction took place in a garage surrounded by crumpled cars and burned-out buildings used for police and fire training. Prospective bidders filling the parking lot were met with echoing thuds from a shooting range nearly. Morris County is a very wealthy part of the state, but the DiPascali auction was decidedly down-market, with more tattoos, mullets, and pickup trucks than luxuries such as the Audi and two BMWs that Franks was forced to surrender.

The local press had touted Frank's arcade game collection prior to the auction, but the foosball table, poker table, Lord of the Rings pinball machine, and Big Buck Hunter II game took up only one corner of the garage. Otherwise, the cavernous space was filled mostly with the DiPascali family's orphaned chairs: ten tall black wicker chairs in the middle of the garage, six upholstered dining chairs, swivel chairs, brass chairs, corner chairs, reclining theater chairs, armchairs, barstools. There were a good number of chintzy gold-themed tables and dressers. There were a couple of oversized paintings wrapped in cellophane, and a handful of maybe-antique urns. A sad little collection of workout equipment—an outdated elliptical, a set of hand weights, a Bosu ball, and a disassembled home gym—included a strength training clock with "Body Solid" printed on top that resembled a barbell's weight plate.

Near the entrance to the garage sat DiPascali's ATV collection—three Yamahas—and a snowblower that had attracted the attention of a significant percentage of the male attendees. Bidding started slowly, the auctioneer taking his time, ratcheting up the bid on the snowblower in increments of $50, from $100 to its final tally of $625. Quickly, though, the hopefuls in the crowd began to realize that they were being consistently outbid by two particular parties. Number 67 bought the first ATV for $800, smiled triumphantly, and went on to bid on nearly every lot that followed. She looked local, with blonde hair dyed several shades lighter than her skin. But Number 67 had nothing on Number 33, the auction's power couple—a large man with a Bluetooth implanted in his ear and a slender, pretty woman in a brown wrap dress. At first, the audience giggled at the bidding war between 67 and 33. But by the end, the crowd was grumbling each time they were outbid.

In a minor victory for the masses, the arcade games went to other attendees. One guy dropped $2,400 on the Ping-Pong table, foosball table, and Super Chexx bubble electronic hockey table. He knew he could have bought the same games in a store for that price, but liked the idea of the money going to compensate Madoff losers. The collection was destined, he said, for his "man cave."

As bizarre as the DiPascali auction was, it was like a bake sale compared with the auctions of Bernie and Ruth's worldly wealth. The first of these, at the Sheraton New York Hotel & Towers in November 2009, drew more than 500 people, plus 1,000 online bidders. Thousands of items (comprising nearly 200 lots) were auctioned off, from a pair of Ruth's diamond earrings that garnered $70,000, more than four times the presale estimate, to a half-used pad of Post-its. Among the items that (understandably) generated the greatest interest was their yacht's white rescue-ring buoy, with the words "Bullship N.Y." painted on the front. It went for $7,500—fifty times the estimated sales price. All the loot had been seized from the Madoffs' homes in Manhattan, Montauk, and Palm Beach. Bernie's yachts were sold in Florida a week later.

The next round came on November 10, 2010, at the Brooklyn Navy Yard, with many items having also come from the Montauk estate. The preview attracted hundreds of people to a warehouse the size of a football field, with the impounded possessions lined up in two rows, behind red velvet ropes, like a gallery in the Museum of Gaudy Junk.

Jenny Crane, the US Marshall in charge of the auction, walked me around, explaining that she was inside the Madoffs' penthouse— with Ruth—when many of the items were first being inventoried. "She's a very little lady, very New York," Crane observed. "She's been through a lot, you could tell. She walked through paparazzi to get up there [the penthouse]; she was moving out at that point. . . . She seemed very taken care of her whole life—from my point of view, anyway. I'm a government worker."

Crane explained the scale of the task facing her and her fellow marshalls: "This is a very large case; thousands of items, houses. Certainly, the largest case for the United States Marshall Service in my five years there. The way it works is that the proceeds go to the victims, with thirty percent to the feds to cover their expenses. Her [Ruth's] engagement ring will bring in the most—up to three hundred thousand dollars. After all, a plastic Igloo cooler went for six hundred dollars at last year's Madoff auction. A big one, but not worth six hundred dollars." People hovered around the ring like it was the Hope Diamond.

It became pretty clear pretty quickly—to me and to many people I chatted with—that the Madoffs had lousy taste. Crane gestured around at the dubious items on offer: Rustic Navajo type rugs, as you walked in the front door. A taxidermied coyote that was standing. A leopard settee. "Yes, well, someone will buy it," said Crane, pointing to what I called a grotesque flowered bedroom set and marble-topped gold mirror.

And so on and so forth. You can take the thief out of suburban Queens, but apparently you can't take Queens out of the thief.

Alan Richardson attended the spectacle in his capacity as a buyer from estatebuyer.com. "Prices will be really stupid," he assured me, adding that between the novelty value of the Madoff connection and the impending holidays, the average bidder would have a rough time competing. "There's a new high in the stock market and Xmas is around corner—and based on the crazy prices at the *last* Madoff auction. . . ."

Richardson wasn't exactly impressed by the loot around him. "For the amount of money he had, the taste doesn't match the dollars," he said. "Not necessarily '*ughh*,' but . . ." Richardson's primary expertise is jewelry, diamonds, and wristwatches, and plenty of Bernie's Rolexes would soon be auctioned: "All the watches have a problem," he pointed out. "On five of them, the dials were redone, not original. The difference as a result will be seventy-five thousand dollars to one hundred thousand dollars per watch. If I'm Bernie Madoff, I'm not buying redone watches. Did they [the sellers] tell him the dials

were redone? Did he know, or did he *not* know and get ripped off?"
As for the furniture, said Richardson, "none of it is important; the
best piece is the piano. Among the finest pianos in world, Steinway."
Madoff had retrofitted it with a cassette player.

And Ruth's engagement ring? "Compared to the money they had,
it's not an expensive stone," Richardson opined, estimating that it
would sell for "under six hundred thousand dollars on Forty-seventh
Street [the city's diamond district]. I can bring you five of them today.
There's already a three hundred five thousand dollar bid on it—*my
bid*. I bought almost every one of her purses at the last auction."

A couple of the items for sale were remarkable for their unre-
markability. Bernie's desk, for example, was quite small—perhaps fittingly, for a man who did no legitimate work at it. Bernie and Ruth's
penthouse canopy bed, too—a nineteenth-century custom-made
George III, with inlaid mahogany and satinwood—is shorter than a
queen, not what one would have expected from a Bernie. The bed
was scooped up on auction day by an attorney named Tally Wiener,
who was working on a Madoff feeder fund liquidation case in the Ca-
ribbean. She explained to me that she was buying it in order to return
it to Ruth. "Ruth should have her bed back," she insisted matter-of-
factly.

(When I caught up again with Wiener in January 2024, she said
that she tried, through one of Ruth's lawyers, to get a message to her
about the bed's availability. But she never heard back. Tally's been
sleeping in it ever since, but says she feels like an "interloper" in their
marriage by doing so. She periodically puts it up on eBay, for about
$20,000. But nobody seems interested.)

The parade of crap continued. There was the rusting "BLM"
branding iron for steaks, ideal for a losing investor looking to self-
harm with an enduring symbol of his or her misfortune. But one
man's junk is another man's treasure, as the cliché goes. Just ask
young Westin Lord, whom I found rummaging around. Lord is

twenty-seven, was living in Aspen, and was ecstatic about the opportunities around him. "Hell yes, I'd like to buy many lots," he enthused.

He walked with me from table to table, hurling jokes at Bernie's expense, as many attendees enjoyed doing. "I'd love to have a pair of his socks—put it in a frame. Or to drink a glass of Scotch out of his brandy sifter? There's only one here. The massage table—perhaps it's where he worked out all his guilt," said Lord. "An American flag— that's ridiculous. It says 'Ruth Madoff' on her putter—in script engraved. I'd use that putter in a second. I'd regrip it. Boxers? No, I don't want my man parts too close to his. Do you think the Monopoly game is fixed."

And finally: "That steak branding iron, that golf bag, that umbrella—for fascination's sakes, to have later in life. The biggest financial scandal in the history of the world!"

Sheila Israel, from Smithtown, Long Island, came "purely out of prurient interest," she confessed. "Why would I want his junk? I have my own junk. When I cleaned out my mother's apartment, I threw out this stuff." Her husband, Mark, concurred: "Why would you want to own something from somebody so notorious? Who would actually wear a shoe that was worn by a man named Bernie Madoff? The one saving grace of this whole charade is money to victims."

It turned out that artist Andres Serrano—creator of the infamous *Piss Christ*, a work that flustered many delicate types back in the eighties—*did* want to own a shoe worn by a man named Bernie Madoff. In fact, he apparently wanted to own many, many of them, because three days later at the auction, he plunked down $700 for twenty-two pairs.

November 13, 2010. Sheraton ballroom, New York City. There are hundreds of people here, with about 1,000 bidding online. This event will raise $2 million for Bernie's losers; the previous auctions of their goods pulled in almost $8 million.

A leather footstool shaped like a bull goes for $3,300. A giggling blonde is applauded loudly by her pals after she nabs a humidor for $900. A Brazilian couple in their twenties, in jeans and sneakers—Gustavo and Clara—are sitting next to me; she's a physical therapist, he's a lawyer. This is the first auction she's ever attended. She wants to spend up to $500 to get Gustavo a Christmas present to add to his collection of strange memorabilia, like his pens from the fallen Lehman Brothers and Bear Stearns.

It's hard for newbies to follow the auctioneer's patter. He is yelling "*Yeah!*" The whole vibe feels like an NFL game, the chaos subtly pushing people to make fiscally unsound decisions, just like the investors who paid for all this detritus. An American flag stands to the right of the auctioneers, next to an oversized US Marshall poster.

Lot 18 includes a fireplace screen and utensils. "You never know what they burned in that fireplace," says the auctioneer to cheers and laughter. It goes for $2,900.

Bernie's desk sells for $7,000.

Lot 27: "So ugly" says Clara, the Brazilian. It's a flowery transparent Lalique crystal clock. "Gross," she adds. "Oh, absolutely," pipes in a man behind me—Walter, from Brookville, Long Island, a former Viacom TV salesman now doing economic development on Long Island. He's here for the "novelty" of it. His wife works on Wall Street. People were hurt so bad by Madoff on the North Shore near him, he says.

Lot 71 is an award from Hofstra University for Alumni Achievement, made out to Bernard L. Madoff, Class of '60.

"*Yeah!*" screams the auctioneer.

A watch goes for $64,000. "That's almost what I pay to go to school," marvels Rob Hochberg, a student at NYU Dental. He's twenty-two, and he's here with a friend from Washington, DC. He also says: "I think it's ironic—these religious items. . . . I want to have his mezuzah. That's what we're here for."

Suddenly a hush comes over the room. Ruth's engagement ring is next. A $550,000 bid. The winner, wearing a tweed jacket, who made that bid online, rushes out of the ballroom saying, oddly, "The press will know shortly, but not today." Doesn't want to give his name. "It has zero significance to me," he says, referring to the fact that it's Ruth's. A gaggle of photographers are following him halfway down West Fifty-third Street, until he barks at them to stop.

Half the room empties after the ring is sold.

Bernie clearly had a shoe fetish; he owned about 250 pairs, way more than Ruth did! Made in Italy, France, and Belgium; many were never worn. Ten pairs of used designer shoes of his sold for $900.

The day after the auction, I visit Serrano, the *Piss Christ* creator, to see the twenty-two pairs of Bernie shoes he'd won, the last lot of the day. He got them for $700, which seems crazy cheap. Included among them: two pair of sneakers and "several high-end slippers." The slippers are French. Some are very expensive shoes. Some from Belgium. Also, nice-looking loafers, including a leopard-print pair. "It was the last lot, and probably people were exhausted by then, and so I got a good price," Serrano says. "I wanted Ruth's shoes, as well, but they were pretty pricey. Bernie's shoes were the most important, so I just went with him. Some are worn, some not."

Less than twenty-four hours after the auction, some of Bregards Bernie's shoes are already up on eBay. Serrano says he has no interest in reselling his. "In the case of Bernard Madoff, I find nothing aesthetic about him," he explains, "but the financial ruin in the aftermath, the devastation he caused, is what is of interest to me."

Serrano keeps Bernie's shoes surprisingly close. "My [own] boots are Gianni Barbato, and I have all of Bernie's shoes next to them, around my bed. My work [artwork] deals with juxtapositions of good and evil, beautiful and vulgar, and duality here—my shoes on one side, and Bernie's shoes on the other. Like I'm holding shoes for Bernie, waiting for him. But the truth is, Bernie will never get his shoes."

In 2014, a federal judge ordered the sale of assets belonging to Peter and his wife, Marion, as well as their daughter and princess, Shana, a shopaholic who clomped loudly around the BLMIS offices in high heels. (As part of Peter's guilty plea agreement, Shana was also required to part with all her assets.) Among the bric-a-brac: Numerous watches from Bulgari, Cartier, and Patek Philippe, and jewelry from Hermès, Cartier, Judith Ripka, and David Yurman. A 9.03-carat diamond ring went for $400,000. Peter's vintage Aston Martin, which he had bought in 2008, shortly before his life came tumbling down, sold for $225,000.

6

The Final Word . . .
on the Losers

| | | | | | | | | | | | |

The Question: Why are the clients who lost money when they knew better (or should have known better) called "victims"?

Monday, June 29, 2009: It is a nasty scene at five in the morning outside 500 Pearl Street. We're here for Bernie's sentencing, and the ugliness is not weather related. Dozens, and eventually hundreds, of people line up outside the building. Lawyers, reporters, photographers, Madoff investors. A hefty cop with thin, blood-red hair is showing everyone that he's in charge. "You *are* moving!" he yells to reporters to keep within barriers. "Get away, get away from the building!"

"Douchebag," mumbles a local Fox reporter. The contempt that court security has for the press is highest on special days like this.

Reporters who woke up early to be first in line hail from outlets ranging from the *Financial Times* to a Quebec newspaper, from CNN to CNBC. ABC's investigative correspondent Brian Ross is getting rigged up with a mike. A circus of tents has spread out on Pearl Street. Everyone wants to hear from the losers.

"My accountant had us use Quicken [software] at end of year for all transactions, and it all worked—every single transaction went in," Madoff investor Carol Baer tells the press. She says she asked Bernie himself ten years ago how safe her money is with him. "He told me, 'It's safe unless I run off with your money.'" Carol drives an imaginary knife into her own heart and gives it a twist.

Another investor, a lawyer named Lia, gives anyone who will listen an earful about how Madoff's lawyer, Ike Sorkin, is a "dirtbag" for taking on the case—a strange reaction from a fellow member of the bar. One man cries that he accumulated "piles and piles of trading slips—and, after awhile, I never opened the envelopes Bernie Madoff sent. It was nuts!"

In the packed courtroom, twenty "victims" of Madoff's Ponzi fill the first two rows. It's an emotional scene, as half of them have been given the opportunity to speak before the judge decides what to do with Bernie. Someone shouts "Crook!" when Madoff enters the room. He faces forward and—except for a quick five-second moment during his own speech—never looks at his accusers.

Bernie appears shrunken, thinner than he did during his arraignment, when he'd pled guilty, months earlier. The judge, Denny Chin, announces that he's received hundreds of letters and emails from investors encouraging him to toss the max at Bernie, but not a single letter on Bernie's behalf. This seems shocking, even though Bernie and Sorkin say later that nobody would dare do so even if he or she was inclined—for fear that it would draw unwelcome attention from Clawback Picard. That almost makes sense.

Judge Chin only allowed nine of the net losers to speak—one after another, in tears, some trembling—and it sends shudders throughout the courtroom. Reporters can't take notes fast enough, but it hardly matters, as the pattern is repeated over and over again until all the voices seem to blend together in a single chorus. If you mix in the highlights from investors' emails and letters to the judge, it goes like this:

"Nightmare, wife told me the news . . . entire life savings . . . how can someone do this to us . . . this can't be real . . . indescribable. We did nothing wrong. Wife lived in house twenty-seven years and sold it . . . motor home . . . pension that is our lifeline . . . hearing loss . . . wife foot run over by a van . . . don't know what I'm gonna do afterwards . . . we have no credit now and can't get mortgage . . . now forced to use people's homes when they are away . . . our govt has failed me and thousands of others . . . SEC totally criminal negligence . . . widow now working fulltime . . . to a psychopath lost my home . . . lost ability to care for myself in my old age . . . lost ability to donate to charity, so Bernie Madoff could buy his wife another Cartier watch . . . worked so we could leave something behind . . . couldn't sleep, eat, rapid heartrate, weight loss, insomnia, crying spells, and this horrible feeling that I had been pushed into the great black abyss . . . he has not truly cooperated . . . he would steal again today . . . evil lowlife . . . a violent crime without the use of a tangible weapon . . . the scope of the devastation he has reaped . . . true justice is maximum sentence in maximum security . . . that monster took it away . . . you have left your children a legacy of shame . . . may god spare you no mercy in hell . . ."

Through it all—through the very real anguish of dozens of investors who lost tons of money, representing thousands more—Madoff is motionless. (In every Madoff-related guilty plea or jury conviction I attended, the defendants all stood still as trees, something I had trouble understanding.) Bernie swears to the judge that he hasn't taken any drugs or alcohol in the previous twenty-four hours, although it would be hard to blame him for being stoned out of his mind in the face of all this. Even when he speaks, Madoff is wooden. "I was already cried out," he insisted to me later, during our first meeting.

As odious as his crimes were, Bernie Madoff did not kill, like his prison pals Persico and Scarfo, nor did he physically assault or sexually abuse anyone. And the one thing missing from the tongue-lashings directed at Bernie was a sense of *any* personal responsibility or agency on the part of his "victims" for what they themselves had done. In many, if not most, cases, after all, these poor unfortunates had been pulling in massive, impossibly consistent profits without a peep—often for decades. It was the very visible elephant in the room, had they been paying attention.

Instead, we got more of this:

"When he sank so low as to steal from Elie Wiesel, as if Wiesel hasn't suffered enough in his lifetime." . . . "Life has been a living hell . . . it feels like a nightmare you can't wake from . . . junior in college works two jobs . . . please your honor, do not fail us . . . this is not a man who deserves a federal country club . . . he's killed my spirit and shattered my dreams . . . he destroyed my trust in people . . . hope that his sentence is long enough that his jail cell becomes his coffin . . . he discarded me like roadkill . . . his stunning indifference . . . I manage on food stamps . . . at end of month I sometimes scavenge in dumpsters . . . I shine my shoes each night afraid they will wear out, drag cans to redemption centers . . . face and acknowledge the murderous aspects of your life's work . . ."

The kicker was a speech by Sheryl Weinstein, the CFO of Hadassah—her pain, her suffering, her losses, her hostility. What she failed to mention was that she'd soon be publishing a memoir alleging a three-decade-long affair with Bernie, which may be why she snapped at a reporter seated behind her who wanted to ask her questions. She was keeping it all for her tell-all. (In an email from prison, which Ruth was cc'd on, Bernie referred to the former Hadassah exec as a "psychotic stalker whose affair was nothing but a fantasy in her own warped mind. . . . I apologize to my wife for bringing up this painful subject once again. It is only because I would hope that my grandchildren would some day hear the truth.")

Fortunately, there are some losers who refuse to be portrayed as victims and who take responsibility for what they did. They see what happened to them as an opportunity to learn and begin a new journey. But in the courthouse that day, and in the months to follow, it seemed that the louder the anger, the less willingness there was to search within themselves for what led them to this sad place.

The losers saved some of their contempt for the man retained to defend Bernie: Ira "Ike" Sorkin, the former SEC official. This was odd, as Sorkin was basically a warm body in the chair, given that Madoff decided to confess immediately and spare Ruth and his sons a trial he was likely to lose or plead out of in the eleventh hour. But if Ike's role was short and limited—essentially just trying to get his client the lowest-possible prison sentence—the will of the mob prevailed nevertheless, reinforcing the judge's determination to set an example with a 150-year sentence.

That sentence looks even more severe today, given that net losers in the Ponzi have already gotten back more than 75 percent of their principal and may get far more by the time the feds, Clawback Picard, and other trustees wrap up their work. In fact, many experts considered Sorkin's argument to the court for why Madoff deserved less than twenty years to be reasonable. He felt that given Madoff's age (seventy-one), a lower sentence might allow him a chance for some freedom before he died. After all, said Sorkin, he pled guilty immediately and took "full acceptance" of responsibility.

Yet Sorkin, like Madoff, was the subject of a deluge of hate mail and emails simply for having defended Bernie. The attorney was so aghast that he collected them—as well as some of the letters addressed to Madoff himself—and copied them into a large loose-leaf binder.

YOU GOD DAMN BASTARDS DESERVE TO ROT TO DEATH IN JAIL!! . . . I hope that the combined miseries of all those swindled by Madoff BEFALL YOU AND YOUR

CLIENT 1000 TIMES OVER, AND THAT YOU BOTH DIE
THE MOST HORRIFIC DEATHS IMAGINABLE.

House arrest . . . fuck you Sorkin, you sleaze bastard typical
jew.

I hope someone kicks the crap out of you. . . . I hope you
and Bernie spontaneously combust. Your wife and children
should be horrified and hate you. . . . How can you live with
yourself?

Mark Schwartz, a Madoff investor, wrote that his infant daughter
lost her college savings and that he and his wife were now broke, "including our wedding money." He added that they had twenty family
members invested in Madoff and that they all lost everything. "Because of you [Sorkin] personally I have lost all faith in the US judicial
system."

As Bernie would put it: And so on and so forth.

One bitter loser, among many dozens I met, was Harriet Rubin,
who, along with her husband, Lee, agreed to dine with me near their
house in Las Vegas in June 2010. (I had chosen Sin City as one of
several places to visit to try to round up losers from Picard's master
list.) It was an expensive fish restaurant, and I was happy to treat,
since they were now pretty much reduced to twofers, or pizza, when
they ventured out. "I used to buy asparagus a lot," said Harriet, aged
seventy. "Not now." Added Lee, eighty-one: "We were living the good
life before—all the best restaurants." They lost everything to Bernie:
$770,000.

Frank DiPascali told FBI agents that Madoff had revealed to him
that the fraud "goes back" to Abe and Moe, whom we met in chapter 2.

As chance had it for me in Vegas, Harriet, originally from Brooklyn, revealed that Abe Hershson was her uncle and that her involvement with Madoff began with him. As she told the story, the Madoffs and Hershsons were nearby neighbors in Queens in the early 1960s, when Ralph Madoff asked Abe if he would invest with his son Bernie, who was just starting out on Wall Street. "Abe did," she told me, "and then Abe got my parents to invest five thousand dollars, which grew to fifteen thousand. Abe was wealthy and controlled the distribution to my parents." It's an intriguing fact, as it suggests that her parents were under Abe's umbrella rather than enjoying their own accounts—more confirmation that Hershson was one of the first feeders.

Harriet's father died in 1984, and her brother, Irwin Salbe, "wanted to do away with the account, but Abe said, 'You don't want to give it up,' so my brother didn't." Instead, he put his, Harriet's, and another sister's names on the account. He also brought in others as the years passed. "My brother had thirty people in it," she estimated.

All went swimmingly until the news of Bernie's arrest. "My husband and son-in-law had to pick me up off the floor," she recalled, her eyes watering. "I was hysterical." Within two days, she was suffering from depression. "I lost everything. My IRA was $450,000, and [a] second account was $320,000—both with Bernie Madoff. Dumb!" Husband Lee had owned a smoked fish and cheese-making business. After fifty-three years of working, he'd put his retirement money into Madoff, too.

The clues were there, though: In 1999 Harriet decided she wanted her own account, separate from Irwin's. At first, Madoff declined to do it, but he relented eventually. Oddly, however, she started noticing that Irwin was earning more money than she was, despite having the same stocks on the statements. "I'd call Jodi [Crupi]. She said, 'Maybe we bought his at a fraction less or sold at a fraction more, by ten minutes.' I said, 'It's the same basket [of stocks]; I don't understand.' This went on every month, and I could not understand it." It was a clue that could have cracked open the Ponzi, but Harriet ultimately ignored it.

Immediately after realizing they'd lost it all, Harriet canceled two cruises that she and Lee had planned. She asked her son to try to refinance their home mortgage, as they weren't able to make the payments. She called the electric company to ask that it put her on an energy budget, and did the same with the gas company. She got rid of call-waiting on her phone. Every penny now counted. They have huge medical expenses, including for high blood pressure and cancer care.

She used to enjoy playing blackjack, but that's just a memory now. Harriet hunts for work every day, while Lee started working one day a week at $9.45 per hour putting magazines into racks at grocery stores. "He reads all the cruise brochures, and I say, 'Why? We can't go.' So I get crazy." Responded Lee: "She's at my neck twenty-four hours a day."

Anger over Madoff drove both Rubins into therapy. She takes Xanax for anxiety attacks; he prays at a local synagogue. "'This guy [Bernie] did what Hitler couldn't do to the Jews,' my CPA told me when it happened," said Harriet.

It was only when Harriet excused herself to use the restroom that Lee opened up about something that goes to the very heart of the fraud, and why—despite my sympathy and empathy—investors like the Rubins cannot be considered victims. "Harriet kept getting huge returns with the market up and down; it didn't make sense," he conceded. "I blame myself as well for the loss." They drove me to my hotel, squabbling over the directions.

Two months after the Ponzi collapsed, the *Chicago Sun-Times* quoted several local investors who were on the "Victim's List." One of them was an elderly woman in Lake Forest, Illinois, named Patti Gerber. It turns out that she's a daughter of Abe Hershson. "I'm not an angry person," she told the newspaper. "I believe in forgiveness. But I'd like to see him [Madoff] burn in hell. I hope he doesn't have an easy death. Isn't that terrible." She said her father began investing with Madoff decades ago and that in good times those investments generated "amazing" returns of up to 30 percent. Gerber ran into Madoff over the years on social outings, including at The Breakers, the luxurious Palm Beach resort. Bernie even cosponsored her in 2008 when she decided to become a member of the exclusive Palm Beach Country Club.

Meanwhile, in Pompano Beach, Florida, Harriet's brother and his son Steve wouldn't concede any responsibility for the loss. In 2009, in a three-minute video testimonial for *Vanity Fair*, they blamed everyone but themselves. (The magazine conducted such testimonials with a handful of Madoff losers, not unlike what museums have done with Holocaust survivors.) By Irwin's reckoning, the account was opened by Abe circa 1963–64, just a few years after Madoff began on Wall Street. "We're the little people that counted on this for the rest of our lives. . . . [We received] a quarterly statement telling me exactly what I have in there; how could it not have that?"

Irwin always talked about this account "and how wonderful it was," son Steve added. "So back in 1996, I had jumped into it also. It's always been there for us. . . . We never think [*sic*] there was anything not normal about it."

Steve went on to decry what he called "the complete negligence of our SEC. . . . If Americans cannot rely on our federal government to protect us, *who* can we?" Building up a good head of steam, he went on to state what seemed pretty obvious by this point: "We want our money. We want justice *done*. We want the government to step in and do what's right, release funds. Get TARP involved." He was referring to the Troubled Asset Relief Program established by the US Treasury in October 2008 in order to strengthen the financial sector and prevent home foreclosures during the economic crisis triggered by the collapse of the housing market.

Steve's pain and anger toward the federal government, and in particular the SEC, is something that thousands of investors felt and continue to feel.

        ▬

On the other end of the Vegas Strip sat an entirely different viewpoint. Kenneth Brinkman sat at a blackjack table in the Stratosphere Club, advising me on what moves to make. Brinkman himself couldn't play his own hand, as he'd lost everything he had to Madoff.

We spent a night on the town. He was a lively man with a tremendous sense of humor and seemed at least twenty years younger than his age of sixty-nine. He showed up wearing shorts and a black T-shirt emblazoned with the acronym *CSI*, for the popular TV drama series *Crime Scene Investigation*. Gray hair, gray goatee, floppy ears, a gold pinky ring. Thick hands and warm eyes. "I don't have a cell anymore, thanks to Bernie," he had said initially from his landline. Soon after greeting, he raised his arms in the air and said: "I should be pissed off and angry. In a way, I gotta respect the guy in terms of being the number one scam artist ever. I'm impressed with the way he did it. He ran a class scam!"

Kenn, who died in 2023 at age eighty-two, worked for decades as a commercial real estate broker and had been invested with Bernie for more than twenty years. He'd made the investment with his father, David, then a vice president for retail stockbroker EF Hutton, which gave his dad some understanding of how markets were supposed to work and how trades cleared.

David once co-owned a 1950s-style motel in town called the Desert Rose with an aunt and uncle. David did the accounting for the motel, until casino tycoon Steve Wynn bought it from them for $10 million, which they all plunked into a Madoff feeder.

Kenn said neither he nor his father knew at first that it was Madoff at the end of the feeder. Eventually he found that out, and phoned

Bernie directly to ask if an aunt and uncle could also get in on the action. "Bernie asked how much. I said three hundred thousand dollars total. He said it was not enough."

Kenn's father had let the account grow without taking out any funds after an initial investment of about $100,000 to $150,000. After Kenn started making decent money, David invited his son to invest into the account, which he did. As an accountant, his father would meticulously examine the monthly statements, but clearly not meticulously enough. Nonetheless, "Dad was old-school; the most level-headed guy I ever knew. 'You want something, you pay cash.' I was the opposite. I lived on plastic for a long time, and married a Vegas showgirl, which didn't last long; I still call her what's-her-name."

At one stage, both Kenn and his father visited the Madoff operation and were given the tour by Frank DiPascali. He put on the usual show, keeping Kenn away from the seventeenth floor, while showing off the state-of-the-art nineteenth-floor trading room, where, as we know, none of Kenn's trading was actually taking place. They were introduced to Shana and met one of Bernie's sons. Kenn recalls the visit lasting more than two hours. DiPascali mentioned that it was a "hedge fund," which Bernie always denied to others. "I just took it for granted," Kenn said, adding, "I took a lot of things for granted."

According to Kenn, he and his father dealt almost entirely with Frank regarding their investments. Their money doubled in four and a half years at 18 percent, then doubled and doubled again. His ex-wife got in on the fun and put in more than $200,000. "When my daughter Danielle wanted to buy a Jeep, I called Frank for ten thousand dollars. He was always there." The riches flowed. Costa Rica for three weeks; Bangkok, three weeks; Panama. Kenn joined the Las Vegas Country Club, where he played tennis. It's a story that one could repeat with thousands upon thousands of investors and their families, the details differing but the main story line the same.

All of that would come to an abrupt end for Brinkman in December 2008, when he was called by a cousin who was also invested with Bernie. "Kenn, it's all gone. There's nothing there." His first reaction? "'Where am I gonna get my stipend?' It was like clockwork, every quarter I had gotten a check in the mail [representing his "earnings"]. The principal I could care less about; it was going to my kids."

Did Kenn sleep that month? "Oh, sure. What was I gonna do? Shit happens. I had a nice run. Life threw a curveball, and I struck out."

He handed a bank the keys to his house, moved into a cheap apartment, and sent out résumés, only to be told he was overqualified. So, he took a training course to work out of his home for a call center for products being sold on TV. He also started buying up domain names in hopes of hitting it big. "It's coach all the way," Brinkman said. "No more first class." He was getting a little more than a grand a month from Social Security. "It's a pisser to start over, but every day we start over, and we fuck up a little too." Decent wisdom. Unlike Irving and Steve Rubin, he doesn't blame the SEC or expect a bailout from the government.

Being Jewish, Kenn did bear a degree of cultural resentment toward Bernie. "I thought he should have a bit more integrity—you don't fuck over people in the tribe, because we are such a small percentage of people that we've got to look out for each other in some way. I don't forgive Bernie on Yom Kippur." The Jewish Day of Atonement.

"Sorry about your aunt," Bernie once told me. "No, I don't remember her, but please tell her I'm sorry and never meant this to happen."

When my cousin broke the news to me that his mom—my then-eighty-year-old aunt Adele (Yetta) Behar—had lost her life savings to some guy I'd never heard of named Madoff, I found it hard to fathom. *Everything?!* "Everything," he responded. "Every dollar. She's now living on Social Security."

At that moment—one of those times in life where you recall forever where you were when you heard seismic, life-altering news—I was at the skyscraping Lower Manhattan offices of *Fast Company* magazine, staring out a window at Ground Zero being rebuilt. I had recently completed an article for the magazine likening China's and the West's financial conquests of sub-Saharan Africa to parasites, a topic that also helps shed some light on Bernie. I didn't realize at the time—nobody did—that the Madoff fraud was the 9-11 of fraud, as the vice chairman of the New York Stock Exchange would later call it. In the days ahead, I'd learn to my surprise that, in my aunt's case, "everything" meant $16 million that she and about twelve of her friends were under an illusion they had accumulated in several accounts. (I was never an heir to any of it.)

"Richard, it's only money, a false measurement of something," she would later tell me with a laugh, adding, "It's quite an exciting trip. I know people think I'm crazy when I say that, but it's true. It's pointing me in new directions. I've got new things to consider, such as how I'm gonna earn the next dollar. I only wish that Bernie had told me that he's actually running a *bank*—a cash-transfer machine no different than any other bank—so that I could have decided if I wanted to stay or not."

Adele Behar's attitude was a healthy one, not unlike how actor John Malkovich feels about losing his life savings to Bernie. He told a reporter that he was initially angry but then decided he simply needed to work and earn more. "After a couple or three days, you go: 'You're lucky to be alive, you're lucky to have a job,'" he said. "Almost no one has money in the banks. I read somewhere that a huge percentage of Americans wouldn't have four hundred dollars to put between their hands in an emergency."

In Malkovich's case, it was his business manager who had stupidly sunk his entire fortune into Madoff. My aunt, on the other hand, acted alone. But how could she put *everything* with him? She was raised in a public housing project in the Bronx. Her mother came over from Poland's Warsaw Ghetto to work in a paper-box factory. Her dad peddled his fruits from a pushcart. A dozen close relatives had died in the Holocaust. This is where the buck stops? With Bernie Madoff?

We know that growing up is a process where one myth after another is shattered. I never knew my own parents, and considered Adele a surrogate mom, as well as the savviest person in my external family on financial matters—right up to the day before this catastrophe. She had built a successful interior design practice. She was a mentor for SCORE, the nationwide nonprofit that helps people create small businesses. She was active with the University of Arizona's esteemed Center for Consciousness Studies, which brings together experts from around the world in many fields— such as nuclear physicists, biophysicists, psychologists, artificial intelligence experts—to try to isolate the "neural underpinnings of consciousness." She attended meetings and conferences, and (with Bernie's money, it turns out) sponsored research by some of the scientists.

Even in her final years (she died in 2016 at eighty-eight), she was still sharper than most people I know half her age. How could she be so reckless? So unconscious? Had she only asked me, an investigative reporter whom she so often tapped to probe things for her, to take a peek into Madoff, I would have found enough in an hour—such as a skeptical 2001 article in *MARHedge*, a financial newsletter, and another in *Barron's*—to advise her to put her money elsewhere. Or to limit her exposure, at least. Why didn't she ask? Why didn't she want to know? Why didn't any of the investors who lost in the end want to know? Why did they decide to push away the obvious?

During the five years prior to Bernie's collapse and confession, his fraud became a Ponzi on steroids, expanding exponentially over-seas to several continents. But until then, the fraud was still mainly an affinity crime, as most Ponzis are. And Adele's story was the story of many Jews through the centuries who, due to persecutions in country after country, tend to trust fellow Jews more than others simply because they are Jewish. She continued to refer to Madoff as a "mensch"—a Yiddish word for a person of integrity, dignity, morality—even weeks after his arrest. "Bernie's a good man, Rich-ard," she insisted. "He really is. Somebody must have jammed him up in some way." Her blind faith in Madoff was something that we proceeded to examine together, and she did it with an open mind and plenty of laughter. "I call Bernie 'My Little Gonif,' she said, using the Yiddish word for a thief or scoundrel. "A gonif steals someone's lollypop but does it cutely. I think of the people on Delancey Street who would lend ten dollars to someone who needed it and get ten fifty back. And I see him that way, but with bigger numbers."

Fast-forward from the tenements to her work with neuroscien-tists in consciousness studies, and she would have relished a window into her little gonif's brain. "Now that we know how to measure neu-ronal transfer and neuronal stimulation areas, if we could just get a brain like Bernie's and examine it," she once said. "I would love to talk to him and see what he *thought*. Did he see himself as a thief? Did he get tired of running?"

Fleeing persecution and destitution, Adele's parents had come to the United States with nothing; the same was true of her husband's mother and father. Both generations had pulled themselves up by their proverbial bootstraps, building their savings through prudence and frugality. She and my uncle Albert were artistic, self-employed entre-preneurs who bought some real estate, worked very hard all of their lives, and managed to sock away roughly $1 million by the time Al died in 1989—just a few years after they'd started investing with BLMIS.

At first, Adele and Al put in 10 percent of their wealth with Bernie, then 20 percent, then 30. It was the usual pattern for Madoff investors, who were lured in slowly. The returns were so consistent and bountiful that it was not long before Adele had her entire savings with him. So successful was Madoff that, by the time of his undoing, those personal savings had grown to $6 million (on fake paper). Like so many others, though, Adele had also invested her friends' and children's savings—another $10 million that was 100 percent committed to Bernie Madoff. And, in the end, 100 percent worthless. (In the end, she was a net loser, not winner, so she didn't face a clawback from hungry Irving.)

Adele never met Bernie or Frank—they did their best to avoid such encounters—but she dealt with the latter a lot by phone in the years ahead. She found DiPascali to be "gruff," as did many investors (as well as BLMIS employees on the floors above him). Nevertheless, she overlooked his attitude, and even dropped off little Christmas goodies for him once at the BLMIS front desk. After all, as DiPascali told the FBI: "Many of these investors had tremendous returns that enabled them to over time buy expensive homes, send their children to college, and spend lavishly on other items."

As it turns out, that included me. After Bernie's arrest, much to my horror, Aunt Adele revealed how Madoff's money had occasionally helped me. That's because she generously assisted me during tough times in my life that—I know now—were, in effect, "gifts" from Bernie. Madoff, it turned out, was responsible for $20,000 that Aunt Adele gave me for a down payment on an apartment I bought in 1993, plus $4,000 in new furniture six years later. Bernie also paid for a chunk of my medical care when I caught a life-threatening parasite while in Africa doing the reporting for that *Fast Company* story cited above. Parasite Bernie helped get rid of my African parasite.

Madoff could have played an even bigger part in my life if the timing of his downfall had been different. A few weeks before his arrest, I was bemoaning the fate of my IRA, which required a submarine for me to see it—as was the fate for many people due to the

2008 financial collapse. "You should have my mom manage your money," said my cousin. "She does very well for herself and a lot of others." Indeed, around that same time, I had asked Adele how she was weathering the storm financially, and she had said (echoing the feelings of thousands of Madoff investors), "Oh, I'm fine. Markets go up, markets go down, and I make a little money." All she would add was that she was in a "closed" fund, meaning it wasn't easily accessible to just anybody.

It was never about greed for Adele and Al, who didn't live extravagantly. They grew up during the Depression, and they viewed the 14 to 15 percent per year in profits that Madoff consistently provided them as a kind of solid CD. They thought they could probably earn a little more elsewhere but didn't want to take the risk. They were hurt, as millions were, in the 1987 stock market crash. And now they just wanted to be able to sleep at night, with confidence in a network of people who were taking care of one other. To them, Madoff was steady and safe. But in the end, it was an illusion of safety, since the double-digit returns they were getting—in up and down markets—were simply too good to be true.

In the wake of the fraud, Adele sent me a pile of the customer statements that she, like other investors, had received on a monthly or quarterly basis, as well as a BLMIS customer agreement that she'd signed in 1993. After examining those documents for this book, an investigative forensic accountant named Bruce Dubinsky, who has probed Madoff's operation for the court-appointed trustee, concluded that had any of these investors done minimal due diligence, or handed them off to an expert, the fraud could have been uncovered. Case in point: on one stock trading "confirmation" ticket, the company listed is spelled wrong, which took place on many statements for customers. Had House 17 actually been connected to the outside stock exchange that handled the trade—it wasn't—this error would have been impossible.

On another trade confirmation ticket sent to Adele, Bernie had it all "backward," says Dubinsky, as it contradicts what appears on the quarterly account statement that accompanied the tickets. Specifically, the ticket states that two shares of the S&P 100 Index were bought on November 15, 1994, while the statement shows they were sold. So, which was it? Neither, of course.

The SEC rules on this subject are simple enough: Customer confirmations must disclose the trade in such a way that the customer understands the transaction that occurred. If a customer were to buy—say—1,000 shares of IBM at $100, the confirmation the customer receives from a legitimate firm would state "You bought" or simply "bought" 1,000 shares of IBM at $100.

But BLMIS confirmations didn't read that way. "Bernie Madoff didn't do that," says Dubinsky. "Maybe he was lazy, he didn't care, he didn't think anybody would notice. It makes no sense."

Here's how the BLMIS statements read: If one of his customers (purportedly) bought 1,000 IBM shares, instead of saying "You bought" or simply "bought," it stated "We sold." The use of the word "we," in a convoluted way, explained that BLMIS was the counterparty to the trade, in that "BLMIS sold to you" 1,000 IBM at $100. However, that is counterintuitive and skirts the requirements of an SEC rule that states you must confirm to the customer what "THEY" did, not what YOU, as the brokerage firm counterparty, did.

Another customer statement of Adele's shows 100 percent success in all of the stocks traded during that period: Walmart, Ford Motor, General Motors, American International Group (AIG), and McDonald's. "It's nice to be able to *always* buy low, sell high," says Dubinsky. "In this case, he sold high by 'going short,' then five days later he bought low. This always happened. Nice way to make money. Easy to do when fake."

The customer agreements that Adele and others signed when they began investing through Madoff should also have raised eyebrows.

Specifically, the trading authorization documents they were required to sign were on BLMIS letterhead. But the first sentence in the document states: "The undersigned hereby authorizes Bernard L. Madoff (whose signature appears below) as his agent and attorney in fact to buy, sell, and trade in stocks." According to Dubinsky, who also once worked as an investment advisor, it was strange to have customers authorize only Bernie and not the firm itself. "If somebody had sent me that, I would have said, 'Why is he the only guy? What happens if he had a heart attack—no one can trade my money?' It makes no sense. No one would ever do that."

Not long after Bernie's arrest, Madoff prosecutors, FBI agents, and forensic accountants found themselves in a conference room trying to make sense of the BLMIS account statements. "They didn't look like normal brokerage statements," recalls prosecutor Baroni. "We couldn't initially understand them. I had to get a tutorial from agents on how to *decode* them." And yet for Adele and virtually every other Madoff investor, this didn't raise any flags.

This is what unfolded, in document after document.

Dubinsky, whose prior work included taking apart Enron, conducted a meaty probe of Madoff that resulted in an exhaustive two-hundred-page report in 2019 for Picard. He not only analyzed trade confirmations and customer statements going back to the mid-1970s but also restored and reconstructed major portions of an outdated IBM AS/400 computer system that House 17 relied on for the Ponzi. He also took apart portions of the prop-trading computerized systems on the eighteenth and nineteenth floors. He discovered that BLMIS as a whole was insolvent from at least late 2002 until it collapsed, and there's some evidence that it may have been broke as far back as 1983.

Dubinsky also found that no trading at all was done using Bernie's convertible arbitrage strategy that he purportedly implemented in the 1970s for his Big Four and others—and that the trades were

fabricated on the customer statements. He also came across no evidence whatsoever that the purported convertible securities were
ever actually *converted*, as those customer statements claimed. Similarly, starting in the 1990s, when Bernie instituted his "split-strike
conversion strategy," no real trading actually occurred—and many of
his purported trades exceeded the *entire* reported market volume for
particular securities (ranging from Apple, to IBM, to GM) on many
trading days, and were recorded at prices that were outside the range
of reported trading prices on the days listed on customer statements.
Had customers such as Aunt Adele and thousands of others checked
their statements carefully and compared the buys and sells for securities against what appeared in the *Wall Street Journal* or on the
Internet, they would have spotted this. They might also have noticed
that many trades were recorded on their statements as being settled
on weekends or holidays, when US stock and options exchanges were
closed. Moreover, billions of dollars of purported dividends that were
reported on their statements were never received by BLMIS.

In many talks over the years, Bernie referred to Bruce derisively
as "This guy Dubinsky" who "doesn't understand the industry" and
whose report was "a joke." Some joke.

Aunt Adele's involvement with Madoff had roots to his first official
feeder fund. It was known as Avellino & Bienes (A&B), an entity
owned by two accountants: Frank Avellino and Michael Bienes. A&B
grew out of Alpern & Avellino (A&A), the former of whom was accountant Saul Alpern—Ruth's father. How it all worked in my aunt's
case is a perfect example of how many of Bernie's sub-rackets did.
And the A&A and A&B stories are critical to the early days of Bernie's fraud.

While Adele always knew she was invested with Madoff, she'd
never heard of A&B. Instead, it was a related entity called Telfran,

owned by yet another group of accountants whom she dealt with directly. Starting in 1989, Telfran—a limited partnership formed in Fort Lauderdale that can be viewed as a kind of A&B subcontractor within the pyramid—had been pooling funds from investors, including Adele and more than eight hundred other people and entities. In return for these funds, Telfran issued investors promissory notes with an average *fixed* interest rate of 15 percent, which was nearly twice what they could earn in a six-month bank CD.

Putting aside the guaranteed, 100 percent risk-free return, which *should* have led all Telfran's customers to laugh (and run for the nearest SEC office), the whole concept of issuing notes (a debt instrument) should have raised its own alarms. In essence, this meant that Telfran was technically borrowing the money from its investors, with a promise in writing to pay a 15 percent return each year as a result of the "loan." Telfran then invested those funds with A&B, which paid Telfran approximately 19 percent interest on those notes. The company kept 4 percent for itself and gave the remaining 15 percent to its investors. "At no time is a trade made that puts your money at risk," wrote A&B in a typical letter to investors. "In over 20 years, there has never been a losing transaction. . . . The funds are send [*sic*] to a New York broker [meaning Madoff, of course, although he's *unnamed*] who invests same on behalf of Avellino & Bienes."

A&B and Telfran also issued letters to investors, terming those investments "loans." For instance, in a letter to one of my cousins, a Telfran staffer wrote in August 1991 to confirm that $31,200 had been transferred "from the Behar Family Limited Partnership . . . [a] transaction that will bring your compound loan account to $53,056."

Why was it done that way for Al and Adele and others? Why term them *loans*? Just like Bernie, who didn't want to register as an "investment company," which would (and ultimately did) result in more scrutiny from the SEC, A&B figured that using notes was a way to avoid having to do so, as notes might be viewed differently from securities. But they were mistaken, and in 1992 the SEC shut down Telfran and A&B for acting as unregistered investment advisors and for unlawfully selling securities—hundreds of millions of dollars' worth. At the time, the SEC learned that it was Madoff, not Avellino and Bienes, who was making all the investment decisions. The agency suspected that A&B might be running a Ponzi scheme, but when Madoff returned all the funds to their investors, the case concluded.

To this day, Frank Avellino has portrayed himself as a victim like just about everyone else, as had Michael Bienes, who died at age eighty in 2017. But the facts tell a different story. In a TV interview with the PBS news program *Frontline* in 2009, Bienes conceded willful blindness (although a prosecutor on the Madoff Five case told me it wasn't quite *enough* of an admission to bring an indictment).

"So you were willing to blind yourself to what might have cost you that money?" correspondent Martin Smith asked Bienes.

"Yes."

"That's greed."

"Yes."

"That's nothing else but greed, right?"

"Yes. And fear. Fear of him."

Him being Bernie Madoff.

Fear of violence or being sucked into a future criminal case? Nope. It was fear of Madoff tossing him out of the gold mine. Asked if he ever conducted any inquiry of Madoff and the implausible returns, Bienes said he wouldn't dare. "I was gonna walk in and say, 'Bernie, let me see your books?' He'd show me the door. He was my income. He was my life. . . . Bernie was the well; I just turned on the spigot, sent him the fax, the money came. . . . Easy peasy, like a money machine."

Bienes conceded that he never worked hard in the operation, "never lifted any weights." So how and why did Bienes get so lucky in life? Did the gods simply favor him? Yes, it turns out. "God gave us this," he said about his Madoff-created wealth. (Bernie's take on Bienes: "total nutjob." Yes, it seems. But an indispensable one.)

Michael Bienes never opened his mouth to a reporter again, with good reason. For years afterward, his various lawyers, who likely did everything they could to shut him up, told me they had no idea how to get a message to him. Some rumors once had him hiding out in London. As for Avellino, now eighty-one, he's been in a court battle since 2009 with the trustee to try to keep his ill-gotten spoils, and he's not returning phone calls. Irving Picard estimates that at least $905 million of customer funds were collectively received, directly or indirectly, by Avellino and Bienes and several family members.

While admitting to greed, Bienes patted himself on the back for not being as greedy as he *could* have been. "That's one thing that kept us going," he said to *Frontline*. "We were never pigs. We were never pigs." But he and Avellino were among the biggest gluttons in the game. Lifestyle tells only part of the story. Avellino and his wife, Nancy, who own or have owned multimillion-dollar homes in Palm Beach, Manhattan, and Nantucket, Massachusetts, like to adorn their dwellings with paintings and sculptures by Pablo Picasso, Edgar Degas, and Giacomo Manzù. All of it courtesy of the Ponzi scheme.

As for Bienes and his wife, Dianne, they were widely known in Fort Lauderdale, Florida, for their opulent, spectacular parties at their $7 million, six-thousand-square-foot home in the exclusive Bay Colony neighborhood, where, in the early 1990s—around the same time the SEC shut down A&B—they built a ten-thousand-square-foot entertainment pavilion. Guests swam in a pool in the living room, which was converted at night into a dance floor. Moreover, the house boasted a cold storage compartment to keep Dianne's furs happy.

They had a second home in England, where they were known to mingle with royalty. After Bienes's death from cancer, one of his lawyers told a local obit writer that Michael was a "remarkable man, generous to friends and social causes, engaging and welcoming to all, whether his friend Prince Charles or the shoeshine man."

With his ill-gotten gains, he was indeed one of the best-known philanthropists in Broward County. His and Dianne's names still adorn buildings and rooms at the county's main library. So, too, a major Catholic hospital wing: the Michael and Dianne Bienes Comprehensive Cancer Center, whose core stated values include "Justice. . . . We foster right relationships to promote the common good, including sustainability of Earth."

Following her husband's death, Dianne told the local paper that her Michael "was never a man who would take advantage of anybody, simply because he was afraid of doing anything wrong." While there can be no question that Bienes was one of the major players who perpetuated and benefited from the Madoff Ponzi scheme for decades, he insisted he had no idea it was a Ponzi scheme—nor saw any signs that anything was amiss at BLMIS. "As God is my only judge, on my mother's grave, not an inkling, not a tickle. May he strike me dead."

By 1992, when the SEC shut down A&B, despite its having billed itself as an exclusive opportunity limited to "relatives, friends and former [accountancy] clients," the entity had, in fact, obtained hundreds of millions of dollars from at least three thousand individuals throughout the United States. And in the weeks before it was put out of business, Avellino and Bienes provided the SEC with closed-door testimony and documents representing that their entity owed its investors just over $413 million—based on the total value of the "loans" it had received from the investors, and all of which they claimed they had invested with Bernie. (For its part, Telfran, the conduit to Aunt Adele and Uncle Al, owned $88 million worth of those A&B notes.)

There was just one big problem: BLMIS's own records reflected that the purported (we now know *phony*) value of the A&B accounts held by Bernie was only $364 million. That created a shortfall of nearly $44 million.

The last thing Avellino and Bienes (both of whom were certified CPAs for decades) wanted was for the SEC to see that the books were a mess—and they *were* a mess—especially after they had sworn to SEC agents that they made certain there was always an adequate cushion of about 20 percent for customer redemptions. "[We] examine the account statements and do our due diligence on a monthly basis," Avellino testified, ". . . and we make sure, and this is where we are very positive, we make sure that that value is always in excess of the loans payable."

If the SEC found a $44 million shortfall, the agency would likely have widened its probe to include BLMIS, increasing the likelihood that the Ponzi would have been discovered. (But without a shortfall, it would be viewed as an illegal scheme that simply glommed on to Madoff, just as small Ponzi schemes have long attached themselves to major banks such as HSBC and Citibank, and, more recently, to firms such as Airbnb and Facebook.) What to do? No problem: Bernie simply created a phony IA account for them, separate from the others they had, in which a phony monthly statement showed well over $44 million in phony funds. After all, when you're a magician, you can simply pull any number out of thin air.

Bernie then directed his employees to manufacture fake and backdated securities transactions on monthly account statements for that newly created phony IA account—for a three-year period, from 1989 to 1992. The statements included dozens of fictitious stock and options transactions designed to show gains of about $66 million— the amount needed to hide the shortfall *and* provide the purported cushion.

When the SEC received the three years' worth of recrafted and backdated customer account statements for the phony new account, Avellino's and Bienes's (and Bernie's) problem was over. The subterfuge worked.

Just to be extra safe, and, given how Annette Bongiorno, one of

Madoff's key employees, was herself prone to making errors on fake statements, she got Avellino to send her back three years' worth of prior statements for *all* A&B accounts. For what purpose? In order to redo *them* as well—to catch any prior shortfalls. She spotted a $32 million shortfall for the 1989–90 period. So, she papered that over with a bogus $86 million addition of phony risk-free US Treasury notes. Done. Another goal of redoing all of the A&B statements: to make sure the transactions on them were consistent with what Avellino and Bienes told the SEC about Madoff's purported conservative investment strategy.

The subterfuge grew even more intriguing when Madoff made sure that Ruth's father, Saul, wasn't drawn into the mess. He did this by altering a monthly statement from 1989 to eliminate an entry that reflected a transfer of money from an IA account held in the name of "Alpern & Avellino." Bernie simply changed it to a dividend payment from General Motors—down to the exact penny.

Had the SEC decided to question him about the identity of Alpern, this could have called into question Bernie's own representations to the SEC at the time that his client base was very small. That's because the company name Alpern & Avellino on any account statement takes the IA business back to the early 1960s.

What's more, the SEC's 1992 complaint against A&B had alleged that unregistered securities had been sold since 1962. That was three years after Avellino had joined Alpern's accounting firm, and only one year after Bernie had moved his brokerage business out of Alpern's office—although Saul continued to encourage people to invest with his son-in-law for decades (and charge them accounting/ bookkeeping fees for doing so). And why not? As Avellino told the SEC thirty years later: "I could honestly say, and you could check any [BLMIS] record that you want with me from 1962 to today, in thousands of transactions, of what I call arbitrage, which is bona fide convertible buying and selling, there has never been a loss."

What Saul's role was, and what he knew and when, may always remain murky. But at the very least, he most certainly knew by the SEC action of 1992—seven years before he died—that something was seriously amiss. Moreover, just why his and Avellino's names were on an IA account as late as 1992 remains a mystery, as their accounting partnership had ended nearly two decades earlier.

While Avellino and Bienes were testifying to the SEC, a BLMIS employee faxed a series of documents for them to sign—papers that should have been signed years if not decades earlier. They ranged from blank partnership account agreements to account opening agreements and options-trading authorizations. Once those papers were in order, yet another bullet had been dodged.

But the SEC was not the only headache for A&B and Bernie. As part of a court order that Avellino and Bienes had consented to, a receiver overseeing A&B's liquidation sought to audit its books and records for an *eight*-year period, from 1984 to 1992. However, they produced accounting records and documents for only 1989 to 1992, the precise period of the altered statements that Bongiorno had concocted for them. Remarkably, despite their having done hundreds of audits for clients until they ditched their accountancy to focus on their Madoff funds, Avellino was able to look the trustee in the eye and say that they "did not maintain detailed financial records"— and, furthermore, that all of their accounting records through 1988 had been trashed. The Big Four accounting giant PriceWaterhouse-Coopers, retained by the receiver to audit the A&B books, expressed frustration over the missing books and records. According to a PW report, Avellino "refuse[d] to prepare financial statements" and instructed the firm to cease and desist questioning a computer service bureau that had maintained A&B's ledger of noteholders.

At a hearing, John Sprizzo, a federal judge in New York famous for his combustible temper, had little use for Avellino. "I don't believe your client," he snapped to his lawyer at one stage. "I heard his testimony, I saw his demeanor, I heard his inconsistencies on direct [examination] and cross. I don't believe him. So, to the extent there are credibility issues to resolve, I resolve them against your client." He ordered Avellino and Bienes to pay civil penalties totaling $300,000, small potatoes even then but nonetheless the highest penalties ever imposed by the SEC at the time.

The judge also ordered that all A&B investors had to be redeemed. In order to provide the funds for this purpose, Bernie obtained cash and securities from other customers—that is, after all, what a Ponzi scheme is—and used the securities as collateral for loans. Most of the bailout money came from Jeffry Picower via large stock positions he held at an account at Goldman Sachs, which Bernie pledged to a bank in order to obtain a loan to pay off the A&B investors.

In his sit-downs with the FBI, Frank DiPascali provided multiple details about the 1992 A&B fiasco and how it unfolded. Until that year, he said, he had never heard of A&B. When he asked Madoff what was going on, he was told: "Those two assholes were selling unsecured securities. It's a deep pile of shit." The truth is that it was *Bernie* who had instructed them not to register with the SEC, just as Bernie himself failed to do with his IA business. *And* just as Madoff's parents failed to do when they operated their own securities firm out of the family's Laurelton home.

Bernie insisted to me that he had no idea that "those idiots" Avellino and Bienes were structuring the securities as "loans." But his claim is inconceivable, given the importance of A&B's clients to the Ponzi scheme at that stage in time. Madoff also said that A&B led him to believe that it was investing money only from a handful of clients and friends and their families. He maintained further that he informed the two men that they had to keep the number of investors below fifteen—the level that would have required A&B to register as an investment company and thus be subject to SEC enforcement. Bearing in mind how much money A&B had with Madoff by 1992 ($400 million), it's too far-fetched to believe that Bernie wouldn't know that the company needed to register. Before he died, Bienes contended that Bernie told him never to register—a far more believable scenario.

Bernie also insisted that it was *he*, and not the SEC, who forced Avellino & Bienes to liquidate rather than simply comply with registration rules. Not surprisingly, SEC records do not back up Madoff's version of history.

But one aspect of Bernie's account of events raises some questions about his father-in-law. In a letter to me, he wrote: "I was so pissed at both Avellino and Bienes for changing their method of doing business from the way Saul Alpern did that I insisted on liquidation. At a later date, my father-in-law pleaded with me to take in his clients' customer accounts directly."

Was this a slip of Bernie's tongue: that Ruth's father pled with him, after the SEC shut down A&B, to take his accounting clients directly? So, did Saul know that the *whole* thing was a fraud? Some investigators on the case believe that he did—and that he even may have initiated it—but the answer to those questions may have long ago turned to ash.

Frank DiPascali told the feds that Bernie directed his IA employees to put the A&B accounts "in order" for the SEC, which entailed looking up past stock prices in the *Wall Street Journal*. That was easy. A bigger problem was that Bernie knew he couldn't keep fibbing that an arbitrage strategy was delivering the consistently high returns. Such an approach can be highly profitable only on teeny scales. So Bernie came up with a new invention called split-strike conversion strategy, based on index options—just as more than a thousand individual A&B investors decided to invest with him directly. Split-strike may have sounded magical, but it was nothing new on Wall Street, where it's more popularly known as a "collar." It entails buying stocks that are highly correlated with a tradable index such as the S&P 100.

Frank presented Bernie with a strategy of twenty-five to thirty stocks to check their correlations with the underlying index options.

But he determined that the correlation between the two was not consistent enough, and so he needed to find more stocks that moved consistently with the general market. He discussed the process with Bernie and began experimenting and implementing the policy simultaneously because many of the individual A&B investors were investing quickly with Madoff.

DiPascali explained to his boss that he didn't have sufficient staff to handle all the new accounts, even though the "trades" would not actually be physically executed. He was also concerned because the few employees who worked for him were, in his view, "not very smart." As a result of taking on the former A&B accounts, the number of BLMIS accounts under Frank's control increased from a couple dozen to more than a thousand.

Bernie told Frank the parameters to use for selecting prices for transactions. One parameter was not using the high and low price for any particular day. Back then, Frank said he assumed Bernie was simply not telling customers *where* the trades actually occurred. But they believed they were occurring *somewhere*.

Starting in 1993, Bernie himself was phoning the former A&B clients to invite them to invest directly with him. His approach was the soft sell. "He told me that the SEC asked him to do this, to make sure all the clients were all well taken care of," Aunt Adele recalled. It was clearly a lie, as the agency would never have done so. "He said I should take my time, and do I understand the risks?" Of course, she told him. Of course she did.

7

The Favored Clients: Shtupped!

I I I I I I I I I I I I

The Question: Why were some Madoff clients fucked (in a good way) for Christmas and Hanukkah?

In one of his FBI debriefings, DiPascali regaled agents and prosecutors with details about how certain special customers (and feeders) each December would get extra gelt. Starting in the mid-1990s, he kept the growing list in a folder in a top desk drawer in his seventeenth-floor office. He labeled the envelope "Schupt"—the Yiddish word for "pushed, or plugged, or slipped in," particularly in the context of sex. If you were getting shtupped at BLMIS, you were among the chosen few. (As an Italian-American who wasn't raised around Jews, Frank should be cut some slack on the spelling.)

The shtup folder, which the FBI retrieved from Frank's office, contained calculations about whose IA accounts would receive extra fake trades at year-end. This included some BLMIS employees (what Frank called "the little people") but was reserved mainly for rewarding certain sub-feeders who'd brought in customers. The shtupping, according to Frank, also brought the sub-feeders in line with the percentage returns that Bernie had promised they'd see each year.

The feds were bewildered when he first brought up the subject. "We'd take the file out of the drawer and we'd shtup them," he explained matter-of-factly. "We were like, '*Shtup?* What are you talking about?'" recalls an FBI agent at the session. "He said it's like an extra shmear of cream cheese on a bagel. We were like, 'Wait, is it a shmear? Or is it a shtup?' We were hysterical. We were all laughing; he was laughing. We couldn't understand what he was talking about."

The shtup list was not unlike the Screw List that Bernie, Peter, and Frank hurriedly compiled in the final few days of BLMIS to determine which lucky customers should get the remaining $250 million in assets before the feds showed up.

But why a need for *year-end* fake trades for favored customers? The answer is that it was sometimes mathematically impossible to create BLMIS account statements the same way for every client participating in the basket trading by using the same fake trades and *still* ladling out more gravy to the special people or the little people. Doing so would have been a computer programming nightmare that even their two leading computer programmers (who were convicted in the Madoff Five case) would have had a hard time pulling off.

When asked by FBI agents whether somebody without any special training could recognize from the account statements that something strange was going on, Frank remarked, "There is not a sane person in the world that did not know they were getting shtupped."

The *shtupees*, if you will, were very aware of these year-end gifts, and were not shy about reminding Bernie or Frank when they were due. Case in point: Steve Mendelow, a BLMIS-affiliated accountant and a co-owner of Telfran, the entity through which Adele Behar got involved with Madoff. (It was Mendelow who, with Adele's blessing, steered her investment directly to Madoff after the SEC shut down A&B/Telfran.)

DiPascali told the feds that when he made year-end adjustments to Mendelow's personal account, he computed that Steve was getting a return 2 percent higher than everyone else. Moreover, he was taking additional fees directly from the customers. Shtupped on all sides.

When I asked Bernie about the shtup file, he claimed implausibly that he had no idea what it was and that Frank himself must have come up with the name.

One of the documents the feds showed Frank contained calculations "handwritten by Mendelow to determine his shtup for the years 1993 to 1995," according to an FBI interview summary. (It's a fair bet that the words "determine his shtup" had not made it into any 302 in the FBI's history before the Madoff case.) Mendelow had sent the documents to Frank to help him figure out "how to retroactively catch up Mendelow's accounts with shtup for the years it had not been shtupped." One of his accounts was an IRA. By placing the extra money into that particular account, DiPascali explained, Steve wouldn't have to report the shtup as taxable income for that year. Investigators then handed Frank a second document, in which Mendelow had referred to the extra money as "vig"—short for *vigorish,* or "the juice," in gambling parlance.

Almost every year, Mendelow called Frank to tell him "how he wanted his shtup divided between his wife and himself." According to Frank, "Mendelow would say something like 'On that thing you do, I want a hundred fifteen for me and a hundred fifteen for my wife.'"

What did Mendelow know about that *thing* Frank did? Did he know the whole thing was a fraud? In 2010 the trustee commenced an action against Mendelow, his wife, and their two daughters, seeking the return of more than $20 million. That represented fraudulent transfers for merely the six years prior to Bernie's arrest, which was the period Picard sought to claw back from winners, until a federal appeals court in 2014 limited him to two years, and not any further.

During an examination by the trustee in 2010, Mendelow invoked his Fifth Amendment right nearly four hundred times, refusing to answer questions. Among the questions he declined to address was why, starting in 1998, he structured the investments from his clients as "loans" but failed to use the term in his letters to them. The most likely reason? To avoid the appearance of violating the 1992 SEC injunction against him when A&B was shut down. Instead, the letters he sent to clients vaguely cited their "arrangements" that they had with him. *Arrangements.* Just like *that thing* you do.

In September 2016, three months after Mendelow died of a blood disease at age seventy-three, a bankruptcy judge found that allegations by the trustee "plausibly showed" that Mendelow had "actual knowledge that BLMIS was not engaged in securities trading." In doing so, the judge declined to toss out the case, as Mendelow's lawyers had requested. But it was still up to the trustee to prove at a trial that Mendelow did indeed have that actual knowledge. Then, the following June, his wife died, and the case for recovering the loot was settled with their estate seven months later. Fight over.

Not only the trustee but also prosecutors had looked into whether proof existed that Mendelow knew it was a Ponzi scheme. But they closed the inquiry. "If you can't indict Avellino, you can't indict anyone [within the A&B orbit]," says former prosecutor Baroni. "How the hell can we prove Mendelow knew it was a Ponzi, when you can't prove Annette [Bongiorno] knew it was a Ponzi?"

After Madoff's arrest, Aunt Adele reached out to Mendelow and was more concerned with his well-being than her own. It's the way she always was. "He's scared and hurt," she said. "We've talked many times, and I hugged him over the phone. He lost his own fourteen million dollars for himself and his kids' education. I thought he'd commit suicide. I could *feel* it. He told me how desperate he was." Mendelow, she felt, was a good guy who didn't mean to hurt anyone. "He said, 'I'm totally gone, I'm totally broke. I'm dead. I'm killed.'" Adele responded to him: "At least you've got work. You're an accountant, you can work. That's what I tell everybody: Go to work! Forget it. You know, you had a game. It was fun. Now go work."

My aunt said she used to send potential customers to him "because I didn't want to take them on. He charged 0.8 percent a year, depending on what they put in." She herself would charge friends 1 percent for bookkeeping. A little self-shtup.

Adele says she never saw the SEC order against Mendelow's Telfran in 1992. "We heard nothing about orders," she said, adding that it wouldn't have mattered to them. Why not? "Because the guys who were registered, how many of them had thieved us already? When the '87 crash came, I think we were with A. G. Edwards"—a brokerage firm—"and the guy who was handling our account, I fired him on the phone. And I said, 'I want my stuff back.'"

Before that, she added, there was another investment advisor that my uncle Al was "playing with at Bear Stearns who ripped him off. And these are all *registered*. So, *no way* would I go with the registered. I hated the registered. So they got a little piece of paper saying that they were 'approved'—who the hell knows? You go with the guys who you trust. And that's the money business."

At one point, Adele persuaded Mendelow to speak for this book, but he never responded to messages. In 2012 I paid a visit to an old friend named Stanley Arkin, one of the country's top criminal defense lawyers, who had represented Mendelow when he was being investigated by the Madoff trustee. "I got to know him very well and was persuaded that he really didn't know what Bernie was doing," said Arkin. "And if he knew that Bernie was just a complete fraud, he wouldn't have left his own money and his children's money with him. He believed that the guy had some kind of a special touch in the marketplace."

Mendelow's obituary noted that he was a "tireless supporter" of many organizations in the fields of medical research and children's services. Thanks to Bernie, he could afford to be generous. His relationship with A&B stemmed back to at least the 1980s, if not the 1970s. Through most of the 1990s, he received a guaranteed 17 percent return, and he took in $400,000 per year just from the shtup on top of his regular annual profits. Achieving his predetermined levels of "profit" was carried out by Frank, who assigned fictitious S&P 100 put- and call-option transactions to his accounts. *That thing you do.* (In brief: a put option gives the holder the right to sell a stock, while a call option gives the holder the right to buy a stock.)

At one stage, for reasons unknown (and somewhat comically), in December 1999 Mendelow's BLMIS IRA account statement showed a cash balance of just 31 cents. No problem. To fabricate the extra profit Mendelow expected, BLMIS purported to buy S&P 100 Index call options costing $510,600, which it proceeded to sell on December 28 to generate a profit of $1,169,400.

In December 2007, following up on a phone conversation, Mendelow sent DiPascali a note simply listing the account numbers for his and Nancy's IRA accounts, with an arrow pointing to a "215m"— $215 million—and concluding with "Thanks Merry Christmas Steve."

It turns out that Bernie was also shtupping Noel Levine, who, as noted previously, had pulled in Elie Wiesel, and who was also one of Bernie's first investors, along with Levine's father-in-law, Abe. In a letter found in the shtup envelope, Levine detailed the clients he had brought to BLMIS over the previous year—a not-so-subtle reminder to Bernie that his account was entitled to receive shtup.

Frank also reviewed a document for the FBI agents that consisted of his own notes of a conversation with Bernie about the *concept* of the shtup. It related in part to Frank Avellino. When Avellino transferred the A&B clients directly to Madoff following his company's shutdown, he had worked out an agreement with Bernie concerning his own compensation. Bernie explained to Frank that his investment strategy at the time earned 19 percent. Of that, Bernie pocketed 2 percent; Avellino would get 2 percent, based on the amount of money he brought in; and the clients would receive 15 percent. Avellino understood this to mean that his personal accounts were slotted to earn 17 percent, or 19 minus 2. Bernie "did not have the guts" to tell Avellino otherwise, said Frank, so he had to calculate a 17 percent return for Avellino's personal accounts on top of the annual shtup.

DiPascali recalled meeting Avellino for the first time in Bernie's office in the winter of 1993, when the shtup arrangement was explained. Bernie told DiPascali to use the "current day's" prices for the trades for Avellino, or, if that didn't seem feasible, to use the prior day's prices. What did it matter, in the end? DiPascali would show Bernie the results using both days and let him decide which one to use.

As one might imagine, there was giggling in the courtroom—loudly from Rudy Bongiorno, Annette's husband—when DiPascali revealed the shtupping program at the 2014 Madoff Five trial. (Perhaps he guffawed because his wife sometimes shtupped herself, according to records.) "Is shtupping something sexual?" a confused Bloomberg reporter asked his colleagues sitting nearby. Laughter all around. Meanwhile, the poor court reporter was confounded about the spelling. Is it *shtupping*? Or *schtupping*? Prosecutor John Zach, who had previously discussed the shtup program with Frank at their closed-door meetings, said afterward that he had to force himself to address the subject in court with a straight face. Everybody seemed to love saying the word aloud.

> ZACH: Looking at this cover page, do you recognize the handwriting?
> DIPASCALI: It's mine.

> Q: What does it say?
> A: It says, "I need to shtup."

> Q: What did you mean by "shtup"?
> A: To put funds into clients' accounts.

> Q: Can we turn to page three of this document . . . What is it?

Frank responded that he was being shown typed-out information that had been given to him at the tail end of the Bernie Madoff–Frank Avellino meeting explaining who and in what quantities "we were going to quote-unquote shtup these accounts."

Zach took Frank back to the time when A&B was shut down by the SEC, and how Frank was involved in the process of transferring those A&B clients into *direct* customers of Madoff Securities. The problem Frank and Bernie faced was how to compensate the people (such as Mendelow) who brought in those A&B clients. The solution: "to shtup their personal accounts with extra P&L," said Frank, using the abbreviation for profit and loss.

As DiPascali explained, he and Bernie would design an "option transaction" and they would calculate what the payment should be. Once they'd identified the appropriate figure, they would "write a fictitious buy ticket and a subsequent fictitious sell ticket that would create P&L in their accounts."

"Over time, did the number of folks that were getting shtupped increase?" Zach asked.

"Yes."

Frank said he'd pretty much handled the shtupping process on his own—usually between Christmas and New Year's—for fourteen or fifteen years. And, of course, the shtup trades, like all of Bernie's trades, were fake.

One of Bernie's most-favored investors was Stanley Shapiro (no relation to Carl), who was overlooked following the Madoff Securities collapse. He was not indicted for any crime, but he came very close, prosecutors told me. Even so, for a decade, until his death in 2020 at age ninety-two, he fought vigorously to try to keep his winnings from Irving Picard, who sued him in 2010 in an effort to retrieve $54 million. Perhaps Shapiro, then in his eighties, was trying to outlive the case, because he didn't have much ground to stand on—based on statements throughout a confidential deposition he sat through in 2010.

For some thirty years, Stanley and his wife, Renee, and other family members held a total of at least twenty-four accounts with Bernie, thanks to the recommendation of Horseman Carl Shapiro— owner of the Kay Windsor dressmaker, where Stanley served as the company's longtime president. The two men invested together in the 1970s in limited partnerships in land deals, citrus fruit, and cattle breeding. Bernie may also have been a partner, according to Stanley.

While Stanley was not one of the Big Four—not by far in terms of winnings—his vantage point into the operation was greater than Carl's. Unlike Carl, he was a stock trader, dabbling in fashion company equities, and presumably knew that trading takes talent. He was also hired by Madoff—purportedly as a prop trader—in 1995 and given a nineteenth-floor office adjacent to Bernie's.

"I could never understand why Stanley Shapiro had an office there," Peter Madoff's longtime secretary, Elaine Solomon, said to me. He shared that room with trader David Kugel, the arbitrage expert and future convict. A year later, Madoff suggested that Stanley hire (the also later convicted) accountant Paul Konigsberg to provide "tax planning" and other expertise regarding the accounts. It was a recommendation Bernie made to many other investors, and Stanley heeded the advice.

The friendships among Ruth, Bernie, Stanley, and Renee were close. Records show they traveled together by private jet more than two dozen times just between 2002 and 2008. As Solomon remembers: "Stanley and Renee, Paul Konigsberg and his wife, Eddie and Susan [Blumenfeld, who were among the net winners in the Ponzi], and Peter and Marion—they'd always go to the movies together on a Tuesday; they did things as a group. And they would sort of fight as to who was gonna sit next to Bernie. And Eleanor [Bernie's secretary] would say to Bernie, 'Why does anybody want to sit next to you? You are the most boring man.' Who wants to spend an evening with Bernie?"

Stanley visited the seventeenth floor more than 150 times during the three years prior to Bernie's arrest, according to security "key" information. That's staggering. There is no evidence of anyone else visiting the floor that often, except for those who had desks there. A big question is how close Carl Shapiro and Stanley Shapiro were in recent decades, and whether Stanley told Carl about his *own* dealings at BLMIS.

We don't know, but we can presume they remained close after their Kay Windsor decades together. A 1978 memo shows that Carl was a trustee on one of Stanley's accounts at BLMIS, for the benefit of the latter's children, and that Bernie himself might also have been a trustee on it. In the late 1980s Carl asked Stanley to invest in something called Mountain Farms Mall (likely a strip mall). On another memo, dated 2004, Stanley is named—along with Bernie, Peter, Mark, Andrew, and Carl's grandson and accountant—regarding investing in an amusement company.

Just as he did for Carl, Bernie engaged in black magic for Stanley. While family members deposited less than $2 million into their accounts over thirty years, they pulled out more than $37 million, and the accounts held about $50 million in fake equity at the time Bernie was arrested.

The benchmark rate that Bernie gave Stanley for many years was 29 percent—although he abruptly lowered it to 20 percent in 2003, for reasons unknown. (For the sake of comparison, Carl, being one of the Four Horsemen, received about 40 percent.) Nonetheless, Bernie often exceeded those percentages for Stanley, with one account having an annual rate of more than 68 percent.

Aside from the inconceivably consistent returns, Stanley's deposition, thirteen years ago, shows a kind of moral contortionism by a longtime trader that's hard to believe possible for a normal, socialized human. For example: after being shown a document dated 1998 that was discovered in his office by investigators, Stanley said implausibly that he was clueless what the words "benchmark return" on it mean. And yet at the bottom of the document, it states the annualized return for recent years was 28.09 percent.

> Q: Is that a concept you are aware of at the time you were
> invested with BLMIS?
> A: No.

> Q: So no expectation of possible returns?
> A: I would hope I would make a profit.

But Stanley recalled no specific number that Bernie was aiming for.

Another document states that five thousand shares of Halliburton Corporation, one of the world's largest oil field services companies, was purchased for his account on April 20, 1992, at a price of $21 7/8 per share. And yet Shapiro's May statement from BLMIS shows the same number of shares were sold at the same exact price, only *prior* to the date it was allegedly purchased. "I never analyzed it or looked at it that carefully," stated the former trader about the obvious discrepancy. "It's just what you're saying never entered my mind."

Similarly:

> Q: Any explanation of why in your May statement they're
> reporting trading activity in your account [of shares in
> Fluor Corporation, an engineering construction giant]
> that happened in the previous month?
> A: No, I never noticed it; I don't know why.

> Q: Does it strike you as unusual today?
> A: Yes.

At another point in the deposition, Stanley said he was confused and that "I never really was able to analyze these statements. And this one is confusing me more." Just like with Halliburton, it had to do with canceling a stock transaction that had supposedly occurred a month earlier. A legitimate transaction? "Never thought about it," said Stanley.

Such responses would be more understandable (but not forgivable) if they came from an outside Madoff investor who simply let the statements pile up unopened for years, so long as the fat checks arrived quarterly. But the company's logs show that Stanley wandered down from the nineteenth to the seventeenth floor—where Annette Bongiorno managed his accounts—an average of once per week from 2005 to 2008. What did they talk about? For that matter, did Stanley never raise these issues with Bernie during the dozens of jet flights that the couples took? Stanley may have been entirely blind, but with each response in his deposition, it strains credulity pretty far to give him the benefit of the doubt. No wonder the deposition remains confidential.

Accountant Konigsberg did Stanley's taxes and would annually provide him schedules of unrealized gains and losses from his Madoff accounts, so that he could figure out his taxes. Stanley could then decide whether to accept or alter reality. In a letter to Konigsberg in late February 2000, Stanley stated that he wanted to cancel a December 1999 trade involving more than $1 million worth of shares in Micron Technology. An honest accountant might have raised at least one eyebrow. But not Konigsberg, who had seen plenty of such letters and whose corrupt relationship with Madoff on falsifying statements would lead to his own conviction.

In his January 2000 statement, Stanley pointed out to Konigsberg, there were trades cited that were "creating losses. . . . What should we do about these?" He added that he was "thinking that we would like to cancel these trades. . . . Annette gave me a 'deadline' of today." Indeed, Bongiorno told Stanley she could cancel all the trades if he wanted her to. He ended up canceling one of them. *Poof!* Never happened.

Q: According to the next month's statement, you were able to

give those shares back, the same amount of shares, and
receive the same money in return.

A: It appears so.

Q: Is that effectively canceling the first transaction?
A: It appears so.

Q: And did you view that as something that was legitimate?
A: I never really thought about it or paid much attention to it. . . .

Q: And you wanted it canceled after the fact?
A: I don't know the answer to that.

In many notes written to Bongiorno that investigators found, Stanley
uses the word "need" when he wants something altered after the fact.
In one case, he wrote, "I need a $360K gain." Stanley's explanation
under oath? "It was a word at random."

Q: So, Bernie goes out and buys a stock and sells it three weeks
   later for the gain you want. Do you find that amazing?
A: In retrospect, yes.

Q: And had you looked at the statement, you would have
   realized it, correct?
A: I don't know. I never bothered to analyze any of Bernie
   Madoff's trades.

One note to Bongiorno says, "I could use a loss. Of $125K."

Q: Do you find it amazing that the stock was bought before
   you wrote the note—purportedly acquired—before you
   wrote [the] note to Annette?

A: No, I don't find it amazing.

But Stanley changed his tune when told that the stock trade enabled him to realize exactly a $125,000 loss.

A: I'm flabbergasted. I find it shocking.

For all his shock, it turns out that Stanley himself was sometimes *picking* the stocks for Annette to trade. In a November 2000 note, as part of his advance tax planning, Stanley wrote Bongiorno that he needed a "loss of about $100,000/110,000" in an account held by his daughter, as well as a "loss of about $60,000" in his son's account, and—for good measure—a "loss of about $50,000" in one of his accounts. Stanley suggested to her that she sell Procter & Gamble and Abercrombie & Fitch stocks to achieve it. No problem. Only instead of Stanley's suggested stocks, Bernie or Bongiorno chose computer stocks (Gateway and Oracle), and executed an immediate and remarkable series of fake trades that yielded almost exactly what Stanley needed: a $109K loss for his daughter, a $57K loss for his son, and his own $62K loss.

A year later, on December 12, 2001, Stanley wrote Annette that he needed a $125,000 loss in one of his accounts. This time she came through with a "purchase" of stock in Too, Inc., a specialty retailer of clothing for girls, on November 30—thirteen days *prior* to his request—that was "sold" two days later for a $124,380 loss, just $120 shy of what he'd requested.

And so it went, on and on, in the fantasy world of Shapiroville.

During a stock market downturn in 2002, the net values listed in some of the Shapiro family's accounts had fallen below zero. This was mainly because Bernie was "buying" stock for folks like Stanley on margin. What to do? Upon Madoff's suggestion, Stanley and Konigsberg met with Bongiorno on the seventeenth floor, after which she used a software program that enabled her, with a few keystrokes, to generate a whole series of revised account statements for him. Those new statements reflected fake and backdated short-against-the-box sales (meaning a short sale of stock one already owns) to eliminate the losses in the 2002 crash.

As was Annette's Bongiorno's practice, she asked Stanley and Konigsberg to return the original statements to her, and they did, before she sent the revised statements to them.

One particularly sordid example comes from a December 2002 statement of Stanley's suggesting that 23,400 shares of media conglomerate AOL–Time Warner were sold on his behalf eleven months earlier—on January 14, 2002. Sounds fine, except that his September 2002 statement still listed the 23,400 shares. "I took Paul's word this was the arithmetic and paid the tax," he told investigators, referring to Konigsberg. Asked if he didn't recall receiving a statement in December 2002 "that contained a large amount of backdated trades," Stanley's lawyer felt it was a leading and argumentative question and wouldn't let him answer it.

But the most explosive document of all may be a letter dated April 27, 2003, from Stanley to Konigsberg, that begins, "Paulie Dear." In it, Stanley says that both Bernie and Bongiorno "are aware of the problems we have." The problem: a $27 million short-term capital gains tax he faced. But after Bernie, Bongiorno, and Paulie waved their magic wands, he owed only a few hundred dollars in tax. How so? By conjuring a series of money-losing backdated trades, at a time when the S&P 100 was *soaring*.

"I'm shocked at this," was all Stanley could muster when confronted with it in the deposition room.

The clincher: a letter sent to Stanley stating that "all bad statements have been returned." Yet, at his deposition, Stanley Shapiro didn't recall anybody at BLMIS asking him to return statements, even though it was a common practice by Bongiorno.

Did Stanley have "actual knowledge" that there were no real stock transactions being conducted in any of these cases? That answer may have been determined in a trial in bankruptcy court that had been scheduled for 2025. For many years, he (as well as family members) had resisted turning over to the trustee even basic records—such as documents concerning the opening of his BLMIS accounts, all account statements, all documents concerning any purported investment strategies from Bernie, his compensation as a trader, and all documents and communications between him and either Madoff, Annette Bongiorno, or any other BLMIS employee.

In June 2018 the judge in the case ordered him to stop stonewalling. In April of 2020, he finally settled the case for about $12 million. Eight months later he was dead.

In his testimony during the Madoff Five trial, DiPascali was questioned by Bongiorno's defense lawyer, Roland "Rollie" Riopelle, about Stanley Shapiro. Frank stated that Shapiro had family accounts under his (Frank's) control, that Stanley was a friend of his, and that Stanley *knew* trades were being backdated. He recalled Shapiro saying at times that he wasn't sure if Bernie had trades in his own account that would allow him (Stanley) to get the backdated trades he wanted.

Q: And so when you heard Mr. Shapiro saying this—and, by the way, was he saying this? He wasn't whispering this in anybody's ear, was he?

A: He certainly wasn't whispering in my ear, and I don't recall when, the location of the conversation. It wouldn't be something that he would whisper.

Q: It wasn't something he felt he had to keep a secret, correct?

A: Correct.

Q: And as you understood it, what Mr. Shapiro was describing was a process by which Mr. Madoff was giving Mr. Shapiro trades from Mr. Madoff's account after the fact, correct?

A: That was my understanding of what Stanley's understanding was.

Q: And these would be backdated [trades], correct?

A: By their very nature, yes.

8

Giant Shops of Horrors: The Feeders

| | | | | | | | | | | | |

The Question: Why did those who poured clients into Madoff Securities ignore the obvious?

Because of my earlier success with this model—called a "split-strike conversion"—there was a growing interest. I was approached by a number of European hedge funds to take them on as clients for a new series of funds. There's no question that the model worked, had I done it [*laughs*].

—BERNIE

Bernie Madoff's largest feeder fund conduit was the Fairfield Greenwich Group (FGG), headquartered in Connecticut, which had—it bears repeating—some $7 billion of customer funds invested with him at the time the Ponzi collapsed. The warnings that Fairfield executives ignored were dire, as evidenced by a series of internal company emails dating from 2005 to just a few months before Madoff's 2008 confession. Here are excerpts from five emails:

When asked what he thought of FGG funds [in Madoff], his reply was that CS [Credit Suisse bank] would never do business with

FGG as a firm, as they believe we are not going "by the rules" and soon [*sic*] or later we will end up in jail!!

Little transparency is given about the Madoff models.

The only constructive criticism I would give is to always keep in mind the prime directive and downplay Madoff's role—never to have his name within 30 words of the word manage, as you do in the second paragraph. He is extremely sensitive to this and wants to be referred to merely as our broker and custodian.

I got much more comfortable knowing that it is not just Bernie Madoff with a laptop running the [trading] model. I am inclined to continue investing Madoff, but not bet the business on it.

Unfortunately there are certain aspects of [Madoff's] operations that remain unclear and although we are attempting to obtain responses from Bernie Madoff, this process could take some time.

In one email, an FGG executive alerts colleagues that he has just found out that Madoff's auditor, David Friehling, did not have two hundred clients, as they were told by Bernie. Indeed, Bernie was his *only* client. The exec goes on to write that he's also learned that Friehling, who would eventually go to prison for filing fraudulent annual financial reports, operates out of a tiny strip mall near a Chinese restaurant in a New York City suburb. He asks his colleagues if he should take a drive up there to see what's going on. He is told not to. As of mid-2024, FGG was still embroiled in litigation over its lack of due diligence.

One document entered into a civil case is an eighty-page transcript of a taped conversation between Madoff and Amit Vijayvergiya

(Vijay), Fairfield Greenwich Group's chief risk officer. The context
was that in 2006 the SEC was planning to ask FGG about its relationship with Bernie, prompting company execs to seek Madoff's help on
what they should tell the SEC about his trading model and strategy—
something they presumably should have known already but didn't.

Bill Brodsky, CEO of the Chicago Board Options Exchange
(from 1997 to 2013), and one of the greatest stock options experts
alive, reviewed the document for this book.

"I've read this piece of shit," he says bluntly. "My general view is
that it was a one-sided conversation by Bernie in what I would call
drivel." The problem, he explains, is that the FGG official on the end
of the line with Madoff "either didn't know anything or was so intim-
idated he couldn't say, 'Bernie, time-out, I want to know exactly what
you do.'" So what *did* Brodsky learn from the transcript about Madoff's trading model? "If anyone can tell me what the hell his strategy
was from reading this, they're better than I am," he responds. "I can
go through it line by line, but I'm not gonna spend ten hours with
you. This is the biggest piece of garbage I've ever read."

Similarly, after reading the transcript, Willie Weinstein, one of
the Street's legendary traders from the 1970s through the 1990s, concludes: "It looks to me like a strategic plan for a giant cover-up." It's
an understandable observation, considering that Madoff opened the
conversation by having the FGG official agree that nobody should
know that the two of them spoke. That's usually how cover-ups begin.

Excerpts from the phone conversation reveal Bernie's MO in real
time:

MADOFF: Obviously, first of all, this conversation never took
    place, okay?
VIJAY: Yes, of course.
MADOFF: Whenever we're asked about our relationship
    with any of these funds [such as Vijay's], number one,

we really have never seen any of your documentation, you know, like the stuff you send out to your clients, you know—because we never want to be looked at as the investment manager [note: which Bernie *is*, of course]. . . . [If] we've ever been asked about what our role is with any of these type of funds, it has always been that we are the "executing broker" for these transactions and that you use a proprietary trading model that has certain parameters built into it which have been approved by you and then that's part of the trading directive that you're seen.

VIJAY: Right. *[In fact, FGG had no such trading model, as it didn't have a clue what Bernie did with its money.]*

MADOFF: And by the way, the trading directives that you sent me is an old one, all right—we're going to send you up, actually, we'll messenger it up to you today—a new trading authorization directive that we had actually a couple of years ago—the options are no longer part of the model. *[Readers might ask why Madoff's largest feeder conduit with some $7 billion of investor money with him— has an old document no longer in effect about what Madoff is doing.]* . . . The reason we did that was because the intellectual property that's in the equity piece of it, is stuff that we feel and that our lawyers feel [note: no such lawyers existed!] is our property and we could always claim it was our property so that nobody else can use that, but the options piece of it really is too broad that we would never be able to actually successfully claim that that's our own intellectual property if somebody else wanted to use that, so we basically split it off from the model, so the equity is part of the model.

VIJAY: Right. *[Vijay's vocabulary is all but limited to this one word throughout the conversation, as Bernie rambles on.]*

MADOFF: I doubt they'll [the SEC examiners] get into that, but you never know with these guys, so it's basically that, you know, that Madoff uses whatever the last amount that he liquidated for the fund and that's the new amount that he would invest unless money is brought in and taken out and then that's—we get a phone call from the investment manager and change the allocation. . . . The best thing is not to get involved with written instructions, if possible, because any time you say you have something in writing, they [the SEC] ask for it.

VIJAY: Okay.

Readers who can't follow this are excused. Vijay clearly doesn't understand it, either. Nor does anyone. The conversation goes on and on, with Madoff doing 90 percent of the talking—an utterly convoluted, circular, and confusing diatribe about parts of the model . . . "options . . . equity piece . . . liquidity . . . and so on and so forth. I'm sorry, can you just hold on for one second so I can take another call? . . . If I get any more solicitations for charity, I'm going to kill myself. Okay, so what I was saying . . . You know, the less that you know about how we execute, and so on and so forth, the better you are."

Despite all the emails, despite the internal company documents, and taped phone conversation, not one individual from Fairfield Greenwich was indicted. Nor a single person from *any* of the Madoff feeder funds. Are they guilty of anything? I bounced this question off Wall Street's Robert Fagenson, who, in addition to his vice presidency of the NYSE, sat on its board with the likes of Bear Stearns's Ace Greenberg, Goldman Sachs's Hank Paulson, and Lehman Brothers's Dick Fuld as they navigated through many smaller scandals that plagued the markets over the decades.

The feeders, he says, "end up being condemned under the prudent-man rule, if nothing else." (That rule calls for fiduciaries to conduct due diligence and only invest in securities that a reasonable person would.) "Because they were all people who had enough experience or were seasoned enough that from the fiduciary perspective of guarding other people's money, they should have gained the knowledge necessary to understand how he was achieving the returns. At the bare minimum, they owed that to their customers. Do I think any of them knew that Bernie was a crook?

Maurice (Sonny) Cohn, who died a bitter old man in 2015, is a prime example of what Fagenson is talking about. If Cohn wasn't in on the Ponzi, he was one of the blindest of Wall Street "experts" who were closest to Madoff. Not just professionally close, but physically, as he had an office at BLMIS a floor below Bernie's, out of which he ran the Cohmad brokerage, founded by him and Bernie in 1985. In reality, it was little more than a conduit for (mainly foreign) customers who invested in Bernie's IA business—a conduit so large that many billions flowed through it. In short, he was a massive feeder into the Ponzi, whether he knew it or not.

Cohn's brokers were paid commissions based on how much money they brought in for Madoff. And yet Cohmad and BLMIS were supposed to be two completely separate entities. That in itself was illegal—a brokerage firm cannot pay its brokers for business that is not technically the firm's—and for good reason: it would insulate a brokerage firm like Cohmad (just a Madoff feeder), enabling it to tell customers something like, "It's not *our* broker who lied to you."

Peter Madoff was among the directors of Cohmad Securities Corporation, in addition to owning 9 percent of the firm. Its first client: Ruth, whose account there was worth $60 million by 2008. Convicted operations chief Dan Bonventre had an account there as well, as did Sonja Kohn, the Austrian feeder. Kohn, who worked as a stockbroker for Merrill Lynch in New York in the 1980s, also received millions of dollars in hidden fees from BLMIS—filtered through Cohmad—for having steered the Bank of Austria and other institutions to Bernie. Trustee Picard was initially so blown away by the Orthodox grandmother and her labyrinth of shell companies that he labeled her Bernie's "criminal soulmate" when he sued her seeking billions of dollars. Picard's off-the-charts description was removed from subsequent legal filings.

It was actually Cohn who enticed the Fairfield Greenwich Group to leap into Bernie Madoff's web, and it was Cohn who introduced Bernie to Kohn. Some of Ruth's money flowed into Cohmad, as did Jeffry Picower's. In total, some 25 percent to 30 percent of Bernie's total accounts, and the biggest chunk of investor money, can be credited in one way or another to Sonny Cohn.

Prior to Cohmad, Cohn was a stockbroker, as well as an active trader who ran a brokerage entity called Cohn, Delaire Kaufman that did business with the market making side of BLMIS (real trades) as well as with other firms on the Street. Cohn's partner at the time, Alvin Delaire, later became a trader for Bernie and a salesman for Cohmad. He also invested with Bernie, and when the Ponzi exploded, he apparently lost his entire net worth at the time: $34 million.

In 2016, a year after Sonny died, his estate reached a settlement with the trustee, who had been trying for years to claw back money from him and his family. As part of the settlement, the Cohns returned $32 million. Picard says this is more than 100 percent of the funds that had been transferred by BLMIS during the last six years of the company's existence to Sonny, his wife, Marilyn, and their daughter, Marcia, who, as president, ran Cohmad with her dad and also served as its compliance officer.

What the family pocketed in the decades prior to that is unknown, and not "claw-able" due to a federal judge's ruling that Madoff-related clawbacks could go back only six years. When the Ponzi blew up, Cohn told investigators, he had about $50 million in personal assets, while his wife had an IA account with Bernie showing $25 million.

The following Sonny Cohn story illustrates the see-no-evil approach of the feeder funds.

Among the people who knew Sonny well was Steve Rand, a former trader who worked closely with him for more than a decade in the 1970s at Cohn's prior company. (Rand says he met Bernie perhaps a dozen times in Cohn's offices.) Before Sonny died, he was drowning in lawsuits and became a hermit inside a condo he owned in Florida. "They don't let me live! They just don't let me live!" he cried on the phone to Rand, who recalls, "I'd never heard Sonny sound this low. He's very depressed; he stares out at the ocean, and that's it."

Rand described how he constantly warned Sonny over the years about Madoff's arrogance and cheating and lack of stock market knowledge. Among other things, Rand talked about Madoff's making cash payments in envelopes to order clerks on the floor of the NYSE in the 1980s. (As mentioned, Ponzi schemer Maurice Rind, whom I interviewed in Vegas, remembered Madoff doing this as far back as the sixties.)

Rand and his wife joined Sonny and Marilyn for meals from time to time. One night, over dinner in the Hamptons just months after Bernie's arrest, Marilyn was apoplectic. "She said, 'If I had a knife, I would cut his *kishkes* out [Yiddish for guts],'" he recalls. "'I'd like to take a large bread knife, put it in my pocketbook, and visit Bernie in prison. And then when I went to say hello and give him a hug, that would be the end of him. Because he took away everything from us.' But Sonny said, 'Oh, Marilyn, stop it.'"

What did Sonny have to say about Bernie? What did he think Madoff was doing with the billions that Sonny helped funnel to him from feeders? "Sonny told me that he thought Bernie had stumbled onto something—a magic elixir—like an alchemist," says Rand. Cohn's worship of Madoff flabbergasted Rand because Rand had concluded long before that Bernie knew very little about how the stock market worked. He remembers crossing paths with Madoff in a Florida airport while both were en route to a business conference. On the cab ride to the hotel, Rand tried engaging Madoff in a technical discussion about the market. But Bernie changed the subject. "It was because he knew nothing," says Rand.

Bernie sure knew how to insult colleagues, though, as Rand discovered firsthand. "When we first got into the cab, he said something like 'How you doin'?' And I'll never forget this, because before I got the first sentence out about my diabetes, he said, 'Listen to *this*! He's *really* going to tell me!'" Madoff then lectured the trader, "When someone says 'How you doin'?' they don't *really* want to know how you're doin'. It's just something that people say. You think I give a shit?"

A stunned Rand recovered to retort, "Go fuck yourself!"

The story gets even better: As Rand tells it, billionaire Bernie claimed to have no cash on him, so Rand covered the $110 cost of the cab ride, with Madoff promising to reimburse him for his half once they reached the hotel. Rand kept running into Madoff, but Bernie never forked over the money or even mentioned it. On the last day of the conference, Rand spotted Bernie at the pool and reminded him about the $55. "I'm in my bathing suit!" Rand recalls him shouting. "You're shaking me down at the *pool*? Don't you think I'm good for it? I'll pay you later." Not surprisingly, he never did.

Shortly after his arrest, Madoff wrote a rambling letter to Sonny Cohn, apologizing and blaming his Ponzi scheme on the fact that he'd once lost the money invested by family members (his 1960s tale) and couldn't bear it, so he started covering the losses with money from other investors. And then it snowballed. In the letter, he also expressed anger at many of those investors. "All of them were running after me, sliding checks under my door—cashier's checks, $50,000 at a clip, and begging me to take it. Especially that Palm Beach group. I couldn't sit at the beach or the pool there. I couldn't leave the house. I had to get out of Palm Beach because they wouldn't leave me alone."

Sonny never wrote him back, nor would he ever speak publicly about Madoff. Fortunately, a confidential daylong deposition that the SEC conducted with Cohn at its Manhattan headquarters in 2009 sheds a great deal of light on his thinking. The deposition was taken one year prior to the agency's settling a civil fraud case against Cohmad. All these years later, both the trustee and the SEC are still attempting to retrieve funds from some of the brokerage's salesmen.

The deposition, handled by three SEC agents, is a remarkable document for several reasons. It provides a rare window into Bernie and BLMIS by an *unconvicted* friend and Wall Street peer who worked on the same floor with Bernie. "I said I don't need an office that big," Cohn told the agents, "and he said, 'Please take it because if you don't, my sons will fight over it.' So I took it."

Cohn was also given key card access to House 17—Ponzi Central. He visited it maybe twice a year. Sometimes, he added, his daughter or another Cohmad executive "might go down there if there was a problem and they had to [see] Jodi [Crupi] or the others to clean up a problem or something." Key card records show that Marcia accessed the seventeenth floor regularly in the year before the fraud was revealed.

Cohn's deposition belongs in a Hall of Greed museum that could perhaps be built with the funds of people who benefit from frauds, starting with Cohn himself. That he should have known what was going on is not open to argument. That he didn't see it (assuming he didn't) is a tragedy, as he could have blown the lid off the scheme decades earlier.

"I want to go home," the seventy-nine-year-old whined about a half hour into the meeting. That wasn't going to happen.

By all accounts, Cohn was of sound mind right up until his death at age eighty-five. He told investigators that he, his wife, his two daughters, and a foundation all had IA accounts. The family lived near Bernie and Ruth in Laurelton in the early 1960s, and the men would often commute to Manhattan together in a seaplane. Their business relationship began in 1974, he said, when he gave money to Bernie to manage. According to Cohn, he believed at the time that Madoff was doing actual convertible bond arbitrage. Asked by the SEC what gave him comfort to invest with Bernie, he responded: "The comfort was I had known him for approximately ten years, and he was a friend, and I trusted him, and I was sort of a professional myself in convertible bond arbitrage."

Cohn's brokerage was sold in 1985 to S. G. Warburg & Co., a big London-based investment bank, and Cohn told Madoff at the time that he was planning to retire. But Bernie suggested Sonny open an office with him instead. And Cohmad Securities Corporation was born. "So, I decided to be a money manager, which I said, 'Gee, that's easy. You have a sign painted "Money Manager," and you put it on the door.'" Easy peasy.

It was even easier than Sonny imagined. That's because the money he "managed" for his own clients was simply funneled to Bernie to invest—with a cut of the new funds going to Cohmad. Sonny also got a piece outside of the company. Initially, Bernie paid him a commission on new funds from investors that he brought in. At one point, Cohn was raking in $6 million annually, but, later, Bernie changed his compensation to a flat $2 million per year, regardless of who and what he brought in. Why the change? "I don't know," Cohn told the SEC. He estimated that his assets were about $40 million at the time the Ponzi blew up.

Q: Who had the authority to trade these accounts?
A: I don't know. Bernard L. Madoff Investment Securities had the authority. . . .

Q: Do you recall any conversations with Mr. Madoff in which you discussed with him his trading strategy?
A: Probably. I don't know. . . .

Q: Were you aware of what stocks were traded—

A: Can I say something which—off the record?

Q: There is nothing off the record.

Cohn claimed that it was always his opinion that whoever was doing the trading, including Madoff, did not know the difference between "General Motors and General Electric." The trading, he said, was done by "a black box, by an algorithm or something." When asked to identify the brain behind trading decisions, Sonny responded, "I thought it was all Frank DiPascali. Maybe he would use one or two of the other people that were in that area. But it was basically Frank. . . . I have known him for thirty years. And he was a nice little kid, and he was a smart little kid. And he grew and he grew, and Bernie gave him more and more responsibilities, and that's where he ended." The truth is that Frank was such an incompetent prop trader that after just a few years, in the 1980s, Bernie kicked DiPascali off the trading desk.

Cohn insisted that "I had a good reputation as being a good trader." It's hard to believe, though, given his answers that day to the SEC. At one point in the questioning, Cohn told the agents that Cohmad was handling some trading for the market making side of BLMIS, run by Bernie's sons, but that he never inquired whether the company could handle the magic trading that Bernie was doing on floor seventeen for investors. "I don't know why I never inquired," he mused. "It's possible that I knew that it was so big that maybe we couldn't handle hundred-thousand-share orders."

Where did he think Bernie was doing the trades? "This is not the same world that we were in twenty years ago," he said. "There are many different stock exchanges. So, I didn't know where he traded. I don't really care."

Despite working for decades a few doors from Bernie's office,

Cohn said he never tried to find out how much money Bernie was managing apart from the billions that came in via Cohmad. "And [if] you could understand this, I never asked Mr. Madoff how much money he managed," he stated. Why not? "Because people asked me, and I didn't want to know. And if somebody would ask me, I can't lie. . . . Some people would ask me, 'Guess.' And my guesses usually were around seven billion dollars. Of course, I was dead wrong. I knew we had introduced possibly a billion dollars. That I knew."

Cohn maintained that it was only after Bernie's arrest that he "put the numbers together," which showed that if Madoff had actually been trading options in his split-strike strategy, the trades would have been bigger than the entire options exchange.

"Things like that never occurred to me."

When questioned whether he received IA statements for his personal accounts, Cohn undoubtedly spoke for every American who has ignored a bank statement when he responded: "Every once in a while, somebody would come in and throw it on my desk."

"Did you ever endeavor to find out what exactly this was that people put on your desk?" asked one of the agents.

"No. Sounds stupid. I should have, but I didn't."

Cohn may not have known what Bernie was doing with the money or with how much money, but he sent letters to his Cohmad customers describing his "mission" as being to "protect your investment and mine."

To investigators, the most intriguing part of Cohmad was how its structure was unlike that of any other brokerage firm. Commissions to its salesmen, or reps, were calculated based on how much of the *original* principal the client kept in the account. In other words, Madoff didn't care as much if clients pulled out the "fake" money they had earned.

For example, let's say a person invested $100,000, and it grew to $1 million. If the investor withdrew $200,000, the rep would no longer earn a commission on the $800,000 balance. In a real brokerage firm, if a rep brings in a client with $100,000, and the investment grows to $1 million, the rep gets paid on all of it.

Cohmad banned its sales force from communicating with clients about performance results. All questions had to be directed to Madoff's squad on floor seventeen. Reps were not permitted to use email—yet another red flag. "The only one in the office that was permitted to receive or take emails was Marcia," Sonny noted. "The computers were set up so that they couldn't send or receive anything."

Among the deposition's most interesting revelations concerned Ruth Madoff, who Cohn stated had an estimated $50 million (it was actually $60 million) in her own Cohmad account in the fall of 2008, and that "large amounts went out of that account from time to time."

During fierce negotiations in 2009 between Bernie's and Ruth's lawyers and prosecutors over how much money she could keep, Bernie's better half claimed that her father had gifted her $10 million worth of municipal bonds that Bernie had initially bought for Saul in the mid-1970s during New York City's fiscal crisis. "Ruth's father was so happy" at the time, recalled Bernie, who said he'd bought the bonds at just 50 cents on the dollar and that they doubled in value soon thereafter. On top of that, according to Madoff, he bought more bonds for her account until its value eventually topped $30 million.

Thus, the defense lawyers argued, she should be allowed to keep that gift money as well as everything else in the account (which had grown to $60 million by the time of Bernie's arrest, thanks mainly to cash transfers into it over prior decades), because prosecutors at the time could not prove the fraud began prior to 1992.

"Ike assured me she'd be able to keep those bonds," Bernie told me, referring to his main attorney, Ike Sorkin. "I said, 'Listen, I don't have any records—they're bonds we bought at Bear Stearns, which is out of business. I don't know where I'm gonna get the records for [*chuckles*] where the original purchase was. Nobody has those records.' He [Ike] said, 'Don't worry, the burden of proof is on the government and on the trustee.'"

Ultimately, that wasn't the case. In the bankruptcy proceeding, the burden of proof was on the Madoffs. "So we were never able to give evidence on that. And I was furious with him [Sorkin], because she had given [up] one hundred million dollars' worth of assets voluntarily. Originally, the prosecutor wanted to give her a hundred thousand. This was while I was in New York, you know, in the SHU." (Bernie was referring to "special housing units" where inmates are separated from other inmates for their protection.) "I said, 'Ike, look, we're gonna go to court on this. It's ridiculous. These assets [bonds] were bought [in the 1970s]—houses in Montauk and New York were bought in the early eighties. There was no fraud until the nineties.' He said, 'Don't worry about it.'"

But Bernie, of course, had already confessed to the feds—and to Frank DiPascali—too, that the fraud began in the early 1960s. Not the 1990s.

Bernie said that settlement proceedings were going back and forth. "They [prosecutors] admitted to Peter Chavkin [Ruth's lawyer] and Ike that they didn't have any evidence that the crime went back that far. So they said, 'We'll give her $2 1/2 million.' And that's what they did, which, of course, was nothing. But Ruth didn't want to litigate. So I said, 'All right, fine.' But quite frankly, to this day I'm still pissed at Ike because of that, because for her to have $2 1/2 million, when the houses were sold for, like, $30 million, and she had $30 million in that Cohmad account, all of which was hers, is ridiculous."

Did Sorkin really assure his client that the burden of proof was on the feds? "To the best of my recollection, we never had such a conversation," he says today. Did Bernie express bitterness to him over the deal? "Maybe in his mind it happened."

Unfortunately for Ruth, here is where Bernie's story breaks down.

During the settlement negotiations, the FBI's Steve "Garf" Garfinkel (who is also a CPA) performed a masterful forensic analysis of Ruth's Cohmad bonds:

Initially, the defense attorneys contended that she was entitled to $60 million because her father, who died in 1999, had allegedly left the bonds for her as an inheritance.

Estate records, however, showed that Saul's money went mainly to his eldest daughter, Joan Alpern Roman, who lived in Boca Raton, Florida. *But nothing to Ruth.* "Sorkin and Chavkin were claiming the bonds went to Ruth from Saul due to an inheritance," says Garf. "What was I to do? Take their word or check with the Surrogates Court?"

Bernie's lawyer, Sorkin, next argued that Saul had given a $10 million gift of municipal bonds to Ruth, but that she "didn't know about it." Instead, said the attorney, Saul gave the money to Bernie to invest *for* Ruth. But it wasn't true. There were indeed bonds in Ruth's account at Cohmad—thirteen of them in total. But duplicate copies of the exact same bonds also sat in the Cohmad accounts of two of Bernie's largest investors: Horsemen Norman Levy and Jeffry Picower.

How could bonds be in several places at the same time? "In effect, it's like 'What's it matter?'" exclaims Garf. "We've got a Ponzi, so the bonds are in three places at once. Who actually owns it? Who knows!?"

In the end, it was proven that Ruth had no legitimate source of income at all. All of her money stemmed from Bernie's thievery—all of it, therefore, tainted—although she was granted what's known as "innocent spouse" status, which allowed her to keep half of whatever assets were deemed untainted. The government swept away everything except $2.5 million, representing money stemming from her and Bernie's sale of a home in affluent Roslyn Estates, Long Island, back in the 1970s.

9

The Ponzi's Engine: JPMorgan Chase

| | | | | | | | | | | | |

G o to your favorite search engine and type in this name: "Gregory Jude Johnson" and the words "JPMorgan Chase." Next to nothing, right? Well, therein lies a tale.

At the time of the Madoff Ponzi's collapse in 2008, JPMorgan Chase (JPMC, Chase) was the largest bank in the United States and the sixth-largest in the world by total assets, with $2 trillion. By early 2024, it was the world's fifth largest, with assets approaching $4 trillion. In terms of market capitalization (the value of a publicly traded company), it's the world's top bank by far, at just over $500 billion.

While it was hardly the only giant bank to help Bernie facilitate his Ponzi scheme in various ways, it is impossible to overstate JPMC's key role in the fraud. As the bank and several of its predecessor institutions, such as Chemical Bank and Chase Manhattan, sat idly by, Bernie ran his Ponzi primarily out of that single Chase checking account ending in 703.

As for Chase's importance for Bernie to carry out his Ponzi, former prosecutor Lisa Baroni, who was part of a team of federal investigators that dug into Chase's relationship with Madoff, puts it succinctly: "Bernie without Chase doesn't exist. If he had a bank that actually paid attention to the ins and outs of the account, then the Ponzi scheme definitely couldn't have been sustained for so long." No fewer than a dozen executives at JPMC ignored the red flags about the 703 account that landed in their laps—and there were many. The bank's role in history's greatest known fraud should be the subject of a course in the country's top business schools, but not a single one offers it.

For several years after the Ponzi exploded, JPMC publicly maintained that "all personnel acted in good faith" during the decades of its relationship with Madoff. It wasn't true. And in 2014 JPMC, in order to avoid pleading guilty to a criminal indictment, admitted to a set of damning facts about its colossal failures, paying $2.6 billion in fines, penalties, and settlements—representing barely .1 percent of its assets, but a penalty nonetheless. Apart from that deal (known as a "deferred prosecution agreement" or DPA), no bank employees were prosecuted. That fact generated some public outrage at the time, particularly because not a single banker anywhere had gone to prison in relation to the overall 2008 fiscal crisis, which was directly traceable to the banking industry.

Tempting as it is, it is difficult to blame prosecutors for the fact that no bankers were held to account for the Madoff scam. While the collective behavior of those at Chase may have been prosecutable— hence the fines—it is difficult to jail a company, an abstraction. And the behavior of any single individual Chase officer or employee did not appear to cross the sometimes too-forgiving bar for criminality.

There was one exception, almost: the aforementioned Gregory Jude Johnson, head of compliance for JPMC's investment bank in the United States, a title he held there until 2014, when he was put in charge of compliance for the bank's global corporate and investment bank. (In 2018, he went to Citigroup as its chief compliance officer, and then in 2020 had a brief stint for a year in the same position for Citadel, one of the world's largest and most successful hedge funds. He now describes himself as quasi-retired.) As opposed to various other Chase bankers, Johnson doesn't appear in connection with anything to do with Madoff—not in articles, books, or investigative documents. But a source close to the investigation confirms that he came closer than any other Chase employee to facing criminal or civil liability.

Bankers have special legal responsibilities in America. When a private citizen witnesses a rape or murder, he or she is under no legal obligation to report it. US financial institutions, however—under the Bank Secrecy Act of 1970—have obligations ordinary people do not; among them, to actively search out fraud in their operations. Banks and their employees are required by law to *maintain* appropriate systems to facilitate the detection of crimes, make clear and consistent efforts to *detect* suspicious activity, and *report* any detected suspicious activity to regulators—namely the Treasury Department and/or its independent bureau, the Office of the Comptroller of the Currency. Not only that but banks can be prosecuted for what's known as "flagrant organizational indifference" for not having a well-designed anti–money laundering and compliance program.

Put another way, "if your compliance and anti–money laundering program is designed in a way *not* to catch all the suspicious activity, then that can give rise to criminal liability," says Matthew L. Schwartz, who served as the lead prosecutor on the Chase case.

The story of Bernie Madoff and Chase is one of codependency and self-serving systemic failure. It is a record of willfully ignored signals on the rare occasions when anyone *did* raise an alarm, and of the consistent failure to build and maintain precisely those systems of detection just described. It is a tale of mutual back-scratching that made all parties money beyond counting—yet went largely unpunished, apart from that fine, which barely registered on the bank's financial Richter scale.

For instance: between 1986 and 2008, Bernie's 703 checking account received deposits and transfers of about $150 billion, almost all of it from investors. That figure represented more than 7 percent of JPMorgan's total global assets in 2008. And more than $70 billion of that money moved in and out—in rapid-fire, back-and-forth transactions—between Madoff and just one of his four largest investors, Norman Levy, a close friend of Bernie and Ruth's, and one of the Four Horsemen.

But Chase's interests weren't confined to the traffic to and from the 703 account. The bank was a gluttonous hydra when it came to Bernie, with multiple divisions involved with him to one degree or another: the London-based equity "exotics desk," the New York–based private banking unit, the investment bank, the broker-dealer unit—everybody loved Bernie. Oh, there were alarm bells: starting in the late 1990s and right up until the Ponzi's downfall, employees of various units of JPMC (and its predecessor companies) raised questions about Madoff. But ultimately, nobody did anything about him. Perhaps the biggest failure of all was that not even once, until *after* he was arrested, did JPMC file a Suspicious Activity Report (SAR) with the US Treasury Department, as banks are required to do if they find any suspicious or even "potentially suspicious" activity.

Which brings us back to Gregory Jude Johnson, the rare Chase officer who did land on prosecutors' radar. It turns out that there *was* one SAR filed, in October 2008—but in the United Kingdom, not the United States. The British JPMC banker who filed the report noted that Madoff's company lacked transparency, had serious conflicts of interest, had failed to provide information that was requested—and had returns that were "probably too good to be true." A colleague then alerted Johnson, based in New York, to the UK trading desk's suspicions, and sent him a bunch of material about the decades-long relationship between Madoff and Chase.

When Johnson learned about the SAR filed in the UK, he infor-
mally discussed the matter with colleagues in a hallway. But he failed to
raise any of the particulars with the bank's anti–money laundering unit
in New York—a fact that Chase conceded to prosecutors. And that's
one helluva problem, given his position heading up the bank's compliance unit. (That's *compliance,* as in "complying with banking laws.")

In a series of emails Johnson is copied on from November 2008—
four weeks before Bernie's arrest—a Chase officer based in London
made it known that the bank had "lodged a report with the relevant
U.K. authority." One email stated that the bank's global head of compliance had been alerted and would examine the bank's relationship
with Bernie in that jurisdiction, but that "given Madoff is a US broker dealer . . . I've copied Gregory Johnson to keep him apprised."

In the wake of this request, not a single JPMC compliance staffer
in the United States took any action to investigate the bank's business
history with Bernie. Not a single compliance staffer called up BLMIS's
703 account on their computer screen to see the tens of billions wash-
ing in and out. Johnson was apprised and did virtually nothing, according to investigators. And it wasn't as though the UK complaint
was too complex for him to grasp: before he went into banking, from
1990 to 1994 Johnson was an enforcement attorney and then branch
chief with the SEC's Northeast Regional Office. In 1997 he joined
JPMC and was immediately installed as head of compliance for its
global corporate and investment bank. Johnson kept moving up the
company ladder.

"I'm not sure where my name came up," said Johnson when
reached by phone in early 2024. "I don't really have, honestly, much
to offer about it. . . . Otherwise I would tell you. . . . I wasn't really
involved in the Madoff situation whatsoever. That was a different
area of compliance."

True enough, but all roads ultimately led to Johnson.

When asked if the feds interviewed him about the case, he

replied, "I really can't tell you what, honestly, my involvement was in the matter. You know, I'm under a confidentiality agreement. But what I could tell you, though, is that I wasn't involved at *all* in the facts of the case. There are other people I think that *were* involved, and you hopefully have *their* names."

In the deferred prosecution agreement, the many pages of agreed-upon facts do not cite any Chase bankers by name. That's something the bank insisted upon during the negotiations with the US Attorney's office. Johnson is disguised as "Senior IB Compliance Officer." A banker named John Hogan is disguised as "CRO" (or "Investment Bank's Chief Risk Officer"). His significance? During a lunch in June of 2007 with a Chase colleague ["the JPMC Executive"], Hogan sent an email to the "Investment Bank's Global Head of Equities," the head of the "Equity Exotics Desk," and the "Head of Equities" for Europe, the Middle East, and Asia. That email stated the following: "I am sitting here with [the JPMC Executive] who just told me that there is a well-known cloud over the head of Madoff and that his returns are speculated to be part of a ponzi scheme—he said if we google the guy we can see the articles for ourselves."

Those bankers dropped the ball on it, too. But they didn't have the same potential liability as Gregory Johnson did, given his position as one of the bank's highest-ranking compliance officials. That's because Hogan's "ponzi" comment was just a stray remark. It sure sounds like a smoking gun, but "when you press into it, it's just a comment," says one investigator—not a legal duty, like Johnson had, *to act.*

Soon after Bernie's arrest, a Chase official named Michael Cembalist, the "Chief Investment Officer of the Private Bank," wrote to his customers that "we did not do business with the Madoff funds, having never been able to reverse engineer how they made the money—the numbers didn't add up." Unfortunately, Cembalist and his team never provided this information to JPMorgan Chase's anti-money laundering personnel.

"JPMC employees were intentionally siloed," one of the investigators on the Madoff-JPMC case tells me. Surely not to permit crimes to happen? "No, but the problem with all these banks to different degrees is that the *compliance* functions are *cost* centers, not *profit* centers, in what is a profit-seeking enterprise." Translated into plain English, this means that the compliance needs are subjugated to the profit motive as long as someone can justify it to themselves that they are doing the bare legal minimum.

JPMorgan had a compliance function for each part of the bank, each of which reported *up* the chain of command. But information never flowed across and around. "So," the investigator explains, "you had one part of the bank over in Europe that had some information, and in the US, where they were hosting bank accounts, they had other information. And you had investment managers who were actually doing some due diligence only because they were thinking of *adding* Madoff and Madoff feeders to JPMorgan's own investment platform, for the bank's *own* IA clients."

The bottom line is this: if all the information about the Madoff enterprise that sat within JPMC had ever been put together in one place, the investigator concluded, "It would have been *obvious* what was going on." But the bank never did that, for reasons we can only speculate about. (See "profit-seeking enterprise," above.) And in Bernie's case, not only did Chase silo the information, but "they did it despite the fact they knew at certain times that other parts of the bank *had* this information."

Government agencies are lousy at creating central databases. Banks, however, are quite efficient at doing so *if* doing so helps them make money. I asked the investigator how he would suggest solving the problem if he were sitting in a room with Jamie Dimon. "These are very complicated problems," he responds. "You can sort of say the answer, but it's easier said than done. The answer is you have to make sure that different parts of bank are talking to one another." That's not easy at an institution like JPMorgan Chase, which has 250,000 employees—nearly the size of St. Louis. It's almost an IT problem, in other words: banks have to ensure that their recordkeeping resides in a system that lets bankers see that an account in the investment bank, say, also has a relationship with an account holder in the commercial bank and/or private bank. Banks must see to it that the compliance function spans the *entire* organization, rather than being balkanized within particular reporting lines. "It is hard to do," sighs the investigator. "They were not trying enough."

In 2013, in the midst of the negotiations between the Chase and the US Attorney's office, the bank announced that it would spend $4 billion on compliance risks and controls and commit 5,000 extra employees to those units. The question is whether throwing more resources at the problem is an excuse to not have it designed properly. There needs to be an organizational intent to get it right, or a behemoth like JPMorgan Chase may find itself in trouble again.

In the wake of the Madoff scandal, and the 2008 financial crisis generally, many big banks and investment houses smartly began hiring former experts from the US Department of Justice to help prevent costly missteps. (In prior decades, the usual pattern was for prosecutors to go mainly to big law firms.) JPMC's chief compliance officer today is Christina Dugger, a former chief assistant US Attorney for the Eastern District, which covers areas such as Brooklyn, Queens, and Long Island. (In May 2009, Chase hired her away from Goldman and made her an assistant general counsel.) Former Madoff prosecutor Lisa Baroni became the global chief compliance officer for Folger Hill Asset Management, which was cofounded by the chief operating officer at SAC Capital Advisors, a major hedge fund that pled guilty to insider trading in 2013. Richard Zabel, the Deputy US Attorney for the Southern District, was scooped up in 2015 by Elliott Investment Management, a $65 billion (assets) hedge fund. Vincent Tortorella, a former federal prosecutor, runs the compliance and surveillance unit for Point72 Asset Management, a $30 billion hedge fund started in 2014 by Steve Cohen, whose previous company was the aforementioned notorious SAC.

FBI and SEC agents, too. Pat Carroll, who oversaw the bureau's Madoff probe for the SDNY, went to Goldman Sachs; the FBI's Madoff prober Steve Garfinkel went to Citibank; and the SEC's Israel Freedman, who was part of the team that interviewed Madoff in his penthouse apartment, now works at Cerberus Capital Management, a $60 billion hedge fund.

Banking is considered a boring profession for a reason, but we do need to cover some of the other low points in the decades-long BLMIS–JPMC lovefest.

Because while Chase's behavior may not have risen to the level of a criminal conviction, it was very, very bad. *Extremely negligent* would be the kindest phrase one could apply. Over the years spent investigating the bank's role in the Bernie saga, investigators kept turning up more emails, more memos, more bankers expressing to one another something close to terror about what they were involved in. And yet the bank didn't merely continue its relationship with Bernie—it expanded it.

JPMC's policy was to have so-called relationship managers recertify on a periodic basis that the necessary due diligence was being performed regarding each of their Wall Street corporate customers. Madoff's JPMC relationship manager was a man named Richard Cassa. Given that Cassa's job was to know his customer and alert his employer to any concerns, I am going to give Mr. Cassa an effectiveness rating of "vanishingly low."

Cassa testified at the Madoff Five trial. He began by saying he'd worked at Chase from 1968 (when it was still Chemical Bank) through March 2008. During that forty-year tenure, he did stints in private banking and as a relationship manager in the broker-dealer division, where he spent fifteen years managing the Chase-Madoff relationship. Cassa told the court that his contact at BLMIS was Dan Bonventre; nevertheless, in all those years, he'd spoken to or met with the operations chief only three or four times annually, "just to maintain a relationship. They weren't a very big client of the bank," he said. As for big boss Bernie, Cassa recalled speaking with him just three times.

When asked what kind of business Madoff's company did with the bank, Cassa replied, "Primarily it had a checking account, and we did have a small custody account with them"—an investment account created by a person on behalf of someone else. "They used to use the bank's wire transfer system. That's about it."

Asked what he understood to be, prior to Madoff's arrest, the purpose of the 703 account, Cassa testified that it was "a basic checking account, you know. Checks would come in and out, payments would be made, wire transfers would go in and out. It was a pretty normal checking account for that type of firm." He added that it was his understanding that the 703 account was associated with the market making business run by Peter Madoff and the boys.

In fact, as we know, the 703 *was* the Ponzi account—the engine room for history's greatest fraud—and hardly "a pretty normal checking account for that type of firm." Anyone looking closely at the monthly account statements would have seen *zero* securities purchased with it, just customer money moving in and customer money moving out. Later in his testimony, Cassa admitted that, apart from "general business purposes," he had no clue what the account was used for. Asked whether he knew the size of the 703 account, he replied, "Not really." The average balance? "No, I don't—I don't recall."

Did he have even a sense whether it held tens of millions or billions of dollars? "Probably tens of millions."

Banking experts find it astounding that Cassa stated, "We didn't see . . . the activity that goes in and out of the account," particularly because *multiple billions of dollars* were flowing through on a brisk, constant basis. Cassa said he knew Madoff had an IA business but that "we really didn't know much about it."

From a due diligence perspective, things didn't improve much when Cassa retired in early 2008 after four decades at the bank, and the role of Madoff's relationship manager passed to one Mark Doctoroff. In March 2009 Chase sent Doctoroff a pro forma letter from the Compliance Department asking him to certify the bank's *current, ongoing* client relationship with Bernie, as Cassa had done each year. Trouble was, in March 2009 Bernie was three months into his life sentence at Butner.

That kind of Keystone Cops–level bumbling went way, way back at Chase and its progenitors. As early as the mid-1990s, bankers at Chemical Bank, a Chase precursor, had spotted a bunch of suspicious transactions between a Chem Bank account belonging to both Horseman Norman Levy and Madoff's 703. At the time, Levy, with more than $2 billion parked in his own Chemical account, was one of the bank's most important individual clients—so important, in fact, that, years later, JPMC gave Levy his own office at the bank's HQ.

The dodgy activity between Bernie and Levy entailed "round-trip" transactions that typically began with Bernie's writing checks from another account he had then at Manufacturers Hanover Trust Company to Levy's account at Chemical/JPMC. Later that same day, Bernie would transfer funds from the 703 to his Manufacturers Hanover account to cover his entire check to Levy at JPMC. The final leg of the trip occurred when Levy moved funds from his own JPMC account to Bernie's 703, in an amount sufficient to cover the original check from Madoff's Manny Hanny account. Nothing suspicious about that, amirite?

These circular, redolent transactions, each for tens of millions of dollars, took place on an almost daily basis for years. The explanation? A time delay between when the transactions were credited to Bernie and when they actually cleared made his balances look bigger than they were at JPMC. And that provided him with a day or two of inflated bank interest payments on funds that hadn't actually cleared yet. Multiply that by hundreds of days a year, and we're talking real money.

In 1994 a Chemical Bank employee wrote an internal memo complaining that the daily costs to the bank from these dubious transactions were "outrageous" because they typically resulted in overdrafts. The employee phoned Madoff and Levy about it, but Levy persuaded him to back off. The employee's notes reflect that Norman told him: "If Bernie is using the float, it is fine with me; he makes a lot of money for my account."

Chemical and Chase merged in 1996. And while the bankers at the new entity didn't seem to care what Bernie and Levy were up to, their competitors at Manny Hanny did. Staffers at Manufacturers Hanover looked into the round-trip transactions, met with one of Bernie's employees to discuss it, and concluded they had no legitimate business purpose. Its fear was that the scheme was essentially check-kiting, a form of fraud involving the use of nonexistent funds in a bank account to take advantage of the float—which, of course, is exactly what Bernie was doing. Manny Hanny ended its relationship with Madoff, notified JPMC, and even filed a Suspicious Activity Report identifying both Madoff and Levy as being involved with suspicious transactions.

So, hats off to Manny Hanny. Unfortunately, banking regulators

receive mountains of SARS to wade through, just as the SEC is inun-
dated with complaints, and it isn't known if regulators did anything
regarding this one. But had JPMC been on its toes at the time—and it
certainly knew its own behavior had been flagged to regulators—it's
entirely possible that the Ponzi could have been stopped in its tracks
in 1996, more than a decade before it was.

This kind of scarcely concealed fraud just went on and on. In
1998, Levy and Madoff continued to engage in round-trip transactions at JPMC. And the amounts of money increased dramatically,
as the two added an extra scheme to their dealings with the bank: In
or around that year, Chase's private bank conducted a new review
of Madoff because it had been extending credit (loans) to Levy to
invest with Bernie. The review found that the balance in Levy's account statements at BLMIS had grown from $183 million in 1986 to
$1.7 billion in early 1998, an 830 percent increase in twelve years.
The private bank also learned, according to internal bank records,
that Madoff reported consistently positive returns for Levy at *all*
times, including through the '87 crash and all major market corrections that followed. In other words, he was doing the impossible for
his pal.

And it kept growing. During a *single month*, December 2001,
Levy engaged in more than $6.8 billion worth of transactions, all of
them between his own private banking account at Chase and Ber-
nie's 703. During 2002 BLMIS initiated outgoing transactions to
Levy in the precise amount of $986,301 on 318 *separate* occasions.
All told, between December 1998 and September 2005, when Levy
died, nearly *$76 billion* in payments moved between the 703 and
Levy's JPMC account.

It's a wonder that JPMC only gave Levy a private office at the
bank's headquarters—he should have been given his own wing. The
behavior was so brazen, it was as if Bernie and Norman were daring
the bank to do something. Astoundingly, Chase not only declined

to file a single SAR, but the private bank unit didn't even report the transactions to the bank's anti–money laundering unit. The private banking crew simply required Levy to reimburse JPMC for the interest payments the transactions had cost the bank. Unlike Manny Hanny, Chase happily kept the relationship intact.

"How much do we have in Madoff at the moment?" a top Chase banker asked a colleague in an email less than six months before Bernie was carted off in cuffs. "To be honest, the more I think about it, the more concerned I am."

Three months later, JPMG finally pulled all its own money out of Madoff, leaving many of its clients in the private banking unit holding the bag.

A subsequential internal email in October 2008 discussed Madoff's "odd choice" of using a tiny, unknown accounting firm to handle BLMIS's books. (The accountant, Friehling, pled guilty in 2009 to doctoring Bernie's books and was sentenced in 2015 to time served.) And still another October email noted that staffers at one feeder fund seemed "very defensive and almost scared of Madoff. They seem unwilling to ask him any difficult questions and seem to be considering his 'interests' before those of the investors. It's almost a cult he seems to have fostered."

And, finally, there's this: immediately following Bernie's arrest, several emails back and forth among a whole bunch of very relieved JPMC bankers:

We got this one right at least—I said it looked too good to be true on that call with you in Sept.

We actually look like we know what we're doing.

Bobby F-ing Magee wanted to do $1bio [billion] of [Madoff-related products] and we made it $200 mio [million]—thank God.

Perhaps best this never sees the light of day again!!

Perhaps it would have been. For Chase.

It was late 2013 when a JPMC banker finally spoke publicly in a Madoff-related case, the aforementioned Madoff Five trial. That banker was our friend Richard Cassa, the BLMIS relationship manager who knew very, very little about the relationship.

Two Chase lawyers were seated in the second row for Cassa's testimony, speed-writing notes as he spoke. And they would leave happy indeed. That's because an agreement between Chase and the prosecutors had been worked out before Cassa ever took the stand. His testimony would be limited largely to specific loans that one of the Madoff Five, operations chief Bonventre, obtained for Bernie under false pretenses—one of several pieces of evidence that helped convict him in the trial. As for the bank's culpability in the Ponzi, that subject had been ruled *totally* off-limits.

Why? It turns out that Chase had already agreed to the $2.6 billion payout to get the US Attorney (and Irving Picard) off its back. And a then-still-undisclosed deal had been inked preventing prosecutors from bringing up the bank's own liability during their questioning of Cassa. Defense lawyers, too, steered clear of the elephant in the courtroom. But had they posed such a question, they would surely have been shut down by the judge. After about ten minutes on the stand talking about one minor aspect, Cassa walked out unscathed.

Given the obvious centrality of JPMC, as well as several other large banks that fed off the Ponzi in various ways, I asked Madoff early on in our relationship if he would give me an exclusive on the subject of the banks. He agreed, but it wasn't long before he reneged on it, chipping away at the subject with other reporters. But it didn't really matter. He didn't have much to say to any of us on the subject. Or maybe he was simply keeping mum on key things, perhaps protecting individual bankers.

Whether they are true or not, Madoff had a few stories to share about Chase. Like the time a senior Chase executive came to Bernie's office at Lipstick to ask tough questions about his 703 transactions with Levy. "I just basically shut them [Chase] down," said Madoff. "I said to Levy, 'Look, you gotta take care of this, because I'm not gonna go into details with them.' And Norman, a very blustery guy, would say to them, 'Listen, if you guys don't leave Madoff alone, I'm gonna pay off all my loans and take my business elsewhere.' People at the very top [of JPMC] came up to my office. And they absolutely were aware that there was something that was not right, but they chose to ignore it."

On a different day, Bernie said that Chase should have seen things that he was doing "by looking at my balance sheet in the later years." On this, Bernie is 100 percent right: no matter how many years—even decades—Chase bankers (starting with boss Jamie Dimon) spend battening down the hatches and covering their asses, the details of their relationship with Madoff will always haunt the institution. Or at least, they should.

Over the years, I asked Bernie repeatedly if he could name any of the top Chase bankers he met and dealt with. He only mentioned one: Robert "Bob" Lipp, whom he said he dined with in the Grill Room at the Four Seasons in Manhattan, and who he claimed visited his Lipstick office once. Lipp spent twenty-three years with Chemical Bank, where he rose to the position of president. After the bank was sold to Chase in 1996, he stayed on in an advisory capacity. He resigned as a director and officer of JPMC just six weeks before the

Ponzi blew up. Clearly, he would know where bones are buried. In 2017 I spoke with Lipp, then age eighty and running his own hedge fund in Connecticut. It was a brief conversation. After saying he recalled meeting Bernie just once in his life, Lipp quickly hung up the phone. He surely could have shed at least some light on the biggest fraudster in history, as well as put Bernie in perspective. But as with most bankers since time immemorial, Lipp stays tight-lipped.

"Chase will have a hard time getting out of this," Bernie told me. "I had hundreds of millions of dollars going in and out of my account—always ending each quarter with the initial balance I started with. But nobody gave a shit. I met with the president of Chase and others there. They just wanted to kiss the ring." Similarly, one investigator who, along with some colleagues, visited Bernie in prison in 2010 recounted what Madoff told him about the bank. "We asked, 'How can nobody [at Chase] have ever asked you any questions?' He said, 'Oh, they just wanted to kiss the ring. All they wanted was to shake the Wizard of Wall Street's hand. Nobody gave a shit.'"

As for Norman Levy, Bernie told the investigators that, on the one hand, he didn't want attention from Chase, but he was also jealous that his pal was given his own office there. "They used to take him out for fancy dinners, and I was kinda pissed," Madoff admitted. "Because they would come shake my hand, but they didn't kiss my ass as much as they kissed Norman Levy's ass." That's literally the extent of JPMorgan Chase's "Know Your Customer."

10

The Foreign Banks: Bottom Feeders

| | | | | | | | | | | | | |

When it comes to ring kissing, no one tops the Europeans. And it was thanks to European clients and banks that Madoff kept the Ponzi going for at least a decade longer than it likely would have survived. They enabled him to expand heavily and keep the perpetual money machine in motion.

I will focus on only a couple examples here, but they are entirely representative of the ways Bernie got his hooks into the Old World. Imagine these tales repeated in country after country, and you can begin to see how Bernie's American fraud was replicated, adapted, and rolled out across the Continent.

It begins in 1997 with, fittingly, Philippe Junot, the former husband of Monaco's Princess Caroline. Junot, who was looking to drum up business for himself, reached out to one of the wealthiest and most powerful families in France: the Bettencourts, heirs to the multibillion-dollar L'Oréal cosmetics fortune. According to a reliable source close to the family who has asked to remain anonymous, Junot tried to interest them in investing with Madoff, whom he described to the Bettencourts as a Wall Street genius who was essentially minting money.

At the time, Junot was partners with a prominent banker in Europe, Patrick Littaye, whose credentials included high-level stints at France's two largest banks, Banque Paribas and Credit Lyonnais. Together the two men tried to assure the family that Madoff was a sure bet. The Bettencourts appreciated the fact that Madoff was a former chairman of NASDAQ, but they were the archetypal Europeans: clannish, judgy, and extremely conservative financially. They rarely took big risks and certainly not on strangers from the New World. They declined to invest.

A few years later, the two men tried again. Flying the flag of a new company they aptly called Access International Advisors, they made a revised pitch to the family. They now had a major bank behind them: Littaye's alma mater BNP Paribas, one of the largest in Europe. Junot and Littaye proposed to have BNP's Luxembourg subsidiary serve as the "custodian" and "administrator" of a Madoff-related private fund they named Oreades, after the mountain nymphs in Greek mythology. At the time, such banks were openly advertising themselves to new customers with slogans such as "Luxembourg, your money's second home." Access assured the Bettencourts that the bank would physically hold their investment, keeping their money in European hands, as it were. That was enough to sway the reluctant family, and the Bettencourts agreed to invest in Madoff.

Under European laws—which are stricter in theory than in the United States, but really only on paper—banks that serve as custodians are supposed to *physically* hold and look after a fund's actual money, with the fund manager given the exclusive right to invest it. *Custodian* means what it sounds like: custody. Moreover, in Europe, when you invest in a bank-administered fund such as Oreades, by law you are guaranteed at least the return of the principal you invested—a setup that sounds like a fairy tale to Americans raised on the ideas of risk assumption and caveat emptor.

The technical name for what Access was offering the Bettencourts is an "absolute return product." Unlike buying a share in a Google or a Walmart, say, these are what's known as structured products. Think of it as similar to an annuity with a US insurance company, where you're always guaranteed the return of your principal.

Without a major bank in Europe behind him, Madoff would never have stood a chance on the Continent, says Emmanuel Asmar, a lawyer who is close to the Bettencourts and other investors in the Oreades fund. "He didn't come from a wealthy family or go to the best schools," he says about Bernie. "While he's a great example of the American dream, where you can go from nothing to the top, in *Europe* he was nothing. He was nobody. There's an elite here. It's terrible to say that, but here it's the ancient world."

Asmar's description of the European mindset sounds like it could have been written a hundred—maybe a thousand—years ago: "The elite would ask, 'Okay, where do you come from, who's your family?'" he explains. "'You're not coming from the best schools? Okay, I'm not talking with you.' In the US, who cares about this? 'You have a good idea, you can make money.' *Here?* No way. It's that way in England, France, Germany. The fact of him being a genius and market maker—this could never happen here. . . . That's why from the very beginning, investors like the Bettencourts said, 'I don't care about Madoff, or who he was at the time, or his legend. I only trusted UBS or HSBC or Citigroup or these banks. That's the only reason I invested.'"

With the support of BNP Paribas ("The bank for a changing world"), the fund took off. Joining Junot and Littaye was a master salesman named Thierry Magon de la Villehuchet, a third-generation French nobleman who had previously invested $1.4 billion into Madoff on behalf of some of Europe's grandest royals—including

King Juan Carlos of Spain, according to Ian Logie, a major European banker who moved in those circles. An internal shareholders list dated October 2008 includes more than a hundred names, including the Switzerland-based International Olympic Committee as well as a committee of France's national parliament.

The tale took many intriguing and sordid twists and turns. It included not just billionaire Liliane Bettencourt, who lost about $1 billion to Madoff, but led ultimately to de la Villehuchet's killing himself in his Madison Avenue office in New York after Madoff's arrest.

At one point in time, for reasons unclear, BNP dropped out of the game and was replaced by UBS, the Swiss-based multinational bank; the fund's name was also changed, from Oreades to Luxalpha. And that's when the real action began. As internal documents make clear (see exhibits), UBS served not just as the fund's custodian but also as its manager and legal administrator—essentially wearing all *three* hats, in violation of European law. While the custodian required UBS to hold on to the investor's funds, in fact, bank records show that *all* the money was wired to Bernie's 703 checking account at Chase in New York.

What did UBS actually do in exchange for its hefty fees? Nothing, except to sell its name, which gave (false) comfort to European investors. No true oversight or due diligence took place. No quants with pocket protectors were brought in to analyze and reverse engineer Bernie's impossible strategy. (A quant is an expert at analyzing quantitative data, and they are a common sight today at large hedge funds.) No one was responsible for proving that 1 plus 1 does not actually equal 3, and never has and never will.

One internal UBS fund prospectus included a large-print, three-asterisk warning to its bankers that they should *never* contact Bernie directly. Why? Out of fear that Bernie would get angry and kick UBS out of the tent. Not only that, but internal emails advise bankers not to tell certain investors that Bernie Madoff was involved *at all* with the funds. That, of course, was Bernie's standard, ironclad condition for almost everyone he dealt with.

A dive into the documents floating around this UBS arrangement quickly turns up some pretty dubious activity. One internal 2005 operating memorandum—copyrighted by UBS Luxembourg—states that Madoff will provide a UBS executive named Christian Schön with a "backdated" monthly investment recommendation. (This statement is highly suggestive of wrongdoing. Indeed, Annette Bongiorno was for decades responsible for doing her archival *Wall Street Journal* magic to find and relay backdated stock prices for major investors on the other side of the Atlantic.)

A year earlier, in a 2004 email to a colleague, the UBS's Schön was mystified how the bank could "officially" be called the manager of the funds from investors if they "do not have a cent posted to our books." He continued: "To date I had assumed that Madoff certainly makes the trades and executes them, but that the assets lie with us. . . . This way I would have been in a position to exercise a certain oversight function."

Nonetheless, a confidential 2004 letter from UBS to the Access trio of Littaye, de la Villehuchet, and Junot states that the bank would act as a "figure head" to third parties in sponsoring and managing the fund. In other words, despite Luxembourg laws that might have held the bank liable for damages from "irregularities" or "inadequacies," Access was proposing to assume all such risk.

Put another way, UBS was in essence saying to Access: you can borrow our name for a hefty cut, but if the walls come crashing down, it's *your* problem. Unfortunately, that information—that UBS was not a true sponsor maintaining custody of invested funds—was never shared with European investors.

The UBS-Madoff investors were always led to believe that their funds were squirreled away securely inside UBS. Wire records, however, show the funds routinely moving from UBS into Bernie's 703 account at Chase—sometimes more than $100 million at a time. (As Chase was fond of saying at the time, "The right relationship is everything.")

In 2006 Littaye and de la Villehuchet, the principals of the UBS Access feeder fund, brought in a due diligence expert—but only after another partner pressured them to do so. It took that expert, Christopher Cutler, who specializes in advising institutional clients on risks, just four days to discover that Madoff's operation made no sense. For starters, he found that the options volume on the securities that Madoff reported as executed by the funds greatly exceeded the *total* volume of options actually traded in the entire market. But when Cutler met with Littaye and de la Villehuchet to relay his findings, they grew defensive and didn't want to hear it.

"Thierry and Patrick did *not* have market expertise to understand," he recalls, "and I could not have been clearer: there are illegal things going on. I told them, 'Shut it down and focus on your other businesses. I don't care if ninety-five percent of your business is Bernie Madoff.'"

The meeting, which lasted all of twenty minutes, took place over coffee in a private conference room at the University Club, a stately social club in Manhattan that dates back to the mid-nineteenth century. "They kept asking me, 'How do you know the options are impossible?'" says Cutler, who'd worked previously at the Federal Reserve, the central banking system of the United States. Look at the trading tickets, he told them. Moreover, he added, there are "no time-stamped trades," and no verification of trades and assets. "Why are they [Madoff's operation] using paper tickets, and why by mail?" he asked them. They responded, "That's the way Bernie wants it." They "drank the Kool-Aid," says Cutler. "It's hard to disprove that something's possible. To me it was the body of evidence of impossibilities that made it completely impossible." At the meeting, a colleague of Littaye's and de la Villehuchet's responded, "Chris, are you

THE FOREIGN BANKS: BOTTOM FEEDERS

out of your mind? I question your business judgment. You're asking us to give up almost all of our main source of our business!" A source that was worth $6 billion.

The fund's principals not only ignored the recommendation to bail out of BLMIS, but also requested that Cutler not provide them a written report of his findings—only the twenty-minute verbal one—which is very unusual in the due diligence industry.

Curiously, in November 2008 Access changed its name, prompting UBS to insist that it sign a new, stronger ass-covering letter about the bank's lack of actual responsibility. Trouble was on the horizon, and both Access and UBS could apparently sense it. In one alarming email, a UBS executive warns Access's Littaye that "if the analysts in Zurich find out Bernie Madoff is behind the *story*"—banking jargon for what makes a fund or company worth investing in—"we would be killed." A follow-up email expresses relief that the UBS executive told a lie in order to keep what they are doing on the down-low.

Finally, another internal document shows that in 2006 Anglo Irish Bank—then the third-biggest bank in Ireland—wanted in on the Madoff action. (The now-defunct institution later booked the largest corporate loss in the history of that country.) The memo shows that an Anglo Irish Bank executive sent a query to Bernie's top deputy, DiPascali, asking who the "counterparties" were for the stock options Bernie said he was buying and selling. The bank wanted to know, in other words, *who* Bernie was doing these so-called trades with.

DiPascali didn't answer, according to the memo. "Rather than leave the subject in the [sic] limbo," the document reads, they re-sent the query, this time with a cover letter stating it was from Ernst & Young, the auditor for both Anglo Irish Bank and UBS. This got Bernie's attention. According to the memo, he called to say that he simply wouldn't disclose the counterparties. "But what he can say is that there is no risk," reads the memo.

One investor—and this happened a lot—lost $43 million he'd

invested in Madoff after convincing UBS to analyze his Madoff/UBS investments so that he could take a bank loan against them. Because UBS itself was behind the Madoff product, the bank had no problem lending that particular investor a whopping 65 percent of his portfolio's value. And to the extent that the investor poured more money into Madoff's funds in the future, the bank would happily increase that lending value. With such a great deal, any investor would simply invest more and more of the borrowed UBS funds into Madoff. In other words, they borrowed *against* Madoff funds for cash to invest *more* in Madoff funds. That story was repeated throughout Europe.

In many conversations, Madoff pooh-poohed news stories about middle-class investors who lost so much money in the Ponzi that they were having trouble putting food on their tables. "After 1992," he once said, referring to the year he claimed the Ponzi started, "the investment was a minimum of two million dollars. So it defies the imagination why now people all of a sudden claim they're living out of dumpsters and so on. And not one of these people were ever solicited by me." But all across Europe, tens of thousands of small investors came aboard without even knowing that it was Madoff who was handling their money.

Brussels-based lawyer Edouard Fremault is the chief strategy officer at Deminor, a group of companies that helps investors recover funds from all kinds of frauds. They represent thousands of clients who put money into Madoff feeder funds located outside the US—including Luxalpha. "They range from small German savers who lost three thousand euros to large, wealthy Paris-based family offices with tens of millions of losses," he says. "But ninety-nine percent of them had no clue that someone in the Lipstick building was supposed to be managing their money. These folks genuinely believed that they invested in a UBS, Bank Medici [Sonja Kohn's Austrian operation], or HSBC products."

Fremault says Madoff was utilized by feeders in what's known in Europe as the "fund hotel business." Why a hotel? "It means if you're a fund and you need to get an investment structure, you just knock at the door of—for example—UBS in Geneva and say, 'Okay, can I get a room for one or two days.' They will give you all the infrastructure, and they will put their name on it. The bank is 'hosting' the investment, but they're not in charge of anything. And then it can be sold basically to anyone." But if you look at the internal documents, the custodian of the funds was supposed to be UBS, *not* Madoff. This was never disclosed to those investors.

As of early 2024, UBS was still holding on to the fees it took in from the Madoff funds—declining to settle with trustee Picard or with the European investors who were left holding the bag. "UBS is clearly not in the mood to settle," says Fremault, "because they really think of themselves as being a victim."

Over at HSBC, various units had been pushing Madoff feeder funds onto their investing clients since at least 1999. In 2001 a few of the bank's executives were expressing doubts about Bernie, but the record shows they did nothing of significance to investigate them—or him. It took until 2005 for the bank to hire accounting giant KPMG to have a look at the "operational risks" of Bernie's business.

In December 2023, an updated 254-page legal complaint by Picard—in detail after detail—paints a compelling portrait of an out-of-control bank. "[But] despite uncovering increasing evidence of fraud and the red flags raised by HSBC's employees and consultants," writes Picard, "HSBC never took its inquiry to its logical conclusion: it never sought proof of actual trade execution or the existence of purported assets under management. Moreover, rather than retreat from its relationship with BLMIS, as many of its officers recommended, HSBC expanded its relationship with BLMIS."

Sure enough, the report that KPMG provided the bank in February 2006 included a long list of suspicious items. It even mentioned the possibility of fraud. HSBC asked the accounting firm to go back and do a second probe. Nevertheless, the bank kept its close "custodial" relationship with Bernie intact—using its good name to comfort prospective Madoff investors. In reality, HSBC didn't perform the services it was contracted to do, but the bank profited immensely by turning a blind eye to Bernie. He was the real custodian of the funds—a violation of European laws, as well as a staggering betrayal of the bank's fiduciary duties to investors.

HSBC Ireland, a large subsidiary of HSBC, also served as the "custodian" of Madoff's money in the European hedge fund entity Optimal, a subsidiary of Spain's largest bank, Banco Santander. A multipage internal document from the American arm of Santander states to would-be investors that the fund's "trading strategy" is *merely* "executed" by an (unnamed) broker, when, in truth, internal emails show that the bank knew it was *all* Madoff's supposed strategy. That document also includes a graph of Madoff's performance going back a decade: it's a diagonal line into outer space, tracking an 11 percent average annual return after fees, with 90 percent of Madoff's trading months showing positive returns. That is, needless to say, an unobtainable achievement for *any* investment firm on planet Earth.

Banco Santander was the largest bank not only in Spain but also in the Eurozone—and, at $135 billion, one of the largest in the world in terms of market capitalization shortly before the 2008 financial crisis. Santander has long been run by one of Spain's richest and most powerful families, the Botins. Bernie told me he met twice with Ana Botin, one of the bank's top executives. (She took the helm in 2014, upon the death of her father, Emilio.) She declined to discuss Madoff with me, but a well-placed source was happy to share a trove of internal Santander documents that show the ignominious relationship the bank maintained with Madoff through the years—all while reaping hundreds of millions of euros.

These documents, as well as internal emails, reveal that Optimal had identified critical risks in Madoff's operation and, after a cursory investigation, failed to get any real answers from him. One due diligence report by a Santander executive, dated July 2006, begins by stating that the report sums up two years of work researching BLMIS and its counterparties. It reads: Madoff "currently manages $2.2 billion for Optimal SUS," Bank Santander's hedge fund arm. "Madoff Securities' setup for trading client assets is different than that of a regular hedge fund and thus poses several questions which we address in this report. In the following sections we identify and review various aspects of organizational risk and propose risk monitoring steps to address them."

The report goes on to lay out the "aspects of organizational risk" posed by BLMIS's unique structure and approach, including:

» "Privately owned family business shrouded in secrecy."
» "No independent custody of client assets (Madoff is the custodian)."
» "Lack of transparency into client accounts, through either clearing or banking accounts (although this is standard brokerage firm procedure)."
» "No independent verification of trading activity."
» "Not regulated as an investment advisor."
» "Lack of realistically independent auditor—Friehling & Horowitz is a very small firm with Madoff as its only major client."

These institutional qualms about Bernie were no secret, internally. For example, in a 2004 email to several Optimal executives (including fund chief executive Manuel Echeverria), a New York–based Santander executive named Hugh Burnaby-Atkins fired off questions like they were coming out of a machine gun:

"Why are there no Madoff employees out in the market place? Does he really pay them so well that they never leave? . . . Who are the individuals who take receipt of wired funds when they are sent into

Madoff's custody? . . . He has mentioned a team of 12 in the past but are these people dedicated to such accounts? . . . How can he moved $20bn of equities in/out of the market without affecting prices? Has anyone spoken to any of his counterparties [buyers and sellers on the opposite sides of trades]. . . ." Of note, after the collapse of Lehman Brothers but before Madoff was exposed, Optimal sent a letter to all its investors to assure them that the fund has "actively monitored" its brokers, "as well as other counterparties and potential exposure." But they weren't, because they would have found that Madoff had no counterparties.

In his 2004 email to his colleagues, Burnaby-Atkins eventually stated the unthinkable: "SUPPOSE this was the largest Ponzi scheme in history—unpalatable but we are not the first to suggest it. . . . No doubt many of these questions have been asked already but given his size and significance to our business we feel we should be asking them again."

Sometimes, the qualms about Bernie were the stuff of black humor within the ranks of upper management: "I heard that Bernie is in your dreams, or nightmares," wrote the bank's chief risk officer, Gilles Prince, to one of its operational risk managers, Michelle Perry. "That must be a lot of fun! Did he say where he's been hiding the money [winking smiley face here]?"

Perhaps the most damning piece of evidence is a confidential video deposition taken in London of Rajiv Jaitly, a former head of risk for Santander's Optimal fund. Internal emails show that he quit after not being permitted to conduct proper due diligence on Madoff. Among other things, Jaitly stated that he was "chaperoned" by other bank executives at a meeting with Bernie "and that if they determined that I shouldn't push on a particular question, that I needed to shut up." In one email to bank executives who were hamstringing him, Jaitly wrote: "We cannot afford to represent to the world at large that we have processes if the exceptions to these processes become the rule."

In truth, his superiors felt they couldn't afford to upset Bernie with too many questions. They didn't want to risk getting cut off.

So they kept quiet, and kept investing, on behalf of thousands of clients. Ultimately, they lost some $3 billion of customer money. That made Santander Bernie Madoff's second-largest feeder fund, after the roughly $7 billion invested by Fairfield Greenwich Group.

In the wake of Madoff's arrest, Santander was one of the only banks that rushed to offer compensation to its private banking clients: a mere $235 million, to be divided among them.

The due diligence that so many banks, feeders, charities, and even celebrity money managers failed to do on Madoff is made even more glaring by the fact that any number of corporate intelligence and risk management outfits could have done it for them. For as little as $5,000 to $10,000, any leading investigative firm with a global footprint—Kroll, Control Risks, Nardello & Co., FTI Consulting, among others—could have found enough in a basic background check (or, in Madoff's case, *not* enough) to raise questions for their clients.

Inside Nardello's New York headquarters, an investigator named Nick Peck demonstrates what could have been learned prior to Madoff's collapse from simple databases and investigative software tools. Aside from turning up the two financial stories from 2001 that questioned his fanciful investment results, Peck found that Bernie revealed in an SEC filing that he doesn't charge customers fees in the form of a percentage of the profits he made for them—a common practice on Wall Street—but would instead take his cut from commissions off stock trades. "That was extremely strange, and we would have looked at who else was doing that in the industry," says Peck. "It's much more likely that fund managers with his kinds of steady returns would, if anything, use their track records to justify *higher* than normal fees—rather than giving their investors a substantial break."

A lack of information in the public domain is itself a reason to be suspicious. "If certain things are not answered, that is the flag for many investors not to invest," points out Peck. "We'd have told our client we can't give definitive answers, but it doesn't feel right."

Jack Casey, a friend and a former head of marketing for a US unit of Credit Suisse Asset Management, recalls numerous conversations with prospective investors in the mid-2000s who were under Bernie's spell. "Often we would give a forty-five-minute pitch on our Fund of Funds product, and after we were done they would say, 'Very interesting—however, you don't stand up against Madoff. He hasn't had a down month in many years.'"

Casey says Madoff would never let Credit Suisse's due diligence team near him. "So we'd have to say to investors, or at least intimate, that the numbers just didn't make sense to us—and we therefore could not invest our fund capital or the prospect's capital into something we could not thoroughly understand. It was typically the end of the conversation. Far too many chose Madoff."

11

The Madoff Five
(Act 1)

| | | | | | | | | | | |

The Question: Why were the only people tried for the Madoff fraud five mid-level employees?

The case of the "Madoff Five" came down to whether five mid-level employees, who'd never worked anywhere else in their professional lives, and had limited skill sets, knew at some point or *should* have known that what they were doing was criminal. Their defense was that they were victims, and that—while the entire Madoff family also worked at the company (in the highest posts)—aside from Bernie himself, it was only his brother who went to prison. And *that* was in a plea deal that didn't require him to concede that he knew anything of the Ponzi.

The case, which unfolded in Lower Manhattan over a five-year-period, from 2009 to 2014, was one of the greatest slugfests ever in a business fraud case. It simply had to be that way, given the nature of the scandal and the limited intelligence of the defendants. And in the end, the results offered something for everyone: prosecutors got convictions on all five defendants, and on all fifty-nine counts, but the sentences imposed by federal judge Laura Taylor Swain were significantly lighter than they could have been.

It was the "biggest Ponzi scheme known to man," proclaimed Judge Swain. So, when she announced the first prison sentence for the Five on December 8, 2014, FBI agent Paul Takla spat out a breath of air in disgust. As for me, observing from the gallery, my brain did a spit-take. Prosecutors sat stunned. So did defense lawyers, including software programmer George Perez's attorney, Larry Krantz, whose frown instantly reconfigured itself into a broad smile. "*This judge knows justice!*" he rejoiced to a colleague. And by the time it was over, with the fifth and final defendant sentenced a week later, Swain had upended her reputation as a hanging judge.

She went soft because none of the Madoff Five defendants was "a master of the universe" capable of bringing down a nation's currency with the wave of a hand; they weren't hedge fund managers straight out of Harvard Business School or derivatives analysts with multiple degrees from the Massachusetts Institute of Technology.

They were the unseen trolls of Wall Street; the workers in the financial underworld. These are the kinds of people who make Wall Street work. And if these five, that world in microcosm, were on trial for making the Ponzi scheme thrive, the judge felt sympathy for them, even if the jurors did not.

In an email to me, Madoff, then in his fifth year of incarceration, insisted, "Richard, these five loyal and dedicated employees were following the instructions of their immediate supervisor," that being turncoat Frank DiPascali. "They were not SEC-registered brokers and therefore had no reason to believe that they were violating any SEC regulations." Bernie went on to claim that they were always led to believe that the trades and the client assets were effected and held in Europe—a common industrywide practice for this type of transaction, according to Madoff. (It wasn't.) "I alone am responsible for any wrongdoing on their part," he declared, "and will always suffer for the pain I caused my clients, my employees, and their families."

Despite being held in prison before the trial began, Bernie hovered over the Manhattan courtroom like an all-knowing apparition. His employees seemed like ordinary folks you'd stand next to on the subway, except that they'd simply had the misfortune to work for the greatest con man ever. Most of them started with Bernie right out of college—or even high school—and knew nothing about the financial world apart from what Madoff taught them. The company's offices were an insulated universe where the boss stovepiped his two hundred or so employees on a need-to-know basis—trying to keep them encased in separate cocoons. Many BLMIS personnel were instructed not to discuss their job duties with colleagues. When one of the five defendants, Jodi Crupi, who oversaw the Chase 703 Ponzi checking account, screwed up the courage to ask Bernie if she could study for a brokerage license, he told her no way.

"I think it's a Matrix problem," surmised John Zach, one of the Madoff Five prosecutors, during an informal talk with him and his colleagues five years after the trial concluded. (The prosecutors felt enough time had passed for them to open up about the case, and excerpts from the conversation are at the end of "Act 2.") "You're in 'the Matrix.' And in this world, you are accepting it as reality when, if you blink every day, your job is a fraud. It becomes the norm. It's human nature. It doesn't seem like fraud, because it's 'just work.'"

Julian Moore, a former prosecutor who spent dozens of hours debriefing DiPascali, likened the Madoff Five prosecution to an organized crime case—"much of it based on circumstantial evidence. . . . As Frank explained it, it was almost like a Mob organization in the way it worked. Most things operated with a wink and a nod. The avoidance of explicit statements of participation in a criminal enterprise allows for plausible deniability."

The defendants were convicted of a swath of crimes that boiled down to helping to fool investors. Specific charges for each are listed in the profiles below. They ranged from creating and backdating fake trades, to ginning up the company's financial ledgers; from feeding the SEC and outside auditors false information, to devising intricate computer programs that "randomized" numbers for regulators, auditors, and customers; from tax evasion and conspiracy, to the commission of bank fraud.

For five years, the case unspooled itself in the federal courthouse—hearings after hearings after hearings. It was capped by a nearly six-month trial, the only one for a total of fifteen individuals who have either pled or been convicted of crimes connected to Bernie. As such, it was the only case to shed any real light on the $68 billion fraud. That figure includes imaginary money that investors believed they had at the firm at the time of its collapse; the actual loss of principal was roughly $19 billion.

Judge Swain is known for "coming in hard" for the government after defense lawyers lose. Yet to the surprise of just about everyone following the case closely—including a handful of jury members who agreed to be interviewed—that didn't happen here.

The prosecutors won, 5–0 (or 59–0, as the jury convicted all five defendants on *every* count they faced). The defense lawyers then scored a coup of their own after Swain showed compassion for a whole slew of reasons—from the short stature of defendant Bongiorno (four foot seven inches on a good day) that the judge said could create extra problems for her in prison, to what she deemed an overly aggressive final address to the jury by the prosecution.

But the biggest reason seemed to be her conclusion that, while all of them benefited financially by either knowing or willfully blinding themselves to the fraud, they weren't its architects. Bongiorno was even granted a prison sentence lower than what her attorney had requested. Now, *that's* mercy.

At nearly six months, from jury selection to verdicts, the Madoff Five showdown is believed to be the lengthiest white-collar case in the history of the federal court for the Southern District of New York—sometimes called the nation's Mother Court. Notable cases that have been heard in that court range from life insurance claims from the 1912 sinking of the RMS *Titanic*, to the 2018 sentencing of Michael Cohen, who had served as Donald Trump's longtime personal legal counsel and personal fixer. The 1951 espionage trials of husband and wife Julius and Ethel Rosenberg and Alger Hiss. The administration of President Richard M. Nixon's failed attempt to stop the *New York Times* from publishing the damning Pentagon Papers in 1971. The Ivan Boesky insider trading case in 1986. Junk-bond king Michael Milken (1990). Mob boss John Gotti (1992). Omar Abdel Rahman, the "blind sheikh" behind the first terrorist bombing of the World Trade Center, in 1993. Plus dozens of other notable cases.

And now the Madoff Five, a case brought by the most prestigious prosecutorial corps in the world: the US Attorney's Office for New York's Southern District. It produced more than forty witnesses, twelve thousand–plus pages of transcripts, more than 1,242 filings in the court's docket system, and 500 *gigabytes* of government exhibits. Millions of documents—whatever Bernie and Frank hadn't shredded already—were stored in thousands of large banker boxes in a warehouse that was made available to the defense.

Let's meet the five defendants: their finances, plus some facts about their convictions, their sentences, what was predicted (based on an unofficial presentencing survey of many key players and observers), as well as how the prosecution and defense portrayed them.

DANIEL (DANNY) BONVENTRE, AGE SIXTY-EIGHT

Began working for Bernie: 1968.

Portrayed by prosecution as: director of operations at Madoff Securities who cooked the books on a par with Frank DiPascali—Bernie's right-hand man and the government's chief rat.

Portrayed by defense as: an unwitting participant in the fraud, manipulated and lied to for decades by Bernie and Frank.

Crimes convicted of: multiple counts of conspiracy; securities/bank/accounting fraud; falsifying records of a broker-dealer and investment advisor; false SEC filings; obstructing IRS; filing false tax returns.

Money: final salary, $1.3 million (more than $15 million from 1992 to 2008). Investment advisory account had $578K when he closed it in 2006.

Took the stand: yes.

Maximum faced: 220 years (70 years longer than Bernie's sentence).

Offer Danny rejected: no plea offer was ever made.

Courtroom polling: 13 to 17 years.

Prosecution wanted: any sentence above the probation office's recommendation.

Probation office recommended: 20 years.

His attorney, Andrew Frisch, requested: "home confinement and community service or, alternatively, a short term of incarceration."

Sentence: 10 years, with the judge recommending that the Bureau of Prisons allow Bonventre to serve the last year in home confinement.

Must forfeit: $155.6 billion.

JOANN (JODI) CRUPI, AGE FIFTY-THREE

Began working for Bernie: 1983.

Portrayed by prosecution as: comanager of Madoff's investment advisory unit who lied directly to customers, played a key role in deceiving the SEC and outside auditors, and kept meticulous track of the Ponzi bank account.

Portrayed by defense as: gullible employee under the sway of Madoff and DiPascali who was not aware of the fraud in which she participated.

Convicted of: conspiracy; securities and bank fraud; falsifying books and records of a broker-dealer and an investment advisor; tax fraud offenses.

Money: final salary, $290K; bought $2.2 million beach house in 2008 with company funds approved by Bernie.

Took the stand: no.

Maximum faced: 175 years.

Offer Jodi rejected: 10 years.

Courtroom polling: 10 to 12 years.

Prosecution wanted: anything higher than the probation office's recommendation.

Probation office recommended: 14 years.

Her attorney, Eric Breslin, requested: "mercy" and "a sentence that will allow Ms. Crupi at least some opportunity to be part of her children's lives before they are children no longer."

Sentence: 6 years, with the judge's recommendation that the last year be served in home confinement, plus 2 additional years of home confinement.

Must forfeit: $33.8 billion.

ANNETTE BONGIORNO, AGE SIXTY-SEVEN

Began working for Bernie: 1968.

Portrayed by prosecution as: comanager of Madoff's investment advisory unit and essential player in the fraud. Engaged knowingly in fake trading scheme since 1970s and used that knowledge to siphon millions of dollars from the fraud for herself.

Portrayed by defense as: longtime, unsophisticated employee— "naïve" and "foolish"—who idolized and was loyal to Bernie, who in turn betrayed her trust and used her as a puppet.

Convicted of: conspiracy; securities fraud; falsifying books and records of a broker-dealer and an investment advisor; obstructing IRS; filing false tax returns.

Money: final salary, $334K ($18.5 million total up to 2008); withdrew $3.7 million from IA account in 2008; account statement showed more than $50 million when the firm collapsed.

Took the stand: yes.

Maximum faced: 78 years.

Offer Annette rejected: no plea offer made, although her attorney, Roland Riopelle, says the prosecution offered to try to convince its bosses to authorize 15 years.

Courtroom polling: 12 to 15 years.

Prosecution wanted: anything higher than the probation office's recommendation.

Probation office recommended: 20 years.

Her attorney requested: 8 to 10 years.

Sentence: 6 years, with the judge recommending that the Bureau of Prisons allow her to serve the last year in home confinement.

Must forfeit (assuming she wins a lottery someday): $155.2 billion.

JEROME (JERRY) O'HARA, AGE FIFTY-ONE

Began working for Bernie: 1990.

Portrayed by prosecution as: knowing participant in the fraud since he began at Madoff Securities; computer programmer whose skills were limited to the use of a nearly obsolete programming language and who wrote hundreds of programs to create blatantly fraudulent books and records.

Essential player in deceiving the SEC, outside accountants, and the IRS.

Portrayed by defense as: diligent but inexperienced worker who was conned by his bosses, Madoff and DiPascali, and who joined the firm long after the computer system's basic architecture had already been designed and implemented.

Convicted of: multiple counts of conspiracy; securities fraud; falsifying the books and records of a broker-dealer and investment advisory firm.

Money: final salary, $312K; closed investment advisory account in 2006 (final balance: $578K); also closed three family accounts totaling $976K.

Took the stand: no.

Maximum faced: 100 years.

Offer Jerry rejected: a maximum of 5 years.

Courtroom polling: 7 to 8 years.

Prosecution requested: anything higher than the probation office's recommendation.

Probation office recommended: 8 years.

His attorney, Gordon Mehler, requested: "home confinement with community service, or, alternatively, a brief period of imprisonment."

Sentence: 2.5 years, with the judge recommending that the Bureau of Prisons place him in an alcohol treatment program that could trim six months off his sentence.

Must forfeit: $19.7 billion.

GEORGE PEREZ, AGE FORTY-NINE

Began working for Bernie: 1991.

Portrayed by prosecution as: same as O'Hara—a knowing participant in the fraud since he began at Madoff Securities; a computer programmer whose skills were limited to the use of a nearly obsolete programming language and who wrote hundreds of programs to create blatantly fraudulent books and records. Essential player in deceiving the SEC and outside accountants, as well as the IRS.

Portrayed by defense as: like O'Hara, a diligent but inexperienced worker who was conned by his bosses, Madoff and DiPascali, and who joined the firm long after the computer system's basic architecture had already been designed and implemented.

Convicted of: creating computer programs that were used to defraud clients and regulators. Specifically: multiple counts of conspiracy; securities fraud; falsifying the books and records of a broker-dealer and an investment advisory firm.

Money: final salary, $315K; closed investment advisory account in 2006 (final balance: $289K, which included a $120K deposit of his own funds).

Took the stand: no.

Maximum faced: 100 years.

Offer George rejected: a maximum of 5 years.

Courtroom polling: 7 to 8 years.

Prosecution wanted: anything higher than the probation office's recommendation.

Probation office recommended: 8 years.

His attorney, Larry Krantz, recommended: "home confinement or a period of brief incarceration followed by home
confinement."

Sentence: 2.5 years, with the judge recommending that the
Bureau of Prisons place him in the same alcohol treatment
program as O'Hara, which could trim six months off his sentence.

Must forfeit: $19.7 billion.

Prior to the Madoff Five trial, the three lead prosecutors—
Matthew Schwartz, John Zach, and Randall Jackson—worked some
of the biggest headline-generating cases on Wall Street: SAC Capital,
a $1.8 billion recovery after a hedge fund's insider trading guilty plea;
John Rigas and his two sons, for bilking billions from investors in
his family-run cable TV system Adelphia Communications Corporation; and Marc Dreier, perpetrator of a $400 million Ponzi scheme.

Madoff-related cases, too: JPMorgan Chase, without admitting
any wrongdoing, agreed to pay $2 billion to the feds and defrauded
Madoff investors in the largest-ever anti–money laundering pen-
alty. There was also the Jeffry Picower $7.2 billion settlement, the
country's largest-ever forfeiture, achieved in coordination with a
court-appointed bankruptcy trustee tasked with recovering funds
for investors. (The US Justice Department's Madoff Victim Fund received $2.2 billion of it, while $5 billion went to the trustee's fund for
customers.)

The lead defense lawyers, among the most eminent in New York's
criminal bar, brought a combined 150 years of experience into "the
well," the combat zone in front of the judge's bench. Andrew Frisch,
the lead lawyer for Bonventre, has practiced criminal law for more

than thirty years—eleven of them as a federal prosecutor. On the defense side, he obtained acquittals in his first two trials and won five of his first appeals—four of them in the US Court of Appeals for the Second Circuit, where reversals are rare.

Perez's lawyer, Larry Krantz, also has three decades (and two dozen cases) on his CV. As a prosecutor in the same district that tried the Madoff Five, he scored big wins in fraud, bribery, and Mafia cases. Krantz has also repped many criminals in cooperation deals with feds, including none other than Frank Pascali.

Yet another three-decade practitioner, Roland Riopelle (client: Annette Bongiorno), spent seven years prosecuting cases in the same US Attorney's Office, ranging from large commodity frauds to major drug cases. He has a rare chemistry with clients, which was clear enough on the morning of Bongiorno's sentencing. "I love him," she told me in a hallway outside the courtroom. "I called him last night to say that I was going to bake him cookies for today, but that I felt too stressed to do it."

Gordon Mehler, also with thirty years in the ring, is a former prosecutor who served as a deputy assistant attorney general in the President Bill Clinton administration. He is the lead author of a well-respected treatise on federal criminal law that, at 1,300 pages, is not recommended for lay readers.

Crupi's attorney, Eric Breslin, clerked in the early 1980s for a chief justice of the New Jersey Supreme Court and has since worked hundreds of cases. Among his many wins was a trial in Miami in which his client was charged with conspiracy and money laundering. Hearing the jury foreman repeat "Not guilty" more than seventy times for five defendants was one of those instances where, he recalled, "time really stood still, and my decision to become a lawyer seemed the best decision I had ever made."

In this contest, however, it was a boomerang for Breslin, as the jury foreman recited "Guilty" fifty-nine times for the Madoff Five. He and his colleagues had thought they had a good shot at acquittals.

Seesawing like a stock market, a few reporters in the gallery kept vacillating between guilt and innocence. Not the jurors, apparently.

Years after the Madoff Five verdicts, the prosecutors said they never doubted that the government would win. And the defense lawyers said they had little hope that their clients *could* win.

The verdict, reflects Mehler, "was heartbreaking. And, in retrospect, with the severe preexisting prejudice from anything associated with Bernie Madoff, I'm not sure we even had a *chance* with this jury"—a sentiment echoed by defender Riopelle. "From the beginning," he says, "I felt like it was a likely conviction. I didn't feel any different during the jury deliberations. In this case, given the notoriety of the case and nature of the proof, the defendants were gonna have a very hard time. No question."

Defendant Crupi, who almost always kept a roll of Life Savers in front of her on the defense table, shared her candy. Bongiorno baked cookies at Christmastime and passed them around the courtroom. (The prosecutors declined.) On the morning of her sentencing, to my astonishment, Annette greeted me outside the court with a hug and said she was wondering if I'd be showing up. When I told her I'd experienced a kind of post-traumatic stress disorder following the verdicts, she laughed and said, "Me, too!"

Yet, while I found Bongiorno likable, it's worth keeping in mind the unfortunate plight of her cousin Guido Parente, a home builder in Florida. He had invested with Madoff starting in the 1980s, thanks to Bongiorno's encouraging him to do so—and lost $1.2 million when the Ponzi exploded.

Parente and his wife were close to the Bongiornos; the four socialized often. "She thought she was better than everyone else," he recalls about Annette, adding that she was rude to waiters. "We [my family] were laughing a lot when we found out she went to jail. Because every time we went out to dinner, it never failed that she sent the food back. There was always something wrong. 'This is not good, too tough, too rare, too green. Get me another one.' And now that she's in jail, we say, 'I wonder if she sends the food back.'"

But the families were once friendly. "That's what ticks me off," he says. "Every time the stock market went down, I used to ask, 'How's the money doing?' And she used to laugh and say, 'Don't worry, your money's safe, you're doing good.'" Did she ever say how that was possible? "She could never give me a clear answer. Now I see that it didn't make sense. The statements would come every month; there was never a loss."

Following Madoff's arrest, Annette and husband Rudy came down to Florida to stay awhile. Parente says that "she was afraid" to get together with him. But they finally went out to dinner, in February or March 2009. Naturally, Parente had lots of questions for her: What happened? What went on? Why can't Madoff just say he lost money in the stock market if it's a legitimate business? Annette got angry and responded, "I can't talk about it. I won't talk about it."

When Rudy tried to explain the situation and "give me some kind of excuse," Annette "jumped on him, and I haven't talked with them since. Why wouldn't she want to talk about it? She's working for the place when things went bad. If I'm only a worker, why would I get excited and upset—why wouldn't I talk with my cousin and say the company went bad, the boss is bad, or something like that? Why would she be upset with *me*? Now I realize why, because she was involved in the whole thing."

For most of the trial, Rudy sat in a tiny section of the gallery that had the only padded chairs. He often wore the same shlumpy casual clothes, and liked jiggling coins in his pockets. He chortled more than a hundred times during the trial and whispered about the case. Shushing him never helped whenever it appeared that even the judge and jury could hear him. His constant giggling didn't help his wife's case with jurors, some of them told me.

There's an endless amount of tedium to endure when attending a lengthy criminal trial, particularly the longest white-collar trial in the history of the Southern District. (Bongiorno attorney Riopelle played solitaire on his computer during long stretches that focused on other defendants.) But in between the dullest parts, illuminating gems and jewels pop up in testimony and exhibits alike. In this case, some of the revelations concerned the Madoff family and their roles and possible culpability.

The extraordinary length and acrimony of the Madoff Five case also forged strong bonds among defense lawyers and their clients, and among the prosecution team. It was like an episode of the reality-TV show *Survivor*, but with fewer bugs. Indeed, the prosecutors were physically separated for almost a year from their colleagues at the US Attorney's Office, with no rescue in sight.

On the defense side, Kimberly Yuhas, cocounsel for George Perez, struck up a close friendship with defendant Bongiorno, even though she didn't represent her. Before Bongiorno skipped off to prison, the women got together roughly once a month, on some occasions for Broadway shows. (Matinees *only*, as Bongiorno had a court-imposed curfew and had often been required to wear an ankle bracelet monitoring her movements.) They also gathered at Annette's now-forfeited mansion, where she taught Kim her recipe for meatballs.

The two women formed "a mother-daughter-type relationship," says the young attorney. "The way that Annette shows love is to cook for people." Prosecutors could scarcely contain themselves after Bongiorno attorney Riopelle went into detail for the jury about how the childless Annette was "everyone's aunt," spending time in the kitchen whipping up traditional Italian food; you could have seen their eyes roll from as far away as Palermo.

Riopelle, an opera buff, started sharing a Metropolitan Opera subscription with Crupi's lawyer, Breslin, whose father was the manager of the beloved operatic tenor Luciano Pavarotti. (They didn't know each other before this case.) Breslin says that he suffered from a form of post-traumatic stress after the trial ended, and not because his client lost. Several jurors endured similar fates.

"Two weeks after the trial, I went to San Francisco to visit my daughter," recounted Breslin several months later, "and looked at the bay and was like, 'Oh my God, it's over, and I'm alive.' It's a little like being at war, like *The Best Years of Our Lives*, that movie about all the guys who came back from war. I still don't feel like I fit at home anymore, I don't feel in sync with anyone anymore."

Assistant US attorneys in the Southern District typically have a five-year run, at which point they jump to prestigious criminal-defense law firms. Not so the thirty-seven-year-old Matthew Schwartz, who became the lead investigative prosecutor of the Madoff Five case. He spent nearly twice that amount of time honing his skills there on cases such as the JPMorgan Chase–Madoff anti–money laundering prosecution, and a lengthy tug-of-war with Madoff customer Jeffry Picower's estate. A graduate of Columbia Law School, he also clerked for two top judges, including the late Connecticut governor and congressman Thomas ("Tough Tommy") Meskill Jr., who was known for rarely walking away from a good fight.

Throughout this trial, Matt was deadpan, sardonic, not prone to displays of exuberance—and rarely swearing, except strategically. He doesn't telegraph his jokes. "That's because I don't care if you laugh," he once said to a colleague.

That dry wit was on display when he cross-examined a former FBI agent who had been retained by BLMIS computer programmers O'Hara and Perez. Astonishingly, the defendants had written and mailed eerily similar letters to themselves in 2006 stating that they were uncomfortable with certain tasks they were asked to do and feared the consequences of refusing to do them.

"I am writing this letter out of fear. Fear for my job, fear for my family, fear for my life as I know it today," both letters began, before eventually adding: "I cannot afford to quit my job at this time."

Presumably, they wrote the letters as a possible hedge against future problems, such as the pickle they were currently in. Their defense lawyers turned over those letters to prosecutors—a highly risky gamble that backfired with jurors.

On one dramatic afternoon, the defense lawyers played the jury a 2012 video that showed an ex–FBI agent using purple gloves to open the sealed letters, so as not to leave fingerprints. Like one of the PriceWaterhouseCoopers accountants guarding the Oscar envelopes, only in a much better suit.

During his cross of the former G-man, Schwartz made his deadpan move to mock the show. He handed him the original letters—protected by plastic Ziploc bags, courtesy of the defense lawyers—to validate their authenticity.

Q: You were wearing gloves in the video. Is that right?
A: Yes.

Q: And that's so the evidence isn't contaminated in any way?
A: Yes, my fingerprints wouldn't be on the documents.

Q: Right. And were you able to confirm that Mr. O'Hara's fingerprints were the only fingerprints on the letter that purports to be from him?

KRANTZ: Objection, your Honor, scope.
COURT: Overruled.

A: I have no idea about his fingerprints.

Q: Okay. Did you do any fingerprint testing?
A: No.

Q: DNA testing?
A: No.

Q: Handwriting analysis?
A: No.

Q: Okay. So I'm going to ask you to look at the originals. We should probably then preserve their evidentiary value. I brought some gloves, so you can open them up. [*The gloves were purple, just like the pair Dotlo wore in the video.*]

Anyone over the age of forty might now be recalling the everlasting moment during the 1995 murder trial of O. J. Simpson, when a prosecutor asked the football legend to slip on a pair of leather gloves found at the murder scene—prompting his attorney to tell the jury: "If it doesn't fit, you must acquit."

But Krantz was in no mood for laughter. He leapt from his chair, fuming and looking perplexed. After all, the prosecutors had stipulated to the authenticity of the letters before the trial even began. He felt the questions by Schwartz violated the spirit of that stipulation. On the other hand, the prosecutors themselves had already put the letters into evidence, as support for *their* case. So maybe they thought there was no need for the defense lawyers to even bring a former FBI agent—with the credibility such a title has for jurors—into the courtroom, let alone have the elaborate video display, in an attempt to lend heft to their case.

KRANTZ: Your Honor, there is no need for the gloves, it's not—they're no longer in any state that needs to be preserved. They're here! The jury can see and touch them. There's no need for gloves.

COURT: Well, since there's no objection to the handling of them without the gloves, you needn't put the gloves on.

It was too late. The joke went off. Krantz hadn't seen the gloves coming. Nobody did. Jurors were titillated. "He just *gets* it," says Danya Perry, a former prosecutor who worked on big cases with Schwartz. "Obviously, in a case like Madoff, which is massive and involves staggering numbers of documents and witnesses, you need someone who won't be distracted by all the sideshows. Matt has a laser-like focus and precision." His reputation in the office, she says, is possessing a consistent ability to take knotty issues and distill.

To sink the two programmers, Schwartz and an expert from IBM reconstructed how the defendants used special software installed on the outdated IBM AS/400 computer system to create false data for client statements, hoodwinking auditors and SEC regulators.

Schwartz and the IBM-er laid the geekspeak on thick for the jury, rolling out concepts and terms such as "linear congruential generators," plus dozens of programs and data files with names as comprehensible as TRDENT, BKCS48, CASH1702, TRADE17, BTS007, DFC021, DTC021, and M1, M2, M3, M4.

One juror nodded off during the seminar, but the rest sat transfixed. "He explained and proved that many of the computer programs and reports were artificial and consciously created," recalls juror Craig Parise, a fifth-grade schoolteacher. "At the least, he proved Jerry and George had their names all over them. It wasn't a line of mistakes unknowingly designed."

The backdrop to that high-tech material was not unlike the labyrinth of generators, transmission lines, and transformers that deliver power to a juror's light switches at home. It was so complicated that

Schwartz (who has a degree in physics) and FBI agent Paul Roberts (who studied computer science before becoming an actuarial analyst) worked with their IBM expert to devise a presentation for the jury that wasn't ready until midway through the trial.

The demonstration took many hundreds of the computer programs and procedures that had been used on the investment advisory side of Madoff Securities (where the Ponzi scheme lived and breathed) for a fifteen-year-period prior to the firm's demise in 2008 and combined them into a boiled-down, interactive court exhibit. It was such a beast—with thousands of enticing links a user could click on—that defense lawyers and even their own hired computer expert struggled for days to figure it out. "It was easily the most complex exhibit I have ever seen as a trial lawyer," says Krantz, "and it was the only case where I ever had to inspect an exhibit for days, mid-trial." The jury members were shown only a fraction of the exhibit, so as not to overwhelm them.

One of the worst moments for defendant Jodi Crupi, a top manager whose core duties for years included tracking the bank account Madoff used for his Ponzi, came when Schwartz poked fun at her expense (and expenses).

Prosecutors displayed her Madoff Securities corporate American Express card statements on screens throughout the courthouse. They included charges such as $126,113 for travel, including cruises and trips to Disney World; $13,591 at an Italian restaurant near her home in New Jersey; $5,473 at Best Friends Pet Care; even $40,371 spent at one wine store, plus another $4,905 on bottles of alcohol purchased elsewhere. "Very telling," says juror Nancy Goldberg, who works as an instructor for at-risk students. "It was just mind-boggling. I'd like the wine list from Jodi. I'd like to know her favorite wine."

Prosecutor Schwartz made sure that the jurors never forgot about it. Crupi's attorney, Eric Breslin, put only two witnesses on the stand for his client's case. One of them, a close friend of the defendant's for fifteen years, was crossed by the prosecutor for barely one minute.

Q: You like her and think well of her?
A: I adore her. I think she is great. We will be friends forever.

Q: You go to her house, she comes to your house?
A: Yes.

Q: She's a good host, is that right?
A: I like to think we both are, but yes.

Q: She has a great wine collection?

Some jurors giggled quietly.

BRESLIN: *Objection.*
COURT: Sustained. *[Translation: The jury is to disregard that question that it will not be able to disregard.]*
SCHWARTZ: No further questions.

Another longtime friend of Crupi's attested to her honesty, trustworthiness, and their experiences as mothers. Schwartz's cross took well under a minute:

Q: You have gone on vacations together?
A: Yes we have.

Q: She goes on vacations without you?
A: I suppose.

Q: She took her kids to Disney World. Do you remember that?

BRESLIN: *Objection,* your honor.

COURT: Sustained.

SCHWARTZ: Nothing further.

The government's main witness in the Madoff Five case was, of course, Frank DiPascali, Bernie's right hand, who joined the company in 1975. If the jury members needed a lifeline in this complex and interminable case, Frankie was it, as he pointed a finger at each of the defendants. If the jury believed he was telling the truth, they'd convict all five, perhaps quickly. If they thought he was a liar, as the defense tried to show, they might be deliberating for a very long time. Five jurors interviewed afterward (the others wouldn't talk) all say they found him credible.

"I felt that what he [DiPascali] was saying was true," says Antwane Joseph, a disability rehabilitation counselor who served as the jury foreman. "I thought what he was describing, the different conversations he was having with people, seemed as if those things were taking place. It didn't seem like he was creating them."

Jurors also found Frank charismatic. "Like him, I'm a fisherman, and I happen to be a hockey fan of the team he's a fan of as well," says juror Parise. Frank owned expensive sportfishing boats, paid for by Madoff—the last one a sixty-one-footer that cost $2.2 million—and used his corporate AmEx card to charge $25,000 per year on New Jersey Devils tickets. "I related to that guy immediately. I was like, I would love to have dinner with him and listen to his stories.

"But if he was on trial," he adds, "I would have found him guilty too."

FBI agents spent hundreds of hours debriefing DiPascali, as did prosecutor Zach, who holed up with the witness for months in a shabby government war room reviewing the case detail by detail. He then put Frank on the stand for roughly thirty hours of direct testimony, during which they took the jurors on a vivid and intricate journey through BLMIS. DiPascali was straightforward, but nervous during his breaks on a courtroom deck, where he would chain-smoke cigarettes all the way down to the filters. Perhaps he did so because he'd had to forfeit all his assets and had to make the most of each butt.

Juror Gloria Wynn, while finding Frank credible, exploded in heavy laughter as she recalled him testifying. "I think I kept writing in my notes, 'Goodfellas, Goodfellas, Goodfellas,'" says Wynn, a church pastor in the Bronx. "It was just like watching *Goodfellas*. But I think he was very much himself. I don't think he put on any airs. He was just who he was."

The thirty-nine-year-old Zach, born and reared in small towns in the habitually affable Midwest, had lots of prior experience getting criminal witnesses (often gangsters) to bond with him. An amiable, laidback personality also wins over jurors. With DiPascali the central pillar of the government's case, pretty much everything depended on Zach. And he delivered.

"John is a skilled advocate, with an easygoing manner and a lot of jury appeal—not many people can claim that when you're in court," says Antonia Apps, a former top prosecutor who worked cases with Zach, including the corrupt SAC Capital affair. "He's one of the most experienced trial lawyers to come out of the office in a long time."

Early in the trial, Zach set the table for the jury by calling Bruce Dubinsky to the witness box. Dubinsky wore four hats for the occasion: accountant, certified fraud examiner, computer forensics expert, and former registered investment advisor. He worked for years analyzing some fifty million transactions inside Madoff Securities for Picard, the court-appointed trustee. At a warehouse where Madoff didn't get around to shredding papers, Dubinsky spent many weeks climbing in sneakers onto hundreds of banker boxes stacked from floor to ceiling—a forensics expert's dream. Stephen Harbeck, the former president of the Securities Investment Protection Corporation, says that the mental picture he carries with him from his own visits to the banker boxes is that last scene in the action film *Raiders of the Lost Ark*, "where they are taking the ark in a wooden crate and wheeling it into a gigantic warehouse. And that's where Bernie's records were. And everything in there, except the bank deposits and withdrawals, was fiction. So, reconstructing that was just an enormous task, and that's what we had to do with respect to each account to figure out what these people were owed."

In the Madoff Five trial, over the course of four days, Dubinsky laid out his findings on the key mechanisms of the Ponzi. Although Dubinsky was not permitted to opine on wrongdoing by the five defendants, defense lawyers couldn't lay a fingerprint on him. "My antennas were up," says juror Sheila Amato, an art teacher, who remembers feeling that some of the defendants were guilty after Dubinsky's presentation. "But at that point, I wasn't sure if they *all* were."

The trial's *Perry Mason* moment was Zach's cross of Annette Bongiorno. Standing four foot seven, she was within the technical bar for dwarfism; among themselves, FBI agents referred to their investigation of her as Operation Troll Hunt. Sitting in the witness box, her feet didn't touch the floor. Poor Annette was the butt of insults. After a tabloid suggested that Bernie had once had an affair with her, he phoned me in a rage, asking if it was somehow mentioned in court. "As if I'm going to have an affair with her—someone who looks like a fire hydrant!" he huffed.

Annette's attorney, Roland Riopelle, had spoken earlier of his client's "naivete" and "foolishness." On the stand, Bongiorno portrayed herself as a simple Italian American woman from the outer boroughs of New York who enjoyed family, friends, and cooking; and who loved and idolized the company CEO (to the point of keeping a photo of Madoff inscribed "My Hero" on her desk). She was loyal to a fault, said Riopelle, and she had wanted only to be his secretary despite Bernie's insistence on promoting her to manage the department that produced account statements for many of BLMIS's long-term investors. At sentencing, the judge noted her "borderline competence to do the complex clerical work that she had agreed to do" for Madoff.

When reminiscing about her childhood, Annette recalled Frank's mother crying on her stoop about her teenage son's bleak future. According to Bongiorno, she enthusiastically recommended DiPascali to Madoff, saying, "He's a very smart young man, and he's pumping gas, and he needs a job. . . . I know him for many, many years. He's a good kid."

Riopelle, speaking to me after the trial, says he was dumbfounded. "I mean, Jesus, that's one of the best, most ironic tidbits in the whole story." Mrs. DiPascali's "ne'er-do-well son was failing in school. My client gets the guy a job where he earns and steals millions, and then he turns on her and tries to dig himself out of the hole he got himself into by testifying against her. As far as I am concerned, Mr. DiPascali is a disgrace to the Italian people."

DiPascali declined to be interviewed—he wouldn't even take my business card outside the courtroom; FBI agent Paul Takla spread out his arms to prevent anyone from getting close to Frank.

In describing her lifestyle, Annette told the jury that she wasn't a big spender on luxuries such as clothes and holidays. Zach pounced. He reminded Bongiorno that her lawyer had previously asked her questions about the $50 million listed on her final IA:

Q: Your answer was, no, it didn't seem ridiculous to you. Do
    you recall that answer?
A: Yes.

Q: The reason—one of the reasons—that you said having that high amount in your account didn't seem ridiculous to you was because you were, quote, someone who never splurged on anything major. You said you didn't spend money on shoes and pocketbooks and vacations. Do you recall saying that?

A: I said I didn't buy, you know, top of the line. I didn't go overboard with those things. I wasn't, like, really spending a fortune on them.

Zach approached the witness box to show her a photo.

Q: Is that your car?
A: Yes.

ZACH: The government offers 6000-111.
RIOPELLE: Objection.

Both teams headed into the Judge Swain's robing room for a pow-wow out of the jury's sight.

The car in question was a *Bentley*—by most anyone's definition, a top-of-the-line vehicle. At the start of the trial, Riopelle had succeeded in convincing the judge that the jury should *not* be told about specific luxury items, such as her Gatsbyesque house or the Bentley, because it might unduly prejudice them against her. But Annette's having mentioned her spending habits regarding pocketbooks and shoes put that favorable ruling in jeopardy. It had made her lawyer cringe, while the prosecutors looked at one another and smiled. They knew instantly that the Bentley would now be allowed to be introduced to jurors.

It didn't take long, but what took place behind those closed doors between prosecutors, Riopelle, and the judge was in effect a burial service for his client. If Bongiorno had even the faintest chance with jurors, this snuffed it out permanently.

In the robing room:

"Your Honor," said Riopelle, "this is the Bentley automobile that I think the court precluded proof relating to my client's expenditures on what Karl Marx would have described as needless luxuries. . . . I think Mr. Zach takes the position that I have opened the door."

JUDGE SWAIN: And you have.
RIOPELLE: Fair enough.

A late-model silver Bentley owned by Bongiorno soon appeared on the screens, and the jury learned next that she also owned two Mercedes-Benzes. After that, Zach handed jurors copies of a brochure for Annette's planned condo in Boca Raton.

Q: When you testified on direct that you didn't splurge on anything major, that did not include the Bentley?
A: What I believe I said was—

Q: Ms. Bongiorno, "yes," "no," or "I can't answer."
A: I did not include the Bentley because I wasn't answering . . . What is the question? I'm sorry.

Bongiorno then confirmed that it was "one" of her cars—adding quickly that it had been confiscated by the government—thus inviting the prosecutor to ask about other cars. She conceded she owned two Mercedes.

Q: On your direct examination, you were asked about homes that you owned and that you were moving in 2007 and 2008. Do you recall that?
A: Yes.

1

Bernie, age twenty-two, giving a toast at a friend's wedding in Manhattan in 1960 (the year he launched BLMIS).

Ruth and Bernie's engagement announcement. He was twenty; she was seventeen. It's hard to imagine that the ring mentioned in this 1958 article is the same "engagement ring" that was valued at about $300,000 after Bernie's arrest (and sold at auction for $550,000). But anything's possible.

Long Island Daily Press

MONDAY, DECEMBER 8, 1958

Madoff—Alpern

The engagement of Laurelton students Ruth Alpern and Bernard L. Madoff was today announced by her parents, Mr. and Mrs. Saul Alpern of 137-25 224th St.

Both are graduates of Far Rockaway High School.

Miss Alpern is now attending Queens College.

Her fiance, the son of Mr. and Mrs. Ralph Madoff of 139-54 228th St., is in his senior year at Hofstra College.

2

RUTH ALPERN
Wears New Ring

3

The Madoffs on May 18, 1974, at a friend's son's Bar Mitzvah in Roslyn, New York, where Bernie and Ruth lived at the time. It was also the day of Ruth's thirty-third birthday. Standing (left to right) are brothers Peter, then age twenty-seven, and Bernie, then thirty-five. Seated (left to right) are Ruth and Peter's wife, Marion, then twenty-six. The man in the back is Aaron Korman, a Dreyfus mutual fund manager and close family friend who was one of Bernie's first backers in the early 1960s.

The nineteenth floor BLMIS trading room, circa 1990s, where the *real* trades were being done by the broker-dealer unit. Andrew Madoff is standing with a phone in the middle of the right half of the photo. Bernie is watching from afar—way in the back of the right half of the photo—phone in hand, arm bent at his waist.

Madoff leaves court on January 14, 2009, after a judge ruled that he could continue to remain free on bail—rejecting a bid by prosecutors to jail him pending trial due to his violation of a court order that froze his assets. (He and Ruth had illicitly mailed more than $1 million in jewelry to family and friends over the holidays.)

The media orgy outside the courthouse in Manhattan on June 29, 2009, the day Madoff was sentenced. Inside, a second (overflow) room had to be set up for spectators to watch by closed-circuit TV.

7

A demonstrator displays a placard expressing his feelings toward Madoff as the fraudster is about to leave his Manhattan penthouse apartment to attend a bail hearing on January 14, 2009.

A protestor expresses her view of the SEC outside the courthouse during the sentencing hearing for Madoff, June 29, 2009. An opposing view: "The agency's mandate is not to protect investors from dumb investments," says former SEC attorney Ernest Badway.

9

An illustration of Ponzi "monster" Madoff portrayed as the Joker from *Batman* is seen on the cover of *New York* magazine at a newsstand, February 24, 2009, in New York City.

10

The front page of the *Daily News* on March 12, 2009, the day Bernie pled guilty. The page reads "RUTH-LESS: Evil Bernie spends final night of luxury with wife Ruth. Today a judge should finally put Ponzi king behind bars."

The federal prison in Butner, North Carolina, where Madoff was housed from July 2009 until his death in April 2021.

12

Bernie's niece, Shana Madoff, attends a benefit hosted by the Central Park Conservancy on June 7, 2006, in Manhattan. As the compliance counsel at BLMIS, she came close to being indicted, according to investigators. Her father, Peter, the chief compliance officer, pled guilty.

13

Bernie's younger brother Peter Madoff, the former senior managing director and head of compliance at BLMIS, exits federal court on June 29, 2012, after pleading guilty to conspiracy and fraud. He received a prenegotiated ten-year prison sentence, which caused heated disagreements inside the US Attorney's Office.

14

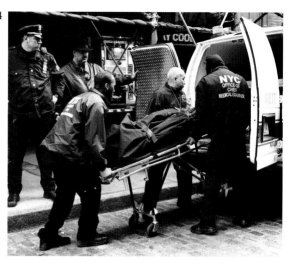

Medical examiners removing the body of Bernie's son Mark Madoff, age forty-six, after he hanged himself in his Manhattan apartment on December 11, 2010—the second anniversary of his father's arrest for perpetrating the Ponzi scheme. "Nobody wants to believe the truth," he said in an email to his attorney.

15

Andrew Madoff on *60 Minutes*, October 30, 2011. His appearance on the show with his mother, Ruth, was the first time they talked publicly after Bernie's 2008 arrest. "I've had absolutely nothing to hide," he stated. "And I've been eager, I would say almost *desperate* to speak out publicly and tell people that I'm absolutely not involved." But he and Ruth never cooperated with law enforcement, and they carefully controlled future media interviews.

16

In this December 2013 photo, DiPascali (in trench coat) is en route to the courthouse, accompanied by his main FBI handler, Shannon Fish. Government investigators considered him one of the best and most honest cooperators they ever worked with.

Frank DiPascali, exiting federal court on December 4, 2013. He was Bernie's chief deputy-in-crime, as well as the feds' top turncoat against the "Madoff Five"—the only criminal trial for the fifteen individuals who either pled guilty or were convicted for crimes.

The Madoff Five's Dan Bonventre, leaving court following a hearing in February 2010. The former operations chief was convicted of crimes including conspiracy, bank and accounting fraud, falsifying records of an investment advisor, and falsifying SEC filings.

17

18

19

The Madoff Five's Jerry O'Hara (left) and George Perez, outside the courthouse on December 9, 2014, following their sentencing hearing. The two computer programmers wrote or modified hundreds of programs that were used to create fraudulent books and records.

20

The Madoff Five's Jodi Crupi arriving at court on October 8, 2013. She rose from a job as a keypuncher to overseeing the Ponzi's Chase checking account. She was sentenced to six years for conspiracy, securities and bank fraud, falsifying the books of an investment advisor, and other crimes.

21

The Madoff Five's Annette Bongiorno exits the courthouse on March 24, 2014, with her attorney, Roland Riopelle, after her conviction on charges that she helped facilitate Madoff's Ponzi scheme. Poor Annette: FBI agents nicknamed their investigation of her "Operation Troll Hunt."

22

Suited up: Madoff Five prosecutors Matthew Schwartz (left), Randall "Action" Jackson (center), and John Zach (right) after their big win. Schwartz: "You could investigate this case for fifty years and not be done."

23

RUN, IT'S THE FEDS!: On August 4, 2010, the feds on many Madoff-related cases enjoyed a "team dinner" at Montebello restaurant in Manhattan. Among the attendees are, front row (left to right): prosecutor Lisa Baroni; FBI agents Julia Hanish, Keith Kelly, and Steven "Garf" Garfinkel. Back row, far left, is FBI agent Jared Thompson. FBI agent Paul "Tak" Takla is in front of the painting in the center. Behind him is prosecutor Julian Moore. Beneath the right sconce is FBI agent Paul Roberts, and next to him in the necktie is prosecutor Matt Schwartz.

The Ponzi "trading desk": This unassuming table on the seventeenth floor was Ground Zero for history's greatest financial fraud. Several employees sat there, churning out false account statements for thousands of customers. The central mechanism was the backdated trade confirmation slip. It doesn't take a genius to predict the past.

24

25

Starting in 1987, Bernie's business was housed on three floors in the iconic Lipstick Building, named as such because the thirty-four-story red-granite skyscraper resembles a giant tube of lipstick. Fred Wilpon, co-owner of the New York Mets, co-owned the building and gave him a sweet deal. Wilpon and his brother-in-law Saul Katz opened and administered nearly 500 Madoff accounts.

26

Dimon in the rough: JPMorgan Chase CEO Jamie Dimon looks on during the inauguration of the bank's new French headquarters in Paris on June 29, 2021. Bernie ran his [latest estimate] $68 billion Ponzi mainly out of a single Chase checking account. The bank publicly maintained that "all personnel acted in good faith" during the decades of its relationship with Madoff." It wasn't true.

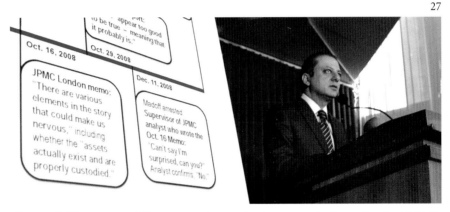

27

Close call: There was public outrage that no bankers were indicted for the 2008 financial crisis. It turns out that one Chase banker came close, although he's not identified by name in the deferred prosecution agreement (DPA) that the bank signed with the feds. A poster board details key events in the Madoff-Chase timeline, as US Attorney Preet Bharara announced at a press conference on January 7, 2014, that the bank would pay a record-breaking $2.6 billion in fines, penalties, and settlements for having overlooked the obvious.

28

Not Bernie's "criminal soulmate" but . . . Trustee Irving Picard went too far when he tagged Orthodox Jewish grandmother Sonja Kohn with that label in a lawsuit he filed against her in December 2010, seeking $19 billion. (He removed those words in an amended complaint.) Nonetheless, the Austrian businesswoman, who owned a bank in Vienna, overlooked the obvious while helping funnel many billions to Bernie.

Bernie's actual criminal soulmate may have been Jeffry Picower, who drowned to death a year after Madoff was arrested. He had $7.2 billion in ill-gotten gains (most of it parked at Goldman Sachs), the most Ponzi loot for any single Madoff investor. When his widow, Barbara, reluctantly returned the money, it was the largest civil forfeiture in history.

29

30

31

Enjoying a laugh: New York Mets' co-owners Fred Wilpon (right) and his brother-in-law Saul Katz exiting federal court on March 19, 2012, the day that a lawsuit against them by Madoff trustee Irving Picard (seeking $303 million in Ponzi winnings) was set to begin. Instead, they settled for $162 million.

Ruth Madoff stepping out for grocery and pharmacy shopping on June 28, 2017, in Old Greenwich, Connecticut, one day after the feds and trustee Irving Picard recovered $23 million in assets from the estates of her and Bernie's late sons Mark and Andrew. Ruth herself was allowed to keep $2.5 million.

At a warehouse in Long Island City, Queens, where Bernie didn't get around to shredding papers, thousands of boxes of BLMIS documents were discovered by feds. These rows of banker boxes mostly contained printouts of fake trades.

32

33

At the Tuck-It-Away storage facility in Brooklyn a manager says that from the mid-1990s until 2004, Madoff was the largest tenant—renting twenty-seven rooms, each piled with paper. In Room 310 sat an oversized shredding machine. No other customer at the facility had ever conducted a shredding operation there.

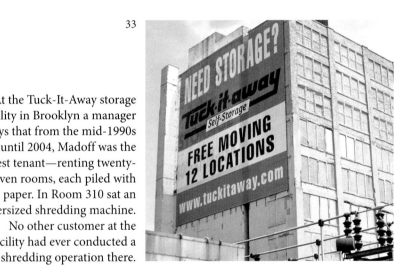

34

In Bernie's warehouse in Queens, in the summer of 2012, forensic fraud expert Bruce Dubinsky is looking at documents to ascertain whether any of Madoff's trades were real. He laid out his findings for jurors in a presentation during the Madoff Five criminal trial, as well as in voluminous reports for trustee Picard's civil cases.

35

The Madoffs' seized oceanfront house in Montauk, Long Island, was sold for $9.4 million at auction in 2009. Their Manhattan penthouse went for $8 million; the Palm Beach house for $5.6 million; and their apartment in the south of France fetched $1.3 million.

36

The front of Bernie and Ruth's lakefront home in Palm Beach on December 15, 2008, four days after his arrest.

37

Shoe fetish: More than 400 lots of Bernie and Ruth's personal possessions were auctioned off in November 2010 in New York (one of several auctions). Pictured are some of the roughly 250 pairs of shoes he owned, many of them never worn.

A life ring marked "BULLSHIP" aboard one of Bernie's boats. In case his friends and investors missed that memo, he also kept a Claes Oldenberg sculpture of a "soft" screw behind his office desk.

Protestors stringing up a banner across Bernie's yacht (aptly named *Bull*) in Antibes, southern France, on May 16, 2009. It was during a gathering to ask for a tax on the tonnage of yachts in Europe. The banner reads: "We won't pay for swindlers."

Ruth's 10.54-carat diamond "engagement ring," estimated to be worth about $300,000 to $350,000, fetched $550,000 at auction in 2010.

41

Bernie's closet in his Manhattan penthouse (pictured here shortly after his arrest) contained a large amount of clothing and shoes that were never worn. A self-described obsessive-compulsive, he owned dozens of the same shirt, all in blue.

42

Clawback Irving: Madoff trustee Picard leaves US Bankruptcy Court in New York on February 2, 2010. By his latest calculations, of the $19 billion in loss of principal invested directly by individual customers (and excluding the $49 billion in phantom profits they thought they had), a bankruptcy record-smashing 75 percent had been recovered by spring 2024. Those figures exclude the indirect investors in feeder funds.

43

Whistleblower Harry Markopolos tries out a whistle before speaking at a business ethics forum at Suffolk University in Boston on April 1, 2010. He may go down in history as the heroic "no one would listen to" tipster about Madoff. But he doesn't deserve to be.

44

Uncle Al and Aunt Adele Behar in 1973, pre-Madoff: Adele lost everything to Bernie, but—unlike most investors—she took full responsibility for it and didn't blame the SEC for not catching the fraudster. "*No way* am I a victim," she said shortly after his arrest. "I'm a survivor. The government owes me nothing."

45

A protestor holds a sign that reads "Santander, where is my money?" during a demonstration in front of the Central Bank of Spain in Madrid on February 28, 2009. Santander clients had huge losses from financial products linked to failing companies such as Madoff and Lehman Brothers.

Continuation of FD-302 of ___FRANK DIPASCALI___ , On _4/15-06/09/09_ , Page _46_

went upstairs and was looking at MADOFF in his office just staring at his computer screen like he was comatose. DIPASCALI had noticed that MADOFF was under tremendous stress for the past few weeks. DIPASCALI went into MADOFF's office eventually and MADOFF finally said: "I'm at the end of my rope." DIPASCALI did not know what he meant. MADOFF said: "I don't have any money." DIPASCALI could not believe what he was hearing. MADOFF went on: "The whole business has been a scam. It goes all the way back to MOE (STEINBERG) and goes back to ABE (HERSHON)." Even though DIPASCALI had long ago realized the trades were not real, he still believed, and had been convinced by MADOFF, that the money was somewhere. MADOFF was telling him there was no money. DIPASCALI was frantic. MADOFF seemed at peace with it by this time, but DIPASCALI kept yelling at him, not believing what was happening. MADOFF told him he was making a scene and that he should calm down. Then DIPASCALI knew he had to calm down and start thinking. He felt they needed to

What DiPascali told the FBI: In hundreds of hours of meetings with the feds, Frank DiPascali, Bernie's chief deputy-in-crime, laid out the details. Above is an excerpt from the more than 100 pages of confidential documents known as FBI 302s. In this particular session, attended by nine prosecutors and FBI agents, DiPascali recounted the moment Bernie first told him that he was out of money—and that the fraud went "all the way back to Moe and goes back to Abe."

Q: I think you also testified when you were being asked about the amount in your IA account that the homes that you had were not decorated like palaces?

A: Right.

And so it went for poor, mega-rich Annette. Jurors had been told previously that Bongiorno had more than $50 million (in largely fictional money, of course) in various investment accounts with Bernie on the day the firm collapsed. She had also withdrawn more than $10 million over the years. Considering her thin résumé and only a high school diploma, jurors wondered how she could not have ever asked herself whether a fortune in the middle eight figures was possible for someone like her without it all being a huge fraud. That $50 million exceeded the combined accounts, on the day of the company's meltdown, of the *entire* Madoff family. (In fairness to Annette, they withdrew tens of millions *prior* to Bernie's arrest.)

Zach introduced a document that had the words "Fake Sales" on it in her handwriting. It was about to get even worse for Annette, and, in many ways, this next moment in the courtroom could stand out for historians as the essence of the Madoff Five phenomena.

Zach displayed records showing that in October 2008 Bongiorno had backdated one of her own account statements to reflect that she'd sold Lehman Brothers stock in August. There was just one problem: Lehman had *imploded* in September and was bankrupt *before* she backdated the phony stock sale. Zach's goal was to persuade jurors that everyone working on Wall Street knew that Lehman no longer existed, but that in the anything-goes Willy Wonka wonderland of BLMIS, a manager like Bongiorno could decide that she wouldn't have to take a loss in Lehman if she could revise reality to show that she had gotten out of the stock in the nick of time.

Q: Do you see there it says that you've got fifty-six hundred
shares of Lehman Brothers as of August 31, 2008?

A: That's what the statement says, and I guess so.

Q: And very, very briefly, I'd like to go to government exhibit
2000-201. And this is your husband's account, right?

This time, not a single guffaw emanated from Rudy Bongiorno in the
gallery. It seemed as if he'd stopped breathing. Annette confirmed
that her husband, too, had Lehman stock in his IA account that
month. She also confirmed, while looking at the statement, that the
trade date of their Lehman stock said August 28, 2008, with a settlement date of September 3.

Zach then displayed headlines from various major newspapers,
in September 2008, highlighting Lehman's filing of the largest bankruptcy case in American history. The tiny woman on the witness
stand seemed to shrink in her chair.

Q: It was at this time that Lehman Brothers, one of the oldest investment banks in the United States, went bankrupt,
didn't it?

A: Yes.

Q: You, in your account as of August 31, 2008, had Lehman
Brothers stock, right?

A: Right.

Q: After it went bankrupt, in the beginning of October of
2008, you went back and backdated a sale of Lehman
Brothers shares to August 2008, before it went bankrupt?

A: If I was told to do it, I did it, right.

Q: That didn't raise any red flags in your mind?
A: Everything was backdated.

Q: Ms. Bongiorno, that company was bankrupt.
A: Well, it didn't raise a red flag.

Q: It was in every newspaper in the country.
A: It didn't raise a red flag.

Q: You went back and backdated a sale before it went bankrupt?
A: I don't know. I guess so.

Bongiorno's position: it was Bernard L. Madoff who called the shots—even regarding her own personal investment accounts, and even if she was the one who dealt with the paperwork for her backdated trades. Was Annette as stupid as her lawyer portrayed her to be? Possibly. Even probably. But the jurors apparently couldn't believe it, and, ultimately, that proved to be a judgment Bongiorno couldn't escape.

The closing rebuttal was by the third prosecutor, Randall Jackson, nicknamed "Action Jackson" by his colleagues. He's built like a football player. Each morning of the trial, Jackson would eat a spoonful of ground coffee beans, as if he were Popeye the Sailor Man wolfing down a can of spinach for strength. The son of a Detroit cop, he'd worked his way through Harvard Law School.

Jackson was only thirty-nine, but, by then, he was already known as one of the best case closers in the US Attorney's Office. His summation felt more like a rampage than a legal proceeding. Sometimes it upset Judge Swain, but just about *every* word infuriated the defense lawyers, who rose and objected *forty-two* times. That's approximately forty times more than what's typical in a federal criminal rebuttal, as there's long been an unspoken code among defense lawyers and prosecutors to do their best not to interrupt closing statements.

When it was all over, the courtroom had the pleasant atmosphere of a stalled, packed subway train. Jackson talked about an extraordinarily generous man named Santa Claus, who "loved to bring great wealth to everyone who would invest in him with milk and cookies . . . who kept meticulous books and records on who had been naughty and who had been nice." It's a lie that parents tell their children, said Jackson, a lie that "probably everybody in this courtroom believed at some point in their life." But kids always figure it out; they start asking questions, like: "Mommy, how can Santa fit enough toys in his sleigh to cover all of the billions of transactions he claims to be completed each night?"

When kids start asking these questions, the prosecutor went on, "then the entire thing falls apart in their mind, and they accept the truth." Except, of course, those kids who refuse to stop believing because they love getting all the presents. But BLMIS was not Santa's factory, and the defendants in this case were not children. "Still, they somehow believed in Bernie Claus," not to mention "the notion that they could have created literally hundreds of computer programs that had no purpose other than creating entirely fictitious records; that they could have backdated every day by hand literally thousands of fake trades. Entirely fraudulent transactions every year, year after year."

By this point, Jackson's voice was booming so loudly that the judge had to ask him to turn down the volume. The closer implored jurors to use common sense—to use the same lens they use in their everyday lives—to examine the defendants' conduct. Based on what jurors know about the way the world works, he asked, is it plausible that their activity is consistent with people who were just trying to work at what they thought was a legitimate investment company? "Or is it consistent with people who were knowingly engaging in and concealing a fraud?"

Jackson analogized aspects of the defendants' criminal conduct to that of drug dealers and bank robbers, then invoked the crime dramas *The Godfather* and *The Sopranos*, both of them unsparing in their depictions of mobsters as amoral sociopaths. Given that three of the defendants, Bongiorno, Bonventre, and Crupi, were Italian Americans, the references left their defense lawyers boiling.

Was Jackson's presentation excessive? Did U.S. Attorney Preet Bharara share the judge's view of Jackson's speech? Not likely. According to Sean O'Shea, a former head of the white-collar-crimes unit at the US Attorney's Office for the Eastern District of New York, almost anything goes during final arguments. As a prosecutor, O'Shea was known for being a killer in the courtroom, just like Jackson. "Trial lawyers are not little wilting-flower consensus types," he explained after the Madoff Five verdicts. "And their bosses want them to win. I would think that Bharara is patting Jackson on the back and saying, 'Dude, you brought it home.' It's *Madoff*—the biggest crime of the century. *Everybody's* gotta go!"

During his rebuttal, Action Jackson had made four factual errors that the judge corrected before the jury. Did the jurors care? "Not at all," says juror Goldberg. "I personally wanted it [the rebuttal] to go on because I was enjoying it." As for the forty-two objections, surely this could have hurt the prosecutors, by perhaps raising doubts among many jurors about Jackson's fairness. The opposite, though, was true, says Sheila Amato. "I felt it was like the defense's last-ditch effort to throw him off his game. I wanted to push their heads down, like that game Whac-A-Mole."

12

The Madoff Five
(Act 2)

| | | | | | | | | | | |

The Question: How did the defense lawyers generate sympathy for their guilty clients that paid off at the sentencings?

One especially unsympathetic Madoff official was Enrica Cotellessa-Pitz, the company's former controller, or chief accounting officer. Unlike DiPascali, who had dropped out of St. John's University after being awarded five incompletes, Cotellessa-Pitz graduated from that college with a degree in economics in 1980 (two years after she started working part-time for Madoff). She toiled at BLMIS for thirty years, and at the time the firm went under, she was earning more than $450,000 per year. Cotellessa-Pitz pled guilty and agreed to cooperate with prosecutors, although her value to them was debatable.

While at the company, she reported to Daniel Bonventre, the director of operations, who was Andrew Frisch's client. On the witness stand, the fifty-five-year-old woman from Queens testified against her former boss, accusing him of using bonds belonging to customers as collateral to obtain bank loans for the company; altering records to bamboozle the SEC; and phonying up the firm's financials. Thus, Frisch had to tear her apart in the courtroom. And he did.

It was Frisch's contention that Enrica was innocent but succumbed to pressure to plead guilty because prosecutors needed her. (He believes she lied on the stand about Bonventre to try to lighten her own sentence if she was ultimately sent to the clink.) It's not an uncommon defense strategy, and the jury didn't buy this idea that she was strong-armed. However, there's no disputing the fact that Frisch helped eliminate her as a credible source for the government.

Here's how: During his barbecuing of her, Enrica appeared to have little grasp on what the truth was, and couldn't remember key statements she'd told prosecutors and FBI agents during fourteen meetings with them—after which they decided to charge her. She recalled FBI agents holding pens but couldn't recall them writing anything. She had no memory of having written letters about her problems to prominent individuals just a few years earlier.

It was painful to watch Pitz squirm. She sometimes sat silently for agonizing lengths of time when asked a question, causing some observers in the gallery to squirm along with her. Worse, she once wrote a letter to the prosecutors begging them not to indict her. In it, she accused them of forcing her to plead guilty even though she didn't know, she insisted, that anything she'd been doing was wrong. But when asked on the stand if her allegation against the US Attorney's Office was true, she admitted she'd lied in that letter. "I felt no pity," says juror Nancy Goldberg, recalling Pitz's performance as a government cooperator.

With the ex-controller out of the way, Frisch did his best to take down DiPascali. He couldn't—nobody could—but he scored some points. DiPascali had told the jury that one reason he decided to cooperate with prosecutors was to help the government "provide some remedy for victims" of the fraud.

Perhaps. But Frisch read a portion of a transcript from a civil suit brought by defrauded investors trying to recover money. Instead of telling the lawyers for those investors what happened at BLMIS, DiPascali pled the Fifth, as per the advice of his lawyer, Marc Mukasey. This was in 2012, three years after he had signed his cooperation agreement and just a year before the Madoff Five trial started.

Prosecutors argued to Judge Swain that Frisch shouldn't be permitted to share that with jurors, as the theatrics might confuse them into thinking that DiPascali was not being forthright with his answers in the current case. But the judge allowed Frisch to fire away. Did it matter in the end to the jury panel? No, but it made Frank look bad at the time. In large part, that was because the plaintiffs who had brought the case were retired police officers, firemen, and other employees of Fairfield County, Connecticut, as Frisch explained to the jury in his closing summation. When DiPascali was asked whether—since signing his cooperation agreement in 2009—he'd ever met with any victims or representatives of victims, Frank said he hadn't, "other than my mother and people that were victims that in the normal course of my life I have run into."

When you're on the stand, bringing your mom into a case can backfire. "He could have answered the question 'No,'" Frisch said to the jury. "But he brings his mother into it. That's how despicable he is. To give you an answer designed to lure you in, to make it believable, he brings his mother into it." But, he went on, "Even if you completely distrust DiPascali at the moment you hear his testimony, this answer seems plausible and believable."

Frisch kept hammering. "Later, I asked him if he'd given testimony in any lawsuit brought by a victim. He said, 'Yes, I took a conference call, and I was deposed.' Even though you were already skeptical of DiPascali, it all seems plausible." However, it turns out that it was only *technically* true. DiPascali *had* met with representatives of victims other than his mother and those he ran into in the normal course of life—in a case brought by a Madoff investor in 2012, the year before the trial started. But he asserted his Fifth Amendment rights to even innocuous questions, such as whether he worked for Madoff. "DiPascali couldn't care less about victims," said Frisch. "He couldn't care less about the retired policemen and firemen of Fairfield County. He is completely out for himself."

At another point in the trial, while the prosecutors took some flesh off Jodi Crupi for her expenditures on the company's AmEx card, her attorney, Breslin, had his revenge on DiPascali, the key witness against his client.

DiPascali had testified about his lifestyle, which included million-dollar boats with full-time boat captains, all paid for by Madoff. At first, Frank said he didn't know if the word "lavish" would describe his home in upscale Bridgewater, New Jersey: five bedrooms on seven acres; a pool with a cascading waterfall; a pond for ice-skating; a theater and a pinball arcade; even an outdoor sports court under construction. Perhaps the adjective threw him off, or in his mind he felt that his home didn't stack up against the four that Bernie and Ruth owned in 2008, before it all came crashing down. Or perhaps in a moment of self-awareness, he realized how disingenuous he must have sounded to the jury. So he quickly reversed course and conceded to Breslin that, yes, "lavish" was an acceptable word to describe his sprawling home, appraised at nearly $1.5 million.

What attorney Breslin did masterfully was to show DiPascali, like a sailor on perpetual leave, couldn't stop spending investors' money—not even in early December 2008, after he says Madoff told him the enterprise was broke and that he was preparing to turn himself in. In short, Breslin exposed Frank's greed in a palpable way that jurors could not ignore.

"He had an epiphany on December 3," Breslin scoffed one day in his office, after the trial ended. "He realized that all the money was stolen—'Oh my God, he didn't know!' The customers have all been deprived and cheated—'Oh my God!' But notwithstanding his great epiphany and sorrow for the fact that he'd been stealing from people for thirty years, notwithstanding his realization that it was a Ponzi scheme—'*Oh my God!*'—it didn't mean he stopped stealing."

During that week of December 3, until Madoff's arrest on the eleventh, DiPascali spent nearly $500 on cigars (mostly for his eldest son for Christmas, he said); more than $1,000 for limousines; nearly $600 at a tea shop; plus fancy restaurant dinners. Meanwhile, about $40 million of new investor money poured into the company during that short window of time.

While grilling DiPascali on the witness stand, Breslin noted, "I see a charge to Ticketmaster on 12-2-08 for Britney Spears. Do you see that for $688?"

A: I do.

Q: I'm hoping that wasn't for you.
A: It wasn't.

After the trial ended, Breslin told me he suspected that prosecutors didn't prepare DiPascali for the credit card pummeling, and thinks they had put in the AmEx bills in the belief that they would be used only against his client, Crupi. They didn't think that anyone would "take the time to sit down and plot out the chronology of Frank's *bullshit* and see what *he* had bought during those days." Madoff's December 3 confession to DiPascali "was supposedly Frank's come-to-Jesus moment," he added. "How can you have a come-to-Jesus moment when you're charging it to the company—because who are you *really* charging it to? It just shows what an unredeemed and unredeemable liar he is."

THE MADOFF FIVE (ACT 2)

It's hard to imagine there was anyone in the courtroom who didn't conclude that Annette Bongiorno was going to prison after the government put up exhibit 105-B22: one of the trial's most incriminating documents, with the words "Fake Sales" scrawled at the top of Jeffry Picower's stock record. A former employee named Winifred "Wini" Jackson, who worked for Madoff Securities from 1987 until its demise, was in the box at the time. She identified the handwriting as belonging to Bongiorno, one of her immediate bosses (the other being Crupi). It was a startling moment, and one that stuck with jurors throughout the trial. When Bongiorno's attorney, Roland Riopelle, stood up to cross the witness, however, he somehow pulled off a coup de théâtre.

It turned out that the smoking piece of paper was actually part of a collection of hundreds of pages of documents. Deep inside the pile was a note that Bongiorno had written to herself. It read: "Use this run just to see what percentage new buys are up as of May 22, then cancel." When Riopelle asked Wini Jackson if this meant the numbers were to be canceled, she replied affirmatively. Moreover, there were additional handwritten notes by Bongiorno with the letters *CXL*, which Wini said meant cancel. What Riopelle did, in short, was take a toxic word ("Fake") and make it sound plausible that his client had been doing little more than a math exercise—and that, by canceling the exercise, it was never a part of the firm's record. It was artfully done, and he had the added advantage of this revelation dropping early in the trial, when both sides were still exchanging first-round jabs, trying to encapsulate the story to jurors. Dubinsky, the prosecution's fraud expert, hadn't testified yet. Nor had DiPascali.

Riopelle asked the witness: "Having looked at all these various pieces of paper, is it your belief, knowing what you know of Ms. Bongiorno and knowing what you've seen now on this paper, that there's anything nefarious about the phrase 'Fake Sales'?"

"In this particular document?" responded Jackson. "No."

"Thank you. I have no further questions."

Seasoned defense lawyers know when to stop. But given the nature of that alarming document, why even take the risk to highlight it for jurors? "The short answer is there was some risk," he acknowledges today. "But in a case where the evidence is pretty overwhelming, and our chances [of winning] were slim going in, you have to be willing to take risks. . . . At that point, you are kind of in a corner, and you better throw the Hail Mary pass, don't you think? Showing a witness something that says 'Fake Trades' is pretty awful in a Ponzi case, so if you were ever going to take your shot, this was the time."

During Matt Schwartz's opening statement to jurors, he said that "year after year after year, they [the five defendants] lied and stole and they lied again for the most simple reason of all: Greed." For many weeks afterward, this grated on Gordon Mehler, the attorney for programmer Jerry O'Hara, who, in 2006, had expressed agitation and discomfort directly to Madoff and DiPascali about the computer programs he'd been writing for them. Recall that he and his colleague Perez had also written and sent letters to themselves that they kept unopened to memorialize their feelings. Additionally, O'Hara penned the following in a personal notebook, after having discussed the matter with Bernie: "I won't lie any longer. Next time, I say, 'Ask Frank.'"

O'Hara and Perez were unlike any programmers you've ever met. Hired in 1990 and 1991, respectively, their only expertise—decades out of date—was the ability to program the prehistoric IBMs that underpinned the Ponzi. They were utterly unqualified anywhere outside the confines of the seventeenth floor. But they were a jolly pair—good friends, if not best friends—and everyone was fond of them. Frank referred to them as "my boys."

The case against O'Hara and Perez was especially riveting. For example, Mehler disagrees strongly with the government's contention that his client's "I won't lie any longer" written statement proved his participation in the fraud. On the contrary, he says, O'Hara was simply making a record of the fact that he would no longer lie to *Madoff* about whether he was doing the dirty work Bernie *wanted* him to do, and that, in the future, he would tell the CEO, "Ask Frank," because DiPascali knew already that O'Hara had refused to work on certain projects.

The two programmers never earned anywhere near as much money as DiPascali, who told the jury that he had once coaxed them with bigger salaries to get them to continue creating devious software code for so-named "special programs."

Mehler had his chance to soften the blow for his client when he rose to the podium to confront the government's top songbird on the notion that his client was greedy. "To cross-examine someone as wily as Frank was intimidating," he says today. "He had been preparing to testify for years." Gordon presented Frank with photocopies of bank checks and deposit slips showing that in 2006 O'Hara had paid back a $687,000 bridge loan that Madoff gave him a few months earlier to purchase a house.

In contrast, DiPascali admitted that Madoff had lent *him* $800,000 for the construction of a house that he never repaid. "And Madoff told you that if the IRS questioned this eight-hundred-thousand-dollar payment that he, Madoff, could always write it up as a loan, correct?" he asked Frank.

A: That is what he implied, yes.

Q: So there would be no tax consequences for you, right?
A: Correct.

Q: And that Madoff did this sort of thing with his sons, Andy
    and Mark, true?
A: He told me he did, yes.

The fact that O'Hara promptly repaid his loan to Madoff "just completely gutted the notion that Jerry was greedy and that Bernie could be extorted by Jerry, which is what prosecutors suggested," says Mehler. "If you're shakin' him down, why doesn't Jerry say to Bernie, 'Hey, let's just forget about that loan?'"

O'Hara's and Perez's lawyers decided to turn over those missives to the government, in the hope that jurors would view the programmers as having sent themselves open-in-case-of-emergency envelopes. In other words, to be used for protection in case Madoff retaliated against them for refusing to take part in measures that the boss used to trick clients as well as the SEC. The attorneys argued in court that, in fact, their clients had acted courageously in refusing to work on some shady stuff in 2006, that they told this to Bernie's face, and then deleted the programs from the computer system. The government's take: the two guys deleted the programs merely to try saving their own hides, so that they could *continue* to work on the shady stuff without leaving any fingerprints.

Not one of the five jurors who agreed to talk about the case saw any courage on display; they accepted the government's case that the programmers—following juicy salary hikes, plus six-figure bonuses in 2004 after an SEC audit—had stayed the course in the deceit. As for the letters, they viewed them as confessions, and faulted the programmers for not having the good sense to find jobs elsewhere, or even contact law enforcement. "I wasn't too sure about the computer guys for a while, until that letter [of O'Hara's] came out," says juror Amato. But at that moment, she says, she wrote "He is guilty" on her legal pad. "I remember writing that down because I didn't want him to be guilty," she explains. "I kind of felt sorry for him in some ways."

Ultimately, Jerry O'Hara and George Perez, the two lowest-level Madoff employees on trial, were *clearly* the guiltiest—thanks to the letters they sent to themselves.

In his rebuttal, prosecutor Action Jackson hilariously called the letters "the most boneheaded attempts to insulate one's self from criminal liability possibly in history." (One wonders if they were also booze-headed when they wrote them, as both men suffered from alcohol abuse.) But here's some irony: while the letters played a significant factor in the two men's jury convictions, Judge Laura Taylor Swain decided to use them as the benchmark for when they knew that their work was being used to defraud all of the firm's clients: in 2006, not earlier.

As noted in the profiles above, this led to their receiving mere three-year sentences, after initially rejecting plea offers of five years maximum. And O'Hara and Perez were back home in little more than a year, thanks to good behavior in prison, as well as a substance-abuse program that shaved some time off their sentences. Not a bad outcome for the programmers, all things considered.

Who flayed Frank the worst? It was probably Perez's lawyer, Larry Krantz. Although calm and mild-mannered outside the courtroom, he was the fieriest of all the defense attorneys in the case—which also made him the least liked by jurors. He once grabbed the podium and yelled at a consultant to the bankruptcy trustee who testified that Perez had confessed his guilt to him only a few weeks after investigators had taken over the BLMIS office. Krantz thought this alleged confession had been disclosed to the prosecutors a few days prior to his consultant's trial testimony, and felt he should have had more notice to prepare for it. "Krantz scared me," recalls Sheila Amato. "I thought he was going to strangle him."

The attorney downshifted his tone with DiPascali, who got tangled up in his answers about when precisely he realized the company's fake trading had begun. Fraud expert Dubinsky, after examining financial documents, had concluded *conservatively* that the Ponzi began in the 1970s. Madoff, at his 2009 sentencing, continued to maintain that the fraud hadn't started until the early 1990s. As for Frank's view of when the fraud started, it . . . *matured*—just like his bank account did.

Asked by Krantz for an approximate date when he learned for himself that the trades weren't real, DiPascali said he suspected it was sometime in the late 1970s, a few years after he started working at BLMIS. However, when Frank pled guilty in August 2009, he had told the FBI that "from at least the early 1990s through December of 2008, there was one simple fact that Bernie Madoff knew that I knew, and that other people knew, but we never told the clients—nor did we tell the regulators, like the SEC." That simple fact? "No purchases or sales of securities were actually taking place in their accounts. It was all fake. It was all fictitious. It was wrong, and I knew it at the time."

Why the discrepancy in years? "Because at the time, that was my assessment of the situation, and that was a truthful answer," he replied. "I have subsequently come to realize, after four and a half years of thinking of this massacre, that actually my crimes occurred in the late seventies." Fair enough. Frank had made that evolution in his understanding—and his involvement in the fraud—pretty clear to the bureau in his many sessions with agents.

Krantz asked DiPascali if he thought that in his life he had "generally been a trustworthy person." He responded that he had "never done that evaluation" and didn't recall "specifically thinking of that exact question." It was an interesting moment, as it may remain the only glimpse of whatever level of introspection Bernie's number two was capable of:

Q: Do you agree with me, Mr. DiPascali, that for most of your adult life as an employee at Madoff Securities, you were a con man?

A: I never thought of myself as one. . . . I did indeed violate the trust of many people during my career at Madoff. I'm not in a position right now to grapple with that question and assign myself that title.

Like Bernie, Frank had the ability to compartmentalize his evil behavior, a common enough human trait but taken to a height few people ever go.

> Q: But if we define "con man" as regularly gaining people's confidence and then violating their trust for your own benefit, you would agree that that definition does describe your conduct at Madoff Securities, true?
> A: At times, yes.
> Q: On practically a daily basis?
> A: Yes.
> Q: And that extends for some thirty or so years?
> A: It does.

Krantz's cross also bolstered his and Mehler's argument that the programmers had at times been hoodwinked by DiPascali about SEC requirements.

> Q: You were their friend, true?
> A: Very.

> Q: Isn't it a fact, Mr. DiPascali, that you were manipulating them in order to have them participate in what you knew to be a massive fraud without them knowing it?
> A: Yes.

> Q: Didn't you think that as a boss and a friend you owed them better than that?
> A: During that short time frame when I had to make that decision, that did not cross my mind.

Krantz calls his cross-examination of DiPascali one of the most memorable moments of his years as a trial lawyer. But it didn't bear fruit until sentencing. "The government was not a check in the system, and Judge Swain *was*," he says. The prosecutors "just quoted his testimony as if they were quoting Scripture."

In the end, it hardly mattered. The jury *loved* Frank.

As the jurors sat behind closed doors to begin deliberating, they held hands and prayed.

"It *needed* prayer," says juror Reverend Wynn, who led the invocation. "We asked God to give us the strength to make the right decision."

Did all of her fellow adjudicators feel the same way about the defendants' guilt? All except one, but she left the courthouse a day and a half into deliberations and never returned. According to several panelists, the holdout, Michelle Forman, didn't feel the prosecutors had met their burden of guilt beyond a reasonable doubt, but she wasn't able to articulate hard reasons why she felt that way. She had temporary support from a second juror, until he was quickly swayed by the others.

"Where the hell have you been all these months?" one juror snapped at Forman, according to Wynn. "You've been sitting here like us, and you don't hear anything that's been presented to us. You've seen everything we've seen, and you heard everything we heard. How could you even *think* that these people were not guilty?"

Forman became ill on the second day of deliberations—several jurors say she vomited in a restroom—and went home early. Two days later, she contacted Judge Swain to say she'd broken a toe and had limited mobility for at least a few days. She asked the judge not to provide any medical details to the public, and Swain honored her request. A decision was made to excuse her, and the jury resumed its deliberations with only eleven members. (The judge, prosecutors, and defense lawyers did not know what her views of the case were.)

Had Forman remained on the panel, and had she maintained

her position, it might have turned out to be a hung jury. Or, conceivably, though unlikely, a *12 Angry Men* scenario: the 1957 movie drama in which a lone juror, played by Henry Fonda, refuses to believe the young defendant is guilty of murder, sparking a bizarre musical-chairs scrimmage that leads to the twelve ultimately finding the defendant *not* guilty.

Forman did not respond to several requests for an interview.

So why the unexpectedly light prison terms? Judge Swain gave many reasons for the sentences, among them that none of the defendants instigated the fraud or knew it was a Ponzi scheme; nor were they fundamentally corrupt or evil. But the biggest factor may have been DiPascali.

During one of the sentencings, she hammered Frank, but used very few words to do so. The judge stated that she accepted his testimony regarding the "overall structure and methodology" of the Madoff fraud as "generally credible" and "widely corroborated." However, she added, "his more salacious details . . . are not. Mr. DiPascali is a glib storyteller, and is an admitted and convicted perjurer."

Aside from the fact that jurors, and subsequent judges in related cases, felt differently, the problem with Swain's analysis is that she never drilled down for public consumption into exactly *what* she had a problem with—and *why*. She simply left everyone with her gut feeling that some of the more colorful things that Frankie said simply didn't have the ring of truth to them. And that's not enough from a judge; certainly not in a case of this historic importance.

⬛

What?! For Annette? How the hell did that happen!? Oh my God, I can't believe Annette got only six years. Don't tell me it's gonna be like two months for Jerry and George. That pisses me off, I'm sorry. I thought she was more guilty than all of them. The prosecutors must have been devastated. It's kind of like a slap in the face to everybody who worked so hard getting these guys con-victed, and for the jury who had to listen to the evidence for nearly six months.

—JUROR SHEILA AMATO, ON THE SENTENCE
   IMPOSED ON BONGIORNO

Monday, December 8, 2014: On the morning of Dan Bonventre's sentencing—the first on Judge Swain's list—a group of smiling and upbeat FBI agents enjoyed an unexpected reunion in the back of the courtroom with two former prosecutors who'd popped in to watch. One of them, Lisa Baroni, led the Madoff Five case for four years prior to the start of the trial, while the other ex-prosecutor who showed up that day—Julian Moore—partnered with her for three of them. (They both had left the US Attorney's Office for private practice.)

Before long, the current prosecutors strolled in confidently, one at a time, to take their seats in front. "And here they are, Team USA! Dah, dah, da-da-da-*da*-da!" said *Newsday* reporter John Riley, hum-ming NBC's theme song for its coverage of the 2014 Sochi Winter Olympic Games earlier in the year. But midway through the sen-tencing, one could almost feel the gold medal slipping through the prosecutors' hands when the judge ripped DiPascali. In fact, it was one of the coldest days of the autumn, and, as if on cue, an intense nor'easter hit the next morning, thrashing the city with a record amount of rain and umbrella-destroying wind.

"This billion-dollar fraud could not have survived but for their [the defendants] galling illegal acts," Moore said to me. "The gov-ernment understandably pressed for higher sentences because, as they ably demonstrated at trial, the defendants were an integral part of the fraud." One factor in Swain's thinking, says Moore: she may have viewed a ten-year plea deal given to Peter Madoff as "the upper bar" for sentencing. If so, then the US Attorney's Office may have shortchanged itself with that deal. On the other hand, prosecutors had argued that Peter was less culpable than these other defendants. However, the judge called that argument "disingenuous."

One day after Bonventre's sentence—a decade in prison—it was Bongiorno's turn. She was given six years. O'Hara then got less than three—"a slap on the wrist, almost," juror Goldberg expressed on the phone that night, although the judge called all of the sentences "harsh" but just. It was now pretty transparent to everyone in the courtroom that fellow programmer Perez would receive the same sentence the following day. With that in mind, Team USA's Schwartz rose to the podium. He stated that any finding that Perez's participation in the conspiracies at the firm began only in 2006 would be "clearly erroneous" and that a sentence of just two or three years would "simply not be reasonable, and it would not be just . . . and it would not be consistent with other sentences under the fraud guidelines or at large.

"And I think what is likely to happen going forward with the next fraud defendant," he continued, "the next insider trading defendant, the next Ponzi scheme defendant, they are going to point to the sentences in this case, and they are going to say, 'I didn't participate in the Madoff fraud—my crime didn't last years, my crime didn't have thousands of victims, my crime did not expose someone to the risk of billions of dollars of losses—certainly I can't be sentenced to more than George Perez or Jerome O'Hara or Annette Bongiorno or Daniel Bonventre. The judges in this district will either have to explain, and I'm not sure how they could, how small-time crooks in front of them were somehow worse than the defendants in this case, or they will have to sentence those defendants in a way that is at odds with your Honor's sentences in this case. And that is contrary to the purposes of sentencing."

It was a whopping reproach of Swain—and highly unusual for a prosecutor to do in that courthouse, as sentencing is normally an area where the feds don't challenge judges. Even more pointed, to those in the know, was Schwartz's use of loaded legalese ("clearly erroneous," "not reasonable") to indicate that the government was seriously considering an appeal of the sentences—also something rarely done by the US Attorney's Office. Swain didn't expect the rebuke. Her response: bring it on. "I'm sure you are looking forward to the seventeenth floor across the road," she said drily, referring to the US Court of Appeals, "and I shall eagerly await the newspaper reports of those proceedings on appeal."

Juror Parise was happy when he read some of Schwartz's comments in a newspaper. "I think he hit it *dead*—head-on," he says. "All this time spent, the money, we found them guilty. I was shocked by the low sentences for all of them."

Finally, Jodi Crupi was sentenced on Monday, December 15. Before the punishment was announced, prosecutor Zach took the microphone in a last-ditch effort to land a lengthy prison term. The defendant, he stated, "was daily confronted with a choice as that knowledge [of the fraud] increased. Each day, with that knowledge, she decided to go back to work and to continue to participate in that. . . . To be confronted with that choice—'Do I do the right thing, walk away, tell somebody about it? Or do I just continue on this path where I'm feeling good, where my life is getting better, where I can put my head in the sand, I can affirmatively lie, I can keep this going for myself. . . .'

"Because that is something that is not unique to fraud. It is something that we all, I think, deal with in our own lives," he went on. "That is why the government thinks punishment needs to be substantial in this case. This is a position that lots of people find themselves in. It is a decision that—it may or may not be fair that a given person is put in. But society expects of them to do the right thing, to not contribute, to not participate in the fraud."

Swain sentenced Crupi to an eight-year combination of prison and home confinement, far less than what just about everyone close

to the case initially expected she'd get, but more than what was antic-
ipated, given what her codefendants secured. Was Swain moved by
Zach? We'll never know.

Crupi, incidentally, was viewed by four of the five jurors I interviewed as the most likable of the defendants; the fifth juror didn't
have feelings one way or another on the matter of likability. She
sometimes smiled at jurors when passing through the courthouse's
front doors at the end of each day. "I didn't feel like the smile was
a manipulation, either," reflects juror Amato. "It's like, that was her
personality, she was a nice person, basically. Crupi was the most
redeeming one." Echoes juror Goldberg: "Based on looks, which is
very shallow, I think that JoAnn Crupi had a very puritan, or pure
look about herself. I don't really know how to explain it. She looked
less likely to be guilty. I struggled with her puritan look. And she
smiled at us when we were going to get our phones at the end of the
day, and I didn't like the closeness there. It didn't feel right. Because
it made me soften for, like, a second."

Judge Swain cited a distinction between *actual knowledge* of the
fraud and *conscious avoidance* of the fraud in declining to impose
obstruction-of-justice "enhancements" on not only Crupi, who did
not testify at trial but had been interviewed by investigators years
before, but also Bonventre and Bongiorno, both of whom did testify.
An obstruction-of-justice enhancement is an increase in the potential prison sentence for telling a lie. However, the judge found that
the government couldn't meet its burden of proof in demonstrating
that the defendants lied because it was possible that they were telling the truth when they denied actual knowledge of the fraud at the
company. Perez and O'Hara were exempt, as neither man testified on
the stand or sat for interviews with the feds.

However, even if Judge Swain had found obstruction, it would
have been largely just a symbolic move here, as the sentencing guidelines for each of the Madoff Five already called for life behind bars.

Of all the defendants' sentences, Bongiorno's six years, with a recommendation that she serve the last year in home detention, was the most surprising—given her forty years of work at the firm, the $50 million–plus (largely fictional) in her investment accounts at the time of Madoff's confession and arrest, and the many millions she withdrew over the decades. Despite a guideline calling for life, the Probation Department's recommendation of twenty years, and the government's request for more than twenty, the judge "was still persuaded that Mrs. Bongiorno was not beyond redemption at sixty-seven years of age—and that she deserved a merciful, albeit 'harsh' sentence," says her attorney, Riopelle. The judge expressed similar views of all the defendants.

Not every juror thinks all of the sentences were light. Gloria Wynn felt the punishments for Bongiorno and the computer programmers were "understandable," but that Bonventre's ten years was too low. "I'm surprised that he only got that," she says. "He was a shaker and a mover, and he benefited an awful lot from the whole thing—more so than a lot of them." Overall, however, she is satisfied with the judge's punishments. The sentences didn't surprise her, she says, "because some of them were not completely totally '*guilty*'-guilty. Some of them didn't start off guilty but got caught up and just stayed on the bandwagon."

And what a bandwagon it was. Approximately $170 billion moving in and out of one single JPMorgan Chase checking account that was used for the Ponzi. Some $20 billion ripped off from customers. Roughly fifty thousand customers sent to the cleaners, including investors in feeder funds, and put through the agony of the restitution process—a trial by fire that is likely to continue for years to come.

But for the Madoff Five, their own bandwagon came to an ugly end—just not nearly as ugly as it could have been.

A Prosecutorial Post-Mortem

Four years after the Madoff Five trial concluded, in 2018, the three prosecutors who conducted it—Matthew Schwartz, John Zach, and Randall Jackson—agreed to go on the record with their reflections on the case. All five defendants had exhausted their legal appeals by this point, and the trio at last felt comfortable opening up. Considering that the trial turned out to be the only one to flow from the Bernie Madoff scandal, their collective insights seem not only invaluable today, but necessary.

We met for many hours over two days around a conference table at the Manhattan headquarters of the law firm where all three worked, Boies Schiller Flexner, known widely as one of the most aggressive firms in the country. The idea for the sessions had been planted soon after the trial when I spotted Zach leaving Campagnola, an uptown Manhattan hangout for journalists, law enforcers, and mobsters. I told him I was struggling with how, in particular, someone extremely likable such as Jodi Crupi could work at the company for decades without bolting despite its boss's ongoing criminal wrongdoing. I had recently spent two hours with Crupi in her lawyer's office. She answered all my questions, never flinched, and there wasn't a moment where I felt she wasn't telling the truth—exactly the way I, and the jury, had felt about DiPascali. (No other Madoff Fivers ever discussed the case and its outcome.)

The daughter of a bartender, Jodi had a lower-middle-class child-hood on Staten Island until seventh grade, when her family moved to Las Vegas. Right after earning a bachelor's degree from the University of Arizona, she landed her first job through a temp agency as a keypunch operator at BLMIS. It was 1983, and the company was then operating out of offices on Wall Street. A keypunch operator, a long-obsolete job done mainly by women, took data that was on paper cards with holes punched in them and entered the information into computers. Jodi didn't know it at the time, but she was posting fake convertible arbitrage trades to the customer accounts of Bernie's IA unit.

Upon her hiring, she told Bernie and Annette that she'd stay only six months; that she wanted some experience but didn't want to be a keypuncher. However, she was quickly promoted to an IA bookkeeper job and then kept rising for twenty-five years until the collapse. Ultimately, she oversaw the 703 Ponzi account, known internally as "Jodi's checkbook." Each day, she'd create a file card for Madoff that showed money in, money out, and a current balance. By the time of the fall, Jodi was pulling down a six-figure salary and bonuses, and had a $2.7 million beach house that Bernie had given her the year before as a gift.

Crupi was convicted of backdating customer statements and deceiving auditors. She even added a fake trade to her own IA account to show phony tax losses. When I told her that Bernie was obsessed with his legacy—with proving that he was a legitimate trader before he started faking it—she laughed and said, "I thought it was *all* real. I thought he was a great trader. I thought the trades were being done up in the trading room. And Frank was on that trading desk for a while."

"Jodi presents very sympathetically, and I don't think anybody's going to debate that," Zach had told me that night, on the sidewalk outside the restaurant. "How does someone like that, who is nice and grounded—you *like* her—go to work every day on the seventeenth floor? She's got a job that's a little above her station. She climbed up from being a keypunch operator, and she's making money, and she's getting responsibilities. And each day you go into work, you are getting further into that lifestyle and that comfort zone, and it can become hard to find the courage at some point to say, 'Shit, this is too much. I need to back out of this; I need to do something else.'

"Your life is already on this path in terms of your income, your station in life, and once you're down that road too far it can be impossible to get off," he observed. "And she just couldn't do it. So, you have a really good person who is now having to go in every day and pretend like she's not doing what she's doing."

Three years later, recalling Zach's possibly cocktail-fueled candor, I proposed the sit-down that would eventually take shape around the Boies Schiller conference table. When I asked how such a seemingly harmless group of people could do such lasting damage, prosecutor Schwartz agreed with Zach's earlier assessment of Jodi: it had been a long process of indoctrination, he said, unfolding over years or even decades: "No one sat down on Day One and said, 'Welcome to the Madoff Ponzi. What we do here is steal people's money and commit fraud. And there's your desk.'"

Randall Jackson had a more skeptical take. On Wall Street, of course, everybody is out to make money, and there is tremendous competition for talent, especially in terms of hotshot traders and financial managers. People get poached all the time. Why, asked Jackson, didn't that ever happen to Bernie's crew? "I think it's hard to imagine that you [Madoff's employees] wouldn't be asking yourselves, 'How come nobody has ever tried to hire away Annette?'" he chimed in sarcastically. "I mean, you've got this woman who is like a wizard. Or Frank?! Or *any* of these people. Or 'Why don't you just start your own fund? You're a genius.' None of them left, none of them wanted to demand they get to start their *own* fund? When that is literally what everybody who is good at this kind of stuff does, because you could make exponentially more money. If you [fellow employees] are not asking that question, then something weird is going on."

Q: You guys interviewed so many employees, some of whom didn't even testify. Was there something almost cult-like happening in the office? Bernie as a kind of Charlie Manson of Wall Street, or an L. Ron Hubbard from the Church of Scientology? The Temple of Bernie?

SCHWARTZ: It's not like brainwashing. But there was an element of cult of personality, and, as you saw at the trial, everyone's defense was "He's revered, he had this credibility, he was a larger-than-life persona. He knew the SEC chairmen and was head of a stock exchange." That's part of it.

Q: Is it plausible that Jodi and Frank never sat down together through the decades and said, "What are we doing here? Where the fuck is this all going to lead?" They maintain they never knew it was a Ponzi, but how could they not at least use the word *fraud* with each other in conversations? I can't put myself on the seventeenth floor just watching this unfold, with none of these people having drinks with each other and acknowledging on a regular basis that it was all a fraud.

SCHWARTZ: Well, I suspect they may have. Certainly, you heard testimony that when things got shaky, they had these kinds of conversations, and not just at the very end. There's the example at trial when DiPascali told the story of a drink he had with Dan Bonventre during the 2006 audits when everyone sort of thought the walls were gonna come down, and they talked about their "exit strategies." But whenever things got a little bit shaky, even at the dinner when they were toasting to fooling the auditors, those are

moments of stress when you sort of can't help but acknowledge the reality of what you're doing—and that's when you
talk about it. I don't think every day you sit around and
talk about "this big fraud we're committing." The way that
people commit crimes over and over and over every day—
unless they are sociopaths—is to try to normalize it and
try and put some distance between themselves and what
they're doing. Certainly, putting distance between themselves and their victims, in this case. At least in times of
stress they talked about it. When times are good, why talk
about it? No one really wants to think about it.

JACKSON: I don't think they had to [speak about the fraud
with one another].

ZACH: I like Randall's analogy. It's not like you sit down and
say, "How is the cocaine trade today?" They just go to
work every day. And it's worked forever. It's been working
for twenty-five years. What's to suggest it's not going to
work *tomorrow*? That was the weird thing about the case,
and, in some ways, it makes it hard to grasp because people are going about their day-to-day jobs like they *were*
day-to-day jobs instead of day-to-day frauds. But if you
step back from the mundane day-to-day work and take
stock, what these workers were doing was impossible in
the real financial world. The conduct could only happen
through fraud or magic: "Okay, let's just transfer, let's just
change the nature of the trades. They weren't real. They
would backdate and manipulate and change."

JACKSON: John, I see your point about how it's different from
the cocaine factory. But if you talk to anyone who has
ever worked in a cocaine factory, they never use the word
cocaine. The word is never said. You know what they always refer to it as? "The product." It's a little, subtle thing

that you are doing that is sort of pushing you away—that gives you this little bit of distance from the horror of like, "What is your day-to-day?"

I once put a witness on the stand who was a hit man. I asked, "What is your job?" He said: "I was a frogger." I was, like, "What's a frogger?"

"You know, they'd tell me we have to take care of some frogs."

"What do you mean by frogs? You are talking about going and killing people, right?"

And he started laughing maniacally—and he said "Yes," but he couldn't believe he was saying it, even on the witness stand. It freaked the jurors out. He was just, like, "I'm a frogger."

Q: But a dozen employees and accountants pled guilty or were convicted. I'm not sure I'll ever fully grasp why they *all* did it. "I'm a frogger" becomes "I'm just an accountant"?

JACKSON: The "why" questions you ask are different at different stages. I spoke quite a bit with Madoff's accountant [David Friehling, who pled guilty], who testified at trial. He had no idea what was going on, except for a massive tax fraud. He never asked *why*. Why does this guy need to go to these extremes? The real secret of the case, which was lost on a lot of people, is that Madoff may have known less about the mechanics of the fraud than the others. I'm not sure, but we talked about it a lot. Madoff was bad at math and did not know how to use a computer. He did not have the technical sophistication to have executed the mechanics of the tax stuff or the computer stuff or what was going on in the accounting department.

Q: He was also a terrible trader throughout his life, from all the evidence I've seen and collected, despite his claims to be a virtual genius at it.

JACKSON: The actual fraud was simple. What was complex is what they had to engage in to not get caught. To make sure they were not triggering an insider trading investigation, for example; to make sure there were not earnings announcements by companies when picking the stocks to backdate.

Q: Frank and the others are adamant that they always believed that Bernie had assets somewhere, mainly overseas, to back up all the fake trading. This is something I may never be able to wrap my head around. And none of them were asked in court why they felt Bernie had to even *do* fake trades if he had assets to back it all up. Maybe they all thought he simply wanted to be revered as a great trader?

ZACH: If you [as an employee] believe the statements are all fake—that there's no Apple or IBM or whatever stock trades—but that there *is* real money behind this, then [you think] all the investors are coming out ahead, because they are all making money on paper, and when they ask to withdraw it, they are able to. So, it's asset backed. You can sort of convince yourself, and maybe this is part of the rationalization that no one is getting hurt. "Yeah, technically it's a fraud, but no one is getting hurt by this." Everyone is making money, and no one is being exposed really to risk of loss—because all the money is *someplace else*. That's a very different thing than coming to grips with "Yeah, we stole billions of dollars."

Q: But again, if they believe the assets are elsewhere, why do they think Bernie is even *doing* this?

SCHWARTZ: Yeah, and if the assets are somewhere else, why every so often does he run out of money and have a cash crisis? If you really have a billion dollars sitting overseas, even if it's not liquid, there's a way to monetize that in a short-term situation, right? Look, I'm not saying that anyone is being untruthful when they say they believed this. I'm saying that it's an act of self-delusion that makes it easier to do that job every single day. And it's an act of self-delusion that they did not subject to any scrutiny. Because if you just think about that theory [Bernie having the assets overseas] for more than a minute, there are like ten different holes in it.

ZACH: It's really not a typical securities fraud case, it's an OC [organized crime] case. The crime was simple. There was no advanced market sophistication. The players are all uneducated.

Q: One thing the world has long wanted to know is when the Ponzi began, and who knew?

JACKSON: I think in the 1960s. Day One. There was never a point where it's not a Ponzi.

ZACH: I think it's the wrong question. The Ponzi is the deepest, darkest fraud. And in all of this other incredibly serious fraud, there's an orbit around it. A gravitational pull of the serious fraud has brought in all of this *other* criminal conduct. [For example, Peter Madoff's using different-colored pens to backdate compliance reports, and lawyer-accountant Paul Konigsberg's preparing phony tax returns for foundations.] So, for each person who is in the Madoff universe, you have to ask *which* of these frauds are they participating in? All of them are serious, all of them are detrimental. But it's not a yes-or-no question. It's a *series* of yes-or-no questions.

JACKSON: I think that's a great analogy. But I wouldn't say that the Ponzi scheme is the deepest, darkest fraud. I would say the Ponzi scheme is *all* of the frauds together. It's almost like a solar system, right? The Ponzi scheme is our solar system. And there were all these different things that make up the solar system. There is the sun, there's Earth, there's all these different planets. There's an asteroid. And it's like somebody is asking, "Do you know about the solar system?" It's a weird question. Someone could legitimately say, "Well, I live on Earth, I'm aware of the moon, I'm aware of Saturn. I see the sun every day. But I don't know about a solar system." That's a name that you are giving to a bigger reality that sort of dominates everything that is circling around you. It's kind of metaphysical. And each one of the people involved had access to various pieces of it.

ZACH: I see the Ponzi more like the sun, and all of the other frauds are kind of revolving around it. This was an entity [BLMIS] that was wholly corrupt to its core. There was a Ponzi scheme in the middle of this, but in order to keep that Ponzi running, there were a series of related but really fundamentally separate frauds that were done. But they were all in service of the Ponzi scheme. The accounting fraud that allowed them to move money up into the market making business [run by Peter, Andrew, and Mark] and prop it up, that was in service of obscuring the Ponzi scheme. The fraud on the SEC, on KPMG, and by Madoff's auditors [Friehling and Konigsberg], that was in service of maintaining the Ponzi scheme. Some of the side frauds were really totally separate, like Madoff's tax fraud. In addition to him taking in all this money illegitimately through a Ponzi scheme, he also failed to accurately report his income, even according to his own *fake* books.

Q: Then you have Peter putting his wife on the payroll as a ghost employee. That's not in the service of the Ponzi.

SCHWARTZ: No, but look, it goes to a corrupt institution. It *is* a corrupt institution. When you have a business where you can do whatever you want, no one is really caring about expenses like you would in the legitimate business. "Throw someone else onto the payroll." Where any of the paperwork can be falsified, sure, why not also fail to report a hundred million dollars in income?

Q: Plus individuals backdating trades in their own IA accounts.

SCHWARTZ: Exactly. That's what John meant when he said this is an OC case. This is a corrupt organization in the same sense like a RICO is a corrupt organization.

13

Solved: Who Knew What in the Madoff Family

| | | | | | | | | | | | |

The Question: Was Ruth Madoff honest about her role in the company—or lack thereof? Did Madoff's brother, sons, and niece do anything wrong?

R uth "Ruthie Books" Madoff. That's the nickname FBI agents privately gave her, and it's a fitting one, given that she lied like a mobster on the witness stand when she appeared on *60 Minutes*—one of the only interviews she's granted since Bernie's arrest.

On the show, which aired on October 30, 2011, she told correspondent Morley Safer that she worked as a receptionist and bookkeeper at the firm from 1961 to 1963, but then left to raise their sons. "And later on, when the boys started to work there," she added, "we lived within walking distance, and I had an office there where I took care of decorating things and house things and boat bills and managing those things. But I was never the bookkeeper after 1963."

Financial records (with her handwriting on them) and testimony from former employees reveal that Ruth did plenty of work to maintain some of the critical Ponzi bank accounts for decades after the 1960s—and right up until early 2008, the year their bubble busted. "I remember thinking, as I was watching the show, '*Oh my God*, she's on *60 Minutes* lying about her role in the company!'" exclaims former prosecutor Lisa Baroni, who oversaw several years of investigations on Madoff family and employee cases. "What she said was untrue."

Nobody gave Ruthie Books's TV claim a second thought at the time, but the feds knew the truth as early as 2009, thanks to information and paperwork from underboss DiPascali. "When asked about Ruth's work with BLMIS, Frank understood that her role was the person who reconciled the Chase 703," according to an FBI agent who interviewed him in 2009 and included the observation on a 302 form. The 703 was the nickname for the JPMorgan Chase checking account that housed all the Ponzi money, the account number of which ended with those three digits. (Reconciliation, as explained earlier, is an accounting term for, in this context, matching bank statements with other company records [mainly paper checks] of money flowing in and out.)

As the FBI summarized, Frank recalled Ruth speaking to Jodi Crupi "often to get answers about checks that had not cleared or were out of numerical order." But in 2008, months before the Ponzi exploded, Ruth seemed to curtail her involvement, he said. The account records were all kept in the office of Dan Bonventre. "These were the records he [Bonventre] brought to investigators on the day of Bernie's arrest," DiPascali told the feds.

In mid-December 2013, when Frank took the stand to testify in the Madoff Five trial, I emailed Bernie some of the highlights of his versions of history and asked if he could tell me what was true or false. I included DiPascali's claim that it was both Ruth and Bonventre who reconciled the 703 account. But Bernie wasn't going anywhere near that subject, and his response was terse.

"I have been asked by the attorneys to refrain from making statements regarding the open trials due to the fact that I could be asked to give depositions on these matters," he began in one email. Bernie added that while he wanted me to continue supplying him with court updates, he'd prefer not to go on the record for the time being. "I hope you can understand. I will tell you this much: it is quite obvious that Frank is not being truthful for all the obvious reasons. Bernie."

Madoff was fibbing again about his lawyers. Just two days earlier, he had indeed answered a series of my questions regarding Frank's testimony about each of the five defendants. And he often responded to testimony from witnesses (such as former employees) during the Madoff Five trial, although he never addressed *anything* in which a family member was mentioned.

Amusingly, within hours of Bernie's sending me that email about his lawyers, he wrote to *both* me and Krantz (the attorney for defendant Perez), bashing DiPascali—in light of the highlights of Frank's testimony that I had just shared with him.

"To both Larry Krantz and Richard," his email read, "after reading the testimony of Frank it is obvious what he is doing. He is super imposing me on the events and activities that were both initiated and conceived by him." In other discussions, Bernie would claim the opposite: that Frank was taking credit for things relating to the fraud that Bernie himself had conceived. "His trying to lay off the blame on the others"—for instance, Ruth or other former employees—"is nothing more than supplying false and grossly exaggerated information to the gov't to reduce his sentence."

So much for "refraining" from making statements while the trial was ongoing. (Long after the trial ended, I asked Krantz about his communications with Madoff. "Honestly," he replied, "I understand about 10 percent of what that guy wrote to me.")

Frank was hardly the only employee who could speak to Ruth's role with the 703 account. In early 2018 I asked Eric Lipkin, who had earlier pled guilty to falsifying records, how long Ruth was doing bookkeeping work from the time he joined the firm in 1992. "Forever," he said. "She would do reconciliations with the bank checking account records and statements—with all the checks that came back from the bank. She was in the office quite a bit."

While both Bernie and Ruth have always vigorously insisted she didn't know anything about anything, it bears repeating that the 703 account at Chase bank *was* the Ponzi. All of the funds that came from investors flowed into that one account, and all the redemptions flowed out of it. In total, during the life of the 703, more than $150 *billion* moved in and out—both from and to IA investors. On one day alone, more than $100 million, at jackhammer speed, shuffled back and forth between the Chase account and one of Bernie's biggest investors. FBI agents, suspecting a crime known as check-kiting, later probed the bank about it but couldn't reach a conclusion about what was going on. What did *Ruth* think while she tallied the figures—day after day after day—from her company office she claimed was mainly used for "decorating things and house things and boat bills"? She was known to have been great at math since her high school days, so that kind of rapid-fire money movement must have raised red flags. Did she ever ask her husband about it? She's never said.

This does not mean, of course, that Ruth knew it was a Ponzi scheme, specifically, as opposed to just some very shady activity. There is no evidence she did. So why lie on *60 Minutes* about the bookkeeping? And given that lie, how and why should we take her word on anything important?

"She'd been trained as a bookkeeper, and her father, an accountant, was ground zero for the whole fraud," says an FBI agent I spoke with a decade ago. "It starts with him. I believe the Ponzi started in the 1960s. . . . But I don't think she [Ruth] necessarily knew it was a fraud. She was not asking questions." Madoff Five prosecutor Randall Jackson says that when Bonventre wasn't reconciling the 703 account, Ruth was. Not only that, but her fingerprints, so to speak, were all over it. During the Madoff Five trial, former BLMIS controller Enrica Cotellessa-Pitz was shown a government exhibit she identified as a bank reconciliation document for the 703. It was dated December 2000—thirty-seven years after 1963, the year that Ruth claimed on TV that she stopped being the bookkeeper. Few reporters were in the court for Cortellessa-Pitz's testimony, and the following exchange between her and prosecutor Jackson didn't make the newspapers:

Q: Do you recognize the handwriting on this page?
A: Yes.

Q: Whose handwriting is it?
A: It's Ruth Madoff.

Q: And when you say a bank reconciliation, what does that mean?
A: It's balancing your checkbook. It's taking your opening balance and going through all your canceled checks, and the checks that are open and haven't cleared are part of your bank reconciliation for the month.

Q: Can you go to page ninety-three of this document. . . . Do you recognize the handwriting?
A: Well, most of it is Ruth's, and the "okay" is Dan's.

The prosecutor put up another document on the screen. This time it was a bank reconciliation for 2004, four years later, which Pitz also identified as having Ruth's and Bonventre's handwriting on it.

In his own testimony on the stand, Bonventre revealed that Ruth would sometimes run into difficulties with the reconciliations because "there were thousands and thousands of entries on any given month . . . and I would help her out with that." He added that if she was out of the office on a vacation or any extended trip during the period reconciliations needed to be done, he would handle them.

"The last eleven months or twelve months before the firm collapsed, she asked me to take it over permanently because it was becoming too much for her to handle."

One can only speculate that the massive redemptions from investors during the 2007–08 global fiscal crisis were stressing her out. Whether or not she knew it was all a Ponzi, it was all starting to crumble.

Bonventre, discussing the procedure in more depth, stated that Jodi Crupi kept cash figures on index cards. Regardless of whether he or Ruth took care of the bank reconciliation, when it was completed, he would "go downstairs and take a look at her cards just to make sure that the balance she showed on the card was the same as the one that we were using to do this reconciliation."

Lest a skeptic think that the only people at BLMIS who are offering up Ruthie Books are those who have been convicted of something, there was one witness in the Madoff Five case never charged with a crime: Winifred Jackson. She worked at Madoff Securities for more than ten years, helping out with the 703. She says that when she first began, in 1987, Ruth was the primary reconciler, "catching transposition of numbers, making corrections if need be."

In addition to employees identifying Ruth as the bookkeeper for decades, records from the US Federal Election Commission (FEC) show that, when contributing money to a political campaign, she listed BLMIS as her employer three times: in 1987, 2003, and 2004. In 2003, donating to Missouri senator Richard Gephardt's ill-fated run for the Democratic presidential nomination, she listed her position at the company as a "director." Now, that could possibly be an error, since no internal records located by the feds identify her in that way. Of course, they could've been shredded.

In any case, the reports are inconsistent, in that she lists her occupation as a "homemaker" for contributions in 1997, 1999, 2000, 2002, 2005, and as a "housewife" in 2000.

Ruth and her sons long maintained that they first learned of Bernie's fraud on December 10, a day before his arrest. As their story goes, Bernie said he would turn himself in sometime during the next week, prompting his sons to turn him in themselves right away. While many feds believe the story was a ruse—arranged by Bernie to make his sons appear to be law-abiding citizens—no proof has ever emerged that it was one.

Ruth certainly did not act heroically. After Bernie's supposed confession to the family, she withdrew $10.5 million from one of her BLMIS accounts straightaway. (Three weeks *earlier* she had taken out $5 million.) Of course, this doesn't show that she knew all along it was a fraud—it might even suggest the opposite—but it does speak to her sense of entitlement. She apparently didn't realize (or care) that once Bernie admitted it was a Ponzi scheme, the music must stop *instantly*. No use of the corporate credit card, and no withdrawals from bank accounts with funds that would need to be returned to investors. Any lawyer would have told her that.

But Ruth has her supporters, including Elaine Solomon, who was once a secretary to Bernie and finished her career as secretary to Peter Madoff. "I love Ruth," she says. "I think Ruth has been the biggest victim in all of this. These people who say Ruth should have known—you know, you should walk in somebody's shoes before you make such a comment. She lost everything. The love of her life for fifty years. Her sons, her friends."

None of which explains why she lied when she claimed not to have worked at the company. But ignorance was clearly the party line, as became evident in a discussion I had with Bernie about the loss of his sons:

"I'll never recover" from Mark's suicide, Bernie told me by phone in 2011, adding that he feels responsible for it. "Of course, people tell me I shouldn't. And the psychologist here tells me that I shouldn't. But I have to." As Bernie explained, he created the very situation that was his sons' undoing. "They believed in me; they looked at me a certain way, and then all of a sudden they felt betrayed, and I understand that."

Bernie then launched into a tirade against Mark's lawyers for keeping him away from his mother after the fraud was exposed. "The media attention was brutal for him. He couldn't walk out of the house without being tormented." Financially, said Bernie, it looked like Mark was going to be bankrupted, and when Picard sued Mark's children to recover funds, "that sort of put him over the edge, I guess."

Bernie blames the suicide not only on Picard but also on his son's attorneys, mainly Martin Flumenbaum, who had alerted the SEC the day before Bernie's arrest. "From Day One, they wouldn't let Ruth be in touch with [Mark] whatsoever, even though my wife's attorneys and my attorneys thought they were being ridiculous." Bernie could understand Flumenbaum's not wanting Mark and Andrew to talk to *him*, but he could see no reason for blocking them from speaking with their mother. "She was not in the business, she was not charged with anything. She was not under investigation. It was crazy."

The truth is that Ruth Madoff definitely *was* under investigation. And that she worked in the business. Period.

It was December 11, 2010, the two-year anniversary of Bernie's arrest, when a despondent Mark Madoff was in his loft in the SoHo section of Manhattan—one of several grand homes he owned. With his two-year-old son Nicholas sleeping in the next room, Mark hung himself with the leash of his labradoodle, Grouper. Whatever reason Mark had for ending his life, and we'll never really know, he had been deeply depressed and had tried to take his life earlier that year. His wife, Stephanie, was out of town at the time, spending the joyless anniversary in Disney World with four-year-old Audrey, the second of their two children. Stephanie felt conflicted. She had married Mark in 2004, but shortly before he committed suicide, she was planning to divorce him, according to his ex-wife. (Stephanie denies this.) She also filed court papers asking to change her surname from Madoff to Morgan. Mark was declining to change his last name.

According to friends, Mark found it impossible to figure out how to go on. Scaling back his lifestyle dramatically and committing himself to full-time charity work was one option that might have helped his state of mind, says a close friend who worked as a consultant at BLMIS. Instead, Mark deluded himself into thinking he could continue to work on Wall Street—something even Bernie had told DiPascali would never happen. The friend emailed me a copy of Mark's résumé that he was fruitlessly sending to financial institutions at the time.

When I texted a top FBI agent on the case with the news that Mark had taken his own life, he texted back: "Really?? Well, at least he manned up." That's a helluva response. But when you dig into the paperwork that exists about Mark's and Andrew's careers at BLMIS, it's almost understandable why FBI agents couldn't muster up much sympathy for them. At the time of Mark's suicide, he and his brother—insisting upon total innocence—were declining to return their ill-gotten millions to the trustee.

Indeed, Andrew and Mark asserted that they were still entitled to more than $100 million in deferred compensation. And it was only in June 2017, eight years after their father pled guilty, that their estates settled with the trustee, dropping their demands for the $100 million and instead agreeing to cough up $23 million for losing investors. By then, Mark had been dead for seven years; Andrew, for three.

Nor did Mark or Andrew, or *any* Madoff family member for that matter, ever approach the US Attorney's Office after Bernie's arrest to offer their cooperation in the investigations. Ruth and Peter didn't even alert authorities after Bernie's purported confession to them.

I once greeted Mark at his swanky home in Greenwich, Connecticut. After ringing the doorbell, I could hear Grouper's barking and growling getting louder and louder as he raced around the back of the house toward me. On his doorstep, I explained to Mark that I was en route to Manhattan after attending a nearby funeral and thought no harm in introducing myself. He was half-hidden behind a full beard, and I've rarely seen a sadder man. He reached his hand out to shake mine and was gracious.

"In the nicest way possible, I need to decline and ask that you call—"

"—Marty Flumenbaum, your lawyer. I know. But since he doesn't return calls or emails, I thought I needed to come to you directly."

Mark took my card and said he hoped that one day we could talk.

As I drove slowly out of his driveway, I spotted a woman racing toward me down a hill, arms flailing. Fearing some kind of emergency, I rolled down my window to help, only to hear her shout over and over again, "Get out! Just get out!!" It was haunting. On the balcony, I could see Mark watching the scene of his wife, Stephanie, losing control.

According to police, shortly before ending his life, Mark had sent his attorney, Flumenbaum, an email saying that "nobody wants to believe the truth." But plenty of journalists, not to mention government investigators, wanted to speak with him. Thus, it was ghastly when Flumenbaum released a statement blaming the investigators for the suicide of "an innocent victim of his father's monstrous crime who succumbed to two years of unrelenting pressure from false accusations and innuendo." Prosecutors, FBI agents, and lawyers for Picard were furious but kept their feelings to themselves.

The suicide took place on the day after Picard filed the last of 1,000 clawback suits—including against Mark and his young children—meeting a court-imposed midnight deadline; Picard's deputy, David Sheehan, immediately canceled a party that he'd planned for his exhausted team. "The office was bustling for weeks, everyone was high and then so sad," recalls a Picard insider. "The counterweight of loss and pain versus the pride of the work to make these [Madoff] victims whole—that was a hard reality."

I had breakfast back then with the FBI agent who had metaphorically high-fived Mark Madoff for hanging himself. I wanted to understand his thinking. His feeling about Mark was this: "It's not that 'I'm a doofus, and I should have known [about the Ponzi scheme].' It's 'I'm a greedy fuck. I had a life of privilege, I did whatever I wanted. It's over. I was spoiled, self-centered.'"

Another investigator told me that David Kugel, the former senior trader for Madoff who pled guilty to securities fraud, shared his own views about Madoff's sons to prosecutors. Kugel had testified in the Madoff Five trial that "beginning in the early 1970s," he himself came up with historical data that was used by Madoff and his cronies to create fake trades for customers. While Kugel did not testify in the case about Mark or Andrew, he told prosecutors that he felt the brothers *had* to know about the fraud. Nonetheless, he could provide no firm proof, and prosecutors won't discuss why Kugel believed this. "Obviously, he had nothing concrete because we didn't arrest Mark or Andy," says one prosecutor. As for DiPascali's view of the brothers, says the prosecutor: "Frank thought they knew and just turned a blind eye to it."

Former FBI agent Garfinkel investigated Andrew and Mark and believes the US Attorney's office should have indicted them both. "Oh, absolutely," he says today. "They were on the road to being indicted before Mark's suicide. I thought the evidence was there—not necessarily that they knew that it was a Ponzi scheme, but the way they were benefiting from certain transactions in their IA account statements. They would probably argue they never saw the statements." In the end, however, prosecutors decided there was not enough evidence to prove beyond a reasonable doubt that the sons knew vast and myriad frauds were swirling all around them—and making them rich. "Willful blindness," or intentionally keeping oneself ignorant of crimes, is tough to prove in a court of law. What can't be denied here, however, is that they most certainly should have known about a lot of wrongdoing.

Fagenson, the former NYSE official, offers his helpful take on it:

"Do I support the theory that his kids didn't know? Yes, probably I do. If you had a father who had started a business that was extremely profitable, and you were a recipient of the beneficence of that success, and your father said to you, 'What I'm doing over here is none of your business, that's *my* business. You stay out of it. Do what you're told. And run the business that I've given you,' how inquisitive are you going to be?" He quotes a favorite saying of Dick Grasso, who chaired the New York Stock Exchange from 1995 to 2003: "'It's tough to complain when your mouth is stuffed full of cash.' And if you think about it, it certainly retards dissent and complaint—particularly if you're chewing on fifties and hundreds, and not ones and fives. It has a thicker consistency."

Former SIPC president Steve Harbeck, whose trustee Picard probed the Madoff family for more than a decade, has a similar take on the sons. His view is that Mark and Andrew should have known, but whether they did or not is an open question. "The reason they should have known is that they were supposedly operating the so-called honest side of the business, which was hemorrhaging money and being supported by the criminal aspects of the business," he explains. "If they couldn't figure out that they were losing money on every transaction and trying to make it up on volume, they should have. And, given the lifestyle they were living, yes, they should have known that something was unsustainable there."

Records show that over the last decade of BLMIS's existence, nearly $800 million was diverted from the phony IA business and moved into the market making and proprietary trading businesses the sons ran—businesses that were bleeding out red during those years. The various BLMIS units became financially incestuous.

From the mid-1990s until the end, Mark was paid more than $33 million, including bonuses totaling $14 million just from 2006 and 2007. Not included in that figure is $6.5 million for a house on the island of Nantucket, plus $8.5 million in "loans" from his mother for two Manhattan apartments—money that originated in the 703 Ponzi account at

Chase. Then there's the $860,000 that went to Mark's interior decorators, plus nearly $800,000 in personal expenses charged to his American Express card that was ultimately paid for by investors in the Ponzi.

Andrew did even better. At least $73 million was funneled to him, including $6.8 million in the form of a purported loan from Ruth, with the money transferred to him from the 703—which, as we now know, Ruth was in charge of reconciling. Where did the sons think all this compensation was coming from? They never said.

Additionally, fake and backdated stock trades appeared regularly in the brothers' own IA accounts, while falsified account statements would materialize whenever they needed to show huge assets for their real estate purchases. Those statements would be handed out to the brothers at their trading desk.

When Bernie finally registered his company as a legal investment advisor in 2006, something he should have done by law as far back as the 1960s, BLMIS filed with the SEC a required form called a Uniform Application for Investment Adviser Registration and Report by Exempt Reporting Adviser. The form, known commonly as an ADV, stated falsely that Bernie had only twenty-three customer accounts with assets totaling $17 billion—when there were nearly five thousand accounts with a phantom total of $68 billion in them. Mark and Andrew alone controlled fourteen accounts, never mind the accounts held by their aunt Sondra Madoff Weiner, uncle Marvin Weiner, uncle Peter Madoff, and cousin Shana. Prior to the false ADV filing, DiPascali told the FBI, Bernie met with Peter and Shana since they were the compliance officers and responsible for the submission of the forms. They asked Bernie "how they could get away with only disclosing about 15 [he ultimately disclosed 23] accounts they managed since they both knew Bernie managed thousands. Bernie bullied them, told them to shut up and not worry about it."

Investigators also retrieved deleted emails that could have been damaging to Mark and Andrew had prosecutors decided there was enough evidence to indict them for crimes. In November 2004 a trader at BLMIS asked Andrew if his father was accepting new IA clients, because his father-in-law's girlfriend wanted to invest with Bernie. A handwritten note on a printed copy of the email reads: "Be sure to delete this one." In another deleted email, from 2005, Andrew expressed concern to Mark about the company's financial situation and told him that their father will probably "walk us through the FOCUS"—an SEC filing that Bernie falsified year after year. Investigators have told me that the Madoff brothers tried to conceal these emails and others from SEC auditors. Adds Bruce Dubinsky, the forensic accountant on the many Madoff cases, "Certainly Shana [as the rules and compliance officer] would have to have seen the FOCUS reports."

Even without all that suspicious material, one wonders what Mark and Andrew thought about how their father shielded them from any involvement in the IA business for decades. Former employees say the brothers tried several times to become more active in it. "After years of talking to so many witnesses," says former prosecutor Lisa Baroni, "what was striking to me was the length to which Madoff went to exclude his sons from participating in what was the most profitable part of the business. What did they think was happening on seventeen?" What's more, Madoff Securities never had a succession plan in place. What did the boys think would happen if their father died? Who would run the IA business? Certainly not the mid-level employees in House 17 who Andrew and Mark *knew* couldn't trade stocks to save their lives.

During one of Frank DiPascali's FBI debriefings, in May 2009, he described two events in 2001 that one would think might have alarmed Bernie's sons and other family members. The first was the article in *MARHedge*, in which the author questioned Bernie's eerily consistent returns and intimated that he had to be cheating. The article put Bernie "into a tizzy," recalled Frank, adding that Bernie told him he called "the asshole" who wrote it and tried to defuse the situation. As the publication was a small financial newsletter focused on hedge funds, it's likely that few if any of Bernie's customers read it or heard about it. But right on its heels came the story in *Barron's*, the major Dow Jones weekly, which theorized that Bernie must be "smoothing over" his reported returns in down markets by taking profits from the market making side of the business. When that article ran, BLMIS "fielded hundreds of calls from clients who were concerned," Frank recalled, according to the 302. "Bernie went so far as to address the employees on the trading floor and reassure them that Bernie was 'certainly not doing that.'" Perhaps Andrew and Mark missed that urgent gathering. But, according to Frank, "Bernie's family was concerned and went to him to discuss the article."

Their concerns were apparently short-lived. Four years later, on June 23, 2005, Bernie received a fax from the SEC asking for all relevant documentation—everything from incoming and outgoing email, instant messages, Lotus messages, and notes—for the period of April 1, 2004, through the present day for a small handful of employees that included Frank, Andrew and Mark. The SEC also requested chat and phone directories and a seating chart for the entire firm (excluding the prop trading and market making areas) as well as "all employee files, including but not limited to compensation records, outside business activities and personal brokerage account statements and confirmations for the following individuals . . ."

Instead of reigniting the family's "concern," the SEC's request prompted them to throw a massive document-shredding party, DiPascali told the feds. While Peter, Andrew, Mark, and Shana set about destroying "problematic" emails, which Frank defined for the FBI as any email "that referenced [IA] customers or could trigger further inquiry by the auditors," Bernie ordered the head of the BLMIS computer department (Elizabeth Weintraub, who died three years later) to "clean up" the BLMIS email server so that "any email that referenced IA customers would be removed." Among other things, recalled Frank, "friends of Mark and Andrew who wanted to inquire about opening an IA account sometimes had sent email to them" and "Bernie knew this was a problem so he ordered the scrubbing of the email. . . . Bernie wanted to present them [the SEC] with a sanitized email server."

Weintraub printed out every email for a given period of time for a select group of employees that included Frank and the Madoff family. Each of them (Ruth excluded) was required to go through every email and segregate the "problematic" ones. Afterward, Weintraub told Frank she "shredded" the "problematic" emails and then made a copy of the "cleaned-up server" to present to the auditors as the original one. It was a "mammoth" task that took days, with Frank recalling Weintraub complaining about the workload and how she was "going blind trying to read small line items" on BLMIS's email server.

The FBI once asked DiPascali about the level of knowledge Andrew Madoff had about what Frank and his team were actually doing on the seventeenth floor. Frank recalled several events "that were indicative to him that Andrew knew exactly what was happening on 17," according to one FBI 302.

The first event involved Andrew helping Frank and his seventeenth-floor team resolve a problem with "varying stock prices" on their two Bloomberg terminals. Frank had asked one of his stooges to print out the previous day's prices for a stock so he could use it in (fake) trades for the current day. But when Frank used the prices, they ended up being outside the NYSE's official recorded range for that day for that particular stock. "BLMIS and eventually Frank fielded hundreds of calls about this when the statements went out later that month," reads the 302.

Frank was certain he had not input the wrong price. He then said Andrew had solved the problem by sending an employee to seventeen to "reconfigure" the Bloomberg terminals. When asked by the feds whether, before reconfiguring the terminals, Andrew had questioned why Frank was using historical prices on stocks in those transactions, "Frank stated that Andrew never asked those questions because Andrew knew what Frank was doing on the 17th floor," reads that same 302. Frank also made the point that in an *actual* trade, if there was a discrepancy in the price of the transaction, the two parties involved (buyer and seller) would reach out to each other to confirm the price—not refer to a Bloomberg terminal (let alone "reconfigure" it), which was simply a passive repository for the data.

The second event Frank recalled for the FBI that he said showed Andrew's state of mind was the creation of an "off-site" location in the Bulova Corporate Center in Queens—a historic Art Deco building that was once the headquarters for the Bulova Watch Company. After 9/11, Peter had pushed for such a shadow location where they could operate at full capacity in the event the Manhattan office was ever incapacitated. "Full capacity" also required replicating Frank's operation on the seventeenth floor, of course, and DiPascali remembered Andrew's constantly asking him what equipment his crew needed to replicate the "House 17" server, the old IBM AS/400. So Frank had his seventeenth-floor programmers O'Hara and Perez compile their needs for the server and relay them to Andrew and Peter. There must've been "dozens" of meetings with them to determine what was needed to replicate the business on seventeen, recalled Frank: "To be involved in the creation of the off-site at Bulova was to know without a doubt that the House 17 server was not connected to the outside world. It was a stand-alone system that talked to no one." And, of course, that meant that no real trading was possible.

DiPascali also recalled the day when he said he'd clearly illustrated the massive scope of the IA clients for Peter and Andrew when he told them he "needed enough paper to mail out 4,000 customer statements regularly." Frank also remembered Andrew lecturing him circa 2006–2007 about the need for better security controls on the seventeenth floor "to protect the thousands of clients and large amount of money that was processed there." Andrew told Frank: "We have enormous exposure."

Frank emphasized to the FBI that his discussions with Bernie about what they were trying to accomplish on a day-to-day fake-trading basis were often conducted "in front of Andrew, Peter and Mark, and most anyone at BLMIS. No topics were off-limits. No coded language was used." Case in point: When Frank would tell Bernie that he was having a problem making the desired fake profits for clients, Bernie would respond, "Well, go back and look at yesterday's opening and use that." Then he'd turn to Andrew and ask, "What did the market do yesterday?" Or Bernie might say to Frank, "Check and see if you can get out of the market yesterday." Anybody with any market experience could not interpret those conversations and directions from Bernie as anything other than what they were— picking stocks after the fact and using those prices in the "trades."

At one point in his sessions with the FBI, an agent showed Frank a series of documents detailing account activity for one of Andrew's IA accounts dated July and August 1998. He explained that either Bongiorno or Crupi executed backdated trades for the account, and caused the creation of the backup documentation in the form of statements and tax documents "to create the illusion that this activity had taken place in the past when in fact it had been completed after the dates reflected on the statements." In other words, the statements were fraudulent and the trades were bogus. Frank was also shown a series of documents detailing account activity for one of Andrew's accounts that used the same procedure described above for a "sale" of Microsoft stock in March 2002. The sale used an advantageous "buy" in 2001 to create a large profit for Andrew.

Finally, Frank was shown account statements for an account in the name of Peter Madoff dated March 2002. The statement showed a large purchase of Microsoft stock in January 2001, more than a year earlier. It was bogus, as the 2001 statement never had such a stock purchase listed on it. Frank had never seen these particular statements before but was aware that Annette put through tickets to "purchase" stock for Peter Madoff in Microsoft. At the time, Peter commented to Frank in a distinct joking manner, "My brother is letting loose some of the Microsoft stock he's been holding for me." The fake Microsoft stock, of course—a backdated bogus deal to enrich his brother.

Bernie's brother wasn't in a joking mood the only time I got to see him in person. I watched for long periods of time as a ceiling spotlight illuminated the pinkness of his sweaty bald spot—as if even the top of his head was blushing out shame. It was June 2012, in a packed courtroom that seated more than two hundred. Peter Madoff was about to plead guilty.

He was sixty-six, and wearing a dark brown suit that didn't look expensive, given the estimated $70 million he'd pocketed over the years. Xanax was helping him maintain his composure as he read a thirty-minute-long statement that said little. His voice broke only twice, and only momentarily. "I revered him," he said of his older brother, his voice cracking, "and trusted him implicitly." ("It's the baby brother defense," whispered Allan Dodds Frank, a colleague seated nearby.) Later, as Peter told the court, "I am deeply ashamed of my actions," his voice broke again on the word "ashamed." He referred to Bernie's crimes as "atrocious" but didn't have anything else strong to say about them.

Like Bernie years before in the same courthouse, Peter Madoff was almost certainly lying. He declared emphatically that he had no idea his brother was running a fraud. "I truly believed that my brother was a brilliant securities trader who successfully traded for his customers' accounts," said the computer expert. That's pretty hard to swallow, since few employees ever saw him actually engaged in trading.

One of those employees was Peter Korman (henceforth: Korman), a finance manager for tech companies who spent summers as a teenager in the early 1970s working at BLMIS— when it was located in a small space directly on Wall Street. Korman recalls that "Uncle Bernie" (as he and scores of future investors called him) spent the summers at the beach on Long Island, rarely coming in to the office. And when he did? "I literally sat there and never saw him trade once," says Korman. (So much for the convertible arb trading genius of the 1970s.)

Korman's father, the late Aaron Korman, was an early manager with the original Dreyfus Fund, one of America's first widely marketed mutual funds. He was also one of BLMIS's financial backers in the early 1960s, due to a close relationship with Ruth's father-in-law. "Bernie's original aspiration was to be a trader," says Korman. "but he was trading in very speculative issues, and he lost, consistently. And he kept on running out of money. Uncle Peter [Madoff], who is eight years younger than Bernie, who I was much closer to, joined the firm [in 1970] and steadied the trading floor." Korman also recalls that Bernie had to be bailed out several times, and not just for that first pickle when he lost $30,000 of customer money in the early 1960s. "Uncle Bernie used to sit in my den, and my dad would write $10-20-30,000 checks on a regular basis."

Through the 1970s, the Madoff and Korman families lived in the same affluent village (Roslyn Heights) and became close. So close that Korman says he spoke with Peter Madoff before he went to prison. During the conversation, according to Korman, Peter revealed that A. G. Edwards—a major regional brokerage firm where Peter sat on the board—had in 2005 or 2006 offered to purchase BLMIS for more than $1 billion. But Bernie—who owned 95 percent of BLMIS—wouldn't even consider a sale. "Peter was kind of ambivalent," says Korman. "The kids [who had minor shares in the firm] wanted to sell it. It was a riff. It was a big disagreement, according to Peter. And Bernie killed the deal."

Of course he did! The last thing Bernie needed was a prospective purchaser nosing through the books as part of a due diligence process. A. G. Edwards would surely have discovered what Peter, Mark, and

Andrew should have known (or did know)—that, since at least 2002, hundreds of millions of dollars from IA customers were being used by Bernie to prop up the troubled broker-dealer and prop trading side.

Some of the crimes Peter pled guilty to were big ones, such as filing false statements with the SEC and cheating on his taxes. But some were just moronic, such as putting his wife on the company's payroll so that she could get insurance benefits. In his court statement, he admitted that "at my request, my wife was placed on the BLMIS payroll." Request *to* whom? Bernie? Or another executive? Peter didn't say. During one of my prison visits with Bernie, he sounded exasperated that this happened, saying, "I don't know what my brother was thinking. Crazy."

Of all the people sentenced in Judge Swain's court, it seems that she had the biggest problem believing Peter—and yet she wasn't privy to certain facts that might have made her even more skeptical about him. She was plainly upset that the government had cut a deal that prevented her from giving him more than ten years, essentially tying her hands and turning her into nothing more than an honorable rubber stamp.

"The guidelines sentence here is life imprisonment," she stressed at his sentencing. "The government and the defense, however, have negotiated a carefully crafted set of charges and a guilty plea agreement under which the maximum possible sentence of imprisonment is ten years."

According to numerous sources, heated arguments broke out inside the US Attorney's Office regarding the case against Peter as well as a case against his daughter and deputy, Shana Madoff Swanson. Some prosecutors wanted to indict her, but higher-ups didn't. Some didn't want to see Peter cop to just a ten-year sentence; they would have preferred taking him to trial, reasoning that a mere ten-year sentence might lead to the Madoff Five defendants refusing to plead guilty. And that is precisely what they did—took their chances at trial and got sentences well below the statutory maximum. (Some FBI agents, such as Paul Takla, were among the most furious about going soft.)

On the other hand, Peter made it clear that he would have refused to plead guilty if the feds indicted his daughter, and the US Attorney's office was eager to start wrapping up cases. As the compliance counsel for BLMIS, Shana helped complete and submit a false filing to the SEC. But simply submitting or even signing a false statement is not necessarily a crime. (It depends whether the submitter or signer knew it was false.) Peter, the firm's general counsel and head of compliance, signed most of them himself, and insisted to the feds that it was *he* who was 100 percent responsible for the false information, not Shana.

Today Shana is doing what perhaps any former compliance officer who's avoided indictment should be doing: she runs a yoga studio in Connecticut, as well as a New Age Facebook page where she adds endless heart emojis to those who love her transcendental posts. Reached by phone in early 2024, she was sweet and gracious but declined to discuss anything to do with her BLMIS days. "While I appreciate your call, I just don't revisit that with anyone," she said. "I've moved on and I'm in a very good place, and so I don't need to go back there. . . . If you want to talk about *yoga*, fine [she laughs]. That's what I do and that's who I am."

Fair enough. But she dodged a bullet and got away narrowly, maybe unaware of the infighting and arguments over her fate inside the prosecutor's offices.

For certain, Judge Swain was deeply distrustful of Peter and how much he knew. As to Peter's insistence that he thought Bernie's trades were real, she wasn't buying it—certainly not for "trades" that benefited Peter specifically. "He knew that huge amounts of money that his brother, Bernard, conveyed to him were not the proceeds of the specific trades to which they were attributed," the judge concluded. "He knew that trading records were backdated and falsified."

At the plea hearing, Peter said he was "in total shock" when

Bernie told him it was all a fraud. If so, the shock apparently didn't last very long. Peter's first move, as stated earlier, was not to reach out to law enforcement (he never did) but to go along with Bernie's plan to use the company's remaining funds—some $250 million—to pay friends, colleagues, and family members.

There's also the small matter of Peter's presence at a meeting with Bernie and SEC agents. But you won't read about it in SEC inspector general David Kotz's harsh 477-page report on the history of the agency's ineffectual probes of Madoff. Kotz deposed one of the SEC's longtime and most-respected agents, Alexander Vasilescu. Alex was the lead investigator probing Madoff *after* his arrest, and he revealed something quite telling about Peter. Curiously, Kotz's final report didn't include *any* of Vasilescu's testimony, which, as we'll see later, logically explained how and why the agency could have *legitimately* missed capturing Madoff over the years.

A Freedom of Information Act (FOIA) request for Vasilescu's testimony took months for the agency to turn over. Initially I was provided an unredacted version of his testimony. Within an hour, however, I was sent a redacted copy and urged to use that version instead.

The complete version of the agent's testimony contained a paragraph regarding Peter Madoff that had been fully inked out from the second version. Thanks to the SEC's mistake, I had the original. In it, Vasilescu said that he reviewed a 2005 internal SEC memo that summed up an interview of Bernie at BLMIS offices. "Investigators there were asking about a number of clients, and Peter Madoff, according to the memo, was present. And Bernie said, 'Oh no, we have only, like, these twenty, whatever, institutional clients.' Because certainly having thousands more retail customers that you're doing this strategy for would have, you know, certainly raised greater red flags."

It is, of course, implausible that Peter could have been listening to this fiction from his brother and not known that Bernie was attempting to mislead the SEC. Back in 2005, any investment firm with fewer than twenty-five customers was not required to register with the SEC as an investment advisor—a registration that would have subjected it to more rigorous agency rules. Bernie had far more than twenty-five accounts just among *family* members, let alone his and Peter's friends. Peter knew that.

At the end of his plea hearing, Judge Swain pounded Bernie's brother hard, while also citing some of his accomplishments on Wall Street. "Peter Madoff's contention that he did not know that anything was wrong with the investment advisory business is beneath the dignity of the former vice chairman of NASD, governor of the National Stock Exchange [posts Peter once had], and corporate director, community pillar, and family paradigm about whom I have read so much over the past few days," she said. "It is also, frankly, not believable." She then challenged him to at least be honest in the future about "all that you have done and all that you have seen—in other words, about all that you know."

Peter simply blew her off. At his sentencing four months later, on December 20, 2012, he offered a ninety-one-word statement that provided nothing new. "I have tried to atone by pleading guilty and agreeing to forfeit all my present and future assets and income," he said.

The judge tried again. "To take his story as told when he pled guilty at face value, he knew that the business operation was a little bit crooked, and he was content to go along with that. We all know that a crooked operation is only rarely if ever just a little bit crooked." Swain pointed out that with the collapse of BLMIS, Peter has been on a "personal journey of spiritual examination." She was referring his currently working and studying at a local synagogue. "This is disgusting," hissed Gladys Luria, a Madoff investor sitting behind me, just loud enough that rows of observers heard her. A former Madoff trader told me that back in November 2008, just before Madoff Securities went dark, he'd attended a second Bar Mitzvah that Peter had for himself. As older brother Bernie explained: "In modern times, it's like reaffirming your vows. It's a popular thing to do in his circle."

Judge Swain told Peter and the full courtroom that it was "important for the victim and for society as a whole that the full scope of corrupt activity at BLMIS be uncovered and understood" and that "part of your [religious] redemptive work is determining what if any role you will play in that process." Luria laughed cynically, turned to her husband seated next to her, and said, "The only good thing is that he [Peter] saw me."

In 2020, after having served nine years of his ten-year sentence, Peter Madoff was freed. Today he lives in Palm Beach Gardens, Florida—the other side of the tracks from tony Palm Beach, where he once had a mansion. Just days after his brother's death, Peter was photographed by a UK tabloid, the *Daily Mail*, looking scraggly in shorts and lugging a heavy bag of dog kibble along a sidewalk there. Despite the judge's challenge, he still chooses silence.

At Bernie's suggestion, I sent Peter a letter in 2016, asking if I could visit him in prison. I wanted to speak with him so that he could help me inform readers about BLMIS's positive contributions to Wall Street, an aspect of the Madoff tragedy that most reporters have ignored—and one that Bernie pressed me hard to include in the book. Things such as state-of-the-art trading systems (with "best execution," a legal duty of brokers to execute customers' trades at the best terms possible—which BLMIS excelled at for more than a decade), and using technology to challenge the NYSE's monopoly. At the time, Peter was incarcerated at a federal prison in Devens, Massachusetts, and was four years into his sentence. He wrote back declining to speak and asked that his letter to me (which said nothing) not be disclosed.

Two months later, Peter sent a letter to Bernie laying out many of those accomplishments that I was seeking to learn about, in excruciating techspeak. I doubt Peter knew the actual letter would be shared with me, but who knows? Most interesting to me is how he ended the letter to his big brother: "Love Peter."

A Prosecutorial
Post-Mortem, Part II

Q: Okay, the $68 billion question: What do you believe Bernie's family members knew?

JACKSON: What we can say clearly about the family—and this was made clear during the trial—I think one of the more important parts of the accounting fraud case is that the upstairs business [nineteenth floor] *didn't make money.* So the business that Andy and Mark worked in [overseen by Peter] didn't actually make money, not in any of the years we looked at after 2000.

Q: Prop trading?

ZACH: It was for sure always propped up by the downstairs [IA] business.

JACKSON: In some years, it lost massive amounts of money, and in other years, it lost smaller amounts of money. That was a big part of the accounting fraud, because the fact that it didn't make money was—this is how Enrica, as the controller, gets involved. The people in charge of the accounting had to go through incredibly complex machinations in order to move money from the seventeenth floor into the books and records of the nineteenth

floor in order to make it look like the nineteenth floor
was making money. The only accounts that consistently
made money on the nineteenth floor were the juiced-up
accounts that came from the seventeenth floor. There
were, like, two traders in my recollection in the history
of the nineteenth floor who actually knew how to make
money and who actually *made* money. Everybody else
was losing money. So, if you're asking me what the sons
knew, well, they knew that the business was not making
money, and they knew that they were inflating the numbers through shady accounting to bring seventeenth-
floor-numbers money into the nineteenth floor. So, you
ask yourself: Does that mean that they were standing on
the sun, potentially not aware of the solar system? I don't
know.

SCHWARTZ: It's not crystal clear who saw what. This is not a
normal business, so it's not like every Monday they would
get reports on their financial positions and things like
that. Everything was handled irregularly. So, it's very hard
to say who had access to what information.

Q: But they [Peter, Andrew, and Mark] are *running* it. They
should have known.

SCHWARTZ: Madoff knew it. DiPascali knew it. Bonventre
knew it. That's for certain, because they, along with some
others, did the round-tripping [movement of cash back
and forth] that allowed them to book the Ponzi profits into the market making business. But, I mean, look:
My view is, some people call that [the nineteenth floor]
the "legitimate business," right? And I never subscribed
to that word. It's legitimate in the sense that the stocks
and bonds were real, I guess, but it's also legitimate in the

same way that, you know, that the olive oil shop that Don Corleone sat in the back of was real. Yeah, they had *real* olive oil. You could probably go in and buy the olive oil. But that didn't mean [*laughs*] that it was a legitimate olive oil shop, right?

I don't think there was anything legitimate about that [BLMIS] business. I think it was corrupt top to bottom. One of the things that DiPascali testifies about, and it's well corroborated, is that some of the IA positions are held on the books of the market making business. So, ask yourself for a second: If you have a multibillion-dollar hedge fund downstairs that's "executing" all of its trades, why for a fraction of them do you have to go upstairs [nineteenth floor] to execute?

Q: So, are you willing to say that Peter and the sons *should* have known?

SCHWARTZ: I don't know what that means, "should have known." A lot of people should know things that they don't know. That's not even something I speculate about. I have my opinions about whether they *did* know, but that's a different issue.

Q: Can we know those opinions?

SCHWARTZ: No. Because that's informed by all sorts of things.

Q: The seventeenth-floor people were not allowed to have email addresses, while those on the top floors could. One wonders if that alone should have made all of the family suspicious—from Ruth to Peter, the sons to Shana.

ZACH: And the seventeenth-floor computers were from the eighties.

JACKSON: And everyone who worked at Madoff Securities knew that the seventeenth-floor technology was ridiculously outdated.

ZACH: Many of the people who worked on the nineteenth floor [Bernie's sons included] went to prestigious colleges and had an actual real-world understanding of the financial markets. So, they are not Frank or Annette, they are people who have a mature and academic grasp of how a business would work.

JACKSON: Most of the business on the nineteenth floor is market making. With some prop trading. They were not very successful at the prop trading. The family members know that. If you assume that they believe that this is all legit, they know that the *successful* part of the business, where real successful "trading" is happening, is on the seventeenth floor, right? So, knowing that, you would think that the key nineteenth-floor employees at some point would say, "Can't we work in the part of the business [*laughs*] that *makes money*?"

Q: And Ruth?

JACKSON: I don't know, and I wouldn't speculate about the scope of her knowledge. There was evidence at trial that, when Dan Bonventre wasn't reconciling the main account, Ruth was reconciling the account.

Q: She said on *60 Minutes* that she hadn't worked at the company since 1963. I spoke recently with Eric Lipkin. He confirms that Ruth was in the office constantly since the time he was hired in 1992 until the company imploded in 2008. He says her job was to reconcile the 703 banking records—money in, money out.

JACKSON: There are financial records that came in during the case, and there is testimony that relates to things that she was doing in order to help maintain some of the critical accounts in the 1980s and 1990s. Her handwriting was identified on various documents.

Q: On the day before Bernie's arrest, she withdrew ten million dollars. And that was *also* the same day that Bernie supposedly confessed to the family that it was all a Ponzi. She apparently thought the good times could continue and that nobody would know about the withdrawal, or that she'd somehow be allowed to keep it. Is Ruth just a victim? Or did she know about Bernie's frauds, or *should* she have known?

ZACH: In the trial, one of the things we emphasized is that things always got thrown into focus whenever there was some sort of audit—or external force trying to look in. She is living with Bernie. These are moments of great stress, going back at least to the A&B. [He is referring to the early Madoff feeder, laid out in chapter 6, which was the subject of an SEC probe in 1992.] A&B is connected to *her* family. It's hard to imagine that when they are fucking stuff up, and Bernie is having to spend months of just *full-on* fraud, that he is not complaining to her about her family—that that's not somehow seeping into the home world. But you can never prove that.

Q: Yes, Ruth's father [Saul Alpern] in the 1960s was bringing investors into Bernie's forerunner-IA unit, and he was partners in the accounting firm with Avellino until the mid-1970s. Is it unreasonable to at least ask if Alpern knew it was a fraud going back to the beginning?

SCHWARTZ: I think it's fair to ask whether *anyone* who was associated with this is a crook. But some things are just lost to time. As prosecutors, we were doing something fundamentally different than what you're doing, so we never set out to tell the complete story, the complete history, and certainly [not] as to people against whom prosecution could never be an option. There was just less reason to pay attention to them in a case where there was more than enough to pay attention to. You could investigate this case for fifty years and not be done, and not explore everything there is to explore, and not go down every avenue, and not get to all the truths. You could do this for fifty years and still leave a lot on the table.

Q: Why not ask David Kugel [the BLMIS arbitrage trader who pled guilty] what family members knew? "You admit you concocted all these fake formulas, and gave them to Annette to create and post fake trades on customer statements. Did any of Bernie's family members know this was happening?"

SCHWARTZ: Who says we didn't ask him? You mean at *trial*? Well, that's not an admissible question. *Who* knew? He can't testify to *who* knew. "What conversations did you have with somebody who is not a defendant" is not a relevant question.

Q: Well, did David implicate any family members when you spoke with him?

SCHWARTZ: He was involved in the fraud for decades. So, he had a lot of relevant information to tell us about. But with only a few exceptions, there are not these sort of explicitly conspiratorial conversations—so, when you ask if someone is "implicated," I don't know exactly what that means. Look, all of these people [who pled] were debriefed dozens of times, extensively, about *everything*. Trust me, we bled these people dry.

Q: Let's talk about Shana. She was a compliance officer who filled out false regulatory reports. Clearly not enough to indict?

SCHWARTZ: When Peter pled guilty, he allocuted to a set of facts that was not consistent with Shana's guilt. The question is, *where* do the answers on the forms come from, and who knows that they're false? Shana filled out the form, but Peter took responsibility for the substance of the answers. Whether or not she signs it, the question is, who is the person intentionally putting false information into it? Just signing something that is not true doesn't make you criminally liable; you have to know it's false. Whether Peter's story was true or not is a different question. But prosecutors have a responsibility to only bring charges that they're confident in.

Q: What about when Frank testified that Shana and the boys were shredding emails before an SEC audit? Was that not enough to indict them?

SCHWARTZ: It's a data point. You only want to bring cases if it's the right thing to do, and someone saying there was this one incident where people were "in a room doing something, and this is my understanding"—that's a data point, but does that give you the moral certainty that you need? It all gets considered together and either adds up to give you comfort you are doing the right thing [to indict] or it doesn't. So, the question is, does it pass that threshold?

14

The Final Word . . .
on the SEC

The Question: Did the SEC blow it by not uncovering the fraud? Or did major Wall Street figures such as Ace Greenberg deserve blame?

Despite the ghastly emails that Bernie's lawyer, Ike Sorkin, received from the fraudster's hate-filled losers, most Madoff investors I spoke with expressed no ire toward the attorney. Instead, they directed their anger toward the Securities and Exchange Commission.

The agency had examined and at times investigated Madoff over the years, but never uncovered the Ponzi. What these investors didn't grasp, or refused to accept, is that the agency's mandate has *never* been to protect people from poor investment decisions. Moreover, not one investor of Madoff's ever complained to the SEC, which is almost always how prior Ponzi schemes were exposed.

One Madoff investor who blames the SEC is Arline Altman. For many decades, she was a close friend of my aunt Adele and uncle Al, and she had suggested to them in the late 1980s that they invest with Bernie. She'd started investing with him in the mid-1970s. I spoke with Arline in 2018; she was eighty-five at the time and living in Boca Raton.

"I kept telling Adele and Al what a good deal it was," she recalled.

"I always say I wish he'd [Bernie] waited until I die before they found [arrested] him. Everybody was grabbing what they could. I was living pretty good." Altman said she was earning 19 percent annually, and estimates that Telfran, the sub-feeder that recruited her, Adele, and Al and then fed them into Avellino & Bienes, must have been making 25 percent.

Arline not only faulted the SEC for failing to catch Madoff, but also said "the unbelievable part, of course, is that the SEC secured it. They said he was good. There was no doubt. So, I agreed with that. Why *not*?" Putting aside the fact that the SEC does not *secure* investments, did she ever think at the time that the returns were too good to be true? "Well, they *were* too good to be true, yes, and my brother-in-law questioned it, and a few people did," she replied. "However, when the SEC okayed him, doesn't that tell you something? Wouldn't you think, 'He's *okay*'?"

Arline was referring to 1992, when the SEC shut down A&B, requiring Frank Avellino and Michael Bienes to return money to investors. Bernie then took on those investors directly. The SEC did not examine Madoff at the time. "They *didn't*?" she gasped. I explained to her that BLMIS was by then a big name in the market making business, like Merrill Lynch, and the money hadn't disappeared; the SEC concluded that A&B was the rotten apple but said nothing about Madoff.

In the end, Arline was a net winner; she took out more than she had invested. "I took out more because, '*Why not?*' It was there." Predictably, she was pressured to return money to Picard, which she ultimately did in 2015. "I was told by my lawyer that they [the trustee] will not leave me alone and that if I want to sleep at night, get rid of it."

As we've seen, Bernie's investors, accountants, employees, and banks were all in positions to expose the fraud. But it's time to shatter the myth that the SEC is the villain for failing to have uncovered it. Instead, let's direct some blame to many Wall Street legends who, as leaders of their industry, were not only in a position to know—but did, in fact, conclude (as they admit in the interviews below)—that something wasn't right about Madoff. Yet they chose to stay silent.

Among them: Ace Greenberg, who built Bear Stearns into a global investment powerhouse before it was sold to JPMorgan Chase; David Komansky, who built Merrill Lynch into a global financial behemoth; and Buzzy Geduld, one of the greatest traders who ever lived. One call to the SEC from any of these guys would have had agents knocking on Madoff's door in no time.

But the SEC is a busy place, and a lot of loonies come knocking on its door. And screening out those loonies isn't as easy as you might think. Nearly two decades ago, when I wrote in *Fortune* magazine about Ponzi schemer Dennis Helliwell—the titleholder prior to Bernie's arrest for the longest-running Ponzi (eleven years)—I interviewed Ernest Badway, the SEC enforcement attorney who nailed Dennis. Today Badway heads up the securities unit for a big law firm, Fox Rothschild, and is considered one of the leading defense lawyers in the country for Wall Street crimes. He represented Bernie's older sister, Sondra Madoff Weiner, and her husband, Marvin, in their case before the trustee, who clawed back winnings from them, as well as an employee of Cohmad who was in a similar spot. Given that background, he's among a handful of SEC experts, past or present, who can provide a reality check on what it takes to get the agency to take action.

I caught back up with Badway to discuss the Madoff case in great detail. Over dozens of hours, and several years, he laid out his understanding of the SEC's role and whether the agency actually deserves all the flak it has taken in the post-Bernie years. I've come to agree with his conclusions.

The central question about what, in retrospect, may seem to be the SEC's failure to investigate Madoff is whether it ever received any actionable information to begin with. The US Securities and Exchange Commission doesn't just patrol the financial landscape, looking for evildoers. That landscape is far too vast for that. The agency instead relies on whistleblowers, tipsters, concerned members of the finance community, complaints by people who feel like they've been swindled in some way. It doesn't just spontaneously start digging, even during routine examinations. It doesn't have the budget for that, not by a long shot.

The widely recognized whistleblowing "hero" in the Madoff case is a Boston-based quant named Harry Markopolos. Following Bernie's arrest, Markopolos testified before Congress about the scandal, wrote a book titled *No One Would Listen: A True Financial Thriller*, and starred in a documentary called *Chasing Madoff*. He turned the Bernie saga into his own little PR (and cash) machine.

It is true that Markopolos alerted the SEC on three occasions—in 2000, 2001, and 2005—to his suspicions about Bernie. And he has been lambasting the agency ever since for not catching him in time. Based almost entirely on Markopolos's version of events, many have laid the blame for the Madoff affair—or at least its longevity—squarely on the SEC.

But it ain't that simple. As Badway explained, "The SEC gets tens of thousands of these kinds of letters all the time. Generally speaking, anonymous tips are viewed and reviewed, but it really becomes the *content* that's going to drive any investigation that would be launched. [And] when it's unsigned, it's one of the things that goes *against* it."

Markopolos's initial letter *was* unsigned. And that wasn't all. He was also a direct competitor of Bernie's, a fact that seriously undermined his account in the eyes of investigators after he signed his subsequent letter. When I asked Badway what his reaction would have been, back in his SEC days, to a twenty-five-page, anonymous, single-spaced letter calling someone a fraud, he told me he would have assumed that the complainant was "a quack. He's in the 'crazy zone.' Again, the SEC gets thousands and thousands of letters from people, where, for example, they don't know if it's coming from a competitor. And guess what? Markopolos *was* a competitor."

In his letters to the agency, Markopolos provided no hard evidence. He asked to be paid a bounty. And one time, in an email to an SEC Enforcement Division branch chief, he identified himself deceptively in capital letters with the title of a "Financial Fraud Investigator." He did eventually become one, but not until after Madoff's arrest. All were signs, says Badway, "that he's somebody who is not interested in turning somebody in or correcting a wrong—he's interested in lining his pockets."

(Pocket-lining, and perhaps lunacy, was again at the forefront for Markopolos in 2019, when he released a 169-page explosive report titled "General Electric, A Bigger Fraud than Enron," in which he accused GE of hiding $29 billion in liabilities. He predicted that, as a result, GE wouldn't survive much longer. An exposé in *Fortune* magazine by journalist Shawn Tully concluded that Markopolos was completely wrong. Nonetheless, *prior* to his report's release, Markopolos admitted to giving the results of his "investigation" to a hedge fund that planned to short GE stock and to share its profits with him. He was also fishing for whistleblower rewards from the SEC and the DOJ.)

Badway concedes that, in hindsight, Markopolos was correct in one of his assertions: that Bernie was either running a Ponzi or engaged in what is called front-running, the practice of trading secretly ahead of clients on the broker-dealer side of the business. The latter would have been impossible for Bernie to do without regulators knowing it. But the totality of the Markopolos correspondence made him look like just another toxic wannabe whistleblower. "He says at the top of his letter that he presented these findings to the SEC's Boston office five years earlier, in 1999," Badway notes. "If that's true, they likely concluded he was a kook."

It turns out Markopolos was paranoid, and slept with a gun under his pillow, fearing that Madoff would harm him. He said he was prepared to drive to New York from his home in Boston to kill Madoff if he felt threatened. He also said he feared being murdered by the Russian Mob, despite zero evidence that *any* crime syndicate even invested with Bernie, much less wanted to see Markopolos dead. He may nevertheless go down in history as the "no one would listen" tipster. But he doesn't deserve to be.

Markopolos had a starring role in a post-Ponzi report written in

2009 by David Kotz, who'd recently been made inspector general of the SEC. Kotz had until 2007 worked in the same role for the Peace Corps, where he had zero experience investigating Wall Street fraud cases. But in his new position, he wrote a scathing 477-page account of the agency's failure to detect the Ponzi. Rushed out barely nine months after Madoff's arrest, it came accompanied by thousands of pages of (often redacted) exhibits; mainly pages of depositions that he and his crew conducted with current and former SEC personnel.

Unfortunately, it doesn't appear that anyone ever dissected the report to any significant degree. If they had, they might have concluded that, just as investors were blinded by Madoff, Kotz was himself blinded by Markopolos—so much so that they actually became good friends. This gave the appearance of a conflict of interest, according to a little-noticed 2012 investigation by the US Postal Service's inspector general. (The USPS had been handed the task of compiling the report, given its neutrality and expertise on such probes; the press all but ignored it.)

I met with Kotz in February 2012, several months before a USPS probe of him was under way, to discuss the Madoff case. Immediately upon sitting down, he asked if I'd chatted with Markopolos. I told him that I had left a message for him in 2009, but that he'd never returned the call. "I'll get Harry to talk to you," he said confidently. Kotz then explained why Harry might have been reluctant to call me back: "Harry was paranoid; he had fear the SEC was going to get him."

I thought it was an odd offer at the time, given the importance of Kotz's maintaining distance from the "hero" of the case. How could the IG get Harry to call me? But I didn't think about it again until the USPS report came out. The USPS investigator had been tasked with looking into whether Kotz had become too close, not only to Markopolos but also to an attorney named Dr. Gaytri Kachroo, who represented victims of another Ponzi, this one run by convicted billionaire Allen Stanford until his arrest in 2009. Kachroo, it turns out, had been introduced to Kotz by—you guessed it—Markopolos.

The USPS IG's report states that it found evidence that Kotz had personal relationships with both Kachroo and whistleblower Markopolos. With regard to the latter, investigators referred to Kotz as a "very good friend" of his. It is unclear exactly when they became friends, but documents describe how Markopolos and Kotz developed a friendship through their interactions during the Madoff investigation. "If this relationship began before or during the SEC OIG's investigation into the SEC's failure to uncover or prevent the Madoff Ponzi scheme," reads the report, using the acronym for the Office of Inspector General, "then Kotz would have been in violation of CIGIE's investigative standards and the Standards of Ethical Conduct for Employees of the Executive Branch." CIGIE stands for Council of the Inspectors General on Integrity and Efficiency.

What if Kotz had become close friends with Markopolos after publishing his report, which lionized the whistleblower? Would that have been okay? Not at all, according to SEC insiders. While it wouldn't have violated SEC's ethical rules, it clearly would have been improper because the Madoff cases themselves—in all their various guises and jurisdictions—were not only going strong in 2012, but they still continue today. In addition, Madoff deputy Frank DiPascali didn't testify in the Madoff Five case until late 2013, and his testimony included details on their efforts to fool the SEC. Had DiPascali revealed information that hadn't been previously known to Kotz, the IG likely would have had to recuse himself from any further probes.

As for the Kachroo matter, in January 2010—just four months after Kotz released the Madoff report—the IG penned a personal business plan on his SEC computer that characterized Kachroo not only as a personal business reference but also as a "personal friend." And yet he hadn't even begun his inquiry into the Stanford case, for which Kachroo was an important source. Furthermore, drafts of Kotz's business plan in 2010 listed Markopolos as a personal contact and "very good friend."

Conflicts aside, how much beef was on the bones in those hundreds of pages Kotz churned out about the Madoff fraud? "The investigators he talked to feel it was a hatchet job and unfair," said an SEC official to me in 2011 who was part of a new team brought in to revamp the agency. "They're not happy with what was omitted from the report." In this official's view, Kotz "would reference truth without resolving tension in the evidence," and that he typically exceeded his mandate as IG to write reports that "second-guessed decisions by people [on cases] that are everyday decisions."

Another member of the new SEC team was Lorin Reisner, a former chief of the criminal division at the US Attorney's Office, where he oversaw many Madoff-related cases (including the JPMorgan Chase probe). In 2009, Reisner joined the SEC for a few years as its director of enforcement. "I think David Kotz oversimplified" the agency's failure to nab Madoff, he says, adding that he remains "skeptical" about many of the former IG's assertions in the report. "But there were obvious mistakes that were made," says Reisner. "For the most part, the SEC staff consists of really good people, but they made mistakes. They didn't do everything that could have been done."

It's a view echoed by Andy Calamari, the SEC official who had tipped off the US Attorney's Office the night before Madoff's arrest. "The IG was in a tough spot," says Calamari, who at the time coheaded enforcement for the agency's New York region. "He was given the assignment to go out and find villains, and that's what he did. The press was demanding it, and so was the Congress." The reality, says Calamari, is that the agency receives scores of whistleblower tips every year, and tips are very often hard to evaluate. "The vast majority are not pursued for one reason or another. But in this case, the SEC staff did try to run down the tip's allegations and spent a lot of time on them."

That much is clear in the IG report, which Calamari says shows "mistakes may have been made along the way, but everyone involved was doing his or her best. I think it's sad that some very good people were so vilified for honest mistakes. We all make mistakes, usually with little consequence. It's very unfortunate that the mistakes made here—likely influenced by Madoff's towering reputation—resulted in what was at the time an unimaginable outcome."

A harsher opinion was held by Ed Nordlinger, an attorney who started working for the SEC in 1965 and rose to become the deputy regional director for New York until he retired in 2005. I spoke with Nordlinger a decade ago (he died in 2021), when he referred to Kotz as a "wild guy trying to make a name for himself . . . he says things that just aren't true in the reports that are public." Nordlinger recalled being interviewed for forty-five minutes by a young reporter for *60 Minutes*, but he didn't make the cut for the show. "The kid who interviewed me said that 'If you read the opening and closing report of an SEC investigation of Madoff, and if you do XYZ steps, could you have uncovered the Ponzi?' I said, 'Absolutely, you're *hired!*' The answer is as follows: You can always uncover any Ponzi scheme if you dig deep enough. The question is, based on what you have, does it justify the resources? That's the difficult measure."

Reisner, the former SEC enforcement chief, recalls how the 2008 financial crisis drew a lot of fresh talent aboard: "We were flooded with applications from people on Wall Street who either were disenchanted and wanted to make a positive contribution, or who had lost their jobs or no longer liked their jobs." Management was streamlined, he says, and every specialized unit was provided "a superstar investigative staff who we empowered, creating a more muscular agency."

Unfortunately, a five-member politicized body of commissioners (appointed by US presidents) continues to have too much power to approve or reject cases. While the commission gives recommendations from the agency's enforcement staff "substantial deference," says George Canellos, a former deputy director of the agency's enforcement division, "it's been unwilling to outright delegate to the staff any meaningful authority to make prosecutorial judgments and resolve cases even in very minor matters."

Another big problem for the SEC is how members of Congress hamstring the agency year after year, while complaining that it needs to do more. The agency's budget is decided by Congress annually, but "from year to year, no one really knows what the SEC's budget will be because of the vagaries of the Congressional budgeting process," says Canellos. "You may receive a significant hike in budget one year to hire new staff and address specific needs. Then your budget may be cut the next year, requiring you to freeze all hiring and contemplate layoffs. There's no predictability, which inhibits long-term planning."

And then there's the David-versus-Goliath ratio of SEC staff to entities they need to regulate. The SEC budget is 99 percent smaller than the markets it is expected to regulate. In 2008, the year Madoff was arrested, the agency had a mere $900 million budget, an inadequate 2.8 percent increase over 2007, and just seventy-five investment advisor (IA) inspectors in the field. But there were more than eleven thousand registered advisors, along with sixteen thousand investment companies and registered funds that managed on the order of $34 *trillion*. So that was more than $500 billion per examiner. Given that ratio, the SEC should be applauded for how many criminals it does catch each year.

And since 2008? That ratio has gotten even worse. In 2023 the SEC's budget barely topped $2 billion, just a 3 percent increase over 2022, despite the fact that it garnered $5 billion in penalties and other financial remedies. The SEC generates way more money for the government than the government pays for it, thanks to fees it charges the Wall Street firms it oversees, as well as fines and penalties it levies on offenders. But Congress has long fought against the idea of the agency funding its own budget each year.

"The SEC doesn't directly cost American taxpayers one penny," says Dennis Kelleher, CEO of Better Markets, a well-respected nonpartisan organization often called "Wall Street's Watchdog." In his view, "you've got to double their budget; they have been level-funded basically since

2016." Without the resources, the agency can't keep pace with sophisticated crooks in areas such as cryptocurrency and high-frequency trading. It often comes down to politics—what Kelleher calls "the yin and yang of regulation." Republican administrations tend to pull back, as the administration of President George W. Bush did prior to the 2008 financial crisis. But it was the Clinton administration that enabled the supersizing of banks, so the Democrats don't get off the hook easily.

In 2003 Congress approved "pay parity" at the SEC, which enabled the agency to bring in highly experienced lawyers and industry experts. After that, the employees starting to come into the SEC "had very deep experience," recalls Calamari. "But it took five, six years to build up that experience. Unfortunately, the agency never got the full benefit of pay parity because our budgets in many years were mostly flat, and so we were under a hiring freeze much of the time, with intermittent spurts of hiring." When combined with normal attrition, which was always highest in the New York region, the money capital of the country, those hiring freezes were deeply felt.

"Budget freezes also made it very difficult to do long-term IT planning, and IT is critical nowadays to catching wrongdoing," says Calamari, echoing George Canellos. "We literally had rocket scientists at the SEC who were devising programs to analyze market data, catch front-running, and identify insider trading patterns. But constant budget freezes really hampered this work. Still, the SEC brought many significant cases in the years those freezes were in place, which goes to show just how conscientious and hardworking the SEC staff is."

For this book, former SEC attorney Badway reviewed the letters from Markopolos to the SEC, including the twenty-five-pager in 2005 that ultimately triggered two agency probes. I walked through every paragraph in Harry's letter, stopping to ask Badway if "at this point, would you have opened an investigation?" His answer every time was "No." Badway also reviewed the Kotz report. "I read the IG's report," he said afterward. "Going page after page after page, I don't think you'll find anything. A lot of it is written in complete conjecture."

Much of it is also a kind of reverse engineering, just like Madoff did with his backdated statements. Overall, how does Badway rank the Kotz investigation? "As one of the former SEC enforcement directors used to say, he knew no heights to the barn door. He never really nailed anyone."

Harry's complaints were all they had to go on, unlike in the Helliwell case. "The reason why we at the SEC discovered Helliwell, and I remember it as if it was yesterday, is that we received a two-line fax in 1996 from a Connecticut investor saying, 'I lost my money' after Helliwell had guaranteed him a twenty percent to twenty-five percent return with a Marine Midland Bank investment that was actually just Helliwell's checking accounts. Until the day that Madoff admitted what he was doing, no one ever complained about losing money from Bernie Madoff."

The complaint from the Helliwell customer had been sent to Richard Lee, who at the time was an SEC assistant director of compliance. "Lee handed it to my boss and said, 'This is real,'" recalls Badway. "My boss says, 'Go see Dennis.'" The following day, Badway and two other SEC enforcers were in Helliwell's Manhattan office, watching him shake for nearly ten minutes while his lawyer gave him advice over the phone. Helliwell's assets were frozen five days later.

In his IG report about the Madoff affair, Kotz criticizes the staff for not checking to see if Bernie was doing actual trading. But, says Badway, that's "just not done when there aren't any victims coming forward to say something's wrong." The SEC, he continues, "would have to get a formal order of investigation indicating that they discovered something untoward. It is pretty hard to say something is untoward when no one is complaining about it—no victim. . . . Someone needs to come in and say, 'Something is wrong with this.' Hindsight is twenty-twenty. How do you make the logical leap at that time that it would have been a Ponzi scheme? But the IG ultimately makes fun of the SEC, causes them grief, insults them. But, really, at the end of the day, they can't be faulted."

Still, should the SEC have picked up on this sooner? "Yes," says Badway. "However, the evidence they had before [Madoff's implosion and arrest], was that *enough* to suggest the SEC should have done that? In a perfect world, I wish the SEC had more power to do certain things. If they had that, then they would have picked it up."

Some years after the SEC was ripped apart over the Madoff case, and the furor over the agency was no longer making headlines, several big financial machers—household names on the Street—agreed to share their views about the Madoff scandal with me. Coming from such historic figures, their perspectives are invaluable for generations to come, while also holding a mirror up to themselves. Case in point: Alan "Ace" Greenberg, Wall Street legend and former chairman-CEO of investment bank Bear Stearns, who sat for an interview in 2012, two years before he died at age eighty-six.

It took place, ironically enough, in his office on the first floor of JPMorgan Chase's headquarters on Park Avenue, as JPMC had purchased Bear Stearns during the fiscal crisis of 2008, when the venerable investment bank was collapsing.

Under Greenberg, Bear was one of BLMIS's largest customers on its broker-dealer side. That's because, while Bear cleared over-the-counter trades for many Wall Street firms (hedge funds, other broker-dealers, and so forth), the company used to farm out a lot of business to Madoff—specifically, business that it didn't want its own traders executing, in order to avoid conflicts of interest between competing Bear units.

"Every firm on Wall Street did business with him. *We* certainly did," said Ace. "He was honest, up front." As for any personal relationship with Bernie, however, Greenberg related only one experience, circa 1990. Mets co-owner Fred Wilpon, one of Madoff's biggest clients on the IA side, was on the Bear Stearns board of directors at the time and invited Greenberg to dinner one night with him and Madoff, as well as their wives. "He was a very quiet guy," Greenberg recalled about Bernie. Ruth, too, he said, "was very quiet."

One can speculate that Madoff might have been too nervous to schmooze it up, given that he was returning unfathomable returns to Wilpon on the IA side, and that Greenberg might have been suspicious had the subject veered in that direction. "Look," said Greenberg, "Madoff wouldn't let anyone from the financial area put money with him," with a few exceptions. "He was scared to death they'd look at his [customer] statements and see something was wrong."

Looking back, Greenberg was amused when recalling that his own wife, who compiled scrapbooks of their lives, had inserted a note from Bernie into one of the volumes chronicling the mid-1990s. It read, "Dear Ace, thanks for what you did for me, I'll never forget it. If I can do anything for you, I would enjoy doing it. Thanks again. Your pal, Bernie."

Greenberg laughed. "I have no idea what he was talking about."

Was Greenberg at all suspicious about Madoff through those years? He certainly was. Ace had a friend, also a Bear client, who'd invested a lot of money with BLMIS. "He was always telling me about the returns, and to me it made no sense whatsoever." Sometime around 2000, Greenberg phoned John Mulheren, a Wall Street icon who had earned billions in the 1980s trading stocks and options. "What's the story with this guy Madoff?" he told me he'd asked Mulheren.

"Well, supposedly he does one of two things," replied Mulheren, who died in 2003. "He writes options on big stocks."

"So, *that's* nonsense," snapped Greenberg. "I know something about that, and you can't make any money on that, period. Nonsense."

"The second thing," said Mulheren, "is supposedly he runs ahead of his institutional orders with clients and makes money off that."

"Well, that's illegal. Between the two things you just told me, one is nonsense and the other is illegal. That's enough for me."

Greenberg laughed after recounting the anecdote. "I didn't tell my friend that," he said. "Luckily, my friend died about three months before Madoff blew up. But if he *hadn't* died, this thing would have killed him." Another laugh. "He was such a believer in him. His family lost a ton, but they'll be getting some back."

If Pat Carroll, the FBI supervisor of all the Madoff post-arrest investigations, had been sitting in the room, he wouldn't have laughed. Carroll, a former Wall Streeter himself before joining the bureau (where he spent a quarter century before retiring in 2015), often visited investment firms to encourage traders, brokers, and executives to come forward with tips about wrongdoing. The reason he gave them for doing so: "Their own self-preservation. If they don't turn in their own crooks, then everyone's reputation is ruined."

Unlike the typical old-school law enforcement agent, Carroll had the skills and cred to do this, having worked previously as a broker at Merrill Lynch. So, Wall Street insiders didn't dismiss what he was saying. When I met Carroll in 2010 (accompanied by FBI spokesman Jim Margolin), he felt they were really starting to listen.

In Carroll's view, what's wrong with Wall Street can be reformed only from within. "A shocking flaw is that so many key players in the securities markets were highly suspicious of Bernie Madoff, and there were rumors in the industry that he was 'no good.' And yet not one of them came forward."

Using Madoff as a hypothetical example, Carroll said, he may have had the following kind of exchange with a Wall Street insider:

"There's a rumor that everyone on the Street hypothetically knows that a dirty guy ran a sixty-five-billion-dollar hedge fund. Well, give him to us!"

"'Well, why do I give a shit?' they'd say."

"But do you give a shit now?" Postarrest.

Just how corrupt was Wall Street at the time? "I'm not saying the Street is a criminal enterprise, like La Cosa Nostra," he said in 2010. "But there is a lot of criminal activity. We have convicted so many on pleas." As he told Street insiders, "If a guy is consistently ahead of the market, drill down on it, and your brand will not suffer. Everyone has someone [crooked], even the FBI." He offered the example of Robert Hanssen, the notorious FBI agent who'd been selling US national security secrets to Russia for two decades at the time of his arrest in 2001, in what the bureau called "possibly the worst intelligence disaster in US history." "If we were a public company, imagine our stock [after Hansen's arrest]."

Carroll wished there was more "one-ended dialogue, where they came to us about things they see." Unfortunately, there was (and still is) a mentality on the Street that "you don't want to give up their own, or you'll be a rat."

So why didn't Ace Greenberg of Bear Stearns sound an alarm? Why not alert securities agents that something isn't kosher? Ace's views would surely have held more weight than Harry Markopolos's. Like the difference in weight between a bull and a chicken.

"John [Mulheren] felt the same way I did, like, who cares?" conceded Ace. "I'm not involved, I don't have any money with him. I never *would* have any money with him. I didn't understand it." As for Greenberg's friend, the true believer, it was caveat emptor all the way. Ace didn't even see the need to even share his suspicions with *him*, let alone SEC agents.

Moreover, in Greenberg's mind, it seems there is a line to draw between the two halves of Bernie's operation. The IA side may be filthy and fraudulent, but the retail side (which Bear's business fueled) was—as he put it—"honest . . . up front." It may not have dawned on Ace, or he didn't care, that the IA business thrived in huge part because of the retail side's stature, or that the IA end (as we now know) sometimes financially fueled the retail side.

So did Greenberg's and Mulheren's silence help fuel the Ponzi, just as the JPMorgan Chases of the industry did? It's a fair question. The industry's leaders sitting on their hands.

Another of Greenberg's friends, he said, examined some of

Madoff's customer statements years before Bernie's arrest and concluded, "This guy's a crook." While Greenberg named the exec—a former longtime member of Bear's board—the latter agreed to speak extensively only under the condition that he not be named. So, let's just call him Mr. Pink, after one of the best movie cowards of all time, from director Quentin Tarantino's 1992 film debut, *Reservoir Dogs*. Mr. Pink, played by Steve Buscemi, hides from his partners in crime whenever there's trouble and yet still ends up with the diamonds.

Here's what our Mr. Pink observed:

In the early 2000s a family friend who had previously invested with Madoff was considering putting in $4 million more. "I said, 'Lemme see the [customer] statements,'" recalls Pink. "And I remember that *most* of the trades were 'as-of' trades; meaning as of another date."

Those two little words are written on customer statements throughout Wall Street after trading errors are caught. But it's not common. Bear Stearns handled 10 percent to 11 percent of the volume on the NYSE, and its error factor was 3 percent. But in the case of BLMIS, which did 6 percent to 8 percent of the NYSE volume at its peak, the statements examined by Mr. Pink found that 80 percent to 90 percent of the trades were "as-of."

It is clear *now* that this was because of the incompetence of the staffers (Annette Bongiorno especially) Madoff employed to phony up the statements. But at the time, an 80 percent to 90 percent error factor would have been a red flag to any Wall Street trading expert looking closely at the statements. "This said to me that he's doing something wrong," says Pink. "How can you have so many trades that are not correct? I've been in the business a long time, and if a guy was doing that, he was doing something else where he's matching trades. He's doing something after the fact and putting them through 'as of.' It made me suspicious."

Unlike the example with Greenberg, *this* executive decided to at least warn his friend. Not that it mattered. "I said, 'I wouldn't put money with him. I don't know what he's doing,'" Pink recalls. Did the friend listen? "What do you think? He did it [invested the additional millions.] People are greedy. People had to be greedy not to be cautious about the guy. But I didn't know it was a Ponzi. I talked to a couple of friends—hedge fund guys I know—and some of the real pros didn't feel comfortable. Nobody could replicate what Bernie Madoff said he was doing—that they *heard* he was doing."

Our Mr. Pink also recalls another friend of his, who owned an over-the-counter day-trading firm and was "*very* friendly" with Peter Madoff. "He wanted to get into the [IA] fund, and Peter would never let him get in," says Pink. "And when this thing broke, he said to me, 'Wasn't that nice? Peter saved my ass. He didn't let me in because he knew I'd get screwed.' I said, 'No, he knew you were sophisticated and that you would have looked at what the hell they were doing, and you would have said, "What the fuck is going on?"'"

Maybe. Or perhaps Bernie vetoed it for that very reason, and Peter didn't have the heart to reveal to his dear pal how powerless he was with his older brother. But while Peter may have had little sway with Bernie on those issues, it seems that Bernie sometimes held himself out as running *Peter's* end of the business.

While Peter ostensibly ran the retail trading side of BLMIS, it was Bernie himself who would come and negotiate the deals with Bear Stearns—*not* Peter. At these meetings, which took place two, maybe three times a year, Bernie "would always bitch that we gave him hard business [tough stocks to execute] as well as easy business," recalls Pink. "He didn't want the hard, just the easy. I said, 'Sorry, you either take it all or you don't get any.'" The significance of this? "It tells you that he was involved with the trading [so-called legitimate] side of the firm."

A former Bear Stearns executive who could shed even more light on Madoff is Michael Minikes, the firm's former treasurer, as well as CEO of Bear Stearns Securities Corp. Minikes was very friendly with Bernie through the years, and they played golf together. Like Greenberg, Minikes moved his office to JPMorgan Chase after the bank bought the firm in early 2008. BLMIS phone records reveal that on December 8, 2008—three days prior to Bernie's confession and arrest—Mark Madoff placed a call to Minikes. The subject? Unknown. Bernie twice asked if I could get him a mailing address for Michael and his wife, Cheryl. It was the first and only time Bernie asked for such assistance. Unfortunately, the ex–Bear treasurer declines to talk—on or off the record—about these subjects.

As my interview with Ace Greenberg drew to a close, I asked his view of whether Chase (his current employer) did anything wrong or negligent, given that Bernie's Ponzi was being operated out of a sole Chase checking account. "No, what did they do wrong?" he asked.

Should Chase not have spotted it?

"Umm, no, I mean, who knows?" he says, growing somewhat uncomfortable with the questions. "I'm not gonna tell someone how to spot it. You know, uhhh . . ."

Greenberg was asked to help place Madoff in the context of Wall Street history. "Oh, he's in a class all by himself," he said. "Oh my God, yes. There are Ponzi schemes that come up every day, but none of them the size of this or as far-reaching as this. The monthly job of falsifying five thousand accounts—can you imagine what a job that is? Unbelievable. He had money clamoring to get in, like *crazy*. But he was very smart: his returns were never that big, he just kept them consistent, and that's what sold people on it. And he could *exist* longer because he wasn't having to pay out twenty-five percent of their money."

E. E. "Buzzy" Geduld is another Wall Street legend who didn't think to blow any whistles on Madoff. Among old-school traders, Buzzy needs no introduction. Scrappy like Madoff, he grew up in a middle-class neighborhood in Brooklyn, dropped out of college, and was fired from his first two Wall Street jobs after just a few months at each company. He quit the industry in the early 1960s to launch a successful chain of donut shops called the Donut Pub. But he returned to build a trading behemoth—Herzog, Heine, Geduld, which has roots in the 1920s—into the Street's third-biggest firm linking buyers and sellers on the NASDAQ.

By 2000, Geduld's company was making markets in more than ten thousand stocks—roughly five times the size of BLMIS's market making unit—when it was sold to Merrill Lynch for more than $900 million. At that point, Geduld literally took his dough and went back into the donut business. Today, at seventy-eight, he runs his own venture capital/private equity firm.

Geduld served on industry committees with Madoff and recalls him at meetings as "very smart, very personable, extraordinarily likable," he said during a chat in 2012. "If you knew him, you'd like him; you'd want to have drinks and dinner." That said, just like Greenberg and the others from Bear Stearns, Bernie's IA business didn't pass Buzzy's smell test.

"You can't have those kind of returns when you theoretically do some subset of an arbitrage," he explained. "The returns should have been six percent to seven percent, and not in the teens consistently. So people would ask me, 'What do you think of Bernie Madoff?' I'd say, 'I know him, I like him, I think he's terrific, but either he's selling dope or laundering money.' Something wasn't right. That was my standard line to people: He was selling dope or laundering money. You can't have returns like that unless something is wrong."

Selling dope or laundering money. And yet Geduld never thought to pick up the phone and discuss it with the SEC.

Additionally, Geduld was dumbfounded that "so many very, very smart and sophisticated people gave *so* much of their assets to one person—which is kind of scary. No matter how 'good' he was, why would you give him all or a big chunk of your assets? It's *mind-boggling* to me."

But, as mentioned earlier, Bernie stayed clear of the "smart money": the Ace Greenbergs, John Mulherens, Buzzy Gedulds, and their ilk. "First of all, he wouldn't take Wall Street money," recalled Geduld. "For instance, someone like myself, if you were in the business, he wouldn't take your money. So, Wall Street guys that got caught up in this would have gotten caught up because they invested into a 'fund of funds,' and one of those funds would have given him money. But to my knowledge, Bernie never solicited nor would he take money from working firms. People like that are gonna ask questions or want to know what your strategy is."

Bernie got red-hot whenever people suggested that the "smart money" on Wall Street knew not to invest with him. Sometimes he would name Wall Street pros who he said *did* invest with BLMIS because they believed in him. At other times, he was vague, simply mentioning the names of firms that his top investors supposedly worked for. "Do you think all of these professionals on Wall Street," he said by phone in 2012, "like Jim Simons, [David] Komansky, all these other people— partners of Goldman, and Merrill, and Morgan Stanley—would invest with me if they didn't believe in my strategy? They didn't see anything wrong. Doesn't mean there wasn't something wrong [*laughs*]."

It turns out, however, that it was only a charitable foundation of Jim Simons's that had a small account with Bernie. Once Simons— considered one of the greatest hedge fund traders alive—conducted an analysis of Madoff, he pulled out the funds. As for Komansky, the former chairman and CEO of Merrill Lynch disputed Bernie's claims in an interview I conducted with him in 2017 (four years before his death). According to Komansky, he would never have invested with Madoff because "it's a flimflam." But, like Greenberg and Geduld, he didn't think it was his responsibility as an industry leader to encourage the SEC to look into it.

Whenever Bernie talked about his (fake) split-strike strategy, he'd always say that he never actually *did* the trades, but that they would have made sense if he *had* executed them. "And you can't say that people should have known, because the strategy made sense," he once said, "and a perfect example of why it made sense are people like Jim Simons and David Komansky."

This baffled Komansky. "How the *hell* he got my name is beyond me because I was three levels away from investing directly with him," he said. "I never invested with Bernie." He laughed. "Never." Komansky said he invested in a private partnership that invested in a Madoff feeder fund. "I never even knew I was involved with Bernie until it went down. When you invest in these private partnerships, part of the deal is you don't know what they're investing in. They don't divulge the vehicle."

Komansky maintained he never would have knowingly invested "in a million years" with Madoff. Why not? "Wall Street was a pretty incestuous place, and there weren't many secrets, and certainly when you are the CEO of Merrill Lynch or running the trading areas of Merrill Lynch, there's not a lot that escapes you in the rumor mill." Komansky said he was never approached directly by Bernie, but that three or four people over the years made pitches. "'Hey, why don't you invest with Madoff?' they'd say. 'I can get him to take your money. You know he doesn't like to take more money, but I can work it'—da da da."

But Komansky wasn't going near it. "I was always told that he almost guarantees a twelve percent," he recalled. "Now, growing up, someone once told me that if you are holding a deck of cards, and someone tells you that if you rub it the right way, the jack of spades will jump up and spit in your face and you're gonna get wet . . . My point being, it's a flimflam. How could *anybody* guarantee twelve percent in the stock market over a period of time? And it never went any further than that. But it was ludicrous that people were doing this."

Komansky said he knew plenty of people who *were* invested with Madoff at the time. But he declined to mention who was running the partnership that invested some of his funds into the Madoff feeder. "Let's let it be," he said, shrugging. "I'm not gonna make people look foolish. On Wall Street, if you are an active investor and you're doing a lot of different things, you're gonna hit some home runs and you're going to lose some. But *guarantees*—any time I heard the word 'guarantee,' I looked askance at that opportunity."

One thing Komansky neglected to mention was that beginning

around 2000, while he was CEO of Merrill Lynch, a post he held from 1996 through 2002, the company had a prohibition on investing with Madoff. It was effectively a "No Madoff" policy, and it was instituted because of Bernie's lack of transparency and an abundance of alarming signs. The firm not only didn't invest its own money or its clients' money through BLMIS, but also refused to provide leverage for other investors looking to make an investment in Madoff feeder funds, something that banks such as JPMorgan Chase did happily. It even prohibited executing trades with exposure to Madoff. Ernest Badway, the former SEC attorney, says that had Komansky shared this information with the agency, in all likelihood it would have launched more aggressive probes that would have uncovered the Ponzi.

In an email to a colleague after Bernie was busted, a Merrill Lynch executive wrote: "We all knew there was something wrong at Madoff—I guess now our suspicions have been confirmed."

But while Merrill Lynch, or at least the parent company, wouldn't go near BLMIS after 2000, that didn't stop one of its overseas subsidiaries— London-based Merrill Lynch International—from dabbling in Bernie. MLI sold structured products tied to feeder funds that were funneling billions into Madoff's IA business. Not only that, but MLI and a few other Merrill Lynch overseas entities were involved in constructing several leveraged products using the Fairfield Greenwich Group's extraordinary returns with Madoff as reference funds—just as Chase, HSBC, Nomura Bank, Natixis, and a host of other global banks did. In MLI's case, its clients had to pay only 25 percent of the total amount invested in Bernie's split-strike baskets of stocks, with Merrill Lynch International loaning the rest. However, MLI would pass the first 25 percent of any potential losses onto the clients, which protected it against risks.

Today, in what could surely be termed chutzpah, MLI is declining to turn over a measly $16 million in stolen BLMIS customer property to Irving Picard, in part on the grounds that this pocket change is the result of a subsequent transfer from Fairfield Greenwich.

15

Solved: Bernie's Old New Math

| | | | | | | | | | | | |

The Question: How did Madoff, while sitting in prison for years, volunteer to take a math test that ended up providing yet more proof that his fraud began decades before he claimed it did?

One of downtown Manhattan's famous buildings is the Alexander Hamilton US Custom House, a seven-story Beaux Arts–style mansion intended to be occupied by US presidents. It was never used for that purpose, and today it's designated a National Historic Landmark. It is home to a giant museum devoted to the history of Native Americans, who suffer their own types of affinity frauds. But there is also a small side door, easy to miss, that tourists and the general public never use: the entrance to the region's federal bankruptcy court.

What has been unfolding there quietly for years, and continues today, can be viewed as the trial of Bernie Madoff that—due to his guilty plea in 2009—never took place in a criminal courtroom. That's because some of the active bankruptcy cases ultimately hang on what seems like a simple question: When did Bernie's fraud begin?

And whether Bernie grasped it or not, in 2017 he helped obliterate his own claim that his fraud began in 1992. It was an extremely complex, and yet beautiful, thing to watch—for quants and mathematicians, anyway. Sadly, it was too technical for even the average Wall Streeter to comprehend.

It involved what is known as "fractional shares" and "cash in lieu" in convertible arbitrage and is but one wiggly strand of the snakelike snarl that was Bernie Madoff's Ponzi scheme. Readers may conclude after this chapter that the comment by former federal judge and FBI Director Freeh in the book's introduction—that he had "never seen such a sophisticated, elaborate infrastructure and operation for deceit and deception that served to protect an underlying fraud scheme of such mammoth proportions"—was, if anything, an understatement.

Before trying to disentangle those snakes, it's worth noting that there are at this writing more than eighty Madoff-related cases with billions of dollars at stake still being argued in that Lower Manhattan courtroom. And yet reporters almost never stop in for a look. The complexity (and boredom) of bankruptcy hearings is too much for most news readers and viewers to stomach.

Nevertheless, octogenarian Irving Picard and his team are still—fifteen years after his initial appointment—recouping money for losing investors. By early 2024, they had recovered and reached settlement agreements totaling a whopping $14.7 billion. But that's not because everyone feels bad about letting Bernie line their pockets. To the contrary, plenty of entities are fighting to hold off Picard—and hold on to their booty. The trustee's team may well be battling it out until 2025 or later.

Just who, exactly, is still fighting is one of the most curious aspects of the ongoing duels taking place beneath the Custom House's rotunda. And the defendants come from all quarters: individuals (including former Madoff employees and distant relatives), foundations, feeder funds, and large banks. Hearing after hearing, although they are routinely postponed again and again.

The banks are the most conspicuous and unrelenting combatants, and there are dozens of them represented, from Citibank to Credit Suisse; from the Royal Bank of Canada to the Royal Bank of Scotland; from the National Bank of Kuwait to the National Bank of Korea. Natixis bank (France). First Gulf Bank (United Arab Emirates). The Abu Dhabi Investment Authority. Bank Hapoalim (Israel). Société Générale (France). Nomura (Japan). The list goes on. They have billions in assets and, if they want, can afford to drag out the litigation for the foreseeable future. None of those banks have been found to have been complicit in the fraud; but none will willingly return the money that they have (or *once* had) on behalf of Madoff feeder fund clients.

In most cases, they are known as "subsequent transferees." In simple language, this means they were middlemen to the ultimate investors. Most of these banks were delighted to act as what they thought were "conduits," collecting fees from feeders and investors (or profiting by investing their own money into Madoff). But now that the music has stopped, they are arguing that even if they still hold the tainted assets, they shouldn't be held liable for them. Some of their arguments also involve complex legal concepts such as extraterritoriality and comity (the principle that nations will extend courtesies to other nations for the sake of good relations, even in bankruptcy litigation). Due to the global scope and span of the Madoff case, new law is even being created in many courts. But perhaps not fast enough. The lawyers are getting rich, not unlike Bernie's net winners did.

The fractional share matter mentioned above is also before the bankruptcy judge, and it contains a sweet irony. From prison in 2017, Bernie himself was helping the plaintiff—a former investor (since deceased) named Aaron Blecker who was 105 years old at the time— try to gain money from the trustee that he thought he deserved. But in so doing, Madoff opened a door that revealed that his fraud began decades before he said it did. In a deposition in the case, he slipped up in a way that proved beyond a mathematical doubt that the fraud was in existence by the early 1980s—and not the 1990s, which, as laid out earlier in the book, would have kept Ruth superrich for the rest of her life. (Of course, we know now that the fraud actually began almost from the start of his career, in the early 1960s.)

But before diving into the math, some background about the case he was deposed in will be useful. For more than a decade, an attorney named Helen Chaitman, who herself lost money to Madoff, has been filing lawsuits on behalf of dozens of fellow losers against the trustee. Her main objective, which she has taken unsuccessfully as high as the US Supreme Court, was to challenge the methodology that Irving Picard and his staff use to determine who gets paid from the billions of dollars recovered to date.

One of Chaitman's arguments has been that Bernie's investors should actually be *credited* with the phantom funds that were displayed on their account statements the month before his arrest. On its face, that sounds preposterous—and judges have so ruled—as it would certainly encourage investors to enter and stay in future Ponzi schemes. Chaitman's centenarian client was claiming that he never received and deposited some "profit withdrawal" checks he had requested from BLMIS in the 1980s. No bank records go back that far.

In some ways, Chaitman is a classic breed of defense lawyer who creates alleys and byways to drag people down, and she can afford to do it because her clients aren't paying. The bankruptcy judge doesn't appear to like her very much: he once memorably shouted her back to her seat in the gallery when she literally tried to traverse the court's well to assist a colleague. But he is allowing this drama to play out, which is great for history as it sheds more light, inch by inch, on the Ponzi.

The best thing about it: Bernie was deposed twice in the case, in 2016 and 2017, in an effort to help Chaitman and these losing investors. Why do it? Madoff often described Chaitman to me as a "nutcase." But perhaps he was willing to be deposed for no other reason than boredom and ego, and because he hated the trustee (who is not shy about disputing Bernie's versions of events), and because he understandably found it more pleasant to engage with smart lawyers rather than drug dealer cellmates, of which he had many. But by doing so, he sabotaged himself on a technical issue that undermined when *he* has long claimed publicly that the Ponzi began.

It may be best to peel this onion by providing highlights of Madoff's testimony in an April 2017 deposition. The person asking the questions is David Sheehan, who oversees the Ponzi recovery cases for trustee Picard. It was a chess match—one for the ages—and Sheehan destroyed Bernie.

Q: What's a fractional share?
A: A fractional share is less than one hundred shares.

Out of the gate, Bernie was wrong. Something called an "odd lot" is less than one hundred shares. A fractional share is less than *one* share of stock. It may come about in the case of certain convertible arbitrage transactions—involving convertible preferred stock, convertible bonds, and warrants.

(In a word, preferred stocks are—*well*—more "preferable" than common stocks because they often have perks like mandated dividends. Warrants are similar to stock options.)

The knowledge that a fractional share is less than one share of stock is something elementary for Wall Street traders. And it's certainly a fact that one of the best convertible arbitrage traders for decades—which is how Bernie portrayed himself—ought to have known.

Sheehan asked Bernie how often a fractional share occurs in

an arbitrage situation. Not very often, replied Bernie. Sheehan then asked if "when you convert the bond, preferred, whatever you are converting, does it not always have a fractional share?"

Sometimes yes and sometimes no, said Bernie.

Q: Do you credit a fractional share [to a customer], or what do you do with it? You're now selling this arbitrage strategy to a customer. You go in, buy the arb [also known as "putting on" an arb]. And then you short the stock, and you do it [the arbitrage] simultaneously. And when you do that, you get a fractional share?

A: Yeah, typically, if customers do a fractional share, you would give them the fractional share.

Q: Do you give them the stock or cash?

A: You could do either, both.

Not so, says Steven Adams, one of the world's top arbitrage experts, and an author of a step-by-step guide on how to do it. (The book's been used at the University of Chicago to teach arbitrage.) Adams walked me through Bernie's deposition on these points. "It's either cash *or* it's shares," he explains. "But since nobody on earth has ever actually *seen* a fractional share, and they couldn't trade them on any exchanges until recently, his customers could never have disposed of them. Thus, they could only have legitimately received the cash value of such a fractional share."

Think of them as crumbs.

When does that fractional share occur? Sheehan asked Madoff. "I don't know when," he replied. "I'm not sure." Bernie should have known that. He'd long insisted that he was doing successful convertible arbitrage for friends and family in the 1960s through

the 1980s. Fractional shares occur at the *moment* when the arbitrage instruments—bonds, warrants, options, etc.—are converted,
not before. This conversion could take place within days, or weeks
or even years later. And at that time, instead of clients receiving a
fractional share (which, again, didn't trade on any exchange), they
would be given cash. But a customer would never be given that cash
up front, because nobody has a crystal ball, and there is no way to
know *pre-conversion* what that cash should be—nor where that cash
came from.

And yet that is precisely what BLMIS did for customers, proving
that the customer statements were phony and backdated in the 1980s
and likely earlier. How so? The statements show a credit of "cash in
lieu of fractional shares" for the customers at the wrong time, *prior*
to the *actual* conversion. But when you are running a Ponzi scheme,
without the normal checks and balances of a company on Wall Street,
who cares?

"That's just crazy!" exclaims Adams. "Because you don't know
what the fractional is worth when you do the conversion. The stock
could be trading at one hundred dollars today, but by the time you
do the conversion it could be one dollar. It could be anything." He offers an analogy using stock dividends, which layfolk can better grasp.
"That would be like buying shares of Microsoft *today*, and Bernie
is giving you the quarterly dividend *up front*, when he's not going
to be paid the dividend by Microsoft for another three months. No
legitimate broker would do that. How can anybody know in advance
what a dividend will be? How can anyone know in advance what a
fractional share's value will be?" He laughs. If the trades were real,
says Adams, it would be a cash drain by Bernie, and it "makes no
logical sense in the world."

During the deposition, Sheehan asked, "When would you receive cash in lieu of fractional shares?"

"Actually, you know, I can't really tell you," said Madoff, "because

I didn't handle the operations side of the business. So, you know, I don't know when that was—when that was done."

Bernie was deflecting. In so many of my interviews with him, he made it clear that he saw the customer statements and oversaw the "operations" side in order to make sure the Ponzi didn't have errors that could give him away. And Annette Bongiorno was bungling customer statements constantly. During the Madoff Five trial, both Bongiorno and JoAnn Crupi stated categorically that they followed direct orders from Bernie at all times, and the trial produced no evidence to dispute their accounts.

> Q: But would it be fair to say that there is no fractional share until you sell the convertible security?
> A: So it's only if you were actually converting [that] it would you get the fractional share.

> Q: Why would you do this? Why would you give the customer cash before the conversion even happens?
> A: Well, you know, the client had intentions of converting; therefore, we didn't want to disadvantage the client by not giving him the cash in lieu, because instead of converting, we may have reversed it in the marketplace.

Intentions? Bernie's clients didn't have a clue what their intentions were—except to continue receiving impossible annual rates of return. Few of his clients bothered to carefully review their statements beyond looking at their balances.

(As for "reversing" in the marketplace, if you buy a convertible financial instrument and short the underlying common stock, and you make $5,000, if you have the opportunity to undo that trade, by selling what you bought and buying what you shorted, and make $7,500, you'd do it. And it's known as a reversal.)

Q: There is no fractional share until you actually convert, and
   yet you're showing a fractional share six weeks early. How
   could you do that unless you were backdating the trade?
A: It's . . . Look, I told you that I'm not sure how they . . .

Once again, Bernie shifted responsibility to an unnamed "they" on
his operations team.

Put simply, we have Bernie himself as the one who "set" it all up,
but his customers (who are actually clueless) are the ones who "decide"
if and when they are going to convert the security. What was *really*
happening here was that Madoff was struggling to get himself out of a
pickle—perhaps the last pickle of his life—from Sheehan's questions,
and he was squirming. One constant pattern with Bernie is that any-
time he is cornered, he launches into non sequiturs that go on and on.

Here's checkmate:

Q: In 1984 you were backdating those trades?
A: No, no.

Q: Those convertible arbs never happened?
A: That's not true.

Q: Do you know that there's hundreds of these? This isn't an
   operational flaw. Do you know that?
A: What I'm telling you is I'm not familiar with what their
   procedure was with fractional shares of how many . . .

Again, he's passing the buck onto former staffers, none of whom had
any experience on Wall Street except on the magical seventeenth floor.

Q: You ran the company. You didn't know?

A: I don't know. I'm not part of the Operations Department.

Q: Didn't you tell us that nobody dealt with customers those years except you, in those years, eighties?

A: I dealt with the customers when we . . . when . . . I spoke to the customers. I didn't physically handle the bookkeeping transaction for the customers ever.

Q: You wouldn't look at the customer statements?

A: The customer statements after—no. I mean, I looked at customer statements after they were generated.

Q: But if it's not converted, there is no fractional share, is there?

A: As far as the client is concerned, he'd be entitled to the fractional share. And *had* we converted, I'm giving you a fractional share. As far as the customer is concerned, he makes the profit.

Q: You didn't convert it; why would you give it to them?

A: Because if, in fact, we had converted it, the customer would be entitled to it. So, you know, I don't know how to explain it to you.

Bernie didn't know how to explain it because he couldn't. Again, he was crediting customers with fractional share cash before the arbitrage trades were even finished. That's because the trades never happened.

Attorney Chaitman, whose idea it was to depose Bernie, is, of course, emphatic in the court hearings that he was telling the truth about these matters. At one hearing, the bankruptcy judge asked the trustee's lawyers why they felt Bernie would lie now, at this stage of his life. It was a strange question, and the answer was quite simple. Bernie lied because he had always lied. He lied a decade ago when he wanted Ruth to secure as much money as possible in her settlement with the feds. Lying also served his "legacy" purposes to try to re-write history and show that he wasn't always a bad guy.

The question from the judge should have been: Why *not* lie?

Chaitman passed me a document that, whether she knew it or not, proved the point that Bernie wasn't conducting real trading in the 1980s. It was a customer statement belonging to her then-105-year-old client. It was dated June 30, 1986, and has fractional shares listed on it. I bounced it to Adams, the arbitrage expert, for his read.

The first entry states that 1,501 shares of convertible preferred stock in a company called Interco had been purchased on June 3, and that the underlying common stock behind it was sold two days later. It also reflects that the settlement date for the transaction was June 10.

Here is what's suspicious about this: first, it reflects that Mad-off waited two days to make the sale of the common stock. "That is very atypical when you are talking about convertible arbitrage," says Adams, "especially if you bought the preferred stock at a discount— which is the whole point of this type of convertible arbitrage. And the statement does reflect that it was bought at a discount."

Why is this atypical? Because the nature of convertible arbitrage is for traders to pounce quickly when they spot a slight discrepancy between the pricing of a company's convertible preferred and common stocks. "The point is that they took risk," says Adams. "Can you buy preferred on a Monday, and on Wednesday short the common, in such a way that you will have bought the preferred at a discount? Yeah, you can. But the market has to go in your direction. Now, can it happen once? Sure. But it's rare."

Investigators into the Madoff scam say they have *thousands* of examples where these purported arbitrage trades were done on different days and were always listed on the fake statements as "profitable." And that is virtually a statistical impossibility.

Moreover, says Adams, the bottom of the statement cites fractional shares. How can that be? The *only* time fractional shares would come into the equation, he explains, "is if Madoff executed a conversion where he would hand the convertible preferred to a conversion agent and say, 'Okay, exercise my option. Give me the stock.' And if you end up with an odd amount, that's when you get the fractional share."

Put into plain English, this is a fraudulent entry on the customer's statement. And there are thousands of such statements that investigators have uncovered.

Bernie claimed that in doing convertible arbitrage, he never converted; instead, he always reversed at premiums. But the BLMIS books don't reflect this. During the 1980s, there is actually no evidence at all, not *ever*, of him unwinding the current position in the marketplace and selling the convertible at a premium and covering the common stock—thus reversing the original position.

Such customer statements can be found even as far back as the *1970s*. Trustee Irving Picard knows that, because to prepare for Madoff's 2006 deposition, they broke open dozens more cartons in the *Raiders of the Lost Ark* warehouse that they still hadn't gotten around to or hadn't needed yet.

That's at least a fraction of a smoking gun, but more than enough to bury the Ponzi King's fairy tale.

16

The Forever-Unsolvable: Bernie's Brain

| | | | | | | | | | | | |

The Final Questions: What made Bernie tick? Can FBI "mind hunters" determine when he was lying? And can victims' gullibility when dealing with a con man be contagious?

D id Bernie believe in God? Or was he agnostic or atheist? "I don't know what I believe in," he said at first when I tossed him those questions.

"I do, I guess. Quite frankly, I just don't know. I never really thought that much about it. I don't know what I believe in at this stage."

What made Bernie *Bernie*? If he knew, he never said. Did his childhood offer any clues? That's a famously dangerous approach to decoding an adult's behavior, particularly that of a criminal who seems to lack empathy, but the temptation is too powerful not to at least try.

I tracked down more than a dozen of Bernie's and Ruth's classmates from elementary and high school and asked them to weigh in on Young Bernie. They described their own lives in 1950s Laurelton as Eisenhower-era idyllic, just as Madoff had done. But Bernie's gauzy memories were belied by his parents' serious financial problems—from the business bankruptcy, to the SEC trouble, to the tax lien on their house. Did Bernie (and Peter, for that matter) learn to violate laws at mother Sylvia's knee? Was father Ralph the de facto owner of the broker-dealers, or did he stick at least one of them in his wife's name as a way to try to hold on to the family home? (After all, it was almost unheard-of for a woman then to own her own brokerage firm.)

When asked, Bernie maintained that his mother once registered "as a tiny brokerage but never became active." In a subsequent interview, he said the companies were "never really active; they never filed financials because they never intended to do any business. She filed [registered] the business because my father was going through personal bankruptcy at the time."

This, of course, makes no sense. Why launch brokerage firms if there was never any intention to do business? Bernie's explanation was that his parents "figured" that registering the brokerage firms "would be more likely to insulate the family" from losing their house to the IRS. He insisted his father was never a registered broker but was working at the time, in the early 1960s, as a finder who brought entrepreneurs to underwriters in order to float small, overlooked public stock issues. Ralph Madoff had an office at BLMIS beginning not long after the business opened until his death on July 16, 1972, at age sixty-two. When young Frank DiPascali arrived on the scene three years later, he inherited Ralph's office.

As a child, Bernie began showing signs of an obsessive-compulsive disorder that would later become infamous at BLMIS. His sister, Sondra, mixed up his sock drawers just to rattle him. Similarly, as an adult, Bernie would roam the office and fanatically level the blinds, only to have employees such as Jodi Crupi set them crooked again as a prank. He also patrolled the traders' area to make sure they weren't eating at their desk and to police for stray papers. Once, Madoff marched over to an employee's desk and swept his arm across it, dumping all of the papers onto the floor to make his point. Most trading floors on Wall Street are messy, to put it mildly, but "Bernie wanted everyone to understand that he ran a business that was more technologically advanced and should appear to be when you looked at it," says a former employee.

Outsiders only got to tour the eighteenth and nineteenth floors; they never saw the ancient computers and piles of old newspapers on seventeen. Did those two worlds represent the two halves of Bernie's brain? Bernie the compartmentalizer?

Madoff was spotted doing his own vacuuming. In one instance, an employee got drunk during a holiday party and vomited on a rug, only to later find Bernie on his hands and knees, cleaning it up himself. All office colors had to be monochromatic shades of light and dark gray. Bernie's youthful obsession with organized sock drawers manifested in adulthood in the form of dozens of the same shirt, all in blue, as well as suits, all in gray. That probably also explains the dozens of pairs of unworn shoes found in his penthouse after his arrest.

Obsessive behavior veered into paranoia. Bernie may not have been able to use his computer very well, as he readily admitted, but he spent hours staring at its screen watching the comings and goings of his London employees on closed-circuit television.

Armchair psychoanalysis is cheap, and by no means sufficient to solve the mystery of what forces shaped history's greatest con man. But that isn't going to stop me from trying. By all accounts, Bernie was not outgoing in high school, nor introverted in the classic meaning of the word. He was *alone*, but not a *loner*. Maybe a better word would be *insular*. He expressed little interest in people or ideas outside of his own experience and could often be unkind.

"He was not *aggressive*," recalls Bob Schiffer, a fellow member of the high school swim team who seems to have known Bernie as well as anyone. "He wasn't an in-your-face, confrontational type of person. But there was a certain degree of hostility that, if you looked, you could see."

Schiffer recalls the swim coach matching up him and Bernie for a lifesaving exercise in the Atlantic Ocean, near the school. Madoff was to play the part of the drowning victim, with Schiffer rescuing him. Battling an undertow and waves, the "drowning" Madoff wrapped his arms around Schiffer's neck—as swimmers often do when being rescued. But this exercise got out of control.

"You're in the ocean, there's an undertow, a current, and waves," Schiffer recounted to me. "So, all sorts of forces playing on you, and you've now got someone with his arms wrapped around your neck who is throttling you. And it appeared that Bernie really liked throttling me."

Schiffer recalls that he threw his hands up as best he could, and both boys sank to the bottom. Schiffer waited and waited. "The amount of energy you have to exert holding someone does not allow you to hold your breath very long," he says. "I broke the hold, put my feet on the bottom, pushed up, and turned the position from in front to behind, put my arm across his chest, and put his head on my hip to save him—and he took a swing at me."

In Schiffer's view, Bernie wanted to be in control, not controlled. In other words, "He didn't want to be saved, he wanted to be victorious. He wanted to save *me*. He wanted to show that I could not break his hold, and that he would bring *me* up gasping."

It sounds like Bernie. Another swimmer, Paul Osher, asked Madoff to sign his yearbook. Bernie wrote: "Into the plunge do those laps, you bum. Don't you have any guts?" A third classmate, Michael Yesner, offers this crumb: "My insight about Bernie that will help you the most is ironic. Bernie was a great basketball player, and my favorite memory of Bernie is [of him] stealing the ball. He was absolutely a magician at it. You'd be dribbling down the courts, he'd come up behind you, and the next thing you know, Bernie had the ball and was heading in the opposite direction. He was a master."

Longtime family friend Peter Korman recalls his "Uncle Bernie" engaging in high-risk behavior outside the office, not just inside. In the late 1960s or early 1970s, says Korman, Bernie often raced a boat he owned for the eighty miles from West Palm Beach to Bimini (in the Bahamas)—alone, at full speed, and on automatic pilot. On one trip, he flew off the boat into the middle of the Atlantic. Madoff also owned a Jaguar XKE Coup and "drove it like he was Mario Andretti," says Korman, causing the car to break down regularly. "Bernie was not scared of high-risk behavior. He embraced it with zeal."

Korman says that while Ruth's parents were affluent, Bernie's parents were middle-class, which created extra pressure for him to give her the good life. "Ruth did have greater expectations, to use a notion from Dickens," says Korman. "And Bernie really did feel he needed to match them. He was young, he was ambitious, and he liked high risk. And he had to become *more* ambitious." As for Ruth, he says: "Ruth was not exactly warm and fuzzy. And if you talk to any of her friends, they'll give you the same. She was not a big hugger. She could be very elegant. Not a total lack of warmth, but formal."

Ultimately, such anecdotes don't tell us much. Barring the discovery of some traumatic moments in his childhood that made Bernie into Bernie, and since Bernie didn't leave his brain to science (in the hope that researchers will someday discover the "crook gene" or the "pathological liar gene"), what is history left with? "At some point, clearly the conscience departed the body," says Wall Street's Fagenson. But when, and why?

About nine years into dealing with Bernie, I shared my exasperation with two renowned experts who spent decades in the top-secret national security section of the FBI's Behavioral Analysis Unit. Those who have seen *Mindhunter*, the hit Netflix series based on that unit, might be glad to know that these two bureau veterans consider the show to be a pretty accurate portrayal. The agents proved invaluable for understanding Bernie better, and for detecting his lies; at the same time, however, they laid out for me the difficulties and pitfalls of analyzing him from afar.

There is no hard science in this realm. In order to reach more definitive conclusions, the FBI experts would have needed to sit with Madoff for days at a time and conduct a battery of tests that included a functional magnetic resonance imaging (fMRI) scan of the brain—and that wasn't happening. Nonetheless, their insights make a lot of sense. One of the experts, Joe Navarro, is the author of a book called *Dangerous Personalities: An FBI Profiler Shows You How to Identify and Protect Yourself from Harmful People.* He spent a quarter century as an FBI agent, fifteen of those years in the Behavioral Unit. Navarro was trained in verbal and nonverbal analysis, and taught a course for fellow agents on how to interview espionage suspects.

Despite never having met or spoken with Madoff, he leans toward certain conclusions about the man based on what he's read and studied, and also from watching him on news clips. So, was Bernie a sociopath? A psychopath? Something else? "It depends on who you talk to," Navarro responds. "Because these are terms that are ill-defined." Psychopathy is a very broad term, says Navarro, but in essence, he adds, as Robert Hare, the world expert on psychopathy suggests, such individuals have no conscience. "They can do great harm and not feel bad about it," explains Navarro. "They can be functional. They don't have to be serial killers. Most of the Ponzi schemes were developed by psychopaths."

Was Bernie *probably* a psychopath? "From a pathological standpoint, he had traits in common with predators," says Navarro. "Not just the body language, but overall behaviors, such as his flat affect, the fact he was under federal scrutiny, and he had what we call a narcissistic glee about him." Accuse most normal people of a serious offense, and they will just fall apart. But if you're somewhere between "a malignant narcissist and a full social predator—even a psychopath— then you have certain traits, and he [had] many of them."

A social predator, then? According to Navarro, Madoff was "well within the boundaries of an antisocial personality disorder and a psychopath. He certainly had all the features of what I reduce to the term of 'social predator,' because I think it's easier for the public to understand."

If you look up antisocial personality disorder in the *Diagnostic and Statistical Manual of Mental Disorders,* published by the American Psychiatric Association for clinicians, or if you look at Hare's work on psychopaths, Bernie Madoff is *well* within those two boundaries, concludes Navarro, adding: "I've sat in rooms with psychopaths, and my legs shook because they had reptilian indifference. 'Oh, here's a mouse, I think I'll bite it and eat it as it starts to dissolve. There's another mouse. Well, I think I'll bite that one, too.'

"They can do things for a very long time and take advantage of people who are friends, they can rip off their mothers, and rip off their grandmothers. And people say, 'I'm *shocked* he did that.' No, that's what's to be expected. And it's that lack of remorse, that lack of pity."

That certainly sounds like our Bernie. And it calls to mind the timeless joke about the scorpion and the frog, in which the former asks the latter to carry it across a river on its back. The frog hesitates, fearful of being stung, but the scorpion points out that "If I did, both of us would drown." The frog sees the scorpion's logic and agrees to take him, but midway across, the scorpion stings the frog, and they both begin to go under. "Why?" asked the frog. "It's my nature," came the reply.

Bernie did express remorse over his fraud and the damage it had done. Whether that remorse was heartfelt has always been unclear. There was never even a damp eye during those supposedly remorseful moments when I was face-to-face with him, nor did he ever seem shaken up on the phone. He also had a tendency to neutralize statements of remorse by following them up with attacks on his investors.

At times, he also evinced bitterness at not being appreciated for certain accomplishments on Wall Street that he felt were honestly achieved. He illustrated that bitterness by way of a vile joke: "Two Jewish guys meet on the street," related Vaudeville Bernie. "Mr. Schwartz complains to his friend Harry Cohen and says, 'All my life, I've been a successful real estate developer, building skyscrapers, office towers, all over New York. All I did was suck one cock, and now no one ever says anything about Harry Schwartz, builder of real estate. You suck one cock, and you're a cocksucker for the rest of your life.' That's the joke."

We've learned that when Bernie's world was collapsing and he was

THE FOREVER-UNSOLVABLE: BERNIE'S BRAIN   339

on the verge of arrest and confession, he conspired with his brother, Peter, and Frank DiPascali to cut checks for many employees and investor friends. He felt badly, he told me. Surely this was an indication of remorse and empathy for others? A psychopath wouldn't pay back an old lady he'd swindled, would he? Well, Bernie never mailed those checks—the FBI found them in his desk drawer—but if he had, and had the employees and friends deposited them, the funds would have been quickly clawed back by trustee Picard. The whole gesture was utterly empty, a performance of remorse with zero cost to Bregards Bernie.

"It has the patina of goodness, but niceness is not goodness," says Navarro, the former FBI expert. "Ted Bundy," the handsome, charming convicted killer believed to have kidnapped, raped, and murdered dozens of girls and young women, "was nice to the girls as he approached them. You have to look at the long arc of behavior and ask if there was any behavior prior to [Madoff's] announcement indicative of trying to undo the fraud and make restitution."

There wasn't such behavior, as Bernie conceded to me, saying that he didn't have the courage. Okay, but wasn't Bernie caring and empathetic when it came to his family? That *has* to rule out psychopathy, right? "They don't care in the same way we do," continues Navarro. "What you have to do is weigh that against whether the family is somehow being put in jeopardy [by Bernie's actions]."

As for Peter, there is no evidence that he's in the same mental camp as Bernie. Nor is there any sign that their sister, Sondra, has a cruel bone in her body, a source close to her says. "Not everybody that Mrs. Bundy gave birth to became a serial killer," Navarro points out.

Maybe Bernie simply had a chemical disorder? An out-of-whack frontal cortex? "No, you can't say that," says Navarro, adding that a full physical would be needed to even consider it—including having Bernie take a test to diagnose psychopathy and undergo brain scans. "What you can say is: this is an individual who is severely flawed of character. That's what the pathological narcissist and antisocial personality is. And these are traits that are lifelong, will *not* go away, cannot be cured, and remain fixed and rigid all their lives." Even Bernie's lawyer, Ike Sorkin, conceded his client's character defects when he spoke in court during sentencing. He said the government's request for a 150-year sentence bordered on absurd. He called Madoff a "deeply flawed individual," but a human being nonetheless.

I was primarily interested in learning from the FBI behavioral analysts how to determine when Bernie was lying to me. Almost all of my fifty-plus phone conversations with him were recorded. When transcribed, patterns seemed to emerge. I wanted help decoding them.

The transcripts are riddled with sentences by Bernie that end with "and so on and so forth" following his explanations about things that took place over the decades. Such phrases are what's known in the FBI psych world as "text bridges." As Navarro explains, Bernie's constant use of the phrase is a tic often used by liars to gloss over details. In Bernie's case, it would be a way to paper over the granular-but-vital minutiae of a lie's backstory; a smoke screen to discourage law enforcement from probing the details.

"You often see this with husbands who kill their wives," says Navarro. "'I came home, and I immediately ran over to her and could tell she was dead.' That's text bridging. 'Well, what time did you get to the house? How did you get to the house? When you got to the front door, did you use your key, or was it unlocked? Was the alarm on? Did you have to turn it on or off? Were the lights on? What was your route?—draw it on a piece of paper. When you got to the body, did you lean down, and where did you lean down at? Did you touch her?' Finally, an expert will ask the question that liars are almost never asked: 'When you found her, how did you feel?' You see, the liar doesn't think about how he felt."

I asked Bernie ad nauseam to describe in detail the key moments of when the fraud began. Surely he'd remember the particulars of when he crossed that line from honest man to thief. That had to have been an amazing and hellish moment—unforgettable—in his life. But Bernie never provided those details. Which stock trade created your fraud? Which client? What conversations took place? Where were you? And what happened next? He recounted nothing.

Similarly, when Bernie was asked to recall any conversations he had with the so-called Four Horsemen investors when they were supposedly betraying him, he couldn't. Or perhaps just wouldn't. Who said what to whom? How did he feel at the time? Not one conversation, beyond a rare sentence or two. Liars, Navarro observes, "have difficulty with the details of things that they never would have thought of; with the questions they never thought of.

"Maybe he never thought anybody would ever *ask*, 'What did you guys converse about?' or 'What did you say at first?' Liars think about the big lie. They *don't* think about the little lies. And so they don't know about the emotion that was attached to it. In those interviews, what you're going to find is that there's lack of detail, and if there is anything to do with how he felt about things, or guilt or so forth, it will most likely be superficial."

But why couldn't Bernie simply *make up* the little details as we went along? "Lying is hard work," says Navarro. "It really is. To tell a complete story that sells, we call that a novel. How many John le Carrés are out there?" That level of fabulism, says Navarro, "really causes what we call a cognitive load. It's where they have great difficulty."

If Madoff's tales were true, Navarro explains, he would have no trouble recounting the details of the moment. Instead, being grilled on the mundane particulars is grueling. "Why would a simple question cause you to look like you're doing trigonometry? Because now you've got to—and I've seen this look so many times when they realize, 'Oh, *shit*, this guy knows how to interview'—now you've got to come up with a plethora of answers that still meet the general outlines of the thing."

In addition to his reflexive text bridging, Bernie resorted constantly to a partial laugh, or something between a slight guffaw and a split-second chuckle. "The little laugh is actually a pacifier," says Navarro. "They have nervous tension, and they can't bring themselves to a full laugh, but it's used to dispel the tension. I hate to reduce it to this, but all primates do the nervous laugh, where we show our teeth, pull our lips, and sort of heh-heh-heh so that we will not get eaten alive. We use that to help dispel nervous tension, especially when we hear something that's troubling. It means that something is difficult for him to talk about."

Another problem any interviewer would face with Bernie, whether by phone or in person, would be the need to drastically limit the prepared questions. That's because he almost always drifted off on time-consuming tangents with merely one or two questions. What's that about? "I've interviewed a lot of people," says Navarro. "It's called the Vomit. Here's how it works: You say you want to talk to me about X, and you ask the question. I know you're on a short time frame, so now I vomit all sorts of shit, all sorts of nonsense, to eat the time. Somehow, you're supposed to pick the morsels out of what's on the floor. The Vomit. It's very effective." It's a way to avoid going into detail—or at least not the detail an investigator wants. It's like "We're in there, and there's a little piece of meat you might be able to use, but the rest is vomit."

Finally, I ask Navarro why Madoff seemed rigid as a corpse when he rose in the courtroom. Many humans would cry and toss themselves onto the floor in a fetal position during or after sentencing, or at least have to be held up. "That's because you're a normal person," he says. "People that are flawed of character are unaffected."

Dr. Jack Schafer, Navarro's colleague in the FBI Behavioral Analysis Unit, takes the analysis even deeper. Schafer spent twenty-two years in the unit's national security section and today teaches at Western Illinois University. He's the author of a book called *Psychological Narrative Analysis: A Professional Method to Detect Deception in Written and Oral Communications* and developer of the concept of the text bridge, discussed above.

Schafer likens text bridges to the "yada, yada, yada" filler deployed by characters on TV's *Seinfeld*. Bernie's reliance on them, suggests Schafer, is his way of saying, "I'm bridging over a bunch of stuff that I want to withhold and not tell you." People naturally text bridge while editing or redacting information they don't think is important, he explains, but criminals will do the same thing with the important stuff. So "listen for text bridges."

In 2018, three years before Bernie's death, I sent Schafer full transcripts of three of my phone conversations with Madoff—including every grunt, cough, half-laugh, "um," and "ahh." I was hoping Schafer could help me not only better understand Madoff but also suggest how I might handle him better in the future.

After having read them, Dr. Schafer had this to say: "In all of those conversations, here's what I think is going on. He is suffering from cognitive dissonance." Specifically, Bernie can accept that he committed a fraud, but only *to some degree*. "He's very confident, and he knows how to stay away from hot-button issues," said Schafer, adding that Bernie's implicit plea is "Don't make me out worse than I think I am."

"To be honest with you, he's playing you in these interviews. He has total control of those interviews."

That may also be why Bernie rambled about minutiae, and often got stuck on trivial points. For example, he obsessed about DiPascali's account of him staring into a computer monitor before confessing that all the money was gone. He denied Frank's description of him—it was the "staring" part that bothered him—and wouldn't let it go. "'Why are you even talking about it?'" is what Schafer would have told Bernie. "That was just an anchor point in time. He's going to seize on that, and he's going to filibuster so that you don't dig deeper with the questions."

At the start of my relationship with Bernie, I took a calculated risk when I conveyed anger at him for canceling our first visit after I'd already traveled to the prison. Bernie could have responded by never talking to me again. But I hoped my telling Bernie that he lied about it and that I felt "ill-used" by him might earn me some

grudging respect, since I figured the rest of the press corps was playing as sweet as possible in order to get him to open up.

"I know the approach you are trying to take, but that plays into
his strong suit," warned Schafer. "At some point, you gotta say, 'Bernie,
what you're giving me is nonsense. It's nonsense. Look, Bernie, you've
done all these things—you're an evil man.' Of course, you run the risk
of him saying, 'I don't want to talk to you anymore.' But you're not picking up anything when you talk to him except his version of the truth."
Which, of course, made him look a whole lot better than he really was.

"He is well practiced at parrying any kind of accusations," Schafer
added. "So, if you come at him with a sword, he'll just parry your sword
and put it out of the way. He can do that very easily because he's used
to talking that way in dealing with people. People would no doubt call
and say, 'Where's the money at?' He'd parry it—'Don't worry'—and
filibuster a little bit and then hang up without saying anything, and the
people will think that he said something. And he's doing that to you.
Would I want to cut him off as a source? Probably not. Because he may
slip up and give you a bit of information that you didn't know before.
He's making stuff up, but the nuggets could come out."

And they did. "But if he *admits* it, then he has to tell himself, 'I'm
a worse person than I think I am.' And he's not gonna do that," said
Schafer. "He's just wrapping you around the axle on these *little* issues.
He filibusters. He knows he's got fifteen minutes [per phone call]. I
could double-talk you for fifteen minutes every time you call. But
guess what: I'm still the center of attention."

In looking back, I'm utterly baffled how—during a decade of
meeting, talking, and writing with Bernie—he never once asked a single question about me. Would it not have served his purpose to get to
know something about *me,* even for a moment? "Oh, no, that's because
it's not about you," Schafer explained, "it's about *him.* And then he goes
[on one transcript] into how Robert De Niro was going to be playing
him [in *The Wizard of Lies,* a 2017 TV movie]. 'I am so important,

and I *look* like Robert De Niro, by the way. And I've got another book coming out, by *you*—and people are gonna read all about how clever I am.' So you're actually feeding the fire of his narcissism. But you have to be narcissistic in order to pull off a scam like he did."

Dr. Schafer was referring to a particular phone conversation I had with Bernie, in which the inmate said, "I think he looks somewhat like me, so I think he's probably a good choice. I had always assumed it would be him." Bernie had also expressed joy in a call that actress Michelle Pfeiffer was playing the part of Ruth in that movie, and that Ruth had welcomed the actress into her home to assist with her fictional portrayal. Bernie said he'd been assured long in advance that she and their sons would be positively portrayed, and they were. (Ruth and sons also came off as innocent victims a year earlier in an ABC TV miniseries called *Madoff*—starring Richard Dreyfuss as Bernie and Blythe Danner as Ruth—and they were portrayed in a similar way in a "true crime" Netflix docuseries in 2023 called *Madoff: The Monster of Wall Street*.)

Bernie often raged at court-appointed experts and law enforcement investigators, disputing their conclusions about elements of the fraud. And he had special venom for those who wanted to strip his family members of their assets. Nicknames like "the idiot Picard" are, of course, ad hominem attacks, which Schafer said boil down to this: "If you can't fight the facts, you discredit the person."

It's a practice that former president Donald Trump utilizes, too, no? "Oh, *you think?*" smirked Schafer.

No matter one's politics, there can be little doubt among rational people that the former president is the greatest falsifier who ever held the American presidency. One can admire and approve of Trump in spite of it, and many millions of Americans do. But tens of thousands of falsehoods that he's uttered since running for the office in 2015, as well as throughout his business career, are easily established and not open to debate.

Should there be an attempt at analysis and comparison of Madoff and Trump—arguably the greatest American fabulists of (for Madoff) the contemporary business world and (for Trump) the political world? Do they know when they lie? Do the 2020 presidential election deniers have anything in common with investors who blindly followed Madoff? And can denial be contagious and transmissible across huge segments of a society? This is shaky, if not treacherous, ground to tread, but to Dr. Bandy X. Lee, a psychiatrist who spent many years as a professor at the Yale University School of Medicine, it's ripe for examining.

In 2017, Trump's first year in the White House, Dr. Lee held a conference at Yale on the subject of the new president's mental health, which led to a book titled *The Dangerous Case of Donald Trump: 27 Psychiatrists and Mental Health Experts Assess a President*. She also wrote *Profile of a Nation: Trump's Mind, America's Soul*, published in 2020.

Like most mental health experts, Lee avoids attempting to analyze individuals without having treated them directly. But she and her twenty-six colleagues who assessed Trump in that book concluded that an exception needed to be made given the power he wielded as commander in chief.

Dr. Lee also spent twenty years as a forensic psychiatrist, working with violent criminals, and authored a textbook on public health approaches to violence. She's worked in prisons, and she initiated reforms at Rikers Island, home to New York City's main jail complex. In other words, she has credibility to opine on Bernie types. She writes that she sees the same personality types she has treated in correctional settings in leadership positions outside of prison.

In Lee's view, as spelled out in *Profile of a Nation*, Trump's most ardent followers represent a national mental health crisis that cries out for attention. Do financial fraudsters such as Madoff rise to that same level? Why is it so that so many Ponzi schemes (although not yet of Madoff's size) continue to proliferate, even as investors are warned time after time that if the financial returns claimed seem too good to be true, then they probably aren't? Is the proliferation of predatory fraudsters its own kind of national mental health crisis? Or is that taking things too far?

My talks with Dr. Lee on this subject were conducted in early 2021, three months before Madoff died on April 14, at the age of eighty-two, from heart and kidney disease. Election denialism had started sweeping across the country following the 2020 presidential election, based on lies perpetrated by many but ultimately instigated by the uncontested loser of that election, Donald Trump. In her books, she argues that denial can be contagious and transmissible, and in concluding that Trump's illness is *America's* illness, she laid out critical steps that she felt should be taken as a result. In the same way, should we see Madoff's enduring fraud as symptomatic of a kind of endemic social affliction we need to address?

Bernie Madoff's name is synonymous with the 2008 financial crisis. In Trump's case, most of the people he deceived were on the lower end of the economic spectrum; in Madoff's case, the higher end. But true believers they all were, and in Trump's case, many followers still are.

"Just as Donald Trump was a public health problem more than an individual one, and he represented the dangerous tendencies in our society, so is Bernie Madoff, on a smaller scale," says Lee. Sociopathy, she believes, is more a societal disorder than an individual one, meaning it affects all of us in some way, even if we never directly had contact. "Sometimes it takes over such important structures that it topples an entire economy or a whole nation. The solution is truly to fix the socioeconomic and cultural conditions that give rise to sociopathic individuals."

That sounds hard enough. "Not only is greed a problem," Lee continues, "but the very structure of extreme economic inequality concentrates wealth in the hands of the few, so that ruthless sociopaths who would do anything to get ahead are highly rewarded, favored, and attracted into positions of power, whether in the political or the financial world. Learning to recognize them collectively and not to give into their schemes, to create limits and contain them rather than to give them power, and to prevent such damaged individuals from arising in the first place is what we need to do."

That's an even taller order: fixing cultural, sociological, and economic conditions. But at the very least, some education starting in childhood would help people identify sociopathic individuals who may be out to hurt them in their lives. Such education is nonexistent today.

Dr. Lee thinks it's safe to say that both Madoff and Trump share well-sharpened predatory skills. "Predation is usually the goal and the purpose of life for those who are not bound by human attachments, by goals that others find important, or by a conscience," she explains. "'Getting away with' something is usually more irresistible than legitimately earning it, since it proves that one is 'smart,' able to do things others cannot, and counters the deep-seated sense of inferiority that one would never succeed legitimately."

Madoff's offspring and Trump's three oldest children were in the family business. Nobody went off on their own to do something different and make a name for themselves independent of their father's success. I shared with Lee that, in Madoff's case, his sons (and wife) may either have known of, or blinded themselves to, his fraud. There is proof, I said, that they themselves engaged in certain acts they must have known were wrong, and in some cases, illegal. Could the Trump kids be in the same boat as the Madoffs'? It would probably have taken a lot of strength and courage to break away from these narcissistic men while growing up.

"Children of these personality defects commonly do not fully individuate, because their fathers do not let them," she says. "Even as adults, they remain mere extensions or instruments of the father. The father also needs not to have to hand over important aspects of the business to strangers who are less bound to him and therefore less likely to be 'loyal.' Since everything that the father does is correct, it is possible that they knew or even participated but never recognized what he did as wrong."

Families aside, how much of Bernie's bunkum did *he* believe to be true? Experts such as Dr. Lee can't know. If he tended toward a malignant form of narcissism, he believed it *all*. But if he were somebody with a conscience, he didn't believe *anything*—he just put up a façade. Unfortunately, even if we could determine scientifically when and how history's greatest con man was lying, there may never be a final word on what made Bernie *Bernie*. No expert can answer that question for us today. And it likely will remain an unsolved riddle for the ages.

It is only human to want stories—any story—to come to a tidy end. Bernie was no different. And while to an outsider it might have seemed that Madoff, locked up for a couple of theoretical lifespans, had nothing but time, he clearly felt the need to see his tale told, closed.

Year after year, in one conversation after the next, it was obvious that Bernie cared deeply about his legacy, the value his firm's innovations had delivered to Wall Street from the eighteenth and nineteenth floors of the Lipstick Building. And he was right on that point: he'd tell anyone who'd listen how they'd advanced the field of automated trading (ironic, given his own computer illiteracy); and taken on the white-shoe NYSE more aggressively than any other market maker between the 1960s and '80s. You could almost taste his desperation for some shred of redemption as he sat there in his prison grays.

In February of 2016, Bernie told me he'd just communicated with Ruth, who was "coming apart at the seams," in part because "she doesn't even know whether I'm telling her the truth, and so on—because I kept her in the dark while it [the Ponzi] was going—and she kept saying 'Why isn't somebody give [sic] the facts out?' And I keep on saying that hopefully Richard is gonna, through his book, and I think he'll be able to give the right story." In a confessional mood, he went on to say, "My grandchildren don't speak to me still. It's a nightmare. Quite frankly, I'll tell you the truth, *I'm* coming apart at the seams. What I need to do is I have to get somebody to get this thing [the facts] out there, to do this thing."

Bernie wasn't shy about suggesting that this book was taking too long. "Listen, so what's the status of your [*chuckle*] book? I mean, is it ever coming out, or what?" He joked that, due to his age and worsening health—the hypertension, the kidney failure, the insomnia—he might not live long enough to read it. He was alternately impatient and fatalistic

about the odds of ever reading what he felt sure, somehow, would be the
final word on his legacy. His black humor about his future even took on
a kind of borscht belt vibe: "I haven't called you because I had a heart
attack," he said in 2014, "so I've been sort of out of [*chuckle*] circulation."

But Bernie could be mean, as well. In 2017, he was angry that I
never bought his interpretation of a mathematical formula in a 2012
report that he believed proved the total net loss to his investors was just
a mere $2 billion. (The report, titled "Customer Outcomes in the Ma-
doff Liquidation Proceeding" was from the US Government Accountability Office. And the chief investigator of the report says he doesn't
buy Bernie's interpretation either.) But Bernie wrote me that he'd "just
got through venting my frustration with your emails [about the GAO
report] with the dean of a major business school who suggested that I
am wasting my time with you." I asked to speak with the dean in hopes
he could help me understand it better. Bernie didn't respond at all to
that request, leaving me feeling that a dean hadn't said that at all.

One subject that often threatened to end our relationship (by
him) was his obsession with a story published in the *New York Times*
in 2010—a year before we started communicating—that stated that
about 720,000 Madoff investors outside the United States received
about $15.5 billion in settlements with their banks—an amount that's
more than what Picard has recovered to date. Picard said it never
happened, while many foreign lawyers on the front lines of battles
with foreign banks told me that at most there were small settlements
with banks for just tens of millions of dollars. "Believe me, it's total
crap," said one of those attorneys, the Brussels-based Edouard Fremault, who represented 5,000 Madoff clients at the time.

The article had been triggered by an announcement from a group of
lawyers in Spain as a publicity stunt, he says, in an attempt to attract clients. The lead lawyer behind the stunt kept canceling promises to speak
about it with me, and never did. But Bernie never let it go, pounding away
at me on it like ripping flesh off my bones unless I agreed with him. That's

because if it had been true, every losing investor would have had all their principal back a decade ago—plus more! "Everyone will wind up making 100% whole," exclaimed Bernie at the time. "And if you add in the $15.5 billion, people are going to get a 6% return. . . . Although the trustee refuses to acknowledge the settlement, it was in fact confirmed to me by foreign attorneys," who he said visited him at Butner. Sure.

The last time I communicated with Bernie was on October 8, 2019. It was in person, at Butner. By this time his physical trajectory was painfully clear, and I was almost desperate myself for a tidy ending. It was as though I personally needed some closure after more than a decade of trying to live in his head. I needed to hear him come clean, to untangle the threads of his myriad lies and contradictions—and take responsibility for them. I needed the gaslighting to end. I needed him to acknowledge the extent of what he'd done. I told him he wasn't going to live forever, that he could bring some measure of healing and peace to the investors he fleeced by telling all. He replied that he'd always been honest with me. Then he stood up with what he said was a leg spasm, shuffled to the door where his walker was parked, and said he'd email me about it. He never did. And I never spoke to him again. Not one more robocall from the 909 area code in North Carolina that began: *"You have a collect call from—Bernard Madoff* [his name in his own voice]*—an inmate at a federal prison. This call is being recorded and is subject to monitoring. Hang up to decline the call, or to accept dial five now. If you wish to block any future calls of this nature, dial seven now."*

There was never a full confession. His losers—and history itself— were never offered the catharsis of a detailed final accounting of history's greatest fraud. There was no admission about the moment he became a criminal, the first dirty trade, the real role of his bankers and their underlings, and his family members, the full scope of the complicity that allowed him to do what he did.

It broke my heart that I could never get Bernie to come clean. At the same time, after all those years, I admit I was relieved that our time had come to an end. But I still felt—and do to this day—perversely protective of the old swindler. Thirteen years after I resisted the urge to hug him on the day we first met, I remain weirdly loyal. Now *that's* a long con.

In February 2024, in the New York civil fraud case against Donald Trump, Judge Arthur Engoron invoked Bernie in the course of excoriating the former president and the other defendants, including Trump's two sons, for refusing to admit wrongdoing. "Their complete lack of contrition and remorse borders on pathological," Engoron wrote in his decision, which dinged the Trump Organization for more than $450 million. He went on to lament that while Trump had not committed violent crimes, and "Donald Trump is not Bernard Madoff," the "defendants are incapable of admitting the error of their ways."

Engoron's words struck me as almost unfair—to Bernie. Leaving aside the scale of Madoff's fraud, which seemed to be what the judge was getting at, Bernie at least evinced some facsimile of a conscience. As hard as he tried to shade the dates of the Ponzi's origin and downplay his own greed, he *did* admit the error of his ways. He *did* feel, however shallowly, some pangs of guilt. That's more than we've seen from our former president.

Shortly after Bernie died, I sent him an email, curious whether it would just vanish into the bowels of Butner, or if I'd receive a response. The latter came back to me:

> Inmate 61727054—MADOFF, BERNARD L no longer has access
> to the Trust Fund Limited Inmate Computer System; therefore,
> he/she may not send or receive messages.

The email seemed to suggest that Bernie was still out there somewhere, bumming quarters, a tattered Leon Uris novel in his pocket. In fact, he is nothing but ashes, and only Ike Sorkin, and another person the lawyer won't name, knows where they are. One last mystery to nag at those of us old Bregards Bernie left behind.

And so on and so forth.

Acknowledgments

"I'm like the turtle. I get there."

—HOMICIDAL MOB BOSS NICKY SCARFO, A PRISON
PAL OF BERNIE'S

In anyone's book, fifteen years is a long time. Indeed, my earliest interviews filled seventy-five timeworn standard cassettes. With that in mind, it's not easy to locate the words to adequately express my thanks to several people who came along on the journey.

First and foremost, my wife, Rebecca Sanhueza, for her unwavering support, encouragement, humor, and always flawless insights and advice. I love you. And to our daughter, Isabel, my guiding star. (Ishka, I finished it, and you are with me always.)

To Jon Karp, the CEO of Simon & Schuster, and my editor Ben Loehnen, VP and editor in chief of Avid Reader Press, for believing in this book—and me. Their guidance, expertise, patience, and compassion—particularly at critical times in my life—is more than any writer can hope for. They are the gold standard in the book world. Their team at the publishing house is super-professional and talented and those who I worked closely with are Carolyn Kelly (associate editor), Philip Bashe (copyeditor), Phil Metcalf (production editor), Lewelin Polanco (interior designer), and Dave Kass (senior director of publicity). You all made this book and the process better.

To Richard Abate (at 3Arts Entertainment)—my indefatigable and long-suffering agent—who was the first, and a fearless, champion of the story.

No decent author should be an island, and wisely I'm not. This book benefitted enormously from the expertise of two dear friends. They are two of the best editors I have ever worked with: Will Bourne (my former editor at *Fortune* and *Fast Company* magazines), who helped with various parts of the manuscript; and Randall Lane, the editor of *Forbes*, who came up with a conceptual framework for the story—and also gave the book its title. I owe them a huge debt of gratitude.

Sue Radlauer, the former director of research services at *Forbes*, a night owl who was always ready to jump in to help fact-check and magically locate seemingly endless court documents that are still being filed.

Several people did me the honor of reading early drafts of the manuscript and providing ideas and suggestions: Richard Curtis, Dan Keeler, John Paine, and Mike Selby.

Four seasoned journalists did some spot reporting in the early years in the US or Europe: Allan Dodds Frank, Mark Hollingsworth, Katie Lobosco. and Gary Weiss. Additional reporting or research came from interns Tim Bella, Millie Dent (chief reporter-researcher), Julia Gilban-Cohen, John Gregory Kapetanes, Tess Owen, Gianna Palmer (ace transcriber of cassettes!), and Karla Zabludovsky. In the UK: Yahia Abaza and Roy Revie. Database research whizzes: Anne Mintz and Stephanie Ardito. Finally, my researcher in a 2024 pinch: Zane Mosqueda.

Given the great passage of time, I can rest assured that I'll be leaving out people who belong here, for which I apologize. The list is long of those who provided anything from valuable expertise and history, to inspiration and encouragement, to the deconstruction of legal documents—or even the passing along of a key source or two:

Tom Ajamie; Stanley Arkin; Judi Asch; Ernie Badway; Arlene

Behar-Montefiore; Preet Bharara; Javier Bleichmar; Chris Bowers; Richard Breeden; Eric Breslin; David Brodsky; "The Brothers" (Ernie Corrigan, Russel Pergament, Mike Zonghetti); Bill Callahan; Dan Castleman; Lizzie Cohen; Marcia Cohn; Katie Coleman; Mark Coleman; Paulette Cooper; Jodi Crupi; Marla Daniels, Scott Daniels; Suzanne Dawson; Joe DeMarco; Emanuel Derman; Eric Dezenhall; Bruce Dubinsky; Lita Epstein; Julia Fenwick; Gene Foreman; Cecile Fradkin; Robert Friedman; Michael Gandin; Jim Gialamas; Eddie Goldstein; Thelma Goldstein; Jonathan Greenberg; Howard Greenwald; Sandy Scherzer Gross; Jim Heinzman; Dave Herron, JCCA; Hal Kahn; Dennis Kelleher; Ilene Kent; John Kim; Scott Kimmel; Gretchen King; Andrew Klein; Jessica Klein, David Kohane; Sonja Kohn; Bill Kreisberg; Ken Krys; Rabbi Dov Lerea; Rabbi Aaron Levine; Mark Litt; Donna MacKay; Bob Manchak; Jim Margolin; Valery Marchive; Better Markets; Carol (Solomon) Marston; Tom Martello; Doug Maynard; Bill McCausland; Brigid McMenamin; Dan Nardello; Nick Niehoff; Dr. Willi Okresek; Bill Olshan; Sean O'Shea; Paul Osher; Ben Ossman; Jody Paul; Tim Pfeifer; Irving Picard; John Pinto; Gordon Platt; Irving Pollack; Norman Poser; Phil Pulaski; Mike Ramos; Richard Rampell; Dr. Stephen Reibel; Amanda Remus; Deborah Renner; Ronald Richter; John Riley; Roland "Rollie" Riopelle; Mike Robbins; Susan (Saffer) Rosenzweig; Randy Rothstein; Gerald Rumetshofer; John Ruskay; Jonathan Sarna; Rabbi Moshe Scheiner; Reggie Schneck; Jeff Schoenfeld; Mark Seal; Shabbat on Tap; David Sheehan; Marion (Dickstein) Sherman; Emily Shipe; Marty Smith; Lisa Solbakken, Steve Solomon; Ron Stein; Don Stott; Larry Stybel; Gay Talese; Andreas Theiss; Matthew Torne; Fred Townsend; Sheila Traister; Clemens Trauttenberg; Philippe Vasset; Peter Walker; Harvey Wall; Carol Warner; Sandy Warrick; Oren Warshavsky; Michael Warszawski; Charles Webb; Don Weeden.

Photo Credits

1. No Credit
2. Long Island Daily Press
3. Courtesy: Peter Korman
4. No Credit
5. Timothy A. Clary/AFP via Getty Images
6. Richard Behar
7. Emmanuel Dunand/AFP via Getty Images
8. Richard Behar
9. Timothy A. Clary/AFP via Getty Images
10. NY Daily News Archive via Getty Images
11. Sara D. Davis/Getty Images, 2015
12. Patrick McMullan/Patrick McMullan via Getty Images
13. Louis Lanzano/Bloomberg via Getty Images
14. Emmanuel Dunand/AFP via Getty Images
15. CBS via Getty Images
16. Richard Behar
17. Louis Lanzano/Bloomberg
18. Jin Lee/Bloomberg via Getty Images
19. Richard Behar
20. Peter Foley/Bloomberg via Getty Images
21. REUTERS/Brendan McDermid
22. Richard Behar
23. No Credit
24. No Credit

25. James Leynse/Corbis via Getty Images

26. Michel Euler/Pool/AFP via Getty Images

27. REUTERS/Allison Joyce

28. Ludwig Schedl/APA-Fotoservice

29. Lucien Capehart/Getty Images, in January 2002

30. Peter Foley/Bloomberg via Getty Images

31. Elder Ordonez/Splash News

32. No Credit

33. Richard Behar

34. No Credit

35. Karen Wiles Stabile/Newsday RM via Getty Images, 2009

36. Joe Raedle/Getty Images

37. Mario Tama/Getty Images

38. Daniel Acker/Bloomberg via Getty Images

39. Stephane Danna/AFP via Getty Images

40. Jonathan Fickies/Bloomberg via Getty Images

41. No Credit

42. Daniel Acker/Bloomberg via Getty Images

43. Matthew West/MediaNews Group/Boston Herald via Getty

44. Richard Behar

45. Denis Doyle/Bloomberg via Getty Images

46. Richard Behar

About the Author

Richard Behar is a contributing editor for *Forbes* magazine and an associate producer and narrator of an upcoming docuseries on organized crime in the former Soviet Union. He previously worked on the staffs of *Fortune*, *Time*, and *Forbes*, and carried out probes for *Fast Company*, CNN, and BBC. Over a four-decade career, Behar has garnered more than twenty journalism awards.